The DevelopMentor Series

Don Box, Editor

Addison-Wesley has joined forces with DevelopMentor, a premiere developer resources company, to produce a series of technical books written by developers for developers. DevelopMentor boasts a prestigious technical staff that includes some of the world's best-known computer science professionals.

*"Works in **The DevelopMentor Series** are practical and informative sources on the tools and techniques for applying component-based technologies to real-world, large-scale distributed systems."*
 —Don Box

Titles in the Series:

Bob Beauchemin, *Essential ADO.NET*, 0-201-75866-0

Don Box, *Essential COM*, 0-201-63446-5

Don Box, Aaron Skonnard, and John Lam, *Essential XML: Beyond Markup*, 0-201-70914-7

Keith Brown, *Programming Windows Security*, 0-201-60442-6

Matthew Curland, *Advanced Visual Basic 6: Power Techniques for Everyday Programs*, 0-201-70712-8

Doug Dunn, *Java™ Rules*, 0-201-70916-3

Tim Ewald, *Transactional COM+L: Building Scalable Applications*, 0-201-61594-0

Jon Flanders, *ASP Internals*, 0-201-61618-1

Richard Grimes, *Developing Applications with Visual Studio.NET*, 0-201-70852-3

Martin Gudgin, *Essential IDL: Interface Design for COM*, 0-201-61595-9

Stuart Halloway, *Component Development for the Java™ Platform*, 0-201-75306-5

Joe Hummel, Ted Pattison, Justin Gehtland, Doug Turnure, and Brian A. Randell, *Effective Visual Basic: How to Improve Your VB/COM+ Applications*, 0-201-70476-5

Stanley B. Lippman, *C# Primer: A Practical Approach*, 0-201-72955-5

Everett N. McKay and Mike Woodring, *Debugging Windows Programs: Strategies, Tools, and Techniques for Visual C++ Programmers*, 0-201-70238-X

Aaron Skonnard and Martin Gudgin, *Essential XML Quick Reference: A Programmer's Reference to XML, XPath, XSLT, XML Schema, SOAP, and More*, 0-201-74095-8

Watch for future titles in The DevelopMentor Series.

Essential ADO.NET

Bob Beauchemin

✦▼Addison-Wesley

Boston • San Francisco • New York • Toronto • Montreal
London • Munich • Paris • Madrid
Capetown • Sydney • Tokyo • Singapore • Mexico City

Portions of this book are adapted from "ADO.NET: Building a Custom Data Provider for Use with the .NET Data Access Framework" by Bob Beauchemin, MSDN Magazine, December 2001, copyright Microsoft Corporation and CMP Media, LLC. Reprinted with permission.

The publisher offers discounts on this book when ordered in quantity for special sales. For more information, please contact:

Pearson Education Corporate Sales Division
201 W. 103rd Street
Indianapolis, IN 46290
(800) 428-5331
corpsales@pearsoned.com

Visit AW on the Web: www.aw.com/cseng/

Library of Congress Cataloging-in-Publication Data
Beauchemin, Bob.
  Essential ADO.NET / Bob Beauchemin.
    p. xm. — (DevelopMentor series)
  Includes bibliographical references and index.
  ISBN 0-201-75866-0 (alk. paper)
    1. Database design. 2. Object-oriented programming (Computer science) 3. ActiveX. I.
Title. II. Series.

QA76.9.D26 B42 2002
005.75'8—dc212002024934
Copyright © 2002 Pearson Education, Inc.

0-201-75866-0
Text printed on recycled paper
1 2 3 4 5 6 7 8 9 10—MA—0605040302
First printing, May 2002

*To Mary, who gave me the encouragement
and the space to follow my aspirations.*

Contents

Foreword by Tim Ewald   **xv**
Foreword by Richard Grimes   **xvii**
Preface   **xix**
Acknowledgments   **xxvii**

1   Data: Models, Applications, and APIs   **1**
    1.1   Information, Data Modeling, and Databases   1
    1.2   Database and API Fundamentals   2
    1.3   The Relational Model   5
          1.3.1   Relational Design Rules   6
          1.3.2   Benefits of the Relational Model   7
          1.3.3   Relational Model Support in ADO.NET   8
    1.4   Hierarchies, Objects, and Hybrids   9
          1.4.1   Modern Nonrelational Data   11
          1.4.2   Multidimensional Data   12
          1.4.3   Nonrelational Data and ADO.NET   13
          1.4.4   XML and the Infoset   14
          1.4.5   XML, Databases, and Universal Data Representation   15
    1.5   Data-centric Application Models   16
    1.6   Evolution of Data Access APIs   19
    1.7   Where Are We?   24

2   ADO.NET Basics   **25**
    2.1   Data Access and the .NET Architecture   25
    2.2   Two Patterns of Data Access   26

2.3   Connected Mode   27
    2.3.1   OleDb and SqlClient Data Providers   35
    2.3.2   Writing Generic Data Access Code with ADO.NET
         Data Providers   36
    2.3.3   Cursors in the Data Provider Model   41
2.4   Disconnected Mode and the DataSet   42
2.5   The XML APIs in .NET   46
    2.5.1   Streaming XML   47
    2.5.2   XML Schemas   51
    2.5.3   The XmlDocument, XPath, and XPathNavigators   54
    2.5.4   Mixing XML and Data Providers   60
2.6   Layout of the Managed Data Classes   65
2.7   Where Are We?   67

3 The Connected Model: Streaming Data Access   69
3.1   .NET Data Providers and the Connected Model   69
3.2   Connection Classes   70
3.3   Connection Pooling   73
3.4   Metadata Methods   74
3.5   Commands   77
    3.5.1   Command Behaviors   81
3.6   Using Parameters   82
3.7   Command Preparation, Cancellation, Timeouts, and Cleanup   92
3.8   Streaming Data through a DataReader   94
3.9   Reading Column Values through IDataRecord   97
    3.9.1   Handling Large Data Columns   101
3.10   Error Handling   103
3.11   Using Transactions   107
    3.11.1 Distributed Transactions   111
    3.11.2 How Connection Pooling Works   115
    3.11.3 How Declarative Transactions Work   121
3.12   Permission Classes   124
    3.12.1 Database Security   126
3.13   Where Are We?   126

4   The DataSet Class: Sets of Relational Data   127

4.1   DataSets   127

    4.1.1   DataSet as an In-memory Database   128

    4.1.2   What Can You Do with a DataSet?   129

4.2   The DataSet Object Model   129

    4.2.1   DataColumns, DataRows, and DataTables   131

    4.2.2   DataTable and Its Uses   134

    4.2.3   DataRows   136

    4.2.4   Keys, Relations, and Constraints   139

    4.2.5   Navigating through Relationships: Select and Find   143

    4.2.6   Adding, Retrieving, Changing, and Deleting Rows   146

    4.2.7   Combining Changes   150

    4.2.8   Merging DataSets   152

    4.2.9   DataRow States and Versions   154

    4.2.10 Rules and Relationships   159

    4.2.11 Error Handling   161

    4.2.12 Events   165

    4.2.13 DataSets and Nonrelational Types   171

4.3   Defining an Information Schema   174

4.4   Where Are We?   176

5   DataAdapters: Synchronizing Databases and Datasets   177

5.1   Optimistic Concurrency   177

5.2   DataAdapter Classes   179

5.3   Populating a DataSet from a Managed Provider   179

    5.3.1   Using Fill with Schema and Mapping Information   183

    5.3.2   Error Handling during DataAdapter.Fill   188

5.4   How DataAdapter.Fill Works   190

5.5   ADO Integration in OleDbDataAdapter   195

5.6   Updating a Database through DataAdapter   196

    5.6.1   The CommandBuilder Class   199

    5.6.2   Coding Update Logic Directly   206

5.7   How Update Works   212

    5.7.1   Controlling Updates   213

5.8	The DataSet Event Model	214
	5.8.1 Refreshing DataSet Using Update and Merge	216
5.9	Writing General Customized Commands	218
	5.9.1 The ADOX CommandBuilder	218
	5.9.2 Building a Batch Update Command	219
5.10	DataSets and Nonrelational Data Types Revisited	220
5.11	Should You Use DataSet or DataReader?	221
5.12	Where Are We?	223

6 Data Binding: ADO.NET and Graphical User Interfaces 225

6.1	Windows Forms and Web Forms	225
6.2	Patterns of Data Presentation	226
6.3	Using Databound Controls	227
	6.3.1 Web Forms Data Binding Types	230
	6.3.2 Anatomy of Databound Control Types	233
	6.3.3 Binding to a DataReader	241
6.4	Data Binding with DataSets	243
6.5	DataViews and Common Transformations	246
6.6	Table and Column Mappings	254
6.7	Editable List Controls: DataList and DataGrid	256
	6.7.1 DataList	256
	6.7.2 DataGrid	259
6.8	Nonrelational Data and DataViews	265
6.9	Integrating Visual Studio	266
	6.9.1 Server Explorer and Data Toolbox	267
6.10	Controls and Data Forms	270
6.11	Where Are We?	271

7 XML and Data Access Integration 273

7.1	XML and Traditional Data Access	273
7.2	XML and ADO.NET	274
	7.2.1 Defining a DataSet's Schema	275
	7.2.2 Refining DataSet's XML Schema	280
	7.2.3 Reading XML into DataSet	283
	7.2.4 Writing XML Schemas from DataSet	288

	7.2.5	Microsoft-Specific Annotations	291
	7.2.6	Writing XML Data from DataSet	292
7.3		Serialization, Marshaling, and DataSet	298
7.4		Typed DataSets	302
7.5		The XmlDataDocument Class	322
	7.5.1	XmlDataDocuments and DataSets	324
	7.5.2	XmlDataDocument and DataDocumentXPathNavigator	331
7.6		Why Databases and XML?	333
	7.6.1	XML as a Distinct Type	333
	7.6.2	Document Composition and Decomposition	334
7.7		SQL Server, XML, and Managed Data Access	334
	7.7.1	The FOR XML Keyword	335
	7.7.2	OpenXML	336
	7.7.3	The SQLOLEDB Provider	336
	7.7.4	The SqlXml Managed Classes	337
	7.7.5	The SQLXML Web Application	337
	7.7.6	Updategrams	337
	7.7.7	FOR XML in the SQLXMLOLEDB Provider	339
	7.7.8	Bulk Loading	339
	7.7.9	Future Support	339
7.8		Using SQLXML and .NET	339
7.9		Where Are We?	348

8 Providers: ADO.NET and Data Providers — 351

8.1		What Are Your Choices?	351
8.2		Staying with OLE DB: A Summary of OLE DB Concepts	353
8.3		Staying with OLE DB: Interaction with the OleDb Data Provider	356
	8.3.1	Main Cotypes and Type Mapping	357
	8.3.2	Accessors	358
	8.3.3	Executing Commands, Returning Results, and Using OpenRowset	358
	8.3.4	Command Results Format and Behaviors	359
	8.3.5	Command Dialects	359
	8.3.6	Hierarchical Data	360
	8.3.7	Updating from a Rowset	360

	8.3.8 Errors	361
	8.3.9 Unsupported Functions	361
	8.3.10 Supported and Unsupported Providers	361
8.4	Writing a Data Provider	366
8.5	Implementing the Connection Class	368
	8.5.1 Specification	369
	8.5.2 Implementation	369
	8.5.3 Specialization	370
8.6	Implementing the Command Class	371
	8.6.1 Specification	371
	8.6.2 Implementation	373
	8.6.3 Specialization	374
8.7	Implementing the DataReader Class	375
	8.7.1 Specification	376
	8.7.2 Implementation	377
	8.7.3 Specialization	379
8.8	Implementing the DataAdapter Class	380
	8.8.1 Specification	380
	8.8.2 Implementation	381
	8.8.3 Specialization	382
8.9	Adding Enhanced Functionality	382
8.10	Implementing XML Infoset Providers	383
8.11	Implementing XmlReader	386
8.12	Implementing XPathNavigator	392
8.13	Implementation Alternatives: Conclusions	396
8.14	Is a Single Universal Data Access Model Possible?	398
8.15	Where Are We?	400
9	**Consumers: ADO.NET Migration for Consumers**	**401**
9.1	ADO.NET Migration Paths	401
9.2	ADO.NET for OLE DB Programmers	402
	9.2.1 Cotype Equivalents	403
	9.2.2 Data Provider Transparency	404
	9.2.3 Using Provider-Specific Functionality	405
	9.2.4 Error Handling	405

	9.2.5	System-Supplied Services	406
	9.2.6	System-Supplied Components	406
	9.2.7	Service Providers	407
	9.2.8	Marshaling	407
9.3	A Brief Overview of ADO		407
9.4	ADO.NET for ADO Programmers		410
	9.4.1	Class Equivalences	410
9.5	ADO Connections, Commands, and Transactions		415
	9.5.1	Connections and Connection Strings	416
	9.5.2	Using Transactions	416
	9.5.3	Commands and Command Behaviors	416
	9.5.4	Hierarchical Data	417
	9.5.5	Asynchronous Operations	417
	9.5.6	Properties	417
9.6	ADO.NET Versus ADO Disconnected Model		417
	9.6.1	Class Equivalents	418
	9.6.2	Navigation	419
	9.6.3	What Happened to GetRows in ADO.NET?	420
	9.6.4	Updates	422
	9.6.5	Update Statement Creation	423
	9.6.6	Batch Updates	423
	9.6.7	ADO.NET DataSet Extensions	423
	9.6.8	Column and Table Naming	424
	9.6.9	Sorting and Filtering	424
9.7	ADO DB Interoperability		425
9.8	ADO.NET for ODBC Programmers		433
	9.8.1	Handles and Environment	434
	9.8.2	Commands	435
	9.8.3	Fetching Data	436
	9.8.4	Metadata and Schema Information	436
	9.8.5	Errors	437
9.9	ADO.NET for JDBC Programmers		443
	9.9.1	Generic Code	443
	9.9.2	Provider Types	443

	9.9.3	Connection Pooling	445
	9.9.4	Nonrelational Data Types	445
	9.9.5	Object Databases	445
	9.9.6	Other SQL-99 Extensions	446
	9.9.7	Metadata	446
	9.9.8	Transactions	446
	9.9.9	Commands and Behaviors	447
	9.9.10	Executing Queries and Returning Results	447
	9.9.11	Server Cursors	448
	9.9.12	Errors	448
9.10	ADO.NET JDBC Programmers and the Disconnected Model		456
9.11	SQL/J Part 0 and Typed DataSets		457
9.12	Where Are We?		458

10 ADO.NET and Various Types of Data 459

10.1	Evolution in Data Access	459
10.2	ADO.NET with Server- and File-Based RDBMS	461
10.3	ADO.NET with Homogeneous Hierarchical Data and ORDBMS	464
10.4	ADO.NET and Network Data: Object Graphs, OODBMS, and Network DBMS	465
10.5	ADO.NET and Structured Files, Multidimensional Data, and ORDBMS	467
10.6	ADO.NET Flat Files and Semistructured Files	468
10.7	Where Are We Going?	469

Appendix A Data Types and Type Mappings 471

Appendix B Expression Syntax 483

Appendix C Schema Inference Rules 491

Bibliography 501

Index 503

Foreword by Tim Ewald

Writing a book is hard. My own book took two and a half years to write, from late 1998 and delivered in early 2001, and the process was hell. My goal was to provide a definitive book on the design of scalable distributed systems in general, and in using COM+ in particular. I couldn't have finished my work without Bob's help.

Bob was my *Encyclopedia Data Accessica*. Near the end of my project (or well into the second year, anyway), he endured repeated phone calls and endless questions at all hours of day and night. The conversations were all very similar. I would start, without preamble, "How come when I do *x*, *y* happens—that can't be right?!??" Bob would answer very patiently, "Hold on, let me boot the machine that has *z* running and we'll see. ..." (During this time, I came to believe that Bob has every database ever written running on some partition of some machine in his home. I was tempted to test this hypothesis by asking about databases that don't exist, e.g., QuuxBase, but I never did—for fear he had those too.)

Bob was, quite simply, an invaluable resource. He helped me understand how transaction isolation works in SQL Server and, more importantly, in Oracle; how to use OLE DB and ADO to execute batch statements; how OLE DB implements connection pooling (and how to do better with COM+ pooled objects), and much more.

Bob used to ask me if he should write a book about OLE DB and my answer was always the same: "Only if you have something you cannot not say." By the time Bob was ready to write, OLE DB (like the rest of COM) was on its way to being replaced by ADO.NET and so his focus changed to the brave new world. But it didn't turn out to be so new after all.

Bob knows more about databases and data access techniques past and present than anyone else I know. So he is able to put ADO.NET in perspective relative to ADO, OLE DB, and the rest, as the current iteration of the last data access

API you'll ever need to know. At a time when the classes in the .NET framework are replacing all the APIs you are used to, this link to the past makes understanding this crucial piece of the new Microsoft platform significantly easier.

Whether you write data access consumers or providers, whether you use ADO, OLE DB, or an older or more esoteric API, this is the book for you.

Tim Ewald
Author of *Transactional COM+*

Foreword by Richard Grimes

Just about every part of our lives is controlled by a database. Everything that we do is categorized and persisted and then analyzed and returned back to us as a mailshot or a marketing campaign. If you develop software, then you'll find that a database will be somewhere in the solution. Clearly databases are important and a deep knowledge of how to access them effectively and to manipulate the data that they hold is vitally important. Data comes in all shapes and sizes, and there are various different ways of storing data. If you are lucky enough to work with just one database then you can become an expert with the API to access that database. However, few solutions use a single data source, and even with those that do you cannot guarantee that you will always use that single data source: Your client may choose to use a database from a different vendor for a later version of the solution.

Universal database access is clearly a goal for library providers, allowing you to write the same code using a universal API regardless of the data source that will be used. The last few years have had several universal APIs and those APIs from Microsoft have now stabilized in the form of ADO.NET as part of the .NET framework. The .NET initiative represents a whole new way of programming with a runtime and garbage collection, and the Microsoft database teams have taken this opportunity to integrate XML into the API, not only as a data source, but as a universal format of data, a lingua franca of databases. ADO.NET is a large library and needs comprehensive coverage.

Comprehensive and *authoritative* are the two adjectives that best describe Bob Beauchemin's book on ADO.NET. From the first to the last page you are immersed into the world of ADO.NET with clear, in-depth explanations of how the library works and how to use it in your code. On your first reading you should start at the beginning and devour the book right through to the end. You should only pause to type in the example code and perhaps to eat. This will give you the best grounding that you'll ever receive into what ADO.NET will offer and how to access its facilities. After that you will be able to develop database solutions effectively but you will still find that you will want to return regularly to review a topic before writing your code. Bob Beauchemin effectively "owns" databases, and any text from Bob is a must read because you know that you will get the best explanation of the technology that is available. After reading this book you will not only know how to use ADO.NET, but you will also understand the rationale behind the design of the library. Oh, and you'll learn a lot about .NET too.

Richard Grimes
Author of *Developing Applications with Visual Studio.NET*

Preface

This book is about a new provider-model-based data access library known as ADO.NET, a part of the Microsoft .NET initiative. But this book is also about data—where we store it and how we retrieve it, update it, and index it. Describing the ins and outs of data management turns out to be a larger topic than simply enumerating the use of all the classes, interfaces, properties, and methods in a library. It entails looking at the problem you're trying to solve with the library and determining which application programming interface (API) or portion of the API to use.

Although business problems fall into certain repeating patterns, there are no hard-and-fast rules that encompass a cookbook solution, especially with respect to data access, presentation, and exchange. The lightning-fast solution you're programming today in native assembly language for the ultimate in speed may turn out to be a maintenance nightmare tomorrow. Patterns that work perfectly with a single user may fail with a group of users. Patterns for a small workgroup may flounder when applied to a global enterprise. Although this book contains solutions for certain generic problems, it doesn't give you cut-and-paste solutions.

Generic Versus Specific Programming Models

Until recently, I'd always programmed database access using the most vendor-specific, down-to-the-metal programming interface available, on the (correct) premise that it was always fastest. However, throughout my career I've often made my living doing application conversions when the organization decided to change hardware type or database. In a given long-lived company, hardware and databases seem to change as often as clothing fashions.

I was first convinced of the usefulness of an abstract, provider-style interface when I was asked to convert a company's Web site from a vendor-specific database API to Open Database Connectivity (ODBC), a more abstract API. As with many organizations, the actual database choice depended on the direction of other parts of the company and was outside our project's control. The wisdom of my project lead's choice of ODBC over native API was soon confirmed. I put the finishing touches on our new application and generated the database. The project was on schedule, and the project lead trundled off to a Friday afternoon meeting. Then, on Monday morning, I was informed that the choice of database had changed. Luckily, because we had used ODBC (and because both databases had ODBC drivers) we needed only to generate the new database, make small changes to the programs because of subtle nuances in Structured Query Language (SQL) dialect, retest the programs, and the application was converted. We were lucky.

A provider-based data access API must always balance the problems of abstracting generic functionality with the need to allow vendors enough room so that the API doesn't become an excuse for lowest common denominator coding. ADO.NET seems to do a good job in the latter area: The SQL Server-specific data provider (known as `SqlClient`) seems to be proof of the room afforded to vendor-specific extensions. The real proof will come with future data providers.

Cyclical Technologies and Innovation

I've been doing computerized information processing professionally for a long time. When I went through the interview at my current job (at DevelopMentor) I was asked, "As you get older, does it get more difficult to acquire new skills in the constantly changing world of programming languages, design paradigms, and application programming interfaces?" I laughed and responded that it actually gets easier. After being exposed to multiple generations of "new ideas" in computing, I've realized that the problem domain being abstracted doesn't change, and differences in the abstractions themselves are usually subtle. In addition, the abstractions are sometimes cyclical; today's new idea may be a throwback.

For example, I've always been intrigued by the problems of data access and structure of database management system products. Having lived through using files as databases (or at least data storage), hierarchical databases, CODASYL databases (standardized by the Conference on Data Systems Languages), relational databases, object databases, multidimensional databases, and all their variations, I was intrigued when I was introduced to the use of XML as a data model. I was impressed when I investigated its data abstraction model, its in-memory object model, its rich data manipulation tools, and its query languages, but I also had the feeling I'd been here (or somewhere close) before. Then, thumbing through an old book that compared relational and hierarchical data-bases, I was struck by the similarity of the hierarchical navigation functions in IMS (IBM's flagship database until the mid-1980s) to those used in the XML Doc-ument Object Model (DOM) APIs. Later, I was able to correlate the (old) idea of letting the underlying SQL engine do the navigation with the possibility of using the same concept in the XPath query language. Speed improvements will be based on future query engine improvements, without the need to rewrite the navigation-based program.

As another example, one of the latest technologies seems to be centered on the use of business-to-business data exchange between unlike systems using a known data format (XML). This pattern appears to be similar to a system that I worked on to import and export banking transactions using the well-known auto-matic clearinghouse (ACH) format. This approach used a known data format and telecommunication protocol to exchange data between unlike systems.

It's always helpful to be able to grab on to something familiar in a new tech-nology. I found out, however, that I'd irritated co-workers by overuse of the phrase "It's just like…" when speaking about a new technology. They were irri-tated because I was implying that there was nothing new in the technology, no improvements. On the contrary, there are usually improvements based on new problems to solve and novel ways of looking at an existing problem. What "It's just like…" meant to me was that I had a bridge from the old world into the new world, and I could go from there to consider the improvements. I noticed that when I mentioned the improvements in new technologies, folks were a lot less irritated.

One of my major assignments at DevelopMentor was to develop and teach a course on OLE DB. In my travels, my students would ask, "What makes this dif-ferent from ODBC?" or "Why should I switch to this from JDBC?" In other words, what do I gain, what do I lose, and what's the same? After having to answer these questions many times, and having considered changes in many different technologies, I find myself in a good position to assess the repercussions of the new ADO.NET interface.

(By the way, Sun Microsystems, the inventor of JDBC, claims that JDBC is not an abbreviation for anything. One would think it stands for Java Database Connectivity, but Sun says this is not so, even though some of the company's own documentation uses those words.)

Data Access Has Changed

When giving talks on data access and presentation strategies, I used to joke that a Web browser was "just a multicolor terminal that can sing and dance." Well, maybe sing. But, to borrow a cliché, accessing applications through a Web browser has drastically changed the way we design our data access strategies. Here's how.

First, user volumes can vary wildly and can change without much prior notice. In the days of terminals, user volume was fairly predictable or at least quantifiable, and growth was constrained by the ability to add terminals and users to the private network. The users also had to fill out forms to gain access to corporate applications, something that made it possible to control growth. In the age of Internet commerce, however, the number of users of your application is constrained only by its popularity. This is one of the major selling points of the Internet as a vehicle of commerce. Businesses want to be able to start with a small server and scale up or out to a large user base on limited notice. It changes the way we design and write applications.

Second, users do not "sign off " of Internet applications, and sometimes you cannot physically identify them. Hyperlinks in Internet applications let users branch immediately from the application to checking on their favorite stock or sports team. If that other Web site contains something new and interesting, they may never return to the application. As a result, it's impossible to incorporate signoff logic into Web applications and guarantee its use. Also, users cannot be identified by terminal ID because of the presence of dynamic address assignment protocols such as Dynamic Host Configuration Protocol (DHCP) and proxy server software that obfuscate the end user's address. Combined with the fact that users do not sign off applications, this makes it impossible to set aside a chunk of storage on a per-user basis, based on the location of a computing device. That's another big change.

Third, users do a lot of their own data entry. In older systems, pessimistic concurrency and record locking were based on the premise that data entry was done by an array of terminal operators. If two operators were accessing data tied to your account at the same time and if your data was "busy," one operator could put your slip of paper at the bottom of the pile and key it in later. Web applications, on the other hand, make everyone a data entry clerk. Because there probably won't be "two of you" updating your personal and financial information at the same time, optimistic concurrency is more viable. It also means that data editing techniques and business rules must be more robust because nonprofessional operators key in the darnedest things.

The ADO.NET APIs use data access patterns tuned to the way data access and input are done today. The techniques of connection pooling, disconnected updates, and optimistic concurrency play a large part in shaping functionality to today's problems even when you're using some of yesterday's technologies.

The Structure of This Book

The thesis of Chapter 1, Data: Models, Applications, and APIs, is that a data access API must strike a balance between, on the one hand, being skewed toward a single data storage style or database and, on the other hand, trying to be so all-encompassing that it renders individual classes and methods meaningless. This chapter enumerates the novel functionality in ADO.NET and describes the data storage styles and application types with which it is most useful.

Chapter 2, ADO.NET Basics, divides the landscape into three parts: data providers, the ADO.NET `DataSet` object model, and the XML data access model. A simple program illustrates each part. I include the XML API portions, along with a discussion of XML and ADO.NET integration in Chapter 7, because I consider the XML stack to be an important part of the overall data access stack in the .NET framework.

Chapter 3, The Connected Model, explains that most data access APIs are centered on a provider model that abstracts away the differences between slightly different concrete implementations. This chapter investigates ADO.NET's variation on the familiar connection, command, and results model that is used to access relational data stores. The chapter concludes with an examination of some application-specific features, including connection pooling and automatic distributed transactions.

In Chapter 4, The `DataSet`, you'll learn that most data access APIs include the concept of an in-memory data representation that you can use to populate controls on a form and can traverse and manipulate. In ADO.NET, this model is based on the `DataSet` class and its supporting collection classes, which model a relational database. This chapter introduces the `DataSet` by examining its intricacies as a stand-alone object model.

Although the `DataSet` is a convenient way to represent data in memory, it is most useful as a client-side model of data in a database. Chapter 5, `Data-Adapters`, is about getting data from a data provider into a `DataSet` and persisting offline changes made to the `DataSet` back to the database. Because a database is shared among many users who work on the same data, this chapter explores the problems that ensue when more than one user changes the same data in offline mode, known as the optimistic concurrency conflict resolution problem. In addition, there has been a lot of debate about when to use a direct-from-the-database stream (the ADO.NET `DataReader`) and when to use an offline cache (the ADO.NET `DataSet`) with common application access patterns. This chapter presents guidelines.

If you want to present data to a human via a graphical program or Web page, you must map the bits in the database or data cache to graphical controls such as text boxes, list boxes, and data grids. Chapter 6, Data Binding, looks at ADO.NET's integration with the user interface items. This chapter reprises the `DataReader` versus `DataSet` debate, this time when using the ASP.NET Web Forms presentation style.

Because a large part of the world's data is stored in relational databases, Chapter 7, XML and Data Access Integration, examines the various methods contained in ADO.NET for integrating relational data storage and XML representation and manipulation. Improved XML integration is one of the main advances in ADO.NET. The chapter concludes with information on XML integration with SQL Server, Microsoft's flagship database.

Data access (and other models with multiple similar implementations that differ only in details) is abstracted through a provider model. Chapter 8, Providers, looks at the mapping of the OLE DB provider model to the ADO.NET data provider model. It also explains the concept of XML Infoset providers, an abstraction of the provider model over the XML Infoset model.

Chapter 9, Consumers, provides a useful reference for data consumers (such as programmers writing data access code) who may be moving from other data access APIs, such as ADO, ODBC, and JDBC. It's designed to make members of each group feel at home with ADO.NET by correlating their class X or function Y to ADO.NET's classes and methods.

The book starts in Chapter 1 by describing the various types of data storage and applications that use this data. The book concludes in Chapter 10 by revisiting the landscape presented in Chapter 1 in light of the knowledge gained in the rest of the book, examining whether the data stacks (ADO.NET and XML) really contain a solution for everyone. Then we take a look at future directions in data access.

How to Read This Book

This book falls into three parts. It is part manifesto and analysis, part API reference by example, and part pure reference material for the use of programmers who are involved in data conversions. Ideally, you should read it sequentially, but you need not understand it completely upon first reading. Whenever you find yourself wondering, "Why should I care about this?" or "I have no point of reference to this," read on. The meaning will become clear later.

Chapters 1 and 10 present a manifesto and analysis of database types, database APIs, and application styles in broad brushstrokes. You may not completely understand or agree with every point. Chapters 2 through 7 explain in minute detail how the ADO.NET classes, interfaces, and methods work. You can read these chapters in their entirety or browse through them piecemeal, but it's best to read them in order. Chapters 8 and 9 are designed for provider writers and consumer writers who are using other database libraries and are looking for a way in to ADO.NET. These chapters are reference-oriented; some idiosyncrasies and analogies in Chapter 8 may be a bit detailed for those who have not written OLE DB code. This chapter is for my friends and students with whom I've learned and written OLE DB providers in the past few years. They always complain that no one ever writes books for them.

What you won't find here are hundreds of pages of class, interface, method, and property information arranged by class name. For this information, I suggest you consult the .NET framework software development kit (SDK) documentation. Having spent many hours browsing the Windows platform documentation, my impression is that it seems to mature with the Windows platform itself. The framework SDK documentation is probably the best yet, although the OLE DB programmer's reference docs were also impressive.

Observation Versus Documentation

There are a few reasons this book was not released earlier. One is that I knew the .NET product would change during the beta process, perhaps drastically. I did not want to produce a "programming with the beta" book as my one contribution to this space, even though these books have their place. Such a book would be obsolete or misleading mere months after it had been published.

In addition, I've tried to verify everything in the documentation through direct experimentation with code. I've also tried to describe some internal behaviors of the providers and details of their implementation. These changed (sometimes significantly) during the beta process, and I was forced to rewrite sections of the book and rethink solutions that I'd come up with. I waited until the final product was released so that I could run the code fragments and experiments one more time.

Deduction of internals through experimentation and observation is risky because the implementation of these hidden details will change over time. It will change because software vendors are constantly working to update and improve their products. Where there exists the most risk of change, I've attempted to document my experimentation so that you can repeat the experiment as the software or underlying database changes.

Additional code, errata (in the original or due to product changes), and additional information will be posted on this book's Web site http://staff.develop.com/bobb/adonetbook.

Acknowledgments

Although this is the first book I've written, I've been a reviewer of technical books for a number of years. As a voracious reader and knowledge consumer, I thought it was the best way to help authors while obtaining knowledge in advance of publication. At the same time, it made me aware of the reviewer's role, and therefore I'd like to say a special thanks to my reviewers. Without them, this book wouldn't be nearly as good. Dan Sullivan and Jason Masterman were the first to digest the whole thing, providing timely feedback in the early stages. Fritz Onion provided unique insight and urged me to write more on motivation. Jim Wilson and Vagif Abilov contributed their data access expertise as writers of data providers as well as consumers. Simon Horrell provided a detailed pedagogical and technical analysis; while he claimed to be pedantic, his detailed input was invaluable. Niels Berglund and Daniel Sinclair added their expert perspectives. I'd also like to acknowledge Don Box and Tim Ewald, who told me, "Write a book only if you have something that you absolutely must say."

Bob Beauchemin
January 2002

Chapter 1

Data: Models, Applications, and APIs

The data access method you use depends on how you model your data. Data access patterns used in applications drive data access method functionality.

1.1 Information, Data Modeling, and Databases

Over the years, many different databases, data models, and data access application programming interfaces (APIs) have come and gone. Or at least we thought we'd seen them go. Each one brought something new to the table (or a variation on a familiar theme). Each had its zealots, who approached the technology with an almost religious fervor. "This is the last data technology you'll ever learn, and it will be adopted by everyone," we've been told. Mostly, it didn't happen. This chapter reviews these systems, with an eye toward what the refactored data access stack in .NET adds, deletes, simplifies, and clarifies.

At its simplest, Microsoft's ADO.NET framework is a set of .NET APIs for accessing data. The question we begin with is, What kind of data? Usually, data (and data access) is classified according to three things:

- The paradigm that has been used to model the data
- The medium used to store the data
- The mechanism used to query the data

Data can be modeled as columns and rows and stored in a specialized data management application (a database) and accessed via Structured Query Language (SQL) queries, or it can be stored in files that model data as hierarchies and are accessed by navigation through the file contents. Although many types of data structures exist, the .NET platform concentrates on two popular data access methods used in Internet-enabled and data exchange applications: relational database management systems (RDBMS) and Extensible Markup Language (XML).

The .NET data access stack contains five main new features:

- It separates the *command-based* (connected) and *optimistic update* (disconnected) models of data access and presentation.
- It separates *navigation-based* data access from *set-based* data access.
- It keeps the universal data access concept of OLE DB and ADO (Microsoft's previous pre-.NET data access APIs), while addressing some of their limitations.
- It offers an easier data binding model for tool vendors and developers.
- It integrates traditional data access with XML.

This last point is arguably the most interesting. Although the XML stack is technically not part of ADO.NET, some of the features that integrate XML and traditional relational data access go far beyond the model in which a resultset is represented as an XML document. The centerpieces of this integration are two new *managed data types*, or classes: `XmlDataDocument` and `XPathNavigator`. These classes help to bridge the gap between the relational data model and all other data models, including some you may have thought had been forgotten (or had never heard of).

You now have many data modeling choices. If you don't review the strengths and weaknesses of the available models in light of the problems you're trying to address, it may be difficult to dig yourself out from under a bad design.

Because XML can represent multiple data paradigms in addition to the paradigm it was originally intended to address (separation of data from presentation in Web pages), it's helpful to review these other database and data access types.

1.2 Database and API Fundamentals

A *database* is an application that provides scalable multiuser access and updates of data. Through a combination of locking, logging, and transactions, it enables point-in-time recovery and ensures the atomicity, consistency, isolation, and durability (commonly known as the ACID properties) of multiple related, shared, updatable data items. Data is stored in an efficient but proprietary manner, and access to related data items is very fast. Most enterprise-quality systems that require data persistence use databases.

Because the data storage layout is proprietary, to ensure data consistency databases allow access to their data only through specific APIs. The API may include a high-level command language, such as SQL or OQL (Object Query Language). Relational databases, such as SQL Server and Oracle, use SQL.

SQL commands are usually submitted through APIs and are executed by the database engine, although multiple SQL statements can be composed into *persistent stored modules* (better known as *stored procedures*) that can contain flow control statements and program logic. The basic SQL data commands are SELECT, INSERT, UPDATE, and DELETE. Listing 1–1 shows the syntax (in the Microsoft dialect of Transact-SQL). Listing 1–2 shows concrete examples. Agreed-upon industry *standards*—such as SQL-99, SQL-92, and earlier standards—attempt to codify the SQL command language, persistent stored modules, and other relational database operations.

Listing 1–1   SQL statement syntax

```
INSERT [ INTO] table_name [ ( column_list ) ]
VALUES
   ( { DEFAULT | NULL | expression } [ ,...n] )
        | execute_statement
        | DEFAULT VALUES

UPDATE table_name
  SET
     { column_name = { expression | DEFAULT | NULL }
        | @variable = expression
[ WHERE < search_condition > ]

DELETE [ FROM ] table_name
[ WHERE < search_condition > ]

SELECT select_list
[ INTO new_table ]
FROM table_source
[ WHERE search_condition ]
[ GROUP BY group_by_expression ]
```

```
[ HAVING search_condition ]
[ ORDER BY order_expression [ ASC | DESC ] ]
```

Listing 1–2   Sample SQL statements

```
INSERT INTO jobs (job_desc, min_lvl, max_lvl)
  VALUES ('Teacher', 10, 15)

UPDATE authors
  SET    au_fname = 'Bob'
  WHERE au_lname = 'Smith'

DELETE authors
  WHERE au_lname = 'Jones'

SELECT au_fname, au_lname, age
  FROM authors
  WHERE au_id > '1'
```

Most relational databases support the concept of *parameterized statements*, which let you separate the query parsing and query plan creation (the specific navigation and fetch plan that is made up by the database) from the actual command execution. You can reuse query plans if you parameterize the statements (also known as commands). Listing 1–3 shows an example.

Listing 1–3   Query parameterization

```
-- the SQL parser thinks these are different queries
select * from authors
  where au_lname = 'Smith'
select * from authors
  where au_lname = 'Jones'

-- this can use the same query plan
-- the parameter is filled in at runtime
select * from authors
  where au_lname = ?
parm = 'Smith'
parm = 'Jones'
```

Database products usually have a mechanism for authenticating users, sometimes integrating with the authentication method of the underlying operating system. You can use or combine the operating system's set of security principles with principles defined in the database. Databases almost always have their own granular data authorization mechanism.

To accommodate this scenario, common operations include logging on to (and establishing a session with) the database, issuing commands that retrieve or update data, and obtaining sets of data or counts of updated data items. ADO.NET and other data access APIs support these operations.

In Chapter 3, you'll see how ADO.NET encapsulates these operations using classes, interfaces, properties, and methods. First, let's review relational databases to see why you would use them in your design.

1.3   The Relational Model

Relational databases use the relational data model popularized by E. F. Codd and C. J. Date. The relational model represents data as entities. An *entity* is a real-world object, such as a customer or an order. Each entity is represented by a row in a table. Rows are referred to as *tuples* and consist of a series of *attributes* (columns). Entities have *state*, which consists of the values of the attributes (columns). Each column has a single value drawn from a domain of appropriate values.

Most relational databases have the concept of a *distinct type*, usually a restriction of a simple type such as integer, which comes close to (but does not exactly correspond to) SQL-99's definition of a domain of values. An example of a distinct type is a Social Security number type, which restricts the simple type string to strings of 11 bytes in length, with a specific number-hyphen pattern: 999-99-9999. In ADO.NET, you implement a distinct type by subclassing .NET types.

The distinction between the relational model and other data models is that in the relational model, relationships between entities are represented as relations between columns in one table and columns in another table. Only actual data is represented as columns in tables. In other data management systems, relationships are represented as links or binary associations between entities.

Note also that, compared with object-oriented programming systems, entities in a relational system consist only of state and not of state and behavior. Any behaviors are implied by tying the attributes (columns) to a specific domain (the data type plus additional constraints).

Relational database theory is based on set theory in mathematics, and has a set of simple principles. The first rule is that there is no support for multivalued data. This means that no columns can consist of arrays or structures. In practice, however, some relational databases do support multivalued types. Examples include Oracle 8's `array` data type and SQL Server 2000's `sql_variant`.

Although almost all relational databases support non-unique tuples, some relational theorists make a principle of tuple uniqueness. In a relational data store, no two rows should be identical. One could argue that rows that differ only by an arbitrary system-assigned identifier, such as a globally unique identifier (GUID), are, in fact, non-unique. In a relational data store there is no concept of tuple (or object) identity except that defined through *key columns*. Key columns are used to uniquely identify a tuple.

Unlike hierarchical and network databases, relational databases do not depend on the ordering of the data. Rather than depend on ordering and navigation through the data, relational databases act on sets of data. This means that unless you use the SQL ORDER BY clause, the order of the data returned by a SE-LECT statement is undefined.

There are some exceptions. Some relational databases allow ordering by letting you define CLUSTERED INDEXes or CLUSTERS on a table or tables. A *clustered index* specifies that data in a table is always stored physically in index order. This is done as a performance optimization rather than as a direct violation of relational theory.

1.3.1 Relational Design Rules

Flat file systems (or *structured* flat file systems, such as XML) represent all the attributes of one or many entities in a single file, or a single XML *document*. For example, a single record in a flat file or a single XML element could contain information about a customer, a collection of addresses, a collection of credit history information, and so on. A single XML document can contain information about an order, the line items of the order, prices, and billing and shipping information.

In contrast, data in relational databases is *decomposed* into tuples in tables to reduce functional dependencies among the data items. Order number, customer ID, and date are put into one table; shipping addresses may be put into a separate table from billing addresses. Line items may have a separate table. The goal is to decompose entities into relations (tables) so that each tuple (row) consists of a *primary key* that identifies the row and a set of mutually independent attributes that describe it.

The key words here are "mutually independent." You accomplish this by decomposing the data using a set of rules called the *normal form rules*. As explained by C. J. Date in his 1981 book *An Introduction to Database Systems*, the three main normal form rules are as follows:

1. A relation R is in first normal form (1NF) only if all underlying domains contain atomic values only. (This means that multivalued data is not allowed.)

2. A relation R is in second normal form (2NF) only if it is in 1NF and every nonkey attribute is fully dependent on the primary key.

3. A relation R is in third normal form (3NF) only if it is in 2NF and every nonkey attribute is nontransitively dependent on the primary key. (Simplified, *nontransitively* means that nonkey attributes depend only on the key and not on each other.)

A *relationship* defines dependencies between two (or occasionally, more than two) physical tables. Relationships are defined in terms of multiplicity—that is, how many rows of table X can be *owned* by rows in table Y. The relationships are defined as multiplicity zero-or-one-to-one, one-to-many, and many-to-many. There are no built-in rules that indicate ways to specify arbitrary multiplicities, such as a one-to-five relationship (one entity of type X relates to exactly five entities of type Y).

Many-to-many relationships are usually represented by a specific entity type. This type, called a *relationship table* or *join table*, exists only to represent the many-to-many relationship. It usually contains only keys from each table, but it can contain other attributes that apply to the relationship as opposed to either of the tables.

Another common relationship type is a *self-referencing table*, which is usually used in representing hierarchies. Rows in this table type have a relationship with other rows in the same table. An example is an employee table that contains an employee ID and an ID of that employee's supervisor. The supervisor must also be an employee, and therefore the supervisor ID attribute refers to a row of the same table.

1.3.2 Benefits of the Relational Model

Relational databases exist to make data more *consistent*. Decomposing data into multiple tables eliminates special codes—for example, field EMPLOYEE_ID means `employee_id` when `employee type = 'E'`, and it means `social security number` when `employee type = 'C'`. Decomposition also seeks to represent each item of data in a single location, thereby ensuring data *integrity*; data lacks integrity if your phone number on the employee master file is 555-1212, but on the payroll system it is 555-1213. Decomposition also eliminates *update* anomalies. For example, if I change a special code column (`employee type`), I must also remember to change the `EMPLOYEE_ID`. If I update one and forget to update the other, the data does not make sense as a whole, even though each piece of it may be correct.

Relational tables are always rectangular, a shape that implies the following:

- Each row has the same number of columns.
- Each column consists of values from a single simple data type. The relational model does not support columns that consist of arrays, multiple name-value pairs, or complex "objects."
- Within a table, a single column has the same data type in all rows. There is no support for a table in which the type of column 3 is an integer in row 1 but a character or date type in row 2.

1.3.3 Relational Model Support in ADO.NET

ADO.NET supports the relational model in two ways. First, the *connected* data access model contains all the usual methods for accessing a relational database, including support for parameterized queries, stored procedures, SQL batches, and transactions. This is similar to support in all other data access APIs such as OLE DB, Open Database Connectivity (ODBC), and JDBC.

Second, ADO.NET contains a *disconnected* `DataSet` class that models a relational database even though the data need not originally come from a relational database. `DataSet` supports multiple rectangular tables, relationships, and integrity constraints and even lets you subset tables using a SQL-like query language. The disconnected model also includes the `DataAdapter` class, which uses connections and commands and acts as a *bridge class* between the `DataSet` and the database.

Relational data is so central to ADO.NET that the `XmlDataDocument` class gives you ways to coerce nonrelational data into the relational `DataSet`. You'll see these features as we progress through the model.

1.4 Hierarchies, Objects, and Hybrids

Now let's explore ADO.NET's support for data models that predate the relational model. These ancient data models may bear some resemblance to more modern data models, and so it's instructional to see why they were used (and still are used, although to a lesser extent).

Early databases consisted of flat files with indexes, much like desktop databases such as Microsoft Access and Lotus dBase. IBM introduced the ISAM (Indexed Sequential Access Method) file access method to complement its Basic Direct Access Method (BDAM). BDAM files use pointers to physical cylinders and tracks on disk to index data. To move a file from one place to another, users must employ utilities that "fix" the physical pointers as they move the data, but because of their dependence on physical pointers, BDAM and ISAM (like Data Access Objects (DAO) and the Access Jet Engine) are blazingly fast.

Among the first databases that dealt with structured data were those that use the hierarchical model, such as IBM's Information Management System (IMS), and the CODASYL (also called network or ring) model, such as Cullinane's Integrated Database Management System (IDMS). These databases use navigation-based access and keep physical pointers as references to related items. Because navigation-based data access and nonrelational data models made their way back into the mainstream with the appearance of XML and semistructured data, it may help if we examine them. Navigation through hierarchies is used in ADO.NET's `XPathNavigator`, `XmlDocument`, and related classes.

Hierarchical databases add a parent-child structure to simple file layouts, known as *physical database records*; individual occurrences are called *segments*. IMS uses a set of navigation-based operations, defined by a data manipulation language known as DL/I. Table 1–1 summarizes the DL/I operations. Because each segment at a given level of the hierarchy is of the same type, this is also known as a *homogeneous hierarchy*.

CODASYL databases add to the basic hierarchical structures and operations. A parent and its children form a basic *set* (not to be confused with a set in relational database terms because this set includes the parent). Variants of the

Table 1–1   DL/I operations

Operation	Usage
GET UNIQUE (GU)	Direct retrieval
GET NEXT (GN)	Sequential retrieval
GET NEXT WITHIN PARENT (GNP)	Sequential retrieval under current parent
GET HOLD (GHU, GHN, GHNP)	Like "get for update"
INSERT (ISRT)	Add new segment
DELETE (DLET)	Delete existing segment
REPLACE (REPL)	Replace existing segment

set, known as *multimember set* and *set with multiple ownership*, might include a hierarchy containing more than one set type or a hierarchy containing more than one record type, as shown in Figure 1–1. In this book, hierarchies with multiple

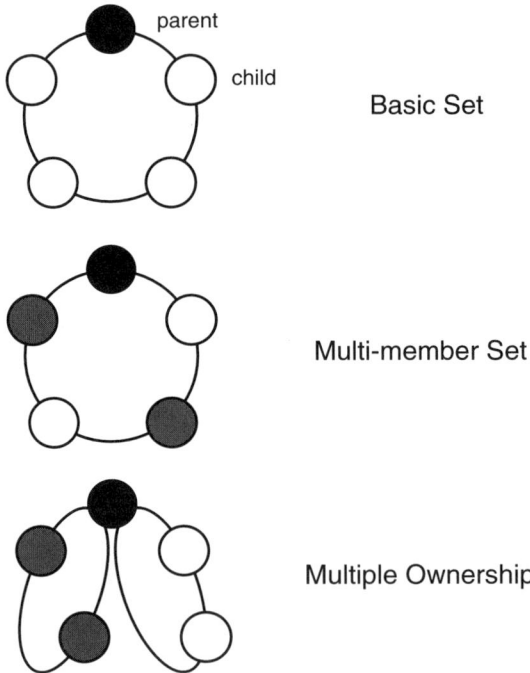

Figure 1–1   IDMS set structures

ownership or record types are called *heterogeneous hierarchies*. They are similar to common patterns in today's object-oriented databases and object application programming systems.

This model uses a rich series of navigation-based operations for data retrieval. The data retrieval results are based on a series of current positions (in the set, area, and so on) known as *currencies positions*. Tables 1–2 and 1–3 show some of the navigation functions and options.

1.4.1 Modern Nonrelational Data

Based on the popularity of object-oriented programming and analysis techniques and the necessity of storing and querying large objects (LOBs) consisting of nonrelational but structured data (such as Graphics Interchange Format (GIF) image

Table 1–2 IDMS navigation options

Operation	Usage
CALC	Locate directly by symbolic key
DB-KEY	Locate directly by database key
CURRENT	Locate directly based on currencies
WITHIN SET	Locate relative to logical relationships with other records
WITHIN AREA	Locate directly or relatively, based on its physical location

Table 1–3 IDMS options for the WITHIN SET operation

Option	Usage
FIRST	First member of the set
LAST	Last member of the set
Nth	Nth member of the set
NEXT	Next record in the set
PRIOR	Previous record in the set
OWNER	Locates parent (or owner) of the set
USING	Locates record by sorted value

data), two new types of databases have sprung up in recent years. They are known as *object database management systems* (ODBMS) and *object-relational database management systems* (ORDBMS). They differ from relational databases in structure and function.

As explained earlier, in a relational database, data from like instances is decomposed into like sets known as tables. The tables are connected by relationships. In object databases, on the other hand, all data pertaining to an individual instance is stored together as a graph of objects. Instances of like classes can be indexed. Object graphs can be homogeneous or heterogeneous hierarchies and can be connected by relationships. They are similar to the data representation in network or hierarchical databases. Queries are written using OQL. Object-relational databases, a hybrid of relational and object databases, are most closely related to relational databases. Although most data in object relational databases is accessed as relational data, specific types such as GIF files or multimedia data are stored as BLOB (*binary large object*) columns and are accessed using special functions, based on knowledge of their internal structure.

An object database more closely models the view of data in a modern object-oriented language, such as a .NET language, and in some cases can outperform a relational database. But relational databases are much more popular because of the speed of most queries based on *just-in-time* (JIT) optimization and the parallelism of set-based queries. In addition, relational databases offer easy schema evolution and a well-known query language, SQL. Relational database schemas are commonly mapped to object graphs via data access APIs or object-relational mapping tools.

Detractors, however, compare the heavy use of decomposition in the relational model to storing a car by removing its wheels and storing them with wheels from all other cars, headlights with other headlights, and so on. To retrieve data, a relational database must gather these parts and rejoin them by using relationships—a complex and possibly time-consuming method that compares unfavorably with storing the car as an organic object and driving it out when ready.

1.4.2 Multidimensional Data

To analyze summarized data, database developers enable queries on data *aggregates* (summaries) in many dimensions, such as by geographic location, time, and so on, something known as *multidimensional data*. Historical data is stored within a *data warehouse*, or *datamart*, in a structure that simplifies what-if queries; this approach is known as *decision support*. Analysis of this summarized data is known as *online analytical processing* (OLAP). OLAP data is not stored in relational tables but rather is stored in multidimensional *cubes*, which consist of a main *fact table* (such as sales) analyzed based on possibly hierarchical dimensions (such as city, within state, within region, and within country).

The unique thing about multidimensional data is that, although data is usually presented in rectangular sets of cells (representing a "slice" through the data cube), the axes are as important as the data, and they are most likely hierarchical. This data type is also best for performance in that it retains as many precalculated aggregations as possible, or at least the most common ones, for ease in querying (hence the name "data warehouse").

Multidimensional data can be queried through a variety of query languages, although Microsoft has led a consortium to standardize on a SQL-like common language known as MDX (Multidimensional Extensions [to SQL]). You can apply various analysis algorithms to further analyze the summarized data for trending purposes, a practice known as *data mining*.

1.4.3   Nonrelational Data and ADO.NET

Because the relational model has overcome its competitors in popularity, every "universal" API has been couched entirely in the relational universe. OLE DB and JDBC, for example, address nonrelational data through extensions to their base models.

ADO.NET addresses the nonrelational world from several angles. Because nonrelational data is integrated somewhat into OLE DB, you can use it in ADO.NET through an OLE DB interoperability layer. However, because .NET contains direct support for two types of XML-based object serialization (in `System.Runtime.Serialization` and `System.Xml.Serialization`) as well as a data-centric XML stack, XML appears to be the interoperability method of choice for nonrelational data. There is also a specification for specifying OLAP queries and query results in XML format; it's known as the XML for Analysis specification.

1.4.4 XML and the Infoset

XML is a popular data transfer and representation method that can handle rectangular data, multivalued data, homogeneous and heterogeneous hierarchies, arbitrary object graphs, and semistructured data. In addition, it has the advantage of being supported on almost every operating system and programming platform.

Note that *semistructured* data is defined as schemaless, or self-describing, data in that the schema exists as part of the data itself rather than in separate structures in a database. Schemaless data has many uses, such as describing data that varies in format (similar in concept to ASN.1 encoding).

It's also useful for *screen scraping*, a process originally designed to procure data from terminal formats such as VT-100 or IBM 3270. With the advent of mountains of data in Hypertext Markup Language (HTML) format, screen scraping has experienced a revival because it lets you obtain text from within HTML tags in Web pages. The problems with scraping HTML were that data was structured based on presentation requirements, and the only data type used was text (character strings). XML solves both problems. Because XML data can be transformed in HTML pages, directly or by use of stylesheets, it is possible to separate presentation from content. In addition, because XML retains the "tags plus text" approach, additional metadata in the form of an XML schema can add type to the text-only data.

XML was meant to serve (and integrate) the needs of the document and data communities, as is obvious in the differences between XML DTDs (document type definitions) and the XML Schema Definition Language (XSD). XML is defined as a series of specifications—that is, how things are intended to work. Many diverse implementations of the specification exist. Interestingly, the original specification for XML (XML 1.0) specified the serialization format in terms of elements, attributes, encodings, and so on. XML structure is defined in terms of an abstract data model known as the XML Information Set (Infoset). The XML schema is used to define simple and complex types within a single XML document or series of XML documents.

The XML specifications include a query language based on hierarchical locations (XPath 1.0) that produces sets of nodes; the specs define how to represent an XML document as a series of nodes—the Document Object Model (DOM)—and include a set of interfaces and methods that provide navigation and allow updating in place. The .NET XML stack adds the `XPathNavigator` type as a refinement of this process. The model and APIs exposed are currency-based and are similar to the hierarchical and network database models discussed earlier. XPath is reminiscent of the SQL language, but queries are also based on the notion of currency. In other words, the same XPath query can produce different results within the same document based on the current position.

1.4.5 XML, Databases, and Universal Data Representation

Relational databases are good for storing data in a controlled, administered manner. They have built-in support for fast concurrent access and optimized set-based query capabilities. However, the protocol and packet formats are database-specific. XML is an almost universally supported method for passing data around. It is supported by unlike architectures. Given that each XML document must have a single root element, the document must be somewhat hierarchical by default.

XML documents can consist of a series of "organic" types. When they do, they most closely represent a graph of objects in an ODBMS or a network DBMS. The information in an XML document can be decomposed into multiple relational tables. This decomposition process reduces database round-trips because the entire document can be passed in at once and parsed into multiple relational tables.

Going the other way, when data needs to be presented as an XML document, *composition* of multiple tables is required. The easiest approach is to use extensions to SQL that know how to produce an XML hierarchy based on the individual tables in a join. Some databases provide extension functions that enable document composition. You can use special logic in stored procedures to add extra data that is provided in the document but doesn't correspond to a specific relational table.

Some databases have XML features built into the server, and integration features may be built into the underlying APIs. An application can facilitate the sending and receiving of SQL results using Hypertext Transfer Protocol (HTTP) and formatting of output as XML, optionally adding stylesheets.

If the XML schema specification can describe all known types in all known type systems (as some of its inventors claim), it is fairly easy to produce XML from any data (relational, hierarchical, object graph, and so on). However, if you must convert XML into a different data model, it is essentially a receiver-makes-right process.

For example, if you wish to transform your XML data into a relational model (because you have a relational database), you must come up with a set of rules for transformation. It's possible to introduce ambiguity by using different rule sets. Microsoft defines a set of rules in .NET for mapping XML data to a (relational) `DataSet` when the method `DataSet.ReadXml` is called. Chapter 7 explains these rules and discusses the extent of XML–relational integration as exposed through ADO.NET.

For more information about XML, see *Essential XML* by Don Box, Aaron Skonnard, and John Lam (Addison-Wesley, 2000).

1.5 Data-centric Application Models

Now let's look at how to use these data designs, and use ADO.NET support, in different types of applications. We'll discuss embedded, client-server, three-tier, and disconnected applications.

Embedded applications are defined as applications in which a single user owns the data store. The data store usually is local, existing as a file on the user's desktop or PDA (personal digital assistant) device. Access, dBase, and other file-based databases—referred to as XBase—are ideally suited for this type of application. Although these data sources understand SQL, they deal in file offset–based records. One record at a time (cursor-based) access is acceptable because the data is local, even though SQL performs much better with set-based operations.

This information relates to traditional relational databases in two ways. First, you may want to run a *client-server* database—such as SQL Server MSDE (Microsoft Data Engine) or Oracle Lite—as a desktop database rather than use a file-based XBase database. Some relational databases now contain optimizations for local operation. SQL Server, for example, has an *in-memory network library* that operates on the buffers of data in SQL Server's memory rather than involving network protocols and data buffer copies. Although it is possible that XBase file displacement-based direct access may be less expensive in terms of resources, MSDE is poised to replace Access and other XBase variants. Nevertheless, there are still many XBase applications that need to be supported or ported in the .NET world.

The other effect on client-server databases is that many programmers attempt to port XBase applications directly to client-server by using the same record-at-a-time data access code and modifying only the data source connection string. Although this technique works, performance is much worse because a round-trip to the remote database is made for each record. SQL Server *netlibs* (libraries that are used to communicate between a SQL Server client and SQL Server) do buffer the fetches, but this is not a solution to the problem. For best performance, you must rewrite the data access code to use set-based data access and minimize round-trips to the data store by using program modules (stored procedures) that execute multiple statements in a single round-trip. Figure 1–2 illustrates this approach.

Three-tier applications are similar to client-server apps with respect to the database but add complications of their own. Large-scale applications usually require at least one dedicated database machine. Although there is no correspondence between three-tier systems and three physical machines, this usually means that the database lives on a different machine from the middle-tier server (the Web server or application server). Three-tier systems can be thought of as two client-server systems. The principles of minimizing round-trips to a remote database apply both to the client-to-app server and app server-to-database layers, as Figure 1–3 illustrates.

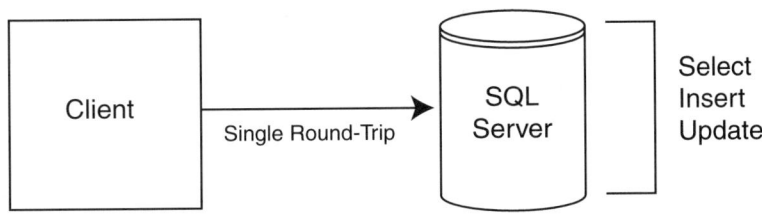

Figure 1–2 Stored procedures in a client-server app

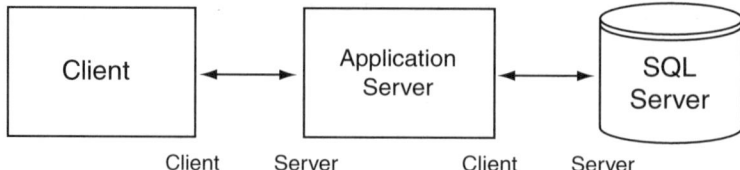

Client	Application Server	SQL Server
Client	Server	Client	Server

Figure 1–3 A three-tier application

In a client-server application, access is limited and controlled, simplifying database session management. Each client connects to the database when the local application is started and uses the same session throughout. Database administrators know exactly how many concurrent connections they need. Administrators can tune for a specific session load. Session settings, such as current database, affect only the current user. Users can use a unique sign-on, and their database activity can be tracked.

Three-tier Web-based applications need a much wider range of session load because the load is unpredictable, and administrators must plan for the busiest case. No one wants a Web site to break when it gets popular. But because many of these applications are public Internet applications, you cannot assign each potential user a unique user ID. For this reason, three-tier applications use short-lived sessions and session pooling. This approach fits in well with DBMS session pooling because a unique session should not be reserved for each potential user. Microsoft data access methods, such as ODBC and OLE DB, enable this pooling on the client (app server) side rather than use server-side connection pooling, as Oracle applications can.

Pooling has repercussions for application coding and implications for session parameters. Suppose that user A allocates connection A to the SQL Server NORTHWIND database. He then changes the current database using the SQL Server directive USE PUBS. When user B acquires the connection through connection pooling, it's possible that she could be in an unexpected database rather than the expected NORTHWIND database. The need for application code to use short-lived connections, enabled by session pooling, also limits the effectiveness of pessimistic locking, cursor-based programming, and other popular techniques. Chapter 3 explains how connection pooling works in ADO.NET data providers and how it handles these problems.

As a final distinction between client-server and three-tier apps, connection pooling works only if all the connections use a single identity. Connections as user "joeuser" would not pool with connections as user "sa" but instead would form two separate pools. To make the most of connection pooling, you must use a single identity. Auditors and database administrators are accustomed to tracking database activity through identity. This practice must change in a three-tier system; they must track identity and enforce security through the app server layer rather than through the database.

Finally, let's look at the disconnected application, a specialized but popular application style. It's a hybrid of an embedded application and a client-server or three-tier application. The canonical example of this type of application is a sales application. While in the main office, salespeople work connected to the central database. They can extract only the subset of the database that they need (in this case, their own customer accounts) to a local database on their laptop for use (and potential updates) while offline. When they return to the office and reconnect, their changes are transmitted to the central database. ADO.NET has specific classes to enable this sort of data access.

1.6 Evolution of Data Access APIs

Database manufacturers have a history of optimizing data access by writing models as specific to their own databases as possible so that they can take advantage of database-specific features. Indeed, until ODBC, the data access API or the embedded SQL precompiler was considered as much a part of the database as the query optimizer or data monitoring tools. Until the advent of SQL and its adoption as a uniform query language for relational databases, each database shipped not only a data access API and tools but also a DBMS-specific query language. Despite claims by inventors of relational theory that SQL is flawed, this common, easy-to-use, powerful query language may be one of the reasons for the success of the relational database model.

There are two main ways to accomplish data access when you're using heterogeneous data stores: universal server and universal data access (UDA). The concept behind *universal server* (Figure 1–4) is to move all data content to a single data store such as an Oracle or DB2 database. The advantage of this

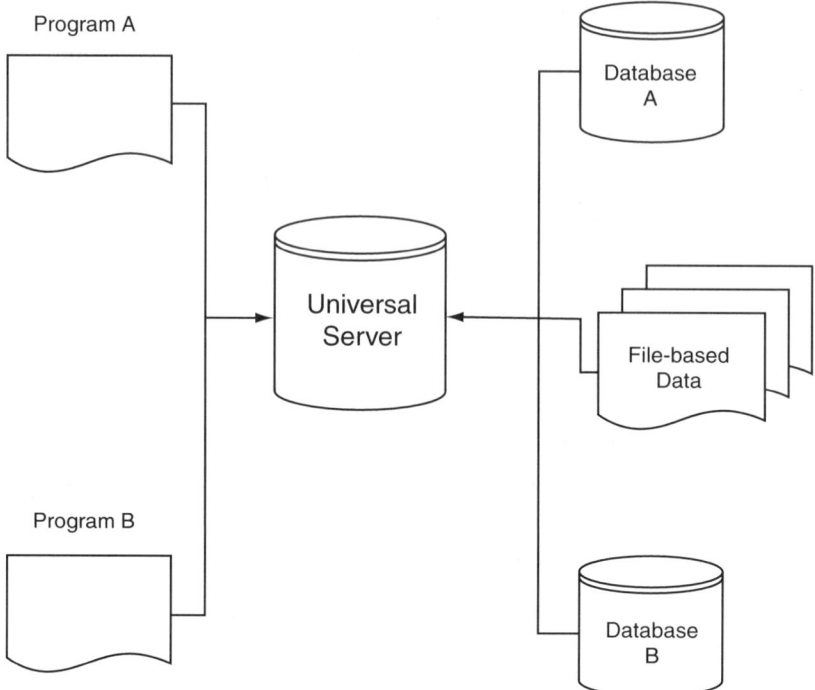

Figure 1–4   Universal server

method is that you can use a single API, optimized to your database implementation, to access all data. The data is also stored together for ease in administration and access control. The disadvantage is that all data must be replicated to the common data store. Because the replication schedule will be different for different subsystems, related data from different stores will always be a little out of sync. This approach might also require reformatting of data, also known as *data cleansing*.

In *universal data access* (Figure 1–5), data is not replicated but instead is accessed through a common generic API. Each provider or driver writer implements the API in a manner optimized for its particular data store. Not only does the common API save programming resources, but also the data is current, although it might be harder to find it and obtain access. Each data source can be accessed in a format close to its native format, although programming can be more difficult based on the subtle differences in format. In each case,

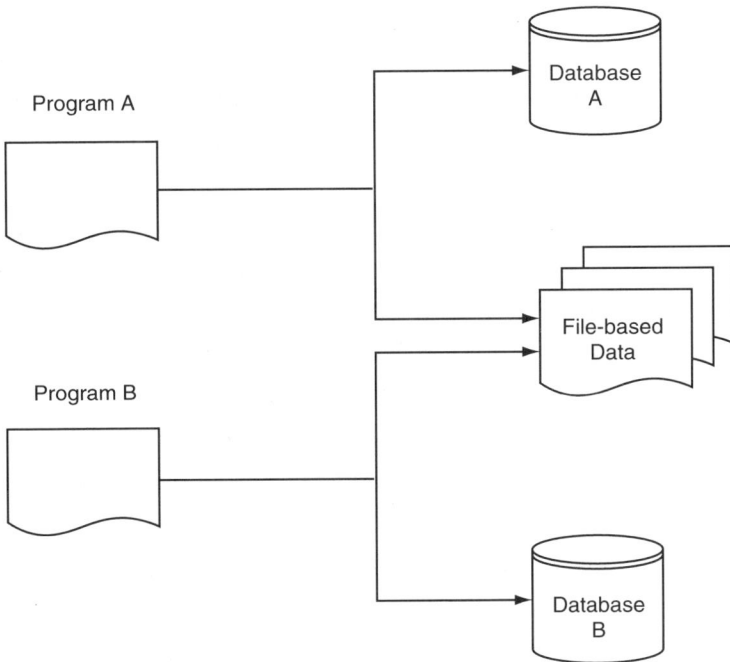

Figure 1–5   Universal data access

data moves across the network. Probably less data is moved when you use UDA because data is fetched only when needed; however, replication is scheduled in the case of a universal server, and ad hoc with UDA. ADO.NET facilitates UDA.

In generic data access APIs, SQL is almost always used. The SQL standard for a data access API is known as SQL-CLI (SQL Call Language Interface). It is most closely related to ODBC. In writing any data access API, you must address three main problems:

- The need to map SQL data types to host language data types and SQL objects to host language objects

- The impedance mismatch between SQL set-based processing and programming languages' record-at-a-time processing

- The need to synchronize host program flow with SQL execution flow, as in implementing SQL error handling versus programming exceptions

Because Microsoft has ruled the desktop and end-user world since the early 1990s, it was only natural that the company would participate and encourage a common data access API that attempts to abstract away the differences among data stores and, with OLE DB, to abstract away the differences among database query languages.

Among Microsoft's first data access APIs were DAO (Data Access Objects) and ODBC. DAO is an object model based on the Microsoft Jet Engine library used by Microsoft Access. Jet Engine technology can also be applied to any data store that uses ISAM data access. The ODBC API is not based on an object model but instead is a traditional handle-based, C-style API. ODBC was the first attempt to standardize data access among unlike databases. Contrary to popular belief, it was not invented by Microsoft but rather by a consortium of database vendors, including not only Microsoft but also Oracle, Sybase, and IBM. Microsoft hoped to use this abstraction to enable easy integration of its suite of end-user tools.

ODBC is a data access method meant to be used by enterprise databases such as Oracle, DB2, Sybase, and Microsoft's own SQL Server. Because ODBC is geared toward providing a common API for databases that speak SQL, it consists of two specifications: one for standard access and one for standard SQL. It was developed at about the same time as the SQL-92 specification series. To ensure universal adaptation, ODBC mirrors the SQL-CLI portion of the SQL-92 spec. ODBC version 3.0 claims almost complete compliance, function by function, with SQL-CLI.

As far as the relational community was concerned, ODBC was nearly perfect. Enterprise relational database and desktop databases alike included ODBC drivers. Even ODBMS (object-oriented database management systems) and hierarchical database vendors developed ODBC drivers, coerced their databases into a pseudo-relational model, and implemented a SQL layer. ODBC is still probably the most widely adopted data access technology.

The problem with ODBC, as far as Microsoft was concerned, was that ODBC did not use the Component Object Model (COM). An early attempt to correct this was called RDO (Remote Data Objects). RDO exposed a thin COM object layer directly over ODBC's connection and statements. Although relatively fast and accessible in any programming language, RDO never caught on in a big way.

OLE DB and ADO are Microsoft's COM-based approach to universal data access. OLE DB abstracts data access into a series of well-defined abstract objects, known as *cotypes*. These cotypes consist of a series of well-factored interfaces. Each provider implements the same cotypes and interfaces, although some cotypes and interfaces are required and others are optional. OLE DB interfaces use pointers, structures, and C-style arrays, along with COM custom interfaces. This means that native OLE DB programming is restricted to a subset of programming languages. OLE DB does not mandate a specific query language or data model, although it is skewed toward the relational model.

ADO is a library layered on top of OLE DB and differs in that there are fewer objects in the model, and each object type has one main interface. This interface is a COM dual interface that can be used by scripting languages as well as low-level languages such as C++. ADO was the API used by most programmers in the days before .NET. In addition to "standard" ADO, some specialized data access functionality is available in companion libraries. RDS (Remote Data Services) deals with the problem of remoting resultsets and commands through firewalls by using port 80 and defines a special binary marshaling format known as Advanced Data TableGram (ADTG). Support for ADTG is built into the Microsoft Internet Explorer Web browser. The ADO Extensions (ADOX) library enables data definition language functionality if this functionality is supported by the underlying provider. The ADO for Multidimensional Data (ADOMD) library extends ADO support to the multidimensional data model for providers that support this model.

Because most database programmers have been using ADO or OLE DB, Chapters 8 and 9 present a detailed overview of ADO and OLE DB along with migration and interoperability strategies. Chapter 8 deals with the problem from the points of view of an OLE DB programmer and also an OLE DB provider writer. Chapter 9 addresses ADO users, as well as users of ADO specialization libraries, and also users of ODBC and its object-oriented Java implementation, JDBC.

ADO.NET takes up where OLE DB and ADO leave off. Code in ADO.NET runs mostly in the .NET managed environment for performance reasons, as well as to benefit from other .NET improvements such as code safety checking and code access security. ADO.NET libraries can be used from any .NET-compliant programming language. Because .NET APIs expose functionality directly in both classes and interfaces—rather than only in interfaces—the ADO.NET classes also reflect this design. Through integration with XML in a variety of ways, the combination of ADO.NET and the XML stack enables access to relational, nonrelational, and other data models.

1.7   Where Are We?

We've defined the various models of data to be reckoned with in a heterogeneous environment: relational, homogeneous, and heterogeneous hierarchies, object graphs, semistructured, and flat files. You've also learned about the methods to access them (roughly, currency- and navigation-based, and set-based) and the types of data access applications you might build. Next, you'll see how the ADO.NET and XML API stacks in the .NET platform provide a programming model that attempts to address the common problems that you might encounter.

Chapter 2

ADO.NET Basics

To codify de facto standards, ADO.NET deals with three data access styles:

- Connected data access
- Disconnected data access with (optional) optimistic concurrency
- Mixing of traditional database access and XML

2.1 Data Access and the .NET Architecture

.NET is the newest Microsoft environment for running code. Instead of having direct access to memory through pointers, code runs inside the .NET execution engine. The engine provides memory management, garbage collection, code security, versioning, and other services. Interoperability with legacy code is provided by means of *COM-callable wrappers* (for COM code) and *platform invoke* (PInvoke) for non-COM code. *Runtime callable wrappers* (RCWs) permit legacy COM code to call managed classes as if they were COM classes.

Where does that leave SQL Server and data access code? Currently, it leaves them mostly outside the runtime. There is no supported way (yet) to have SQL code interoperate completely with managed classes inside SQL Server, although you can manually load the execution engine in SQL Server, load classes, and invoke methods. Running the execution engine under SQL Server and the resultant integration will be a feature of the next version of SQL Server, code-named Yukon. All current APIs and netlibs sit outside the execution engine. Every call that crosses the boundary between managed and unmanaged code involves overhead. A new *data provider* architecture minimizes this overhead by reducing the number of transitions between managed and unmanaged space. A data provider set of classes is similar in concept to OLE DB providers, ODBC drivers, or JDBC drivers.

ADO.NET improves on previous APIs, not so much by adding new functionality (in fact, ADO.NET in version 1.0 is a functional subset of most previous relational APIs) but rather by making it clear to the programmer what is going on in terms of database round-trips, whether or not the results from SQL SELECT statements permit in-place updates and clarifying ownership of those sets of data. A "misunderstanding" that plagued previous data access specifications and libraries was the difference between data access in connected and disconnected mode. ADO.NET addresses this confusion by making them separate object models and providing a bridge class between them.

ADO.NET also attempts to address the difficulties in using data access with graphical user interface elements, known as *databound controls*. A mapping model and new data binding APIs make it easier to expose data through visual controls without writing extensive code.

One last point: Database developers are exposing increasing amounts of data, for interoperability reasons, through XML. The ADO.NET stack features tight integration with pieces of the XML stack, exposing disconnected data in either the XML model or the relational database model. There are a number of integration points in the XML stack that let you either write data providers or XML Infoset providers, or use OLE DB providers to access custom data. Which one is most useful depends on the data store and data access paradigm you're using.

2.2 Two Patterns of Data Access

Data is no good unless you can access it. As a contrived example, suppose I keep a diary in which I record, among all the facets of my personal life, how much I spent on each purchase in my important role as a consumer. If the Internal Revenue Service wants to know how much I spent on charitable contributions, for example, it does not want me to send in the whole diary. Instead, it wants a summary. Similarly, in the manufacturing and sales industries, businesses and consumers want to track the status of their orders. They want to know, for example, whether an order has been received, processed, manufactured, and shipped.

There are two methods of accessing this data: connected and disconnected. In *connected* mode, you install a terminal or client-server application on the user's desk. This connects the user directly to the database. In *disconnected* mode, you use a Web browser. The browser has the following advantages:

- You don't need extra software (except the browser) at each customer site.
- You don't need special cabling because the customers install their own Internet connections.
- You don't need specialized data entry or telephone support staff to enter the customer's data or request. Data entry is performed by the consumer.

The difference between the two approaches is that in disconnected mode the consumer has a connection to the company's Web server and not to its database. In this scenario, customer satisfaction is achieved by letting customers download a subset of data (into, for example, Excel, Quicken, or a personal digital assistant) and work on it using their own device, possibly uploading changes to the central store. Figure 2–1 shows these two access types.

Connected access (to the database) is performed at the Web server (or other *service agent*). Disconnected access—dealing not with a database but with sets, graphs, or trees of data—is implemented at the client. This chapter illustrates each of these modes of data access with a simple example. The examples illustrate how to access an actual database using the `SqlClient` data provider set of classes, optimized for and specific to SQL Server. Other data providers have the same general structure and functions.

2.3 Connected Mode

The `Connection` class in connected mode represents a connection to a data store that uses a proprietary protocol. The connection string identifies which data store the user wishes to log on to and identifies the user. (*User* is an antiquated term in a three-tier scenario; usually, the "user" is a service agent and not the end user.) The following code opens a database connection through the

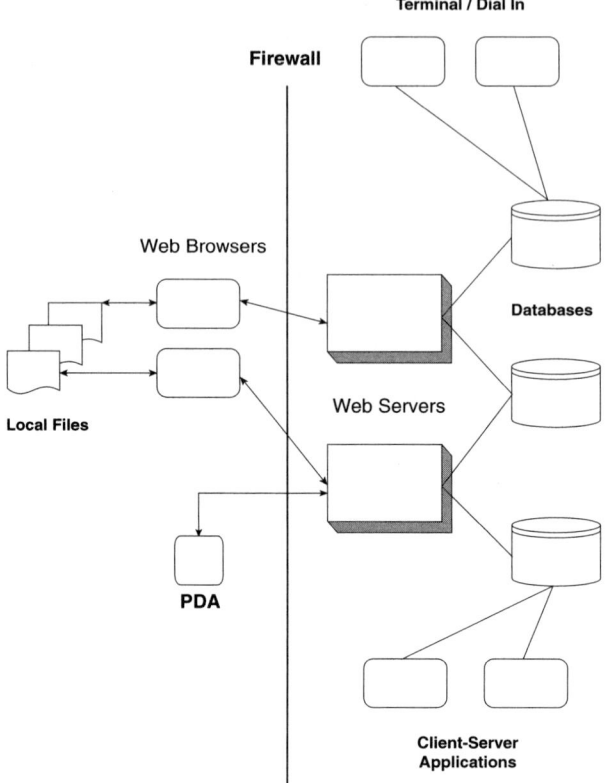

Terminal / Dial In

Firewall

Web Browsers

Databases

Local Files

Web Servers

PDA

Client-Server Applications

Figure 2–1   Two ways of accessing data

`SqlClient` and `OleDb` data providers. This code will look familiar if you've used a data access API.

```
// open a connection to SQL Server
SqlConnection sconn = new SqlConnection(
   "server=myserver;uid=sam;pwd=tc8!at;database=acme");
sconn.Open();

// open a connection to SQL Server
OleDbConnection oconn = new OleDbConnection(
   "provider=sqloledb;data source=myserver;" +
   "user id=sam;password=tc8!at;initial catalog=acme");
oconn.Open();
```

Although these connection strings are analogous, what is going on behind the scenes (and the software required to make it work) is vastly different in the two examples. In the first example, managed code is used to construct a tabular data stream (TDS) packet and ship the TDS to SQL Server. In the second example, managed code calls out to a set of COM components (an OLE DB provider, which must be installed on every user's machine), which constructs the TDS and sends it to a SQL client. The difference is that in the first case each user does not need to have the OLE DB provider installed. Of course, the `SqlClient` and `OleDb` data providers live in `System.Data.dll`, which must be deployed and versioned on every machine. In addition, the SQL client network libraries must be installed on each machine.

From now on in this overview, I refer only to the `Sql` series of classes. If you stick to basic functionality, you can substitute the analogous `OleDb` classes when you require connection to a non-SQL Server database. Remember that the `OleDb` managed provider exists only to provide an immediate path for data sources that don't yet have a native data provider. Of course, most real users won't be connecting directly to the data store at all but instead will be submitting requests and obtaining data through a level of indirection. We'll get back to this.

Listing 2–1 shows a simple console application written in the C# (pronounced "C sharp") programming language.

Listing 2–1 A simple console application

```
using System;
using System.Data;
using System.Data.SqlClient;

namespace Chapter2
{
  class Class1
  {
    static void Main(string[] args) //
    {
      // (1) declarations begin
      SqlConnection conn = new SqlConnection(
        "server=localhost;uid=sa;pwd=;database=pubs");
```

```
SqlCommand cmd1 = new SqlCommand(
  "select au_id, au_fname, au_lname from authors", conn);
SqlCommand cmd2 = new SqlCommand(
  "insert_new_job", conn);
SqlDataReader rdr = null;
// (1) declarations end
try
{
  conn.Open(); // (4)
  rdr = cmd1.ExecuteReader(); // (6)
  while (rdr.Read()) // (7)
  {
    Console.WriteLine("author id is {0}", rdr[0]); // (8)
    Console.WriteLine("author name is {0} {1}",
      rdr["au_fname"], rdr["au_lname"]);
  }
  rdr.Close(); // (9)

  /*
   *   create procedure insert_new_job(
   *     @desc varchar(50),
   *     @max tinyint,
   *     @min tinyint)
   *as
   *   insert into jobs values(@desc, @max, @min)
   */

  cmd2.CommandType = CommandType.StoredProcedure; //(10)
  cmd2.Parameters.Add("@desc", SqlDbType.VarChar); // (11)
  cmd2.Parameters.Add("@max", SqlDbType.TinyInt);
  cmd2.Parameters.Add("@min", SqlDbType.TinyInt);

  cmd2.Parameters[0].Value = "Grand Poobah";
  cmd2.Parameters[1].Value = 50;
  cmd2.Parameters[2].Value = 40;

  int rows = cmd2.ExecuteNonQuery(); //(12)

  Console.WriteLine("{0} rows affected", rows);
}
// (2)
catch (SqlException se)
```

```
      {
        // first exception only
        Console.WriteLine("SQL Exception: {0}", se.Message);
      }
      // (3)
      catch (Exception e)
      {
        // write message
        Console.WriteLine("Exception: {0}", e.Message);
      }
        finally
        {
          // (5)
          if(rdr != null && !rdr.IsClosed)
            rdr.Close();
          cmd1.Dispose();
          cmd2.Dispose();
          if (conn.State == ConnectionState.Open)
            conn.Close();
        }
      }
    }
  }
```

This program serves as an introduction to ADO.NET program structure and also illustrates the most familiar of the data access paradigms, connected data access. Figure 2–2 shows the series of classes exposed by the `SqlClient` data provider for connected data access.

Listing 2–1 is a console application that simply connects to a SQL Server database, issues a `SELECT` command, reads the set of results produced, and then uses the same connection to invoke a parameterized stored procedure that returns only a count of rows affected. It starts by instantiating a `SqlConnection` using the `new` operator, which takes a connection string as a constructor argument. Then it instantiates two `SqlCommand` instances—`cmd1` and `cmd2`—using a constructor that takes two arguments: a command string containing the SQL command to be executed and a `SqlConnection` instance. The first `SqlCommand` consists of a single `SELECT` statement, and the second one names a stored procedure, `insert_new_job`. Finally, the code defines a variable that will hold an instance of a `SqlDataReader` class and initializes the variable to null (1). This example uses types from the `SqlClient` data provider.

You declare these classes outside a C# `try-catch-finally` block so that you can catch exceptions and clean up. If something goes wrong, the `SqlClient` provider throws an exception, usually of type `SqlException`. The code defines multiple catch blocks: one specifically for the `SqlException` (2) and another one for all other types of exceptions (3). The first thing you do inside the try block is to open the `Connection` to the database (4). The `finally` block closes the connection in the normal case and also in case of an exception (5).

After you've opened the `SqlConnection`, you next execute the SELECT command. The `SqlCommand.ExecuteReader` method returns a set of rows or other results (which I refer to as a *resultset*), and you encapsulate this in the `SqlData-Reader` class (6). `SqlDataReader` has a method called `Read()` that reads the

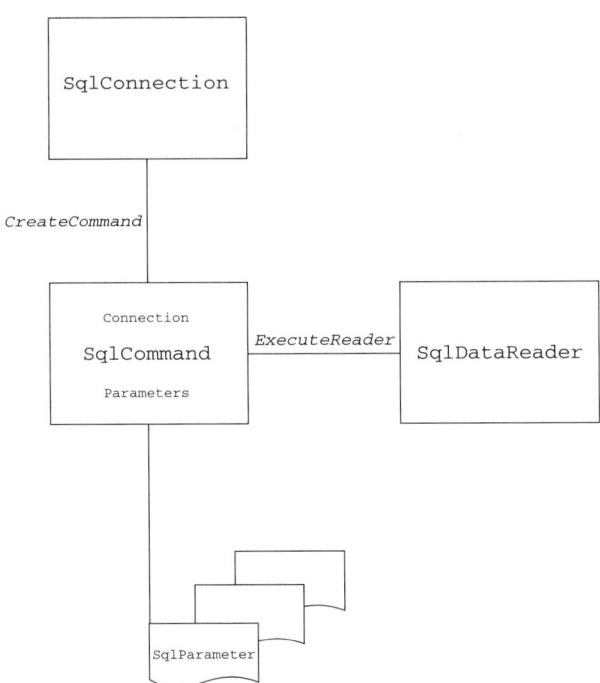

Figure 2–2 `SqlClient` **data provider classes**

ESSENTIAL ADO.NET

next row of data, returning `true` if it is a successful read, and `false` if there are no more rows to read (7). Note that, unlike in ADO, the `DataReader` is not already positioned on the first row; you must call `Read()` to obtain the first row.

The program simply loops through the rows, writing the values of columns to the console. You can refer to columns in the current `SqlDataReader` row by column ordinal or by name. Note that the column ordinal is zero-based rather than 1-based (8). This program illustrates a subtle but often forgotten point. When you access data from a data source, it usually arrives over the network, taking up space and time in the transmission. You should never request more data than you or your client will actually use. This query selects three specific columns from the `authors` table and uses all of them. Using `select * from authors` would be wasteful, transmitting nine columns of data for each row and throwing away six. You use (print the value in) each row that you fetch.

When you're finished with a `SqlDataReader`, it should be explicitly closed (9) (as with a `Connection`) rather than garbage-collected. This is critical for some scenarios and data sources more than others, but it's a good habit to get into. When you're using `SqlDataReader`, it matters. I discuss this (and `Command.Dispose`) further in later chapters, but in this case it results in the `SqlConnection` becoming available to be used with the next `SqlCommand`.

Next, you invoke the stored procedure named in `cmd2`. First, you must set the `SqlCommand`'s `CommandType` property to `CommandType.StoredProcedure` (10). You didn't need to explicitly set it with the preceding command because the default is `CommandType.Text`, that is, a simple text-based command. This stored procedure, as you can see, takes three parameters: a `varchar` and two `tinyint`s. You need to add a `SqlParameter` instance to the `SqlCommand`'s `Parameters` collection for each one, naming the parameter (the name must match the name in the stored procedure in this case) and declaring its data type. The data types in this case represent SQL Server's data types, so you use members from the `SqlDbType` enumeration (11).

You know that this stored procedure does not return a resultset, so you use `Command.ExecuteNonQuery` (12) in this case. This simply returns the number of rows affected by the stored procedure, which in this case should be 1. Finally, you print the value, reach the `finally` block, close the `Connection` if it is open, and the program ends.

To compile the program into an executable, you can add a reference during the compile to the dynamic link library (DLL) that contains the types you're referencing: `System.Data.dll` (for `SqlConnection`, `SqlCommand`, and `SqlDataReader`). The compile line could look like this:

```
csc /r:System.Data.dll chapter2_1.cs
```

However, it turns out that both the C# command-line compiler and Visual Studio reference `System.Data.dll` (as well as `System.Xml.dll` and others) by default, so the compile line could be simply

```
csc chapter2_1.cs
```

Either compile line produces an executable, `chapter2_1.exe`, by default.

This concludes the discussion of our sample program that uses connected access. It's connected because the `Open` and `Close` methods of `SqlConnection` scope a connection to the database, and the user connects to the database directly, using a user ID and password. To execute this program, users would have to have the SQL Server client software on their machines as well as network connectivity to your database.

Obviously, this is not the kind of data access program that you're going to let arbitrary Web users execute, especially when the user ID and password in the connection string allows SQL Server system administrator privileges! Arbitrary users should have access only to the data you want them to see and commands you want them to use, and you can implement this policy by using appropriate database permissions. In addition, allowing users to connect directly to the database means that each user takes up the space required for a connection to SQL Server. In this case, the client would most likely be an internal user (inside the organization) or an ASP.NET (.NET's API for Web applications) page running inside the Web server. But this example does introduce the concept of data providers.

2.3.1 `OleDb` and `SqlClient` Data Providers

Taking advantage of proprietary protocols, .NET provides a connected data access stack. With a few refinements in naming, this stack exposes the familiar connection/command/transaction/results model, or data provider model. No existing provider currently supports server cursors or direct updating of resultsets.

The `SqlClient` data provider is specific to and optimized for SQL Server. The `OleDb` data provider can handle data using any OLE DB provider, including providers for SQL Server, Oracle, Jet, and others. Because the `OleDb` data provider makes more round-trips across the runtime boundary, the `SqlClient` data provider is preferable when you're using SQL Server.

The `SqlClient` data provider uses streamed (noncursor) output only. SQL Server cursors are not supported. Almost everything happens in managed code because the code to parse the TDS messages can live inside the execution engine. The only unmanaged code used is the SQL Server network libraries, as illustrated in Figure 2–3.

The `OleDb` data provider, on the other hand, reads and writes data by using handles to rows and unmanaged structures (known as *accessors*). The accessors are bound to managed variables. Therefore, this provider makes one trip across the managed-unmanaged border per row read (OLE DB's `IRowset::GetData`) in

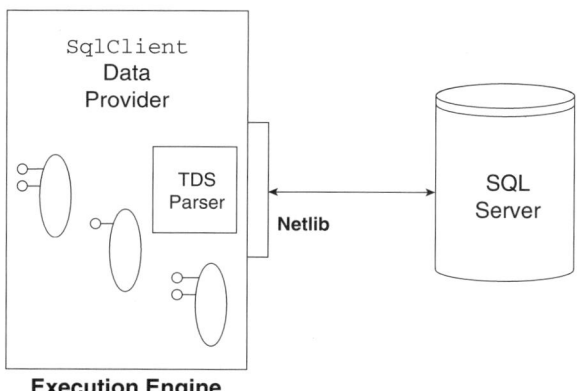

Figure 2–3 The `SqlClient` data provider

addition to calling through the unmanaged OLE DB APIs for almost every other method. This is illustrated in Figure 2–4.

2.3.2 Writing Generic Data Access Code with ADO.NET Data Providers

The data provider portion is factored into common interfaces—which all providers implement—exposed by a series of classes. Each provider may implement these interfaces differently. For example, when you call `IDbConnection.Open` on a data provider, the `OleDb` data provider calls the `IDbInitialize::Initialize` method on the underlying OLE DB provider. In contrast, the `SqlClient` constructs a series of TDS messages that implement a connect protocol sequence for SQL Server.

ODBC, JDBC, OLE DB, and ADO are predicated on defining an identical set of functionality to be implemented by drivers or providers. By permitting extensibility in data types, provider-specific interfaces, cotypes (a notation specific to COM-based OLE DB), and error classes, OLE DB goes the furthest toward defining extensibility points in the architecture. But because Microsoft encouraged consumers to use ADO rather than OLE DB and because ADO does not notice

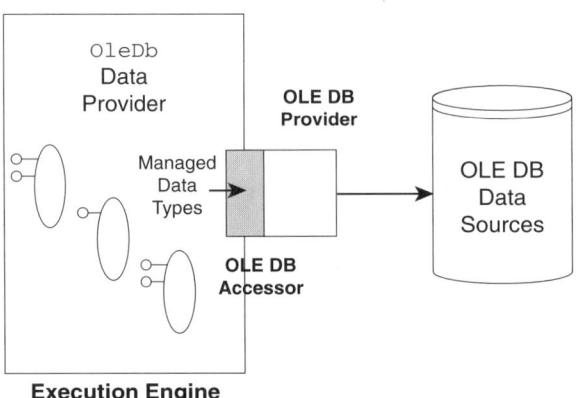

Figure 2–4 The `OleDb` data provider

ESSENTIAL ADO.NET

these extensibility points in general, few provider writers have bothered to implement extensions.

ADO.NET allows data provider writers to extend the model in a way that consumers can understand. This moves the model away from lowest common denominator programming. However, after you've obtained your original IDbConnection interface reference on a data-provider-specific Connection class, you can still write a client that uses only standard interfaces. You can either cast a typed Connection instance back to the IDbConnection interface, or you can use Activator.CreateInstance to instantiate the Connection class. DataAdapter and DbDataAdapter represent the only use of common subclasses in the model; all other generic functionality revolves around common interfaces. Even the mapping of provider data types to .NET Common Language Specification (CLS) types is provider-specific.

Programming generically, however, limits the ways in which you can navigate your way through the common interfaces and types. Listing 2–2 is an example using only generic types.

Listing 2–2 Using generic types

```
namespace DBGeneric
{
  using System;
  using System.Data;
  using System.Data.Common;
  using System.Data.OleDb;
  using System.Data.SqlClient;

  public enum connType {OLEDBConn, SQLConn}

  public class Class1
  {
    public static void Main()
    {
      Client c = new Client();
      c.cMain(connType.SQLConn);
      c.cMain(connType.OLEDBConn);
    }
```

```
public class Client
{
  public void cMain(connType t)
  {
    DBUtil u = new DBUtil();
    IDbConnection iconn = null;
    IDbCommand icmd = null;
    IDataReader irdr = null;
    IDbDataAdapter ida;

    try
    {
      string connStr = "";
      if (t == connType.SQLConn)
        connStr = "server=localhost;" +
          "uid=sa;pwd=;database=pubs";
      else
        if (t == connType.OLEDBConn)
        connStr = "provider=sqloledb;server=localhost;" +
          "uid=sa;pwd=;database=pubs";
      iconn = u.getConn(connStr, t);
      iconn.Open();
      icmd = iconn.CreateCommand();
      icmd.CommandText = "select * from authors";
      irdr = icmd.ExecuteReader();

      while (irdr.Read())
      {
        Console.WriteLine("Author ID = {0}",
          irdr.GetString(0));
      }
      irdr.Close();

      // Parameters
      IDbCommand icmd2;
      icmd2 = iconn.CreateCommand();

      string marker = "";
      if (t == connType.SQLConn)
        marker = "@lname";
      else
```

```csharp
      if (t == connType.OLEDBConn)
        marker = "?";

    icmd2.CommandText =
        "update authors set au_lname = 'Smith' " +
        "where au_lname = " + marker;

    IDataParameter p;
    p = icmd2.CreateParameter();
    p.DbType = DbType.String;
    p.ParameterName = "@lname";
    p.Value = "Smith";
    icmd2.Parameters.Add(p);

    int num = icmd2.ExecuteNonQuery();
    Console.WriteLine("number of authors = {0}", num);

    // DataAdapter
    ida = u.getDA(connStr, "select * from authors", t);

    DataSet ds = new DataSet();
    ida.Fill(ds);
    Console.WriteLine("There is {0} table in the dataset",
        ds.Tables.Count);

    // DataAdapter - better to use base class
    DbDataAdapter da;
    da = u.getDABase(connStr, "select * from authors", t);

    DataSet ds2 = new DataSet();
    da.Fill(ds2, "authors");
    Console.WriteLine("There is {0} table in the dataset",
        ds2.Tables.Count);
}
catch (Exception e)
{
    Console.WriteLine(e.Message);
}
finally
{
    if(irdr != null && !irdr.IsClosed)
        irdr.Close();
```

```
          icmd.Dispose();
          if (iconn != null && iconn.State == ConnectionState.Open)
            iconn.Close();
        }
      }
    }

    public class DBUtil
    {
      public IDbConnection getConn(string s,connType t)
      {
        IDbConnection iconn;
        if (t == connType.SQLConn)
          iconn = new SqlConnection(s);
        else
          iconn = new OleDbConnection(s);
        return iconn;
      }

      public IDbDataAdapter getDA(string conn, string cmd, connType t)
      {
        IDbDataAdapter ida;
        if (t == connType.SQLConn)
          ida = new SqlDataAdapter(cmd, conn);
        else
          ida = new OleDbDataAdapter(cmd, conn);
        return ida;
      }

      public DbDataAdapter getDABase(string conn, string cmd,
        connType t)
      {
        DbDataAdapter da;
        if (t == connType.SQLConn)
          da = new SqlDataAdapter(cmd, conn);
        else
          da = new OleDbDataAdapter(cmd, conn);
        return da;
      }
    }
  }
}
```

2.3.3 Cursors in the Data Provider Model

I mentioned that server cursors are currently not supported in ADO.NET. So what exactly is a cursor? What functionality are you missing out on, and do you really need it?

A *cursor*, at its simplest, is a current position in a set of rows. In some databases, a cursor implies a connection, a currency position, and possibly locking. Currency positions are especially important in systems that have complex type relationships because in addition to navigating to the next row, currency allows navigation at the parent or child level. For example, XML's XPath expressions may produce different results based on the currency position. I discuss XPath in more detail shortly.

The SQL-CLI specification (and the ODBC, OLE DB/ADO, and JDBC implementations) includes the concept of a cursor library to manipulate database cursors (sometimes called server cursors) from API code. In addition, OLE DB/ADO implements the concept of a *client cursor library*. A confusing point is that the client cursor library implements cursor-like functionality by reading an entire set of rows from server to client and implementing cursor-like navigation functions on the client. The *client cursor engine* in OLE DB is actually centered on a COM component (`FX.Rowset`) and two supporting libraries (`msdace.dll` and `msdacer.dll`). Rather than overload the term *client cursor*, which led to confusion in ADO, ADO.NET names the class `DataSet` and adds multitable functionality as well.

Server-side cursors imply a rowset management mechanism in the database itself, along with maintenance of a currency position and a database connection. ADO.NET does not currently support manipulation of server cursors because maintaining a database connection and frequent round-trips to the database to fetch rows based on the database's currency position are not scalable in a three-tier Web-based application.

Unlike ADO, ADO.NET does not attempt to abstract away the differences between client and server "cursors." There are two distinct modes of operation: connected mode and disconnected mode. These modes do not share a

`Recordset` object as in ADO, instead using either a `DataReader` or a `DataSet` to work with sets of data or database query results.

2.4 Disconnected Mode and the `DataSet`

When collecting data for transmission to Web browser or Web service clients, most developers use disconnected mode if the retrieved data can be cached in the middle tier or Web server and reused. This practice eliminates multiple re-dundant round-trips to the database, trading them for the space on the Web server required to store the data in memory. Storing the data on the Web server can be implemented using the ASP.NET `Application`, `Session`, or `Cache` class, subject to concurrency and memory constraints. The replacement for the ADO's client-side, disconnected `Recordset` is the `DataSet`, shown in the next example to illustrate the disconnected mode of data access. The `DataSet` can manage multiple sets of data and relations among them. It is a class that repre-sents data from one or more resultsets. It permits different views on the data and can be persisted to disk or returned to the client. It's also useful in a discon-nected update scenario using optimistic concurrency. Listing 2–3 shows a sim-ple update through a `DataSet`.

Listing 2–3   Disconnected updates

```
using System;
using System.Data;
using System.Data.SqlClient;

namespace Chapter2_3
{
  class Class1
  {
    static void Main(string[] args)
    {
      SqlDataAdapter da = new SqlDataAdapter(
        "select * from authors where au_id > '5%'",
        "server=localhost;uid=sa;pwd=;database=pubs"); // (1)
      SqlCommandBuilder bld = new SqlCommandBuilder(da); // (2)

      DataSet ds = new DataSet(); // (3)
```

```
      try
      {
        da.Fill(ds, "myauthors"); //(4)

        // keep the DataSet around and update it
        ds.Tables["myauthors"].DefaultView.Sort = "au_id"; // (5)
        int idx = // (6)
          ds.Tables["myauthors"].DefaultView.Find("712-45-1867");
          ds.Tables["myauthors"].Rows[idx]["city"] = "Eugene"; //(7)
          ds.Tables["myauthors"].Rows[idx]["state"] = "OR";

        int rows = da.Update(ds, "myauthors"); // (8)
        Console.WriteLine("{0} rows updated", rows);
      }
      catch (SqlException se)
      {
        // first exception only
        Console.WriteLine("SQL Exception: {0}", se.Message);
      }
      catch (Exception e)
      {
        // write message
        Console.WriteLine("Exception: {0}", e.Message);
      }
    }
  }
}
```

This program starts by creating an instance of the SqlDataAdapter class. SqlDataAdapter is used to move data from the database to the DataSet and vice versa. This example uses a constructor that takes two arguments: a SQL command string and a connection string (1). This SELECT statement selects a subset of authors, perhaps to return to a single user, for use while disconnected from the database. After the SqlDataReader, the code declares a SqlCommandBuilder (2). The SqlCommandBuilder class will be used to "automatically" construct SQL INSERT, UPDATE, and DELETE commands when changes to the data are flushed back to the data store. Note that the SqlCommandBuilder takes a SqlDataAdapter instance (which must already be created) in the constructor used here. You also create a new DataSet instance (3).

Calling the `DataAdapter`'s `Fill` method (4) results in the transfer of all matching rows from the database to the `DataSet`. This seemingly simple statement contains a number of interesting aspects. When the `Fill` method is called, it opens the `SqlConnection` to the database using the connection string specified in the constructor. Then the command is executed by means of creating a `SqlCommand` and calling `ExecuteReader`. A new `DataTable` named `"myauthors"` is created inside the `DataSet` using metadata returned by the command to determine the data types of its columns. This `DataTable` is then filled with all the rows read from the database through an implicitly created `SqlDataReader`. When you are finished reading rows, the `SqlDataReader` and the `SqlConnection` are closed. That's quite a lot of work for a single method, although if there were multiple commands to execute, you could use an explicit `SqlConnection` object to more closely manage the connection state.

The `DataSet` has a collection of `DataTable`s. After `SqlDataAdapter.Fill` returns, that collection consists only of the `"myauthors"` `DataTable`. There is no longer any connection between the database and the `DataSet`, and it can be worked on directly, used to populate an ASP.NET `DataGrid` or connected directly to a Windows Forms `DataGrid`, passed over the network, or persisted to disk. In this case, for simplicity you'll work on it directly, but bear in mind that usually clients will see data in a `DataGrid`. The database connection exists only for the amount of time it takes to fill the `DataTable` in the `DataSet`. On the other hand, you now have an in-memory cache that takes up space for the duration of the `DataSet`'s lifetime.

Using a class called `DataView`, you can define multiple views for each `DataTable`. You can sort and filter `DataView`s using a SQL-like syntax. `DataTable`s start with a `DefaultView`, which consists of the entire set of rows in the order in which they were fetched from the database. The next statement sorts the `DefaultView` of the `"myauthors"` `DataTable` by the `au_id` field (5). Note that you can refer to the `DataTable`s in the `DataSet`'s collection by ordinal or by name and that `DefaultView` is a property of the `DataTable` class.

After you've sorted the `DataView` by key, you can use the `DataView`'s `Find` method (6) to locate a row by means of that key. This supposes that author "846-92-7186" has just moved to Eugene, Oregon, and that you want to change her address. The `Find` method returns a row index of the found row. By using the appropriate index, you directly change the columns desired (7).

Note that you're using array syntax rather than navigation to reference the row in memory. The `DataTable` contains collections of `DataRow`s and `DataColumn`s. It's a two-dimensional array. Obviously, because you don't have a connection to the database, only the data in the `DataSet` is affected. In addition, the `DataSet` actually keeps two versions of this `DataRow`: the original version and the one containing the changes. This will be useful for writing back to the database.

Now that you've updated the data in the `DataSet` you can attempt to write it back to the database. You do this by calling the `DataAdapter`'s `Update` method (8). `Update` is another one of those hard-working methods, dense with embedded calls. The following summarizes what happens (Chapter 5 explains this in detail):

1. The `DataSet` iterates through its collection of changed (or new) rows.

2. If the collection is not empty, a connection to the database is opened.

3. `SqlCommandBuilder` creates an insert/update or delete command using the database metadata, the table's primary key, and the values in the original and changed `DataRow`s. The `Command` contains enough information to determine whether the row in the database has been changed since you fetched it into the `DataSet`. This is done by phrasing the SQL command so that it will fail if other users have changed the database row since you fetched it.

4. The SQL command is executed and returns either zero or 1 for the number of rows affected. A command is submitted for each `DataRow` changed. If any command returns zero rows affected, an exception is thrown.

5. The total number of updates is returned.

6. The state of the `DataTable` is updated to reflect the changes you've made if they were successful.

So far, you've investigated one way of streaming data from a data store to a connected client (or Web browser): a data provider's `SqlDataReader`. You can issue SQL commands against the database while connected (through `SqlCommand`) and compose multiple operations into an atomic transaction (through `SqlTransaction`, discussed in Chapter 3). You've also seen a way to cache results in memory, update them while disconnected from the database, and flush back the changes. This is done through the bridge class of a data provider (`SqlDataAdapter`) and a disconnected object model, the `DataSet`. Inside the `DataSet`, you can use a `DataView` to subset the results using a SQL-like syntax.

You can use the .NET XML APIs to implement parallel functionality to everything except the connection, command, and transaction model. Whereas `DataSet`s and data providers are .NET-specific, XML is platform-neutral and much more universal in scope. You can produce an XML Infoset using .NET APIs on a Windows platform and consume the same Infoset on a UNIX or mainframe platform without data conversion. Furthermore, XML Infosets can be used to represent heterogeneous nonrelational data, something that the classes in `System.Data.dll` do with difficulty, if at all.

2.5   The XML APIs in .NET

XML support is pervasive in .NET. Remote method calls can use the Simple Object Access Protocol (SOAP), based on using XML as a transport for remote procedure calls (RPC). Instances of managed types can expose `ISerializable`; if they do, they can be serialized in XML format. You can also use the XML format as a more portable way to marshal .NET managed types through Web Services. Even the various configuration files in .NET are XML-based!

Unless you have used object or object-relational databases before, the notion of storing an object as a database row or column may seem strange. But because most .NET types can be serialized in XML format, this may be a more attractive alternative when you're storing .NET types in databases. For example, because the Java platform defines a standard (Java) object serialization format, an entire series of Java-relational databases (JDBMS) have sprung up that use exactly this storage mechanism.

XML, like databases, supports the notion of using schema to layer type on top of structured or semistructured data. In .NET, this concept is used to map CLR types to XML schema types. There are two supported ways to map XML schema types to CLR types. One takes a CLR-centric view (`System.Runtime.Serialization`). The other takes an XML schema-centric view (`System.Xml.Serialization`).

To prepare you for future discussions about merging XML and data access and also because the XML data access model may not be as familiar as the database API-like models, let's take a look at the XML stack in .NET.

2.5.1 Streaming XML

`XmlReader` is similar to `DataReader` in concept. `XmlReader` exposes the data using the XML Infoset model as a stream of nodes, just as `DataReader` exposes a database resultset as a stream of rows containing columns. As shown in Figure 2–5, however, there are two major distinctions. First, individual resultsets exposed by `DataReader` follow the relational model. This means that rows are homogeneous, each one containing the same number and type of columns. This fact limits type extensibility because only a certain subset of data models can be exposed this way. XML data has no such limitation.

Second, because each XML *document* can have only a single root node and because all other nodes are children of the root, the XML Infoset model is hierarchical by definition. You can represent relational data through an `XmlReader`/`XmlWriter` by ignoring the root node or assuming that it contains (possibly multiple) groupings of relational results. The XML model has limited support for the concept of connections, commands, and transactions, however, so it is more suited to intersecting with the database model at the `DataReader` point.

Note that the XML model usually streams entire nodesets in or out of a data store. There is no support in the streaming model for in-place maintenance of a database-style repository.

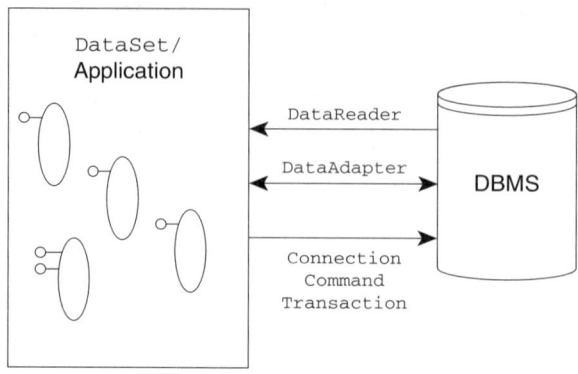

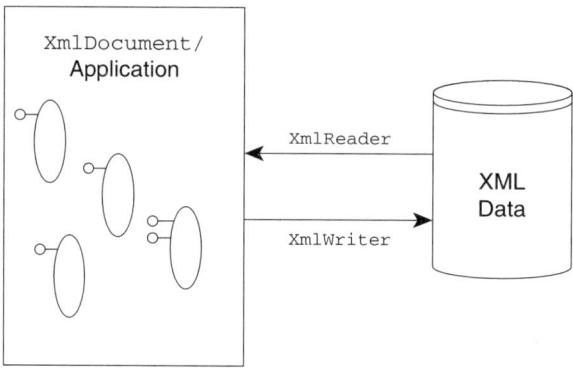

Figure 2–5   Reading and writing with XML and data providers

XmlReader and XmlWriter are abstract base classes, allowing for specialization over any data store. System.Xml contains XmlTextReader and XmlNodeReader, which read into an Infoset model from a text file (or stream) and from a DOM node, respectively. XmlValidatingReader permits validation of the document contents based on a schema. XmlTextWriter writes Infosets to a text file or stream, making it symmetric to XmlTextReader. If your data store need support only reading and writing streams of data, it will be easier to process it through a custom implementation of XmlReader/XmlWriter rather than through a `DataReader`. In addition, there is no symmetric `DataWriter` interface, as there is with `XmlWriter`. Listing 2–4 shows a simple example of using `XmlReader` and `XmlWriter` to read and write text files.

Listing 2–4   Reading XML to and writing XML from text files

```csharp
using System;
using System.IO;
using System.Xml;

namespace Chapter2_4
{
  class Class1
  {
    static void Main(string[] args) // (1)
    {
      Class1 c = new Class1();
      c.instanceMain();
    }

    void instanceMain()
    {
      simplexmlread();
      simplexmlwrite();
    }

    void simplexmlread()
    {
      XmlTextReader rdr = null;
      try
      {
        // Load the file with an XmlTextReader
        rdr = new XmlTextReader ("c:\\jobsemps.xml");

        // Process the supplied XML file
        while (rdr.Read())
        {
          Console.WriteLine("Node Type = {0}",
              rdr.NodeType.ToString());
          Console.WriteLine("Depth = {0}", rdr.Depth);
          Console.WriteLine("Node has {0} attributes",
              rdr.AttributeCount);
```

```csharp
      }
    }
    catch (Exception e)
    {
      Console.WriteLine ("Exception: {0}", e.ToString());
    }
    finally
    {
      // Clean up XmlTextReader
      if (rdr != null)
        rdr.Close();
    }
  }

  void simplexmlwrite()
  {
    XmlTextWriter w = null;
    try
    {
      w = new XmlTextWriter ("c:\\newemp.xml", null);

      w.Formatting = Formatting.Indented;
      w.WriteStartDocument(false);
      w.WriteStartElement("emp");
      w.WriteElementString("empno", null, "9999");
      w.WriteStartElement("ename", null);
      w.WriteElementString("firstname", "Bill");
      w.WriteElementString("lastname", "Melater");
      w.WriteEndElement();
      w.WriteEndElement();
      w.WriteEndDocument();

      //Write the XML to file and close the writer
      w.Flush();
      w.Close();
    }
    catch (Exception e)
    {
      Console.WriteLine ("Exception: {0}", e.ToString());
    }
    finally
    {
```

```
            //Close the writer
            if (w != null)
               w.Close();
          }
        }
      }
    }
```

Note that the code for `XmlTextReader` is almost completely analogous to the `DataReader` code except that `XmlTextReader` is reading nodes instead of rows. You can write nodes in a similar manner using `XmlTextWriter`, including formatting.

If your application or component needs to expose itself as XML, you should consider implementing `XmlReader`. In this way, you can plug it in to XML-based applications without investing the time and resources to convert it to character XML representation. The XML I/O layer of `XmlReader/XmlWriter` provides a symmetric bridge between XML-based applications.

2.5.2   XML Schemas

An XML schema is similar to a schema for a database. An XML schema defines types much as a database schema defines columns in tables. However, an XML schema is identified and located independently of its usage, as opposed to being located with the data as a database schema is. The identity, which is known as the *namespace*, of a schema is determined by a string that conforms to uniform resource identifier (URI) Request for Comments (RFC). In other words, the name of a schema looks like a uniform resource locator (URL) or URI, but it is not intended to be used to physically locate something on the Internet.

The schema is used to document the allowable content of some XML data. For example, a `"person"` element from the namespace `"urn:example-org:peo-ple"` could be validated—that is, tested to make sure it contains proper content—given access to the schema for `"urn:example-org:people"`.

Listing 2–5 shows an example of some typical XML serialized in a form consistent with the XML 1.0 Recommendation—a string of characters—and the corresponding XML schema that defines its type and structure.

Listing 2–5 XML document and schema

```xml
<?xml version="1.0" ?>
<!-- this document -->
<emp xmlns="http://www.emps.com/" >
  <empno>9999</empno>
  <ename>
    <firstname>Bill</firstname>
    <lastname>Melater</lastname>
  </ename>
</emp>
<!-- conforms to this schema -->
<?xml version="1.0" encoding="utf-8"?>
<xsd:schema targetNamespace="http://www.emps.com/"
     xmlns:xsd="http://www.w3.org/2001/XMLSchema">
  <xsd:element name="emp">
    <xsd:complexType>
      <xsd:sequence>
        <xsd:element name="empno" type="xsd:string" />
        <xsd:element name="ename">
          <xsd:complexType>
            <xsd:sequence>
              <xsd:element name="firstname"
                             type="xsd:string" />
              <xsd:element name="lastname"
                             type="xsd:string"  />
            </xsd:sequence>
          </xsd:complexType>
        </xsd:element>
      </xsd:sequence>
    </xsd:complexType>
  </xsd:element>
  <xsd:element name="emps">
    <xsd:complexType>
      <xsd:choice maxOccurs="unbounded">
        <xsd:element ref="emp" />
      </xsd:choice>
    </xsd:complexType>
  </xsd:element>
</xsd:schema>
```

XML schemas are supported in .NET using W3C (World Wide Web Consortium) W3C Recommendation standard XSD (XML schema definition language) as well as Microsoft legacy XDR (XML Data Reduced) format. XDR was a Microsoft-specific predecessor of the XSD schema definition language; it was submitted to the W3C as a Note. (The W3C is the standards organization that defined most of the XML standards.) XDR support provides interoperability with previous APIs, such as "ADO classic" (my term to distinguish ADO from ADO.NET), and data formats (such as BizTalk schemas), but, going forward, XSD schemas are always preferable. Because XSD is a superset of XDR, you can use a .NET software development kit (SDK) utility, `XSD.exe`, to create an XSD schema from the corresponding XDR schema.

The .NET runtime and Microsoft Visual Studio contain extensive support for XML schemas. Most arbitrary XML schemas can be consumed by the `DataSet` to define its structure—inferred from the structure of the incoming data (as discussed in Chapter 7)—or can be produced from a `DataSet` populated by relational resultsets or XML documents. Listing 2–6 shows the XML schema produced by populating a `DataSet` with the SQL query `select * from jobs` in the SQL Server `pubs` database. Listing 2–7 shows the corresponding SQL data definition language (DDL). In addition, Visual Studio or the command-line utility `XSD.exe` can produce, from a corresponding XML schema, a strongly typed subclass of the `DataSet` class containing a description of one or more `DataTable`s.

Listing 2–6 Schema for `DataSet` containing `jobs` table

```xml
<?xml version="1.0" ?>
<xsd:schema id="NewDataSet" xmlns=""
  xmlns:xsd="http://www.w3.org/2001/XMLSchema"
  xmlns:msdata="urn:schemas-microsoft-com:xml-msdata">
  <xsd:element name="NewDataSet" msdata:IsDataSet="true">
    <xsd:complexType>
      <xsd:choice maxOccurs="unbounded">
        <xsd:element name="jobs">
          <xsd:complexType>
            <xsd:sequence>
              <xsd:element name="job_id"
                type="xsd:short"
                msdata:Ordinal="0" />
              <xsd:element name="job_desc"
                msdata:DefaultValue="NULL"
                type="xsd:string"
                minOccurs="0" msdata:Ordinal="1" />
              <xsd:element name="min_lvl"
```

```
                type="xsd:unsignedByte"
                msdata:Ordinal="2" />
            <xsd:element name="max_lvl"
                type="xsd:unsignedByte"
                msdata:Ordinal="3" />
        </xsd:sequence>
      </xsd:complexType>
    </xsd:element>
  </xsd:choice>
  </xsd:complexType>
  </xsd:element>
</xsd:schema>
```

Listing 2–7   SQL data definition language for `jobs` table

```
CREATE TABLE jobs (
  job_id smallint PRIMARY KEY IDENTITY NOT NULL ,
  job_desc varchar (50) ,
  min_lvl tinyint NOT NULL ,
  max_lvl tinyint NOT NULL
  )
```

The .NET XML stack contains a series of classes in `System.Xml.Schema` known as the Schema Object Model (SOM). These classes can be used for synthesizing schemas on-the-fly, and they could be useful for real-time validation or the generation of schemas at runtime from dynamic input. Because the XSD schema type system is a rich superset of the SQL-92 and SQL-99 type systems, this allows data definition through XSD to go beyond the relational model to represent hierarchies, object graphs, or virtually any data pattern or structure.

2.5.3   The `XmlDocument`, XPath, and `XPathNavigators`

In addition to a streaming model, the .NET data access stack supports the W3C standard Document Object Model as well as set-based and navigation-based access using this object model. You implement set-based access by using the XPath query language. You can use XPath to query any XML data; it doesn't require a relational or nested hierarchical structure. XPath uses the hierarchical file system paradigm based on separating levels of hierarchy by forward slashes. In addition to hierarchical search, XPath can use an extended set of data *axes* (an *axis* is defined as a set of nodes relative to the current node) and contains functions, operators, parameters, and a set of well-defined implementation extensibility points. XPath queries can return nodes, sets of nodes, or scalar values. Listing 2–8 shows a sample XPath query and resultset.

Listing 2–8 XPath query

```
<!-- the query /ROOT/Customers/Orders/OrderDetails -->
<!-- when positioned anywhere in the document       -->
<ROOT>
<Customers CustomerID="VINET" ContactName="Paul Henriot">
   <Orders CustomerID="VINET" EmployeeID="5">
      <OrderDetails OrderID="10248" ProductID="11" />
      <OrderDetails OrderID="10248" ProductID="42" />
   </Orders>
</Customers>
<Customers CustomerID="LILAS" ContactName="Carlos Gonzalez">
   <Orders CustomerID="LILAS" EmployeeID="3">
      <OrderDetails OrderID="10283"
                    ProductID="72" Quantity="3"/>
   </Orders>
</Customers>
</ROOT>
<!--                                          -->
<!-- selects the three OrderDetails nodes -->
      <OrderDetails OrderID="10248" ProductID="11" />
      <OrderDetails OrderID="10248" ProductID="42" />
      <OrderDetails OrderID="10283"
                    ProductID="72" Quantity="3"/>
```

`System.Xml.XPath` contains a set of classes that implement an XPath parser and execution engine. As with SQL or OQL, you can separate query parsing from query execution, and you can save compiled (pre-parsed) queries for later use, affording similar benefits to SQL query caches.

Navigation facilities are provided in .NET by the `XmlDocument`, `XPathDocument`, and `XPathNavigator` classes. An `XmlDocument` is similar in concept to a `DataSet`, with the distinction that `XmlDocument` is tree-structured rather than relational-database-structured. The `XmlDocument` class corresponds to the W3C DOM model and provides an entire suite of navigation methods. In addition, you can update an `XmlDocument` in place. The `XmlNode` class is the base class for each information item in the document, and `XmlDocument` is the specialization that represents the containing document. Listing 2–9 shows the navigation methods of XmlDocument (actually XmlNode). Note that these are analogous to the IMS navigation methods shown in Chapter 1. The updating methods are shown in Listing 2–10.

Listing 2–9 `XmlNode` **members for document traversal**

```
public abstract class XmlNode : ICloneable, IEnumerable
{
  ...
  public XmlNodeList ChildNodes {virtual get;}
  public XmlNode FirstChild {virtual get;}
  public XmlNode LastChild {virtual get;}
  public XmlNode NextSibling {virtual get;}
  public XmlNode PreviousSibling {virtual get;}
  public XmlNode ParentNode {virtual get;}
  public XmlDocument OwnerDocument {virtual get;}
  ...
}
```

Listing 2–10 `XmlDocument`/`XmlNode` **members for building documents**

```
public class XmlDocument : XmlNode
{
  ...
  // creating new nodes
  public virtual XmlElement CreateElement(string prefix,
    string localName, string namespaceURI);
  public virtual XmlAttribute CreateAttribute(
    string prefix, string localName, string namespaceURI);
  public virtual XmlText CreateTextNode(string text);
  ...
}

public abstract class XmlNode : ICloneable, IEnumerable
{
  ...
  // inserting, removing, replace nodes in the tree
  public virtual XmlNode AppendChild(XmlNode newChild);
  public virtual XmlNode PrependChild(XmlNode newChild);
  public virtual XmlNode InsertBefore(XmlNode newChild,
    XmlNode refChild);
  public virtual XmlNode InsertAfter(XmlNode newChild,
    XmlNode refChild);
  public virtual XmlNode RemoveChild(XmlNode oldChild);
```

```
    public virtual void RemoveAll();
    public virtual XmlNode ReplaceChild(XmlNode newChild,
      XmlNode oldChild);
  ...
}
```

As with a `DataSet`, the `XmlDocument` can be updated only in place. After it is updated, the entire tree of nodes must be streamed into a data store; no `DataAdapter`-like functionality exists for streaming only the changes. Also note that the `XmlDocument` is a concrete class, and you can't easily specialize it by derivation. As with the `DataSet`, this means that the `XmlDocument` is a dead end for data providers wishing to extend its capabilities by this technique. `XPathDocument` has analogous functionality to `XmlDocument` but is optimized for navigation. It has an advantage over `XmlDocument` in that it does not necessarily read the entire document into memory before the document is used.

Like the `IDbConnection` interface and friends, however, `XPathNavigator` is an abstract base class that requires provider-specific extensions. The .NET framework provides two subclasses of `XPathNavigator`, and a few third-party custom `XPathNavigator`s are available. `XPathNavigator` lets you navigate through any data that is represented in terms of the tree-structured Infoset model. Custom "Infoset providers" can be exposed for any data and can layer over relational, object-relational, hierarchical, or other data stores. Custom `XPathNavigator`s are usually private implementations that are exposed through the `IXPathNavigable` interface. Listing 2–11 shows how to obtain an `XPathNavigator` class by loading a text file into an `XPathDocument` that implements `IXPathNavigable`.

Listing 2–11 Getting an `XPathNavigator`

```
// load an XPathDocument
XPathDocument xpdoc = new XPathDocument("c:\\orders.xml");

// Get an XPathNavigator from the XPathDocument
XPathNavigator xpnav =xpdoc.CreateNavigator();
```

`XPathNavigator` supports a currency position, or cursor, on the current node. It exposes methods (shown in Listing 2–12) for navigation around a hierarchical tree. As you can see, the navigation methods map directly to any of the APIs exposed by hierarchical or object data stores mentioned in Chapter 1. Because `MoveToParent` is available, any of the CODASYL ring structures in IDMS is easily represented. If columns are considered as first-class nodes, the relational data structure is easily mappable; you can use parent-child methods to accommodate hierarchies produced by relations. In this way, you can use the methods of `XPathNavigator` to expose any kind of data.

Listing 2–12 `XPathNavigator` members for document traversal

```
public abstract class XPathNavigator : ICloneable{
    ...
    // move to document / root element
    public abstract void MoveToRoot();

    // move to node by ID
    public abstract bool MoveToId(string id);

    // move to child / parent
    public bool HasChildren {abstract get;}
    public abstract bool MoveToFirstChild();
    public abstract bool MoveToParent();

    // move to siblings
    public abstract bool MoveToFirst();
    public abstract bool MoveToNext();
    public abstract bool MoveToPrevious();
    ...
}
```

`XPathNavigator` is used as an input to XPath queries. So in addition to moving around in a set of data, you can use XPath to extract nodes, nodesets, or scalar values from the underlying data. Listing 2–13 shows how to execute an XPath query against an `XPathNavigator` and process the results using an `XPathNodeIterator`. When used in this manner, XPath becomes an alternative to SQL for reading data; it's more extensible in that it supports nonrelational queries and SQL-like joins without the need to explicitly define relationships through primary-foreign key pairs.

Listing 2–13   Using `Select` to return an iterator

```
xpnav.MoveToRoot();

// select OrderDetail children of Orders
XPathNodeIterator xpiter = xpnav.Select(
            "/Orders/OrderDetail");

// Move through nodeset of results
while(xpiter.MoveNext())
{
   Console.WriteLine("<" + xpiter.Current.Name +
                      ">" + xpiter.Current.Value);
};
```

XPathNavigators also can be fed into a series of declarative instructions, provided in XML format, called XSLT (XML transformation language). XSLT lets you process any data exposed through an XPathNavigator to produce a stream of XML, HTML, or any other text-based format. System.Xml.Xsl contains a series of classes that encapsulate parsing an XSLT transform and processing an input XPathNavigator to produce a result. XSLT *transforms* can be thought of as stored procedures in XML for database aficionados. They can be compiled, and the execution plan cached for future use. However, no method exists in .NET for serializing the compiled format. Other products and utilities, such as the BizTalk mapper, provide such functionality. Listing 2–14 shows an example of using XSLT through an XPathNavigator.

Listing 2–14   Using an XSLT transform

```
// Load document
XPathDocument xpdoc = new XPathDocument ("c:\\newemp.xml");

// Load transform
XslTransform xform = new XslTransform();
xform.Load("c:\\myxslt.xsl");

// Transforming produces a reader
XmlReader rdr = xform.Transform(xpdoc, null);
```

Note that, although XPathNavigator provides the ability to query or navigate, it contains no ability to update in place. You can use XmlDocument (or

XPathDocument) to update data, but you can't directly use XPathNavigator based on XmlDocument (or XPathDocument) to update the underlying data. The current XPathNavigator implementations supplied with .NET are only indirectly accessible via the XPathNavigator abstract base class. To update data, you would need a more specialized XPathNavigator implementation class to be made directly available.

2.5.4 Mixing XML and Data Providers

Let's conclude with a simple example of using a data provider and a DataSet to produce an XML schema and an XML document (Listing 2–15). It uses the DataSet (1) as a way of building a cache of relational data and then acts as an Infoset provider by exposing it as a serialized XML document. You start by instantiating a new SqlDataAdapter and DataSet. The only things that differ from the simple update example are that the command string in this example generates multiple DataTables (one for each SELECT statement) and that the DataSet uses a constructor that specifies its name.

Listing 2–15 Using DataSets to produce XML

```
using System;
using System.Data;
using System.Data.SqlClient;

namespace Chapter2_15
{
  class Class1
  {
    static void Main(string[] args) // (1)
    {
      // (1)
      SqlDataAdapter da = new SqlDataAdapter(
        "select * from jobs;select * from employee",
        "server=localhost;uid=sa;pwd=;database=pubs");
      DataSet ds = new DataSet("AcmeJobs");

      try
      {
```

```
        da.Fill(ds); // (2)
        ds.Tables[0].TableName = "Jobs"; // (3)
        ds.Tables[1].TableName = "EmpInJob";

        ds.Relations.Add(ds.Tables["Jobs"].Columns["job_id"],
          ds.Tables["EmpInJob"].Columns["job_id"]); // (4)

        ds.Relations[0].Nested = true; // (5)
        ds.Namespace = "urn:jobs-emps-com:xml-joblist-1"; // (6)

        ds.WriteXmlSchema("c:\\jobsemps.xsd"); // (7)
          // (8)
        ds.WriteXml("c:\\jobsemps.xml",
        XmlWriteMode.IgnoreSchema);

    }
    catch (SqlException se)
    {
      // first exception only
      Console.WriteLine("SQL Exception: {0}", se.Message);
    }
    catch (Exception e)
    {
      // write message
      Console.WriteLine("Exception: {0}", e.Message);
    }
  }
 }
}
```

When `SqlDataAdapter.Fill` (2) is executed, both resultsets are used to populate the `DataSet`. Because you didn't specify the table name, the names `"Table"` and `"Table1"` are used by default. That's OK because you can rename the `DataSet`'s `DataTables` at any time to more descriptive names (3). You now have two `DataTables`, but the `DataAdapter` doesn't specify that there is a parent-child relationship between the two. You do that by adding a parent-child relationship (of type `DataRelation`) to the `DataSet`'s `Relations` collection (4).

Because you're going to persist the `DataSet`'s contents as XML, you can add some properties to the `DataSet` to shape and define the "XML view" of its data. You specify the hierarchical relationship among the `DataTables` by using the `DataRelation`'s nested property (5). You also specify the default XML namespace for the `DataSet` (and all its contained `DataTables` and `DataColumns`) (6). Now that you have set up the XML view of the data exactly as you want it to appear, you call the `DataSet`'s `WriteXmlSchema` method (7) to persist an XML `Schema` that defines that view. You then use the `DataSet`'s built-in Infoset provider to persist the contents as an XML document on the file system (8). Listing 2–16 shows the resulting XML schema and XML document.

Listing 2–16   XML schema and document produced by Listing 2–15

```
Xml Schema:

<?xml version="1.0" standalone="yes"?>
<xs:schema id="AcmeJobs"
targetNamespace="urn:jobs-emps-com:xml-joblist-1"
xmlns:mstns="urn:jobs-emps-com:xml-joblist-1"
xmlns="urn:jobs-emps-com:xml-joblist-1"
xmlns:xs="http://www.w3.org/2001/XMLSchema"
xmlns:msdata="urn:schemas-microsoft-com:xml-msdata"
attributeFormDefault="qualified" elementFormDefault="qualified">
  <xs:element name="AcmeJobs" msdata:IsDataSet="true">
    <xs:complexType>
      <xs:choice maxOccurs="unbounded">
        <xs:element name="Jobs">
          <xs:complexType>
            <xs:sequence>
              <xs:element name="job_id" type="xs:short"
                  minOccurs="0/>
              <xs:element name="job_desc" type="xs:string"
                  minOccurs="0" />
              <xs:element name="min_lvl" type="xs:unsignedByte"
                  minOccurs="0" />
              <xs:element name="max_lvl" type="xs:unsignedByte"
                  minOccurs="0" />
              <xs:element name="EmpInJob" minOccurs="0"
                  maxOccurs="unbounded">
                <xs:complexType>
```

```
            <xs:sequence>
              <xs:element name="emp_id" type="xs:string"
                minOccurs="0" />
              <xs:element name="fname" type="xs:string"
                minOccurs="0" />
              <xs:element name="minit" type="xs:string"
                minOccurs="0" />
              <xs:element name="lname" type="xs:string"
                minOccurs="0" />
              <xs:element name="job_id" type="xs:short"
                minOccurs="0" />
             <xs:element name="job_lvl" type="xs:unsignedByte"
                minOccurs="0" />
              <xs:element name="pub_id" type="xs:string"
                minOccurs="0" />
             <xs:element name="hire_date" type="xs:dateTime"
                minOccurs="0" />
            </xs:sequence>
          </xs:complexType>
        </xs:element>
      </xs:sequence>
    </xs:complexType>
  </xs:element>
  </xs:choice>
  </xs:complexType>
  <xs:unique name="Constraint1">
    <xs:selector xpath=".//mstns:Jobs" />
    <xs:field xpath="mstns:job_id" />
  </xs:unique>
  <xs:keyref name="Relation1" refer="Constraint1"
        msdata:IsNested="true">
    <xs:selector xpath=".//mstns:EmpInJob" />
    <xs:field xpath="mstns:job_id" />
  </xs:keyref>
  </xs:element>
</xs:schema>

XML Document:

<?xml version="1.0" standalone="yes"?>
<AcmeJobs xmlns="urn:jobs-emps-com:xml-joblist-1">
  <Jobs>
    <job_id>1</job_id>
```

```
      <job_desc>Vice Chairman</job_desc>
      <min_lvl>10</min_lvl>
      <max_lvl>10</max_lvl>
    </Jobs>
    <Jobs>
      <job_id>2</job_id>
      <job_desc>Grand Poobah</job_desc>
      <min_lvl>100</min_lvl>
      <max_lvl>200</max_lvl>
      <EmpInJob>
        <emp_id>PTC11962M</emp_id>
        <fname>Philip</fname>
        <minit>T</minit>
        <lname>Cramer</lname>
        <job_id>2</job_id>
        <job_lvl>215</job_lvl>
        <pub_id>9952</pub_id>
        <hire_date>1989-11-11T00:00:00.0000000-08:00</hire_date>
      </EmpInJob>
    </Jobs>
    <Jobs>
      <job_id>3</job_id>
      <job_desc>Business Operations Manager</job_desc>
      <min_lvl>100</min_lvl>
      <max_lvl>100</max_lvl>
      <EmpInJob>
        <emp_id>AMD15433F</emp_id>
        <fname>Ann</fname>
        <minit>M</minit>
        <lname>Devon</lname>
        <job_id>3</job_id>
        <job_lvl>200</job_lvl>
        <pub_id>9952</pub_id>
        <hire_date>1991-07-16T00:00:00.0000000-07:00</hire_date>
      </EmpInJob>
    </Jobs>
    <!-- remainder of document elided for clarity -->
  </AcmeJobs>
```

This example is interesting for two reasons. The first is its use in applications. Because data that is persisted in XML format is accessible regardless of platform, operating system, or programming language, this is a perfect way to make the data accessible to any user. This data could be saved in a file and taken home to be used offline, or rendered as HTML on a Web server using the XSLT language. It represents a convenient cached subset of the data in the database.

The second reason is the format of the data: hierarchical rather than relational. It is a homogeneous hierarchy, similar to the data on a master-detail report containing children composed along with their parents. It can be accessed, using the `XmlDocument` model, through an Infoset provider that encompasses the hierarchical model (such as an Infoset provider over IMS, as mentioned in Chapter 1), a CODASYL ring model, or an object database model. The data is accessed using a navigation model rather than rows and columns and can be searched (after it is exposed as an `XmlDocument` or `XPathDocument`) using the XPath query language.

Sometimes it is convenient to expose data as both an `XmlDocument` and a `DataSet` simultaneously. For this, you use the `XmlDataDocument`, a hybrid of an `XmlDocument` and a `DataSet`. The `XmlDataDocument` class derives from `XmlDocument` and contains a public `DataSet` member variable, making all the methods of `DataSet` and `XmlDocument` directly available over the same cache of data. Because the `XmlDocument` can handle more types of data, the `XmlDataDocument`'s `DataSet` exposes only that portion of the `XmlDocument` that corresponds to a mapping schema. (Chapter 7 explains this in more detail.) A change made through either `XmlDocument` or `DataSet` will be reflected in both.

To obtain an `XmlDocument` element node from a `DataRow` in a `DataSet` and to obtain the corresponding `DataRow` from an element, the `XmlDataDocument` exposes two extra methods. In addition, a custom `XPathNavigator` retains currency position in both the `XmlDocument` and `DataSet` as the user navigates through the object models.

2.6 Layout of the Managed Data Classes

Now that you've completed a quick overview of the .NET data and XML classes, let's see how they are arranged in terms of assemblies and namespaces.

The core assembly for data access is `System.Data.dll`, which contains the `System.Data` namespace and its sub-namespaces, shown in Figure 2–6. The `System.Data` namespace contains `DataSet` and its subsidiary classes as well as all the enumerations, such as `CommandType`, used in the data provider classes. `System.Data` also contains all the interface definitions—for example, `IDbConnection`—used in data providers. `System.Data.dll` contains four other namespaces. `System.Data.Common` contains a few base classes that are used in the `OleDb` and `SqlClient` data providers, such as `DataAdapter` and `DbDataAdapter`. Each data provider has its own namespace: `System.Data.OleDb` and `System.Data.SqlClient`. `System.Data.SqlTypes` provides classes for SQL Server native data types. An additional ODBC data provider, released through the Web, contains a `Microsoft.Data.Odbc` namespace at the same level as `OleDb` and `SqlClient` and enough of the `System.Data.Common` namespace to provide the core common functionality.

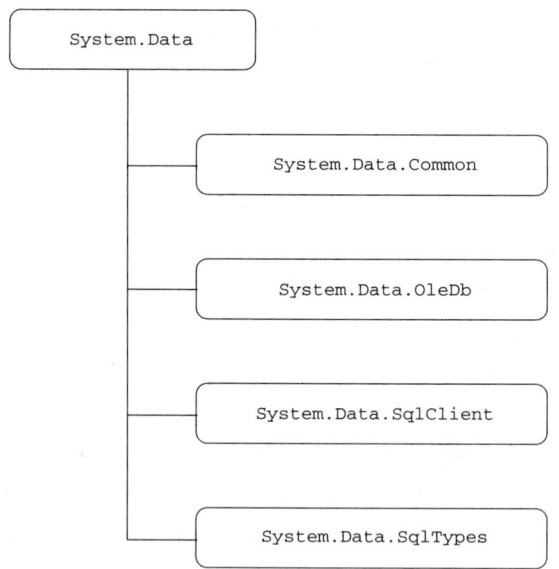

Figure 2–6 The `System.Data` namespace (ODBC is a separate DLL)

The core assembly for XML programming is `System.Xml.dll`. This assembly contains a layered set of types for performing I/O, in-memory traversal and navigation, and XPath and XSLT processing. Figure 2–7 shows the namespaces in `System.Xml.dll`. Interestingly, the `System.Data.dll` assembly also contains a discrete set of classes in the `System.Xml` namespace. This includes `XmlDataDocument` and its support classes and `DataDocumentXPathNavigator`, discussed in Chapter 7.

2.7   Where Are We?

You've taken a brief look at both the ADO.NET and the XML data access stacks. You should now know where everything is and have a basic understanding of the way each model works and how the ADO.NET and XML.NET models complement each other. You should also know how each class library relates to the various data models discussed in Chapter 1.

Next, you'll examine each portion of the ADO.NET models, including ADO.NET and XML integration, in greater depth.

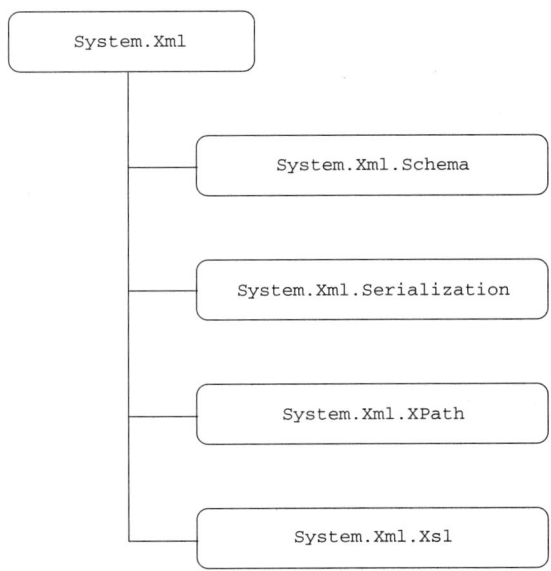

Figure 2–7   The `System.Xml` namespace

Chapter 3

The Connected Model: Streaming Data Access

.NET introduces data providers that run in managed space. Data is read directly using `DataReader` classes.

3.1 .NET Data Providers and the Connected Model

As mentioned in Chapter 2, the connected part of ADO.NET features data providers, a new model for using databases. Microsoft ships two data providers with .NET: the `SqlClient` data provider for SQL Server 7.0 and later, and the `OleDb` data provider for OLE DB data sources. A data provider for ODBC data sources is available as a Microsoft Web release, as are the `SqlXml` managed data classes discussed in Chapter 7; other specialized providers from Microsoft, DataDirect Technologies (formerly MERANT DataDirect), and others will be available by the time you read this. APIs to abstract database access started with ODBC and include OLE DB, ADO (a library that sits atop OLE DB), and JDBC. They all abstract things in almost the same way, but with some subtle differences. This chapter looks at how the "usual" items are abstracted by this new model, with an eye toward the things that set ADO.NET apart as well as the differences between the providers. You can also build your own data provider, as explained in Chapter 8.

Users interact with databases by connecting to a database instance, issuing commands to the database, and disconnecting. This is called the connected model. An alternative access model consists of a user who connects and retrieves data into a cache, disconnects, updates the cache, and reconnects to flush changes to the database. This is called the disconnected model and is discussed in Chapter 5. The disconnected model also uses data providers to retrieve rows from the database and to synchronize changes.

Database connections take up precious resources, such as data buffers, in the database server. When you're writing an application that will scale to a large number of users, the preferred model is to connect to the database, issue commands, retrieve results, and disconnect as soon as possible. ADO.NET is geared toward using the connected and disconnected models in this manner. An alternative way to use a database is to establish one long-lived connection per user and keep state in the database server. This state may consist of row locks or user-specific sets of data with currency positions, known as server cursors. Currently, no ADO.NET data provider supports server cursors because these providers are designed with application scalability in mind.

As we look at the data provider APIs in this chapter, you'll notice that I often use fuzzy terms such as *usually*, *mostly*, and *almost always*. This is because not all of the underlying data stores—or in the case of OLE DB and ODBC, underlying data providers—work in exactly the same way. `Connections`, `Commands`, `Parameters`, and so on are an API generalization. I also mention the specific behavior of data providers over popular data stores such as SQL Server, Oracle, and Access when it is relevant and differs from what you might expect.

3.2 Connection Classes

The connection classes (`SqlConnection` and `OleDbConnection`) are not built around a common base class structure; instead, they're built around implementation of a common interface, `IDbConnection`. You must instantiate a concrete class of the correct type, although it can be cast to the `IDbConnection` interface:

```
IDbConnection conn = new SqlConnection();
IDbConnection oconn = new OleDbConnection();
```

As in ADO classic (also known as ADODB), you can explicitly create and control the `Connection` instances, or you can pass a connection string as a constructor parameter to other objects, such as the `DataAdapter`, in lieu of a `Connection` instance. If a connection string is passed to the `DataAdapter`'s constructor, it implicitly creates the correct `Connection` instance type when needed.

The `Open` and `Close` methods do what the names suggest, although you'll see later that `Close` may not physically break the connection to the database. Because garbage collection is not deterministic, you must explicitly call `Close` or `Dispose` to release the database connection in a timely manner in connected mode. Note that this is different from the `DataAdapter` class discussed in Chapter 2 and Chapter 5, which can implicitly call `Open` and `Close`. The `ConnectionTimeout` property defaults to 15 seconds, but it is settable.

Both providers implement a `Connection.Dispose` method in addition to `Close`. A no-argument overload is available to consumers, along with a protected overload that takes a Boolean parameter that indicates whether unmanaged resources should be released. Examples of unmanaged resources are a COM interface pointer, an ODBC handle, or a cursor inside an Oracle database. `Dispose` calls `Close` if the `Connection` is still open. Because the semantics of reusing an instance after you have called `Dispose` are undefined, in general you should use `Close` rather than `Dispose` if you might want to reuse the `Connection` instance.

The most commonly used constructor of a `Connection` takes a connection string as a parameter. As in OLE DB, connection strings are name-value pairs, but the connection strings are subtly different for the `SqlClient` and `OleDb` data providers. `OleDbConnection` uses the standard OLE DB property names in the connection string, whereas `SqlConnection` can also use SQL Server-specific connection property names. However, the OLE DB provider for SQL Server, `SQLOLEDB`, and only this specific OLE DB provider, can use SQL Server-specific connection property names as well, making things a bit confusing for users of other OLE DB providers. Table 3–1 shows the common names for the same connection properties. The `SqlClient` provider can use OLE DB property names—for example, this will work:

```
IDbConnection conn = new SqlConnection("data source=(local);
    user id=sa;password=mypw;initial catalog=pubs");
```

Data providers can also add their own property names, such as the ODBC data provider's DSN property. Because the OLE DB specification enables OLE DB

Table 3–1   OLE DB properties and SQL Server equivalents

OLE DB Properties	Sql Server Properties
Data Source	Server
User ID	UID
Password	PWD
Initial Catalog	Database

providers to add custom properties, these can also be used in a connection string when `OleDbConnection` is used.

`SqlConnection` does not support certain esoteric `SQLOLEDB` provider connection properties (such as `"use procedure for prepare"`). `SqlConnection` does support a new connection property `AttachDBFilename`, which might be useful in a scenario using the MSDE version of SQL Server; you can use it to execute a SQL Server `attach` to the filename of a SQL Server database file on-the-fly. This moves MSDE one step closer to emulating Microsoft Access's ease of use. `SqlConnection` supports additional properties related to connection pooling, which I discuss shortly.

Because the OLE DB provider for ODBC (`MSDASQL`) is not supported, the `provider=` property of the connection string is required when you're using `OleDbConnection`. Omitting it implicitly selects `MSDASQL`, and this now throws an exception. In addition, OLE DB 2.5 introduced the concept of binding by URL by using a component known as the OLE DB *root binder* and provider-specific `Binder` classes. This was used by the Internet Publishing provider and the OLE DB provider for Exchange. The `OleDb` data provider does not support URL-based connections.

Both OLE DB and ODBC support a mechanism for configuring connection properties and storing them in a file. These are known as the ODBC file DSN (*data source name*) and OLE DB UDL (*universal data link*) files. In addition, ODBC DSNs can be stored in the registry. These files or symbolic names can be referenced in connection strings:

```
IDbConnection conn = new
  OleDbConnection("File=c:\\myconfig.udl");
```

The ODBC Data Sources API and OLE DB Data Links API provide a GUI-based mechanism for configuring and maintaining these files. The data provider APIs have no standard mechanism for accomplishing this, so you must provide a custom solution. The .NET standard solution is to store connection strings in the `appSettings` section of the appropriate configuration files. .NET configuration files always have a `.config` suffix and are reminiscent of Windows `.ini` files or UNIX `.rc` files except that they use an XML-based vocabulary.

3.3 Connection Pooling

Connection pooling refers to the practice of keeping a set of open database connections to be shared by sessions that use the same user ID in the database, thereby avoiding the need to constantly open and close the connection. Connection pooling is especially useful in a three-tier scenario, such as a Web server or forms server environment. It takes a nontrivial amount of time for each user (or middle-tier component) to connect to a database—sometimes longer than it takes to perform the query after the user is connected. In addition, each open connection takes up buffers and resources in the database. In a Web server scenario, users may never actually sign off of your application, so even if you had unlimited resources in your database, holding long-lived database connections is not an alternative. The .NET framework provides client-side connection pooling for both data providers for connections in a single process, and it also contains provisions for working with databases that use server-side connection pooling.

The `SqlClient` and `OleDb` data providers implement connection pooling in completely different ways. To summarize, the `OleDb` provider uses OLE DB Services' native connection pooling through a resource dispenser architecture that is intimately related to .NET Enterprise Services' declarative distributed transactions. The `Odbc` data provider also uses the resource dispenser architecture for connection pooling. In contrast, `SqlClient` uses an internal pooling mechanism that is similar to COM+ object pooling. Because the connection pooling mechanism is tightly coupled with transactions, I save the detailed explanation of how connection pooling works until after I talk about explicit and declarative transactions. For now, Table 3–2 shows a list of `SqlClient` pooling parameters and a summary of their effect on the pool.

Table 3–2 Parameters that effect pooling

Parameter	Default	Description
Connection Lifetime	0	When a connection is returned to the pool, its creation time is compared with the current time, and the connection is destroyed if that time span (in seconds) exceeds the value specified by connection lifetime. Useful in clustered configurations to force load balancing between a running server and a server just brought online.
Connection Reset	true	Determines whether the database connection is reset when being removed from the pool. Setting to `false` avoids making an additional server round-trip when obtaining a connection, but the programmer must be aware that the connection state is not being reset.
Enlist	true	When `true`, the pooler automatically enlists the connection in the creation thread's current transaction context.
Max Pool Size	100	The maximum number of connections allowed in the pool.
Min Pool Size	0	The minimum number of connections allowed in the pool.
Pooling	true	When `true`, the `SqlConnection` object is drawn from the appropriate pool, or if necessary is created and added to the appropriate pool.

3.4 Metadata Methods

The ANSI SQL standards (SQL-92 and SQL-99) define a series of metadata items that should be kept by a relational database. This list, known as the SQL *information schema*, contains data about database items such as tables, columns, primary keys, and stored procedure parameters. This information is presented in special metadata views. The spec describes the views that constitute the information schema and the metadata that should be available. An example (COLUMNS information) is shown in Table 3–3. Such information is especially useful for writing generic clients that present list boxes of information based on this metadata, such as a list of tables.

OLE DB provides a standard way to obtain metadata from the information schema. The OleDb data provider exposes it in a method of the OleDbConnection

Table 3–3 COLUMNS information (subset) from SQL-92 information schema

Column Name	Data Type	Description
TABLE_CATALOG	nvarchar(128)	Table qualifier.
TABLE_SCHEMA	nvarchar(128)	Table owner.
TABLE_NAME	nvarchar(128)	Table name.
COLUMN_NAME	nvarchar(128)	Column name.
ORDINAL_POSITION	smallint	Column identification number.
COLUMN_DEFAULT	nvarchar(4000)	Default value of the column.
IS_NULLABLE	varchar(3)	Nullability of the column. If this column allows NULL, this column returns YES. Otherwise, NO is returned.
DATA_TYPE	nvarchar(128)	System supplied data type.
CHARACTER_MAXIMUM _LENGTH	smallint	Maximum length, in characters, for binary data, character data, or text and image data. Otherwise, NULL is returned.
CHARACTER_OCTET _LENGTH	smallint	Maximum length, in bytes, for binary data, character data, or text and image data. Otherwise, NULL is returned.
NUMERIC_PRECISION	tinyint	Precision of approximate numeric data, exact numeric data, integer data, or monetary data. Otherwise, NULL is returned.
NUMERIC_PRECISION _RADIX	smallint	Precision radix of approximate numeric data, exact numeric data, integer data, or monetary data. Otherwise, NULL is returned.
NUMERIC_SCALE	tinyint	Scale of approximate numeric data, exact numeric data, integer data, or monetary data. Otherwise, NULL is returned.

class called `Connection.GetOleDbSchemaTable`. This method takes the GUID representing the desired metadata view and an array of restrictions and then returns a `DataTable` of information. The restrictions array is used to subset the information returned. For example, you may want to list information only about the columns in the jobs table in the pubs database.

The `OleDbSchemaGuid` class is a helper class that allows easy access to the GUID (defined by the OLE DB spec) for each information schema item. The restrictions differ for each item and are also defined by the OLE DB specification. The following code shows an example of using this method to obtain the column information for the jobs table in the pubs database. The information in the OLE DB schema rowsets corresponds to the SQL-92 information schema with OLE DB-specific extensions. This query yields 33 columns of information:

```
// Get info about the columns in the pubs.dbo.jobs table
OleDbConnection oconn = new OleDbConnection(
  "provider=sqloledb;uid=sa" +
  ";data source=(local);initial catalog=pubs");
oconn.Open();

// restrictions:
// Only the database PUBS. Only owner DBO.
// Only tables named JOBS. All column names.
object[] restrictions = { "pubs", "dbo", "jobs", null };

DataTable t = oconn.GetOleDbSchemaTable(
  OleDbSchemaGuid.Columns, restrictions);
Console.WriteLine("there are {0} columns in the table",
  t.Rows.Count);
Console.WriteLine("there are {0} items of info per column",
  t.Columns.Count);
```

To retrieve metadata through the `SqlClient` provider, you can issue normal commands using the INFORMATION_SCHEMA views contained in SQL Server itself. Following is an example of obtaining standard information about columns using `SqlClient`. Because this is a normal SQL command, you could also use `SqlCommand` to get this information. The information in SQL Server corresponds to the SQL-92 information schema. The following query yields 23 columns of information:

```
// Get info about the columns in the jobs table
string cmd = "select * from INFORMATION_SCHEMA.COLUMNS " +
             "where TABLE_NAME = 'jobs'";
SqlDataAdapter da = new SqlDataAdapter(
   cmd, "data source=(local);uid=sa;pwd=mypw;database=pubs");
DataTable st = new DataTable();
da.Fill(st);
Console.WriteLine("there are {0} columns in the table",
   st.Rows.Count);
Console.WriteLine("there are {0} items of info per column",
   st.Columns.Count);
```

3.5 Commands

Data providers implement a `Command` class, such as `SqlCommand` or `OleDb-Command`, to execute action statements and submit queries to the database. This class must implement the `IDbCommand` interface. You can create the `Command` instance from a `Connection` instance using the `IDbConnection.CreateCommand` method. You can also instantiate it directly using a variety of constructors.

The constructor can specify a command string, or you can set the command string by using the `CommandText` property. The most useful constructor overloads accept an instance of the correct subclass of `Connection`. The `Connection` does not have to be open in order to be used in the `Command` object's constructor. Note that there is not a constructor that takes a command text string and a connection string. Listing 3–1 shows how to initialize a `SqlCommand`.

Listing 3–1 Initializing a Command
```
// This initializes a SqlCommand from an existing
// connection. The Connection must be strongly typed.
SqlConnection conn = new SqlConnection(
   "server=localhost;uid=sa;pwd=mypw;database=pubs");
SqlCommand cmd2 = new SqlCommand(
    "select * from authors", conn);

// This won't compile, need a Connection instance
// not a connection string
//SqlCommand cmd = new SqlCommand(
//   "select * from authors",
//   "server=localhost;uid=sa;pwd=mypw;initial catalog=pubs");
```

You can also set the `Command`'s `Connection` using the `Connection` property instead of passing it in as a constructor parameter. A `Connection` can have many `Command`s, but a `Command` is associated only with a single `Connection` at a time. The `Connection` can be changed at any time, as shown in Listing 3–2. This code could be used to permit a single `Command` to be executed against different database instances with the same schema. This capability is useful when the data in a series of tables is spread across multiple database instances based on geographic server location (such as western employees and eastern employees) and is known as *data directed routing*. The `Command` can also be associated with a single `Transaction` instance, as discussed in the section on transactions.

Listing 3–2 Switching a `Command`'s `Connection`

```
SqlConnection conn1 = new SqlConnection(
  "server=localhost;uid=sa;pwd=mypw;initial catalog=pubs");
SqlConnection conn2 = new SqlConnection(
  "server=localhost;uid=sa;pwd=mypw;initial catalog=northwind");

conn1.Open();
conn2.Open();

SqlCommand cmd = new SqlCommand(
  "insert jobs values('new job', 10, 10)", conn1);

int i = cmd.ExecuteNonQuery();

// switch connection
cmd.Connection = conn2;
cmd.CommandText = "insert region values(5, 'Northeast')";
int j = cmd.ExecuteNonQuery();

conn1.Close();
conn2.Close();
```

The `IDbCommand` interface contains an `ExecuteNonQuery` method that returns only the number of rows affected. For SELECT statements, this number is always –1 when you use SQL Server. When you use `ExecuteNonQuery` with stored procedures that return multiple result with SQL server, the number of rows affected is the sum of all the rows affected by all of the INSERT, UPDATE, and DELETE statements in a stored procedure. This is shown in Listing 3–3.

Listing 3–3 Returning the total number of rows affected

```
-- referenced stored procedure
create procedure ins_sel_ins
as
insert into jobs values('New job', 10, 10)
select * from jobs
insert into jobs values('Another New job', 20, 20)
go

// execute it...
OleDbConnection conn = new OleDbConnection(
  "provider=sqloledb;uid=sa;pwd=mypw;initial catalog=pubs");
OleDbCommand cmd = new OleDbCommand(
  "ins_sel_ins", conn);

cmd.Connection.Open();
cmd.CommandType = CommandType.StoredProcedure;
int i = cmd.ExecuteNonQuery();

// Return the number 2
Console.WriteLine(i + " rows affected");
```

The `CommandText` property can refer to a SQL command (or to other command languages supported by the OLE DB provider when you're using the `OleDbCommand`) or a stored procedure name. Because OLE DB providers need not support commands at all and can fetch data by table name, the `OleDb` data provider (but not the `SqlClient` provider) also supports using only a table name. The `CommandType` property indicates whether the `CommandText` refers to a textual statement, a stored procedure name, or a table name.

`Command.ExecuteReader` is the method for executing commands that return a set of rows from the data store. `ExecuteReader` returns its results through the `IDataReader` interface or a typed `DataReader` instance.

Multiple results are supported when you use a `Command` with the `SqlClient` provider or, if the underlying OLE DB provider supports them, when you use the `OleDb` data provider, as shown in Listing 3–4. If you want individual row counts for multiple results, you must insert a separate command to `SELECT` SQL Server's `@@ROWCOUNT` variable. This is because the `DataReader` only returns results that are rowsets. `SELECT @@ROWCOUNT` will return a one-column, one-row rowset containing the number of rows affected by the last command.

Listing 3–4 Multiple results

```
SqlConnection sconn = new SqlConnection(
    "server=(local);uid=sa;pwd=mypw;database=pubs");
SqlCommand cmd = new SqlCommand(
  "set nocount off;" +
  "select * from jobs;" +
  "insert into jobs values('New job', 10, 10);" +
  "select * from authors",
  sconn);
sconn.Open();

IDataReader rdr = cmd.ExecuteReader();
bool more;
int results = 0;
do
{
  Console.WriteLine("new result");
  results++;
  while(rdr.Read())
  {
    Console.WriteLine("reading...");
  }
  more = rdr.NextResult();
} while(more);

// prints 2 results
Console.WriteLine("There were {0} results", results);

rdr.Close();
sconn.Close();
```

In addition to `ExecuteReader` and `ExecuteNonQuery`, the `IDbCommand.ExecuteScalar` method returns an `Object` that corresponds to the first column of the first row. This is useful for returning counts or other scalar values efficiently. Listing 3–5 shows an example of using `ExecuteScalar`. Notice that if you are casting the result of `ExecuteScalar` from `Object` to a more precise type, you must cast it to the type that is actually returned from the database; otherwise, an `InvalidCastException` will be thrown. Beyond the vanilla methods of `IDbCommand`, the `SqlClient` provider implements some SQL Server-specific functionality. `ExecuteXmlReader` is used with the SQL

Server 2000 FOR XML syntax, which returns the results of a query directly as XML. Chapter 7 looks at this method in more detail.

Listing 3–5 Using `Command.ExecuteScalar`

```
SqlConnection sconn = new SqlConnection(
  "server=(local);uid=sa;pwd=mypw;database=pubs");
SqlCommand cmd = new SqlCommand(
  "select AVG(CAST(royaltyper as real))from titleauthor",
  sconn);
sconn.Open();

double d = (double)cmd.ExecuteScalar();
Console.WriteLine("Average = {0}", d.ToString());
sconn.Close();
```

3.5.1 `Command` Behaviors

`IDbCommand.ExecuteReader` has an overload that accepts a `CommandBehavior` parameter, something you can use for a variety of behaviors. Some of the behaviors provide metadata about results that would be returned from the database, but do not actually execute the command. Others change what is returned in `DataReader`. In addition, you can use the `CloseConnection` behavior to automatically close the `Connection` associated with the `Command` when the `DataReader` produced from the `Command` is closed, and thereby quickly free resources associated with `Command`, `Connection`, and `DataReader`.

`CommandBehavior.SingleRow` is used to return a single row, rather than a resultset, from the database. This can result in a significant performance gain when you're issuing a *singleton select*—that is, a SELECT statement that is known in advance to return only a single row, such as a SELECT statement based on a primary key value. `CommandBehavior.SingleResult` is used to override the default multiple-results retrieving behavior of `Command.ExecuteReader`. The `CommandBehavior.SequentialAccess` method is used to force the columns to be retrieved in sequential order. You need this behavior if you want to use `DataReader` with BLOB or CLOB (character large object) columns (IMAGE or TEXT in SQL Server) so as to permit the data to be retrieved in chunks through data results with stream-like semantics.

`CommandBehavior.SchemaOnly` and `CommandBehavior.KeyInfo` are used to retrieve schema information. They retrieve the schema of the resultsets that are to be retrieved by executing the command; they do not retrieve database schema information. This behavior may be useful in determining whether to use the sequential access behavior (discussed earlier) or when you're collecting metadata for use with `CommandBuilders`, a class used for disconnected updates. We'll investigate how to use this information in later chapters.

Bear in mind that when you're using the `OleDb` data provider, support of extended behaviors and command types is entirely dependent on the capabilities of the underlying OLE DB provider. Although some OLE DB providers do not support command text, stored procedures, sequential access, or returning single rows, all non-OLAP OLE DB providers must support `CommandType.TableDirect`.

3.6 Using Parameters

Parameters are confusing because there are so many different "standards" for them. Parameters are used mainly because of the way the query engine works (and caches) in relational databases. Consider these two queries:

```
select * from authors where au_fname = 'Bob'
select * from authors where au_fname = 'Fred'
```

When a SQL engine executes these commands, it goes through a three-step process (the absolute specifics may vary among databases):

1. The command is parsed into a tree form, and the object names are resolved. This step catches mistakes such as spelling the keyword `SELECT` incorrectly or referring to a table or column that does not exist.

2. The parsed tree form of the command is analyzed by the relational manager, and a query plan is constructed. The programmer may be offered a series of choices, such as using rule-based versus cost-based optimization or choosing which join is to be executed first. In the preceding example, choosing the plan is a trivial process, but in a 16-table join, the order of execution could be critical. In fact, some optimizers (for example, OB2s) allow the programmer to hint at how many times the plan may be used, thereby determining how long to spend optimizing it. Constructing a query plan could possibly take longer than the query itself.

3. The query plan is executed.

As you can see, step 2 requires a nontrivial amount of time in almost all cases, so it would be nice to be able to reuse the query plan. For that reason, databases keep a cache of recently used queries. The two sample queries are so similar that the same plan could be reused, but how is the query analyzer to know that? If it performs a string compare, the two queries will appear to be different.

Enter parameters. Suppose you rewrite the two queries like this:

```
select * from authors where au_fname = ? , parameter = 'Bob'
select * from authors where au_fname = ? , parameter = 'Fred'
```

If you look only at the SQL statement rather than the parameter, the same query plan can be used for both. This is known as a parameterized query. Some databases (such as SQL Server) attempt "auto-parameterization" of queries, but mostly you have to do it yourself.

In addition to using parameterized queries, the SQL-99 standard includes a specification for *persistent stored modules*. The two types of persistent stored modules that are interesting from an API point of view are stored procedures and user-defined functions. If you use stored procedures and functions, both the code and the parsed tree (which can contain procedural statements) are stored in the database, thus eliminating step 1 in the process.

Like function calls in a traditional programming language, stored procedures can contain input parameters, output parameters, or parameters that are both input and output. User-defined functions—and stored procedures in some databases, such as SQL Server—can return only a return value. Some databases, such as Oracle, return resultsets as output parameters of data type `refcursor`, which are usually represented as resultsets by the provider; SQL Server, Sybase, and DB2 return them directly as resultsets. When you use `refcursors` with Oracle stored procedures, they are omitted from the parameters collection and also, if you're using `CommandType.Text`, from the command text. In almost every case, all resultsets from a stored procedure are returned before output parameter values are, and output parameters are not available in ADO.NET until the resulting `DataReader` instance is closed. Listing 3–6 illustrates this behavior. What a parameter is—input, output, inout (both input and output), or a return value—is indicated in the `Parameter`'s `Direction` property.

Listing 3-6 Retrieving result and output parameters

```
/* create procedure ins_sel_parms(
 * @in1 as int,
 * @inout1 as int output,
 * @out1 as int output
 * )
 * as
 * insert into jobs
 *    values('Proc with parms', 20, 20)
 * set @inout1 = @inout1 * 2
 * set @out1 = @in1 * 3
 * select * from authors
 * return 99
 */
SqlConnection conn = new SqlConnection(
  "server=localhost;uid=sa;pwd=mypw;database=pubs");
SqlCommand cmd = new SqlCommand(
  "ins_sel_parms", conn);
SqlDataReader rdr;

conn.Open();
cmd.CommandType = CommandType.StoredProcedure;
cmd.Parameters.Add("@in1", 10);
cmd.Parameters.Add("@inout1", 10);
cmd.Parameters.Add("@out1", SqlDbType.Int);
cmd.Parameters.Add("@ret", SqlDbType.Int);

cmd.Parameters[0].Direction =
  ParameterDirection.Input;
cmd.Parameters[1].Direction =
  ParameterDirection.InputOutput;
cmd.Parameters[2].Direction =
  ParameterDirection.Output;
cmd.Parameters[3].Direction =
  ParameterDirection.ReturnValue;

rdr = cmd.ExecuteReader();

// I see no output parms here..
for (int i=0;i<cmd.Parameters.Count;i++)
  Console.WriteLine("Parameter {0} value is {1}",
    i, cmd.Parameters[i].Value);

rdr.Close();
```

```
// inout, output and return value available now
for (int j=0;j<cmd.Parameters.Count;j++)
  Console.WriteLine("Parameter {0} value is {1}",
    j, cmd.Parameters[j].Value);

conn.Close();
```

Classes that implement IDbCommand can use parameterized statements through the Command's Parameters property, which can point to a collection of instances of classes that encapsulate query parameter functionality. Both the OleDb data provider and the SqlClient data provider implement parameter classes (OleDbParameter and SqlParameter respectively) as well as the corresponding collection classes: OleDbParameterCollection and SqlParameterCollection. The code in Listing 3–7 opens a SqlConnection and a SqlCommand and then executes a SQL statement with parameters. Listing 3–8 shows the definitions of the stored procedures used in this and the next few examples.

Listing 3–7   Stored procedure parameters

```
SqlConnection conn = new SqlConnection(
    "server=localhost;uid=sa;pwd=mypw;database=pubs");
SqlCommand cmd = new SqlCommand("getByAuid", conn);
IDataReader reader;

conn.Open();

cmd.Parameters.Add(
   new SqlParameter("@au_id", SqlDbType.VarChar, 11));
cmd.Parameters["@au_id"].Value = "472-27-2349";

cmd.CommandType = CommandType.StoredProcedure;
reader = cmd.ExecuteReader();
```

Listing 3–8   Stored procedures used in code examples

```
create procedure getByAuid(@au_id as varchar(11))
as
select * from authors
  where au_id = @au_id
go
```

```
create procedure ins_sel_ins
as
insert into jobs values('New job', 10, 10)
select * from jobs
insert into jobs values('Another New job', 20, 20)
go

create procedure ins_upd_del
as
insert into jobs values('Latest job', 10, 10)
update jobs set job_desc = 'Dummy'
  where job_id > 20
delete jobs where job_id > 20
go
```

You can use parameters when the `CommandType` is `Command-Type.StoredProcedure` or when using parameterized queries or stored procedures and `CommandType.Text`. Listing 3–9 illustrates using a stored procedure as `CommandText`.

Listing 3–9 Using a stored procedure as `CommandText`

```
OleDbConnection conn = new OleDbConnection(
  "provider=sqloledb;uid=sa;pwd=mypw;initial catalog=pubs");
OleDbCommand cmd = new OleDbCommand(
  "exec ins_sel_ins", conn);
cmd.Connection.Open();
cmd.CommandType = CommandType.Text;
int i = cmd.ExecuteNonQuery();
```

The `Parameter` and `ParameterCollection` classes are managed types that are meaningless outside their association with a `Command`. The `Command` classes have a `Parameters` property that contains a reference to a `ParameterCollection`. Parameter objects can be instantiated directly and then added to the appropriate `ParameterCollection` or can be added directly using the `Command.Parameters.Add` convenience method. Both ways of using `Parameter`s are illustrated in Listing 3–10.

Listing 3–10 Adding parameters to the collection

```
SqlConnection conn = new SqlConnection(
  "uid=sa;pwd=mypw;pwd=;initial catalog=pubs");
```

```
SqlCommand cmd = new SqlCommand("sel_ins_sel", conn);
cmd.CommandType = CommandType.StoredProcedure;

// create, then add
SqlParameter parm = new SqlParameter();
parm.ParameterName = "@parm";
parm.Value = 8;
cmd.Parameters.Add(parm);

// or just add
cmd.Parameters.Add("@aparm", 10);
```

As shown in Listing 3–11, there are a plethora of overloaded constructors for `Parameter` instances. The last two overloads, useful only in disconnected mode, are used to flush changes from the `DataSet` to the database. In these constructors, `srcColumn` and `DataRowVersion` refer to columns in the `DataSet`'s `DataTable`. Chapter 5 explores the utility of these `Parameter` properties.

Listing 3–11   Constructors of `SqlParameter`
```
SqlParameter()
SqlParameter(string name, SqlDbType dataType)
SqlParameter(string name, object value)
SqlParameter(string name, SqlDbType dataType,
            int size)
SqlParameter(string name, SqlDbType dataType,
            int size, string srcColumn)
SqlParameter(string name, SqlDbType dbType,
            int size,
            ParameterDirection direction,
            Boolean isNullable, Byte precision,
            Byte scale, string srcColumn,
            DataRowVersion srcVersion,
            object value)
```

Parameter values are specified using .NET native (CLS) types, but databases are expecting parameters as database types. The `Parameter` classes therefore contain two data type properties. Both data providers use the property `DbType` to refer to CLS types. The `SqlClient` provider uses `SqlDbType` to refer to the SQL Server native database types, and the `OleDb` data provider uses a `OleDbType` property to refer to OLE DB's type system, known as DBTYPES.

You can specify parameters using a native data type that differs from the one the database is expecting. In this case, you specify both the `DbType` property and the `SqlDbType` or `OleDbType`, and the provider may be able to perform the conversion.

The `Parameter` classes contain additional properties relating to data types. The `IsNullable` property indicates whether the parameter value can be NULL—in other words, whether you can set the `Parameter`'s value to DB-Null.Value. You use `Offset` to indicate an offset into a buffer. The `Precision` and `Scale` properties refer to the total number as numeric digits and the number of decimal digits. They are used only with exact numeric values, such as the CLS `Numeric` type and a relational database's DECIMAL or NUMERIC data type. Bear in mind that some databases (such as Oracle) have no INTEGER data type. Integral values must be expressed as a NUMERIC type with a numeric scale of zero.

The way parameters are specified differs in the `OleDb` and `SqlClient` providers. In the `OleDb` data provider, parameters are passed by left-to-right position. This is specified by the order of the parameters in the `OleDbParameterCollection`. Although `ParameterName` can be specified, it is irrelevant, as shown in Listing 3–12. When using SQL Server—or other databases whose stored procedures return a return code—with the `OleDb` data provider (SQLOLEDB provider), you must specify the return value as the first member of the collection (parameter zero when using zero-based indexers). A return value placeholder cannot be used with a stored procedure (where return values are not used)—for example, with the Oracle OLE DB provider (MSDAORA)—because it will be mistaken for the invocation of an Oracle user-defined function. When using the `OleDb` data provider, you specify parameterized queries as follows:

```
select * from authors where au_id = ?
```

Because OLE DB providers can use any query language or dialect, some of them may accept parameter markers other than `?`. The `Jet` 4.0 OLE DB provider, for example, accepts named parameter markers, as does SQL Server. The `SQLOLEDB` provider, however, requires `?` as a parameter marker when used with the `OleDb` data provider.

Listing 3–12   Using parameters with the `OleDb` data provider

```
OleDbConnection oconn = new OleDbConnection(
  "provider=msdaora;user id=scott;" +
  "password=tiger;data source=orcll");
OleDbCommand cmd = new OleDbCommand("in_parms2", oconn);
cmd.CommandType = CommandType.StoredProcedure;

// you can't use a return value with Oracle
// else it thinks it's a UDF
//cmd.Parameters.Add("return", 0);

// exact names are irrelevant
// but names still must be specified
cmd.Parameters.Add("xxx", 10);
cmd.Parameters.Add("yyy",10);
cmd.Parameters.Add("zzz", 0);

cmd.Parameters["xxx"].DbType = DbType.Int32;
cmd.Parameters["yyy"].Direction =
  ParameterDirection.InputOutput;
cmd.Parameters["zzz"].Direction =
  ParameterDirection.Output;

oconn.Open();
cmd.ExecuteNonQuery();

// SQL Server with OleDb data provider
OleDbConnection sconn = new OleDbConnection(
  "provider=sqloledb;server=(local);" +
  "uid=sa;pwd=mypw;database=pubs");
OleDbCommand scmd = new OleDbCommand(
  "ins_sel_parms2", sconn);
cmd.CommandType = CommandType.StoredProcedure;

// you do need a return value - parameter 0
scmd.Parameters.Add("return", 0);

// the name is not at all significant
scmd.Parameters.Add("@zzy", 10);
scmd.Parameters.Add("@inout1",10);
scmd.Parameters.Add("@out1", 0);
```

The `SqlClient` data provider uses name-based parameters. You can specify the parameters in any order in the `SqlParameterCollection`, but the parameter names *must* be correct, as shown in Listing 3–13. The return value need not be specified, and if it is specified, its name is irrelevant; SQL Server figures out that it is a return value by `Direction` property only. When you're using a parameterized query in the `SqlClient` provider, the only syntax that will work is

```
select * from authors where au_id = @parmname
```

where `@parmname` can be any name that is unique in the statement. You can also use a stored procedure as `CommandType.Text`. In that case, depending on whether you use the `OleDb` or the `SqlClient` data provider, some of the ways of specifying a stored procedure will work. These are shown in Listing 3–14. Note that `SqlClient` does not support ODBC escape clauses at all (`{ call }` format). If you want the same `Command` to be used for nonparameterized statements after using parameters, be sure to call `IDbCommand.Parameters.Clear` before reusing it.

Listing 3–13 Using parameters with the SQL Server provider

```
SqlConnection sconn = new SqlConnection(
  "server=(local);uid=sa;pwd=mypw;database=pubs");
SqlCommand cmd = new SqlCommand(
  "ins_sel_parms2", sconn);
cmd.CommandType = CommandType.StoredProcedure;

// we can put these in any order, but name is significant
// must have the '@', in case you wondered
cmd.Parameters.Add("@inout1", 10);
cmd.Parameters.Add("@in1", 10);
cmd.Parameters.Add("@out1", 0);

// the return value can be named anything
cmd.Parameters.Add("zzz", 0);
cmd.Parameters["@inout1"].Direction =
  ParameterDirection.InputOutput;
cmd.Parameters[2].Direction =
  ParameterDirection.Output;
cmd.Parameters[3].Direction =
  ParameterDirection.ReturnValue;

sconn.Open();
cmd.ExecuteNonQuery();
```

Listing 3–14 Calling a stored procedure

```
// SqlCommand calling stored procedure
// cmd.CommandType = CommandType.Text

// no, no, no
//SqlCommand cmd = new SqlCommand(
//    "exec getjobs ? ", sconn);
//SqlCommand cmd = new SqlCommand(
//    "execute getjobs ? ", sconn);
//SqlCommand cmd = new SqlCommand(
//    "{ call getjobs(?) }", sconn);

// yes, yes..
SqlCommand cmd1 = new SqlCommand(
  "exec getjobs @parm ", sconn);
SqlCommand cmd2 = new SqlCommand(
  "execute getjobs @parm ", sconn);

// no, must have 'exec'
//SqlCommand cmd = new SqlCommand(
//    "getjobs @parm ", sconn);

// this doesn't speak ODBC escape clauses either.
//SqlCommand cmd = new SqlCommand(
//    "{ call getjobs(@parm) }", sconn);

//
// OleDbCommand calling stored procedure
// cmd.CommandType = CommandType.Text

// yes...
OleDbCommand ocmd1 = new OleDbCommand(
  "exec getjobs ? ", oconn);
// yes..
OleDbCommand ocmd2 = new OleDbCommand(
  "execute getjobs ? ", oconn);
// yes..
OleDbCommand ocmd3 = new OleDbCommand(
  "{ call getjobs(?) }", oconn);
```

3.7 Command Preparation, Cancellation, Timeouts, and Cleanup

The `IDbCommand` interface has a method called `Prepare`, which makes a round-trip to the database to tell the database to `Prepare` the statement and cache it in its query cache for later use. Because all modern databases cache query plans without asking, the only thing `Prepare` buys you with most databases is a little faster execution speed the first time the query is executed; you also get some control over the lifetime of the query plan. This comes at the expense of a database round-trip, so its usefulness is questionable—although, on a busy system, a statement that isn't prepared could have its query plan flushed, depending on the query cache management policy of the database. Although `Commands` can be prepared by calling `Prepare`, there is no `Unprepare` method.

When testing or using dynamically entered commands, you may need to find out the number, name, and data type of parameters before execution. You could do this by using the database's information schema, but because this entails an extra round-trip, it is special-purpose and should not be used with known queries in a production environment. The `CommandBuilder` class has a method that automatically fills in a `Parameters` collection, something discussed in Chapter 5.

The `Command` class has a `CommandTimeout` value that is exposed as a settable property. The default is 30 seconds. There is also a method, `ResetCommandTimeout`, to reset it to its default value. Both `OleDbCommand` and `SqlCommand` support a `Cancel` method for canceling `Commands` in progress. The `Command` must be started on a separate thread to be cancelable, and the `Cancel` command should be issued on a separate thread to be effective. Listing 3–15 shows how to cancel a command in progress. This capability is used in ad hoc query tools—for example, to implement the "stop button" functionality in SQL Server Query Analyzer.

Listing 3–15 Canceling a command in progress

```
SqlCommand cmd;

// threads to signal
AutoResetEvent ev1 = new AutoResetEvent(false);
AutoResetEvent ev2 = new AutoResetEvent(false);
```

```
public void DoQuery()
{
    try
    {
      int i = cmd.ExecuteNonQuery();
    }
    catch (Exception e)
    {
      Console.WriteLine(e.Message);
    }
    ev1.Set();
}

public void DoCancel()
{
  System.Threading.Thread.Sleep(100);
  cmd.Cancel();
  ev2.Set();
}

public void CancelCommand()
{
  SqlConnection conn = new SqlConnection(
    "server=localhost;uid=sa;pwd=mypw;database=pubs");
  conn.Open();
  cmd = new SqlCommand(
    "update jobs set min_lvl = 30", conn);

  AutoResetEvent[] evnts = new AutoResetEvent[2];
  evnts[0] = ev1;
  evnts[1] = ev2;

  Thread t1 = new Thread(new ThreadStart(this.DoQuery));
  Thread t2 = new Thread(new ThreadStart(this.DoCancel));

  t1.Start();
  t2.Start();
  WaitHandle.WaitAll(evnts);
  conn.Close();
}
```

When you are finished with a `Command`, you can call `Dispose` on it. There is no `Close` method. In some providers, `Dispose` cleans up internal database resources, although the specifics vary by provider. For example, when you're using the Microsoft OLE DB provider for Oracle (`MSDAORA`), calling `Command.Dispose` frees up internal database cursors in Oracle. When you're using Oracle's OLE DB provider, on the other hand, cursor management works automatically and `Dispose` does not specifically free internal cursors. This is important because if `Dispose` is not called in heavily used systems, Oracle eventually returns an "out of cursors" error message.

3.8   Streaming Data through a `DataReader`

SQL commands and stored procedures often produce sets of rectangular results in addition to output parameters and counts of rows affected by the commands. The results are rectangular in that each row (tuple) has the same number of columns and a column's data type does not vary from row to row. In accordance with the relational model, which mandates no support for multivalued data, columns usually contain only primitive data types. However, ADO.NET supports columns of type `Object`.

Managed providers retrieve rows and column values through the `DataReader` class. `DataReader` is composed of two standard interfaces—`IDataReader` and `IDataRecord`—plus data source-specific functionality. `IDataReader` contains methods to move from row to row and, if multiple results are involved, from resultset to resultset. There are also a few metadata properties and methods that permit you to get descriptive information about the resultset. `IDataRecord` gets data from columns in the current row. Because `IDataReader` extends `IDataRecord`, all methods can be invoked through `IDataReader`.

`DataReader`s, such as `SqlDataReader` and `OleDbDataReader`, implement `IDataReader` to provide forward-only, pull-style access to a resultset. (See Chapter 8 for the formal interface definition of `IDataReader`.) `DataReader` implements the concept of a single current row or cursor over the data, although this does not necessarily correspond to a database cursor. `IDataReader.Read` moves to the next row and returns `false` when there are no more rows to be read. Because some databases (including SQL Server) can expose multiple resultsets from a single command or stored procedure, consumers can use `IDataReader.NextResult` to process multiple discrete resultsets returned from a single command. Listing 3–16 shows the use of `Read` and `NextResult`.

Listing 3–16   Getting multiple results

```
SqlConnection conn = new SqlConnection(
    "server=localhost;uid=sa;pwd=mypw;database=pubs");
SqlCommand cmd = new SqlCommand(
    "select * from authors;select * from jobs", conn);

conn.Open();
IDataReader rdr = cmd.ExecuteReader();

bool more;
int results = 0;
do
{
  Console.WriteLine("new result");
  results++;
  while(rdr.Read())
  {
    Console.WriteLine(Column 0 = " + rdr[0]);
    Console.WriteLine(Column 1 = " + rdr[1]);
  }
  more = rdr.NextResult();
} while(more);
```

When you're using a DataReader, it is not always possible to know the number of rows that will be returned from a SELECT statement immediately after the SELECT returns. This is especially true with SQL Server. When you're using SqlDataReader—and when you're using OleDbDataReader with the SQLOLEDB provider—SQL Server uses a noncursor mode (for speed and to enable support of multiple results) known as *streaming mode*. In most streaming mode operations, SQL Server locks and streams the data as you read it, one buffer at a time. Because other users might insert, change, or delete records while you are reading, and because those changes can appear in the resultset as you read buffers, the number of rows affected is unknown at command execution time. IDataReader.RecordsAffected returns –1 in this case, which is the correct behavior.

Although you can use the same DataReader instance again to process another result from the same Command instance or a different Command instance, you must explicitly close the DataReader before you reuse it. This is because of the way that the underlying database protocol works. For example, if you're using SQL Server's TDS protocol in streaming mode, there is no way to interleave results from multiple commands. Attempting to reuse the `DataReader` without first closing it will produce a `SqlException`: "There is already an open `DataReader` associated with this `Connection` which must be closed first." However, it is entirely possible to `Close` a `DataReader` before you have finished reading all the rows.

Providers of `DataReader` types implement `IEnumerable` to allow iteration through the rows as a collection. This interface also allows data binding to GUI controls such as data grids. When reading through a resultset using `foreach` syntax in C# or `for each` in VB.NET, each iteration through the loop returns a `DbDataRecord` instance. `DbDataRecord`, an internal helper class in `System.Data.Common`, contains the columns for exactly one row. The array of column values are copied into `DbDataRecord`'s `_values` property using `IDataRecord.GetValues`, which is described later.

Reading and writing are not symmetric in data providers. Commands (usually SQL commands) are used to insert, update, or delete data in a database. ADO.NET's data providers do not currently support positioned updates through server cursors, and there is no support for writing an entire set of rows. `System.Data` does not contain a specification for a `DataWriter`.

Because a column's data type does not vary from row to row, there is no need to provide type information on a per-row basis. Type information about each column is provided by a `GetSchemaTable` method. This method produces a `System.Data.DataTable` consisting of columns of schema information (such as data type, column size, and so on). There is one schema metadata row in this table for each column in the resultset. Listing 3–17 shows how to use `SchemaTable` to determine information about the resultset's columns. Note that in the default case, `SchemaTable` does not identify key columns, at least when you're using SQL Server. Chapter 5 explains how you can get more detailed metadata.

Listing 3–17   Getting resultset metadata

```
// this code:
SqlDataReader rdr;
rdr = cmd.ExecuteReader();
```

```
DataTable t = rdr.GetSchemaTable();
foreach(DataRow r in t.Rows)
  foreach(DataColumn c in t.Columns)
    Console.WriteLine(c.ColumnName + ": \t" + r[c]);

// results in this output
// (one row for each column in the resultset)
// (only first row is shown)

ColumnName:        job_id
ColumnOrdinal:     0
ColumnSize:        2
NumericPrecision: 0
NumericScale:      0
IsUnique:
IsKeyColumn:
BaseCatalogName:
BaseColumnName: job_id
BaseSchemaName:
BaseTableName:
DataType:          System.Int16
AllowDBNull:       False
DbType:            16
IsAliased:
IsExpression:
IsIdentity:        True
IsAutoIncrement: True
IsRowVersion:
IsHidden:
IsLong:            False
IsReadOnly:        True
```

3.9 Reading Column Values through `IDataRecord`

Individual column values are read through a `DataReader`'s implementation of the `IDataRecord` interface. `IDataRecord` includes a series of strongly typed accessors (shown in Listing 3–18) that take a zero-based column ordinal and return a CLS type. These methods map data source data types to CLS data types. Providers can choose to expose accessors for data source-specific data types; for example, the `SqlClient` provider's accessors can return instances of structures defined in the `System.Data.SqlTypes` namespace. Strongly typed accessors do not necessarily convert types; using the wrong getter (for example, calling

`GetString` on an integer column) results in an `InvalidCastException`. A special method, `IsDBNull`, indicates whether or not the field contains a (database) null value. If a field can be `NULL`, you should use `IsDBNull` before attempting to get the field's value.

Listing 3–18 Strongly typed accessors

```
public interface IDataRecord
{
... other methods omitted
    bool GetBoolean(int i)
    byte GetByte(int i)
    int GetBytes(int i,
                int fieldoffset,
                byte[] buffer,
                int bufferoffset,
                int length)
    char GetChar(int i)
    int GetChars(int i,
                int fieldoffset,
                char[] buffer,
                int bufferoffset,
                int length)
    IDataReader GetData(int i)
    DateTime GetDateTime(int i)
    decimal GetDecimal(int i)
    double GetDouble(int i)
    float GetFloat(int i)
    Guid GetGuid(int i)
    short GetInt16(int i)
    int GetInt32(int i)
    long GetInt64(int i)
    string GetString(int i)
}
```

In addition to the strongly typed accessors, the `GetValue` and `GetValues` methods can return the values as an `Object` or `Array` of `Object`s, respectively. As with a variant in ADO classic, `System.Object` is not a primitive type and therefore can represent any type. You know how big to allocate the array when calling `GetValues` by using the `FieldCount` property, as shown in Listing 3–19. Because it is often faster to use the corresponding typed getter (for example, `GetInt32`) rather than use `GetValue`, the `GetFieldType` method returns the CLS type that would be returned by `GetValue`. The `Get-DataTypeName` method returns the database type (for example, `integer`) for the specified column.

Listing 3–19 Getting fields as an array of Objects

```
SqlDataReader rdr;

// populate data reader... then
Object[] o = new Object[rdr.FieldCount];
rdr.GetValues(o);
```

Consumers can also use the `Item` property, which allows access to columns by zero-based ordinal or by column name. The `Item` property is accessed using array index notation in VB.NET or C#. Listing 3–20 shows examples of indexed access by ordinal and name. Providers of `DataReader` types implement `IEnumerable` to allow iteration through the columns as a collection. This also allows data binding to GUI controls such as data grids. A single column ordinal can be obtained from a column name (using `GetOrdinal`); conversely, a column name can be obtained from a column ordinal (using `GetName`). When using `GetOrdinal` or using column names in indexers, the provider must search through the array looking for the right name, so it is faster to use the ordinals, although using names enhances code maintainability. How much slower `GetOrdinal` is depends on the number of columns in the resultset. In such cases, calling `GetOrdinal` once and storing the result may improve performance.

Listing 3–20 Using field indexers

```
SqlDataReader rdr;

// populate data reader... then
for (int i=0;i < rdr.FieldCount; i++)
{
    // column name
    String name = rdr.GetName(i);

    // get name and value by ordinal
    Console.WriteLine("column {0}: {1}",
            rdr.GetName(i), rdr[i]);

    // get ordinal and value by name
```

```
      Console.WriteLine("column {0}: {1}",
               rdr.GetOrdinal(name), rdr[name]);
   }
```

When you're using OLE DB (but not when you're using SQL Server), you can return hierarchical results using the special column type DBTYPE_CHAPTER. A *chapter column* is essentially a handle (an implementation is not mandated by the spec) that points to corresponding child rows for a given parent. This type is useful for data sources that natively expose hierarchical data or embedded tables—for example, the OLE DB provider for Unisys's DMS III. In addition, Microsoft has shipped a DataShape OLE DB provider that "creates" hierarchies over any relational data source using a special command syntax known as Shape language.

The OleDb data provider can use chapters through the IDataRecord.GetData method. GetData returns an IDataReader interface that corresponds to the child rowset, as illustrated in Listing 3–21. In addition, IDataReader exposes a Depth property that gets the depth in the hierarchy of the current row.

Listing 3–21   Using IDataReader.GetData with the Shape provider

```
OleDbConnection conn = new OleDbConnection(
  "provider=msdatashape;data provider=sqloledb;" +
  "uid=sa;pwd=mypw;initial catalog=pubs");

// hierarchical with titleauthor as child or author
String thecommand =
     "SHAPE  {select au_id from authors} " +
   "APPEND({select au_id, title_id from titleauthor} " +
   "AS chapter RELATE au_id TO au_id)";
OleDbCommand cmd = new OleDbCommand(thecommand, conn);
OleDbDataReader rdr;

conn.Open();
rdr = cmd.ExecuteReader();

while (rdr.Read())
{
  Console.WriteLine("au_id = " + rdr[0]);

  // read the title_ids for this author
```

```
  OleDbDataReader chapter = rdr.GetData(1);
  while (chapter.Read())
    Console.Write("title_id = " + chapter[1]);
  chapter.Close();
}

rdr.Close();
conn.Close();
```

3.9.1 Handling Large Data Columns

Usually, a single row of data will fit into a buffer streamed from the database. However, most databases support data types that accommodate very large objects, known as BLOB or CLOB columns. Data of this type can be read in user-defined chunks that are streamed directly in multiple contiguous data buffers. You need not allocate a single buffer large enough to allocate the entire contents. ADO.NET supports this by using `CommandType.SequentialAccess` and the `IDataReader.GetChars` or `IDataReader.GetBytes` method.

As discussed in the section "`Command` Behaviors," `CommandBehavior.SequentialAccess` is used to permit streaming columns that can be arbitrarily large, but it mandates that the data in columns for a specific row must be read in ordinal order. `GetChars` or `GetBytes` can then be used to read the data into a stream class—for example, to buffer an object containing multimedia data or to write the data to the file system. Listing 3–22 shows an example of using streamed data.

Listing 3–22 Reading large objects from a database

```
SqlConnection conn = new SqlConnection(
  "server=localhost;uid=sa;pwd=mypw;database=northwind");

string cmdtext = "SELECT employeeid, photo" +
  " from employees" +
  " where employeeid = 1";
SqlCommand cmd = new SqlCommand(cmdtext, conn);

FileStream fs;      // to write to a file
BinaryWriter bw;

long numread;
long startIndex;
```

```
int buffSize = 4096;
byte[] buff = new byte[buffSize];

// must use SequentialAccess
conn.Open();
SqlDataReader rdr =
  cmd.ExecuteReader(CommandBehavior.SequentialAccess);

if (rdr.Read())
{
  // Must get employeeid first
  int empid = rdr.GetInt32(0);

  // Create a file and open a BinaryWriter over it
  fs = new FileStream("c:\\mypic.bmp",
                      FileMode.OpenOrCreate,
                      FileAccess.Write);
  bw = new BinaryWriter(fs);

  // Set the start index
  startIndex = 0;

  // call GetBytes
  numread = rdr.GetBytes(1, startIndex,
                            buff, 0, buffSize);

  // Read and write buffers of data
  while (numread == buffSize)
  {
    bw.Write(numread);
    bw.Flush();

    startIndex+= buffSize;
    numread = rdr.GetBytes(1, startIndex,
                              buff, 0, buffSize);
  }

  // Write the last buffer.
  bw.Write(buff);
  bw.Flush();

  // Close the output file.
  bw.Close();
  fs.Close();
```

```
        }

        rdr.Close();
        conn.Close();
```

Although the runtime doesn't provide a straightforward mechanism for buffering `Command` parameters when you're using large objects, you can use BLOB and CLOB columns (IMAGE and TEXT in SQL Server) as parameters—for example, to upload a file to a SQL Server column over the Internet or from a file. Listing 3–23 shows an example of using a `Command` parameter of `SqlDbType.Image`.

Listing 3–23   Writing a `SqlDbType.Image` column

```
// Create a file and open a binary writer over it
FileStream fs = new FileStream("c:\\mypic.bmp",
                               FileMode.Open,
                               FileAccess.Read);
BinaryReader br = new BinaryReader(fs);

SqlConnection conn = new SqlConnection(
    "server=localhost;uid=sa;pwd=mypw;database=northwind");

string cmdtext = "update employees " +
  "set Photo=@image where EmployeeId=1";
SqlCommand cmd = new SqlCommand(cmdtext, conn);
cmd.Parameters.Add("@image", SqlDbType.Image);

cmd.Parameters["@image"].Value =
    br.ReadBytes((int)br.BaseStream.Length);

conn.Open();
int i = cmd.ExecuteNonQuery();

conn.Close();
```

3.10   Error Handling

If you need to handle only a single error, you can use the generic `Exception` class, which reports a single error message. Sometimes, databases return additional error information or a collection of errors. This is especially true of OLE DB, in which each provider can add information when using the service provider architecture. For this reason, `SqlClient` and `OleDb` each implements its own subclass of `Exception`, which can return a collection of errors.

The OleDb provider's OleDbException exposes an OleDbErrorCollection that is similar to the ADO's Errors collection (OLE DB's IErrorRecord). Each error contains an error message, the provider's native error, and an optional SQLState. The OleDbException is derived from InteropServices.ExternalException.

The SqlClient provider exposes a SqlException derived from SystemException. Because it includes more SQL Server-specific error information, SqlException encapsulates a SqlErrorCollection that exposes a superset of classic ADO's error information. Information available through SqlError includes the SQL Server instance involved, the error's severity, and an optional stored procedure name and line number. Listing 3–24 shows how to handle multiple errors and display the stored procedure name and line number.

Listing 3–24 SqlClient extended error information

```
SqlConnection conn = new SqlConnection(
  "server=(local);uid=sa;pwd=mypw;database=pubs");
SqlCommand cmd = new SqlCommand("ins_sel_ins", conn);
cmd.CommandType = CommandType.StoredProcedure;

try
{
  conn.Open();
  int rows = cmd.ExecuteNonQuery();
}
catch (SqlException se)
{
  Console.WriteLine("Procedure {0} failed at line {1}",
    se.Procedure, se.LineNumber);
  for (int i=0;i<se.Errors.Count;i++)
    Console.WriteLine(se.Errors[i].Message);
}
finally
{
if (conn.State == ConnectionState.Open)
conn.Close();
}
```

Although most errors in the database interrupt the program's flow of control, other errors do not; the program continues even though it has processed the warning message. This concept is a difficult one to map in any data access API.

In ADO.NET, this concept is encapsulated in the difference between an `Exception` (a severe error) and an `InfoMessageEvent` (a warning or information). Figure 3–1 shows this concept. The warnings at `Connection.Open` time and in `Command` statement 2 do not alter the program flow; the program can safely ignore those errors if it wants to. However, `Command` statement 3 produces a severe error that throws an `Exception`, with the result that `Command` statement 4 is never executed. What distinguishes a severe error from a warning is specific to the data source. SQL Server, for example, defines an error severity of 10 or less as a warning.

One of the problems with ADO (classic) is that severe errors (which will and should alter program flow) and SQL warning messages such as "Language changed to US English" (which should not alter program flow) are combined in the `errors` collection. The data provider architecture exposes warnings as an

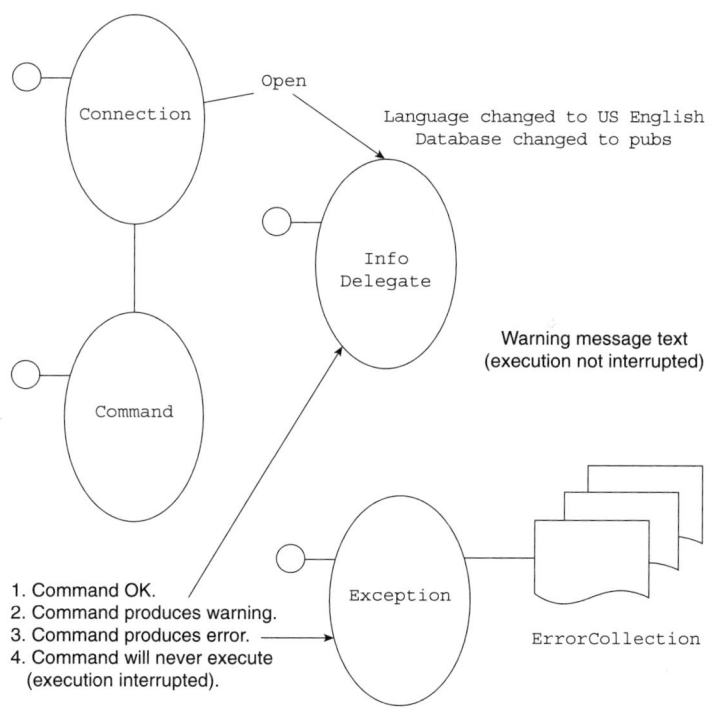

Figure 3–1 Producing errors and warnings

event, separate from errors, that can be caught or ignored. Listing 3–25 shows an example of using `SqlInfoMessageEventHandler` in addition to exception handling.

Listing 3–25 Catching errors and warnings

```
void useInfoHandler()
{
// get a SQLConnection
SqlConnection conn = new SqlConnection(
  "server=(local);uid=sa;pwd=mypw;database=pubs");

// Add InfoMessage event handler
// for additional custom handling
conn.InfoMessage +=
  new SqlInfoMessageEventHandler(this.myInfoHandler);

try
{
  conn.Open();
}
catch (SqlException e)
{
  for (int i=0; i < e.Errors.Count; i++)
  {
    Console.WriteLine("Index #" + i + "\n" +
      "Error: " + e.Errors[i].ToString() + "\n");
  }
}
catch (Exception e)
  {
    Console.WriteLine(e.Message);
  }
finally { conn.Close(); }
return;
}

public void myInfoHandler(
  object conn, SqlInfoMessageEventArgs e)
{
  Console.WriteLine("caught a SQL warning");
  for (int i=0; i < e.Errors.Count; i++)
  {
    Console.WriteLine("Index #" + i + "\n" +
```

```
      "Warning: " + e.Errors[i].ToString() + "\n");
  }
}
```

3.11   Using Transactions

The IDbConnection interface has a single method to begin a local transaction. This method returns an instance of a class that implements IDbTransaction. Classes such as SqlTransaction and OleDbTransaction implement IDbTransaction, which encapsulates operations involving a local transaction such as Commit and Rollback. You can configure the transaction isolation level through an optional parameter of IDbConnection.BeginTransaction. A simple transaction is shown in Listing 3–26.

Listing 3–26   A simple transaction

```
SqlConnection sconn = new SqlConnection(
  "server=(local);uid=sa;pwd=mypw;database=pubs");
SqlCommand cmd = new SqlCommand(
  "insert jobs values('First', 10, 10)", sconn);
SqlTransaction tx = null;
try
{
  sconn.Open();
  tx = sconn.BeginTransaction(
      IsolationLevel.ReadCommitted);
  cmd.Transaction = tx;
  int i = cmd.ExecuteNonQuery();

  cmd.CommandText =
    "insert jobs values('Second', 20, 20)";
  int j = cmd.ExecuteNonQuery();

  tx.Commit();
  sconn.Close();
}
catch (Exception e)
{
  if (tx != null)
    tx.Rollback();
  Console.WriteLine(e.Message);
}
finally
```

```
{
  if (sconn.State == ConnectionState.Open)
    sconn.Close();
}
```

Notice that, although BeginTransaction is called on the Connection class, Commands that use this Connection do not automatically "inherit" the Connection's transaction. The Command.Transaction property must be assigned to a currently executing transaction; otherwise, with most data stores, the Command will fail when executed. An alternative is to specify a Transaction instance in the Command's constructor. Although this seems like overkill for a simple case, it makes the transaction model extremely flexible, accommodating, in data providers that support it, nested transactions and a transaction that can span multiple Connections and multiple Commands. The concept, with the associated references, is shown in Figure 3–2.

Each class that implements IDbTransaction (such as SqlTransaction and OleDbTransaction) can implement different transaction features. Be-

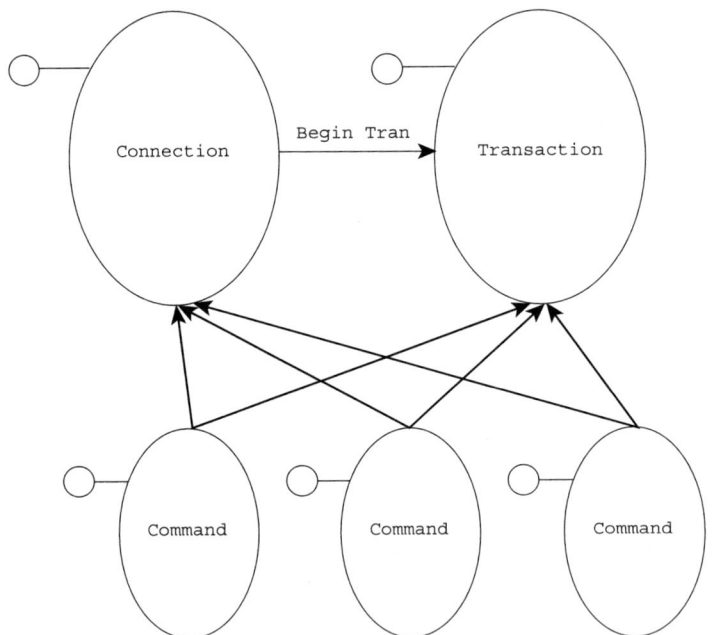

Figure 3–2 Connections, Commands, and Transactions

cause the OLE DB specification mandates the use of the Ole Transaction (OLE TX) object model and because this model supports nested transactions, the OleDb data provider supports beginning a nested transaction by using OleDb-Transaction.Begin, rather than OleDbConnection.BeginTransaction, to start a nested transaction. For example, Microsoft Access is one of the few data stores that supports true nested transactions, in which the inner transaction can be rolled back without rolling back the outer transaction and vice versa. Listing 3–27 shows how to use nested transactions with Microsoft Access. This example also illustrates using the Command constructor overload that uses a Transaction as a parameter.

Listing 3–27   A nested transaction

```
OleDbConnection conn = new OleDbConnection(
  "Provider=Microsoft.Jet.OLEDB.4.0;" +
  "Data Source=C:\\Northwind4.mdb;");
conn.Open();

OleDbTransaction tx1 = conn.BeginTransaction();

string cmdtext1 =
  "update suppliers set city = 'Kobe' " +
  " where supplierid = 4";
OleDbCommand cmd1 = new OleDbCommand(
  cmdtext1, conn, tx1);
int i = cmd1.ExecuteNonQuery();

OleDbTransaction tx2 = tx1.Begin();
string cmdtext2 =
  "update suppliers set city = 'Redding' " +
  " where supplierid = 1";
OleDbCommand cmd2 = new OleDbCommand(
  cmdtext2, conn, tx2);

int j = cmd2.ExecuteNonQuery();

// roll back the inner transaction only
tx2.Rollback();

// commit the outer transaction
tx1.Commit();
```

`SqlTransaction` supports named savepoints through the `Save` method. With *named savepoints*, you can declare a savepoint in the middle of a transaction, do more work, and then roll back only the work done since the savepoint. You can then commit or roll back the rest of the work separately. You can roll back to a named savepoint by using an overload of `SqlTransaction.Rollback`, as shown in Listing 3–28.

Listing 3–28   Using a named savepoint

```
SqlConnection sconn = new SqlConnection(
  "server=(local);uid=sa;pwd=mypw;database=pubs");
sconn.Open();

IDbCommand cmd = sconn.CreateCommand();

cmd.CommandText = "select count(*) from jobs";
int i = (int)cmd.ExecuteScalar();
Console.WriteLine("There are {0} jobs records", i);

SqlTransaction tx = sconn.BeginTransaction();
cmd.Transaction = tx;
cmd.CommandText =
  "insert jobs values('new job', 10, 10)";
i = cmd.ExecuteNonQuery();
  if (i != 1)
    tx.Rollback();
  else
  {
    tx.Save("afterinsert_savepoint");
    cmd.CommandText = "delete jobs where job_id > 14";
    i = cmd.ExecuteNonQuery();

    // oops didn't want to do that...
    // roll back the delete, but not the insert
    tx.Rollback("afterinsert_savepoint");
    tx.Commit();

    // must reset before using Command again
    cmd.Transaction = null;

    // check - it should be more than 9 jobs records
    cmd.CommandText = "select count(*) from jobs";
    int j = (int)cmd.ExecuteScalar();
    Console.WriteLine("There are now {0} jobs records", j);
  }
```

3.11.1 Distributed Transactions

A transaction that encompasses multiple database instances or multiple databases is known as a *distributed* transaction. Because most databases implement transactional semantics by logging changes to a transaction log and because even instances of the same database type (such as multiple instances of SQL Server) cannot share a single transaction log, a third party must manage and coordinate the transaction. SQL Server (and also the Windows 2000 and XP operating systems) includes the Microsoft Distributed Transaction Coordinator (MSDTC), an NT service that manages distributed transactions. This service uses its own log, a transaction dispenser, the OLE TX API, and a standard two-phase commit protocol to manage transactions.

COM+ 1.0 (and before this, Microsoft Transaction Server) introduced a way to use distributed transactions declaratively through context attributes. This technique, which is the only supported way to use distributed transactions with the .NET data providers, uses the .NET System.EnterpriseServices assembly. Without going into all the details of System.EnterpriseServices, I'll describe how to use a distributed transaction with an ADO.NET data provider.

To use declarative distributed transactions, you must instantiate the SqlConnection or OleDbConnection instance from a class of your own that derives from EnterpriseServices.ServicedComponent. This class must be installed in a COM+ application. When using .NET Enterprise Services, you can do this in one of three ways:

- Manually add the class's assembly to an application using COM+ Explorer.
- Use the .NET RegistrationHelper class to add it to the COM+ catalog programmatically.
- Use the automatic registration features provided by .NET.

Although this appears to be the easiest approach, it is useful mostly when you're developing COM+ components in Visual Studio.

The assembly in which your component resides must be a strong named assembly and must either reside in the global assembly cache (GAC) or be in a client-accessible location. In practice, the latter is useful only during development of an application, for ease in testing.

.NET attributes are used to specify behaviors related to `EnterpriseServices`. The `TransactionAttribute` attribute class specifies whether or not a class's methods should be transactional—that is, whether `Connections` used in those methods should participate in a declarative distributed transaction. `TransactionAttribute` has three properties that can be set to affect the transaction:

- `Value`. This is a positional parameter that is set to a value in the `TransactionOption` enumeration. `TransactionOption` contains five options corresponding to the declarative transaction settings in the COM+ catalog.
- `Timeout`. This overrides the default transaction timeout value only if the component is the root of a COM+ transaction stream.
- `Isolation`. This overrides the default transaction isolation level of the DTC transaction only if the component is the root of a COM+ transaction stream.

Information about the transaction (the OLE TX transaction instance pointer) is propagated among components that participate in distributed transactions, subject to the `TransactionOption` specified by each component. The information about the transaction (and other COM+ services) is available through static properties and methods on the `EnterpriseServices.ContextUtil` class. You can have components affect the outcome of an `EnterpriseServices` transaction in one of three ways:

- Use the `ContextUtil.SetComplete` or `ContextUtil.SetAbort` method.
- Use the `ContextUtil.MyTransactionVote` property.
- Use the `AutoCompleteAttribute` in `EnterpriseServices`.

The first two methods are familiar to COM+ programmers. `SetComplete` and `SetAbort` also set a bit that may permit COM+ services to destroy the instance; the `MyTransactionVote` property sets only a bit that votes on the distributed transaction. `AutoCompleteAttribute` sets a transaction vote based on whether the method being invoked throws an exception.

Listing 3–29 shows an example of a simple `ServicedComponent` that uses most of the attributes you've just seen. You should observe a few other caveats when using `EnterpriseServices`. Serviced components usually use a `JustInTimeActivationAttribute` or require the caller to call `Dispose` to reclaim resources in a timely manner. This does not mean, however, that `Connection`, `Command`, and `DataReader` instances need not be cleaned up; even when you call `Dispose` on the `ServicedComponent` instance, you must implement data instance cleanup. You can disable enlistment in distributed transactions by using a connection string parameter on a `Connection`-by-`Connection` basis. Listing 3–30 shows an example of turning off auto-enlistment. Additionally, declarative transactions interact with connection pooling, which is discussed next. For more information about using `System.EnterpriseServices` in .NET, refer to Tim Ewald's COM+ integration article in the October 2001 issue of *MSDN* magazine (see the Bibliography).

Listing 3–29 Using `EnterpriseServices` transactions

```
// require a distributed transaction for this class
// lower the transaction isolation level

[Transaction(TransactionOption.Required,
    Isolation=TransactionIsolationLevel.ReadCommitted)]

public class DoTx : ServicedComponent
{
  // only no-arg constructors
  public DoTx() { }

  // autocomplete true is the default
  [AutoComplete(false)]
  public void DoDatabase()
  {
    SqlConnection conn = null;
    SqlDataReader rdr;

    try
    {
      conn = new SqlConnection(
        "server=localhost;uid=sa;pwd=mypw;database=pubs");
      conn.Open();
      SqlCommand cmd = new SqlCommand(
        "select * from authors", conn);
```

```
      rdr = cmd.ExecuteReader();
      while (rdr.Read())
      { // do something with those rows }
      rdr.Close();

      cmd.CommandText(
        "delete authors where au_id = '999-99-9999'")
      cmd.ExecuteNonQuery();

      // if I get here I vote to commit
      ContextUtil.SetComplete();
    }
    catch (Exception e)
    {
      ContextUtil.SetAbort();
      // rethrow the exception
      throw(e);
    }
    finally
    {
      // this closes the command and datareader
      if ((conn != null) &&
         (conn.State != ConnectionState.Closed))
          conn.Close();
    }
  }
}
```

Listing 3–30 Turning off auto-enlistment

```
// require a distributed transaction for this class

[Transaction(TransactionOption.Required)]
public class DoTx : ServicedComponent
{
  // only no-arg constructors
  public DoTx() { }

  // autocomplete true is the default
  [AutoComplete(true)]
  public void DoDatabaseBad()
  {
    SqlConnection conn = null;
    SqlConnection conn2 = null;
    try
```

```
    {
      // don't autoenlist this one
      conn = new SqlConnection(
      "server=localhost;uid=sa;pwd=mypw;database=pubs;
       enlist='false'");

      conn.Open();
      conn2 = new SqlConnection(
      "server=localhost;uid=sa;pwd=mypw;database=pubs");
      conn2.Open();

      SqlCommand cmd = new SqlCommand();
      cmd.Connection = conn2;
      cmd.CommandText =
        "insert jobs values('new job', 10, 10)";
      cmd.ExecuteNonQuery();

      // this should throw an exception
      // and abort the transaction
      // if joe2 table doesn't exist
      cmd.Connection = conn;
      cmd.CommandText = "insert joe2 values('no')";
      cmd.ExecuteNonQuery();
    }
    finally
    {
      // this closes the command and datareader
      if ((conn != null) &&
          (conn.State != ConnectionState.Closed))
          conn.Close();
    }
  }
}
```

3.11.2 How Connection Pooling Works

On the surface, writing a connection pool appears to be a simple job. But transactions cloud the picture because your connection pool cannot reuse a connection that has a transaction in progress. In addition, enterprise frameworks such as MTS (Microsoft Transaction Server) and EJB (Enterprise Java Beans) encapsulate connection pooling and distributed transaction enlistment, hiding it from the programmer. Because programmers attempt to get the last ounce of performance from enterprise systems, there has been an inordinate amount of interest in the details of connection pooling and declarative transactions. Let's discuss this with respect to the ADO.NET data providers.

In .NET Enterprise Services, COM+, and MTS (all variations on the same theme), a resource manager proxy is a library of functions that is used by consumers to connect to transactional resource managers, such as databases. By this definition, OLE DB providers and ODBC drivers are resource manager proxies. MTS encourages database developers to implement resource manager proxies as resource dispensers. This is also supported under COM+ and .NET Enterprise Services but is somewhat deprecated. A resource dispenser hooks into the system infrastructure to gain system-managed pooling and distributed transaction enlistment. Resource dispensers use the system-supplied dispenser manager (also known as DispMan) to manage pools of named resources. DispMan helps the resource dispenser to manage its pooled resources and their transaction enlistment. When you're using ODBC, the resource dispenser is built into the ODBC driver manager. With OLE DB, the resource dispenser is part of OLE DB Services.

DispMan maintains a separate set of pools for each resource dispenser. They are initially empty and are swept for stale resources every 10 seconds. A resource is represented by an opaque handle and can be anything defined by the dispenser; the resource managed on behalf of SQL Server, for example, is the connection to SQL Server. The pointer to DispMan is exposed to the resource dispenser (such as the OLE DB Service components) as a pointer to a `Holder` object. DispMan gets an `IDispenserDriver` pointer in return, and the pointer permits it to call into the resource dispenser. As shown in Figure 3–3, when a component asks an OLE DB provider for a resource (database connection), the OLE DB Services ask its holder to allocate it. The holder first searches the list of unused resources (inventory) for a suitable connection. If the pool is empty or no match is found, the holder asks the OLE DB provider to create a new resource (connection). The resource returned by the holder is returned to the client.

If a match is found, it is returned to the provider, as shown in Figure 3–4. This method of connection pooling is also hooked in to automatic transaction enlistment in enterprise services. Later in this chapter we'll talk more about how that works.

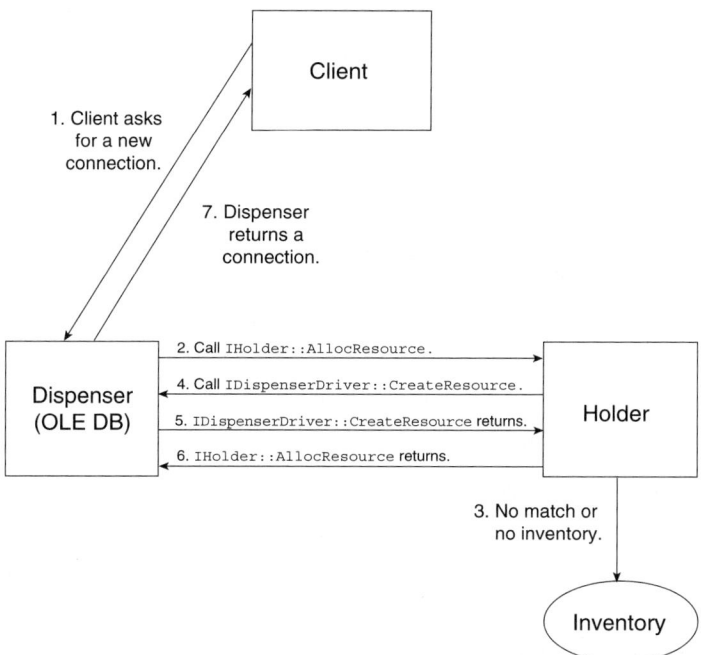

Figure 3–3 Dispenser: No match or no inventory

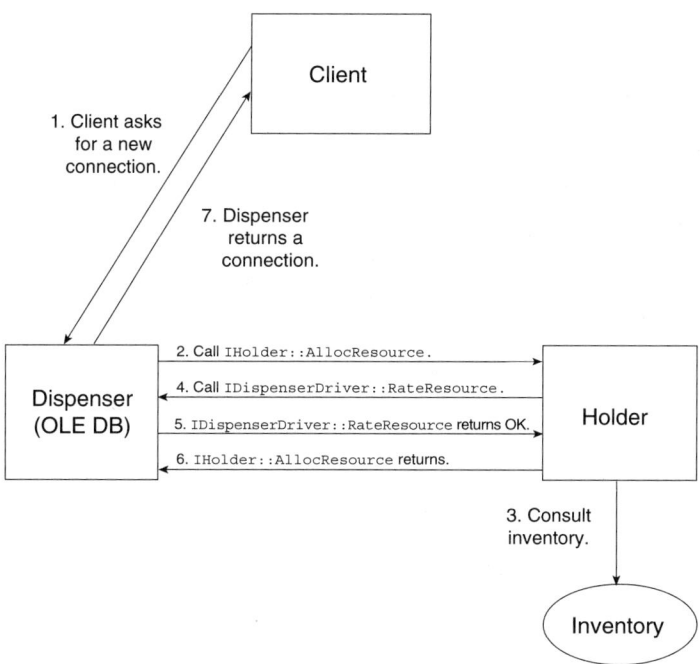

Figure 3–4 Dispenser: Match in inventory

Generic connection pooling from OLE DB or ODBC is often suboptimal. Many connections might need to be examined before a match is found (or not found). The only way to control the size of the pool is indirectly through the pool timeout value. This is set to 60 seconds by default and is configurable via the ODBC administrator tool (ODBC) or in the registry (OLE DB) on a per-provider or per-driver basis.

There is no way to put an upper bound on the number of resources when you're using DispMan for connection pooling. There is no way to preinitialize a working set of connections before a request. In addition, if the pool manager runs out, there is no way to tell it to wait for an available connection.

The `OleDb` data provider uses OLE DB's built-in connection pooling described earlier. An extra reference to the connection pool itself is kept to prevent the pool structures from being garbage-collected when the last connection is closed. `OleDbConnection.ReleaseObjectPool` releases the extra reference if garbage-collecting the pool is the desired behavior. You can disable pooling and automatic transaction enlistment by using the `OLE DB Services` parameter on the connection string.

`SqlConnection` uses a solution that provides more control over pool configuration and management. This is similar to COM+ object pooling, but `SqlConnection` is not a COM+ pooled object class. You can customize the behaviors of the pool by using pool-specific parameters in the connection string, as shown in Listing 3–31. In addition, a parameter exists to allow automatic enlistment of a connection in a transaction managed by Enterprise Services. Connection pooling is the default for the `SqlClient` provider. If the containing class is appropriately configured in the COM+ catalog, automatic transaction enlistment is also the default for the `SqlClient` provider.

Listing 3–31 Pooling connections

```
// build up a connection string
// vanilla parms
String sConn =
  "uid=sa;pwd=mypw;database=pubs;server=localhost";

// add connection pooling and auto enlistment
sConn +=
  ";Pooling='true';Connection Reset='false';Enlist='true'";
```

```
// specify pool parms
sConn +=
  ";Connection Lifetime=5;Min Pool Size=2;Max Pool Size=50";

// open the connection
SqlConnection conn = new SqlConnection(sConn);
```

When a `SqlConnection` is opened, the pool manager checks the connection string (using string comparison rather than parsing it into properties), and if it is an exact match with a current pool and there is a free connection, the pool manager uses a connection from the pool. If you're using the integrated security setting of a data provider, the OS security principle must also match. If there is no matching pool, a new pool is created. If there is no free connection in an existing pool, a new one is created, subject to the pool behavior parameters. Setting up the pooling infrastructure is time-consuming, so after it has been set up, the pool structures will not be torn down until process shutdown. However, connections that are not in use will be released from the pool, and the underlying SQL Server connection will be closed approximately six minutes after `Connection.Close` has been called on them. This action is subject to the `Min Pool Size` parameter; the number of connections in a pool will never drop below `Min Pool Size`. The six-minute release time is based on observation rather than documentation, and it may change in later releases.

The pool parameters give you complete control over the creation and behavior of the pool. The minimum (`Min Pool Size`) is the number of connections created when the pool is initialized. It is useful for "priming" a set of connections so that they remain in memory and users never have to wait for a connection. Listing 3–32 shows an example. The maximum (`Max Pool Size`) is useful for preventing runaway connection-allocating tasks from using too much memory. You can also use `Max Pool Size` to put a lid on memory utilization inside SQL Server.

Listing 3–32   Behavior when `Min Pool Size` is specified

```
SqlConnection conn1 = new SqlConnection(
  "server=.;uid=sa;pwd=mypw;database=pubs;min pool size=5");

// opens 5 connections
conn1.Open();
```

```
// still 5 connections after this
conn1.Close();

SqlConnection conn2 = new SqlConnection(
  "server=.;uid=sa;pwd=mypw;database=pubs;Min Pool Size=5");

// uses an already open connection from the pool
conn2.Open();
```

In an application designed for connection pooling, connection time is not an issue because there is usually an open connection in the pool. Thus, the best practice is to allocate a connection as late as possible and release it as early as possible so that others can use it. If your application is designed this way, it is possible that a connection may not be available (the pool is at its maximum) but one will be available soon. In this case, you want to have the component wait. You can specify Connection Timeout, as in a nonpooled scenario. The pool manager will wait in a separate thread for a connection to become available.

You can specify a discrete total lifetime for your connections using the Connection Lifetime connection string parameter. If this is specified, the pool manager will record the time when your connection was originally created and, each time the connection is returned to the pool, check against the lifetime, aging the connection closed at the appropriate time. This technique is useful in load-balancing scenarios, letting you balance connections among servers more quickly when a new server comes online.

If the SQL Server process is recycled, open connections in a connection pool will now be unusable. The first time you attempt to communicate with the database, the connection pooler will detect that the connection to the (original) SQL Server instance has been broken, and it will remove the connection from the pool.

A final way to tweak the behavior of your SqlConnection is to specify Connection Reset. Because connections are held open across multiple usages, if the user changes a SQL Server *environment variable* such as ANSI_NULLS, this setting (rather than the initial setting) will carry over to the next user. Specifying Connection Reset=true causes the pool manager to issue an sp_reset_connection command so that the next user starts with the appropriate environment. Be aware that, in some versions of SQL Server (such as SQL Server 7), this does require an extra round-trip to the database.

Connection pooling occurs on a per-application domain (`AppDomain`) basis, rather than on a per-process basis. The `SqlClient` data provider exposes performance counters that permit you to detect failed connections and commands and also monitor and tune connection pooling. These performance counters are as follows:

- Current number of pooled and nonpooled connections: total connections using the `SqlClient` data provider
- Current number of pooled connections: total connections using the `SqlClient` data provider with `Pooling=true` specified in the connection string
- Current number of connection pools: total number of pools allocated by the process
- Peak number of pooled connections: peak number of connections in all pools
- Total number of failed connects: total connections that fail, either because a pool is at `Max Pool Size` longer than the connect timeout value for a connection or because a SQL Server instance is unavailable

Note that this activity is measured on a per-process basis, not a per-pool basis. In addition, if a process uses `SqlClient` to connect to multiple instances of SQL Server, these numbers reflect the total for all instances.

A final way to monitor connection state in your own program is to use the `Connection` class's `StateChange` event. Both `SqlConnection` and `OleDbConnection` support this event, and, because the `State` property is part of the `IDbConnection` interface, most future providers will probably support this event as well.

3.11.3 How Declarative Transactions Work

.NET Enterprise Services inherit the implementation of an object context and a transaction stream from MTS and COM+. Contexts that have a transaction stream always have access to a declarative transaction. It is possible to reach into the context and access the transaction directly, but the more common case is to use a resource manager proxy to do this implicitly. The RM proxies used by databases such as SQL Server are services in the ODBC and OLE DB APIs.

The holder will automatically enlist resources (such as database connections) in a distributed transaction if one exists in the object context. This is how .NET Enterprise Services, COM+, and MTS control transactional semantics through declarative attributes. Each holder maintains a separate subpool for each transaction and a separate unenlisted pool. The holder first searches inventory enlisted in the component's transaction (if present). If a match is found, the resource is already enlisted and the resource is returned directly, as shown in Figure 3–5. This is a substantial time-saver because enlistment in a distributed transaction is network-intensive.

If no match is found in the correct per-transaction enlisted pool, unenlisted inventory is searched. If a match is found in unenlisted inventory, the holder asks the resource dispenser to enlist the resource using `IResourceDispenser::EnlistResource`, as shown in Figure 3–6. In OLE DB, this results in the OLE DB services' calling the provider's `ITransactionJoin::JoinTransaction` method. If no match is found, both resource creation and enlistment must occur, as shown in Figure 3–7.

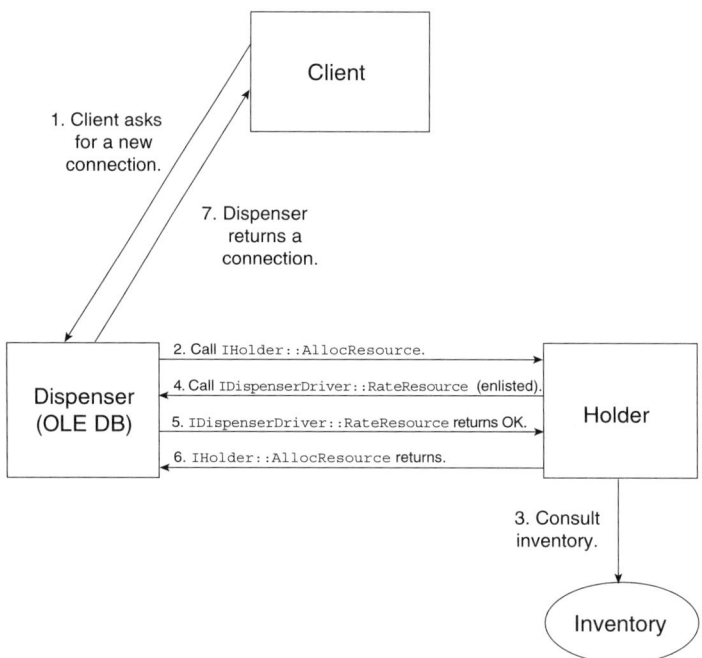

Figure 3–5 Dispenser: Match in enlisted inventory

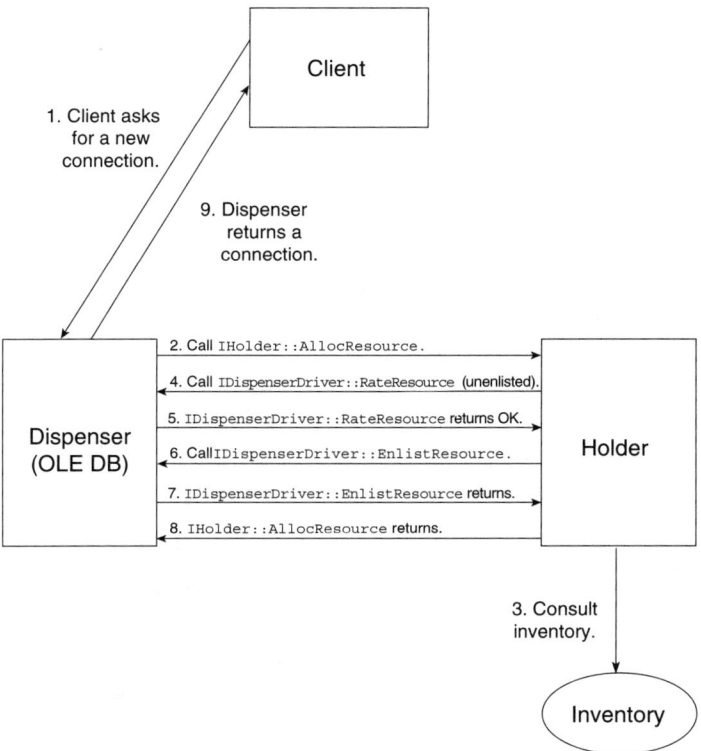

Figure 3–6 Dispenser: Match in unenlisted inventory

To preserve correct transactional semantics, enlisted inventory is unavailable outside its transaction. Connections are moved to unenlisted inventory when the transaction is over.

`IHolder::AllocResource` asks the resource dispenser to rate each resource in inventory until a match is found. The resource dispenser is presented with initial connection parameters and a resource. It returns a suitability index between 0 and 100. For example, the ODBC and OLE DB dispensers might return 0 when the connection parameters are different, 50 when the parameters are the same but the connection is unenlisted, and 100 when the connection parameters are same and the resource is enlisted on the correct transaction.

When you're using the subclasses of `ServicedComponent`, it means that `OleDbConnection` instances will always participate in a declarative distributed

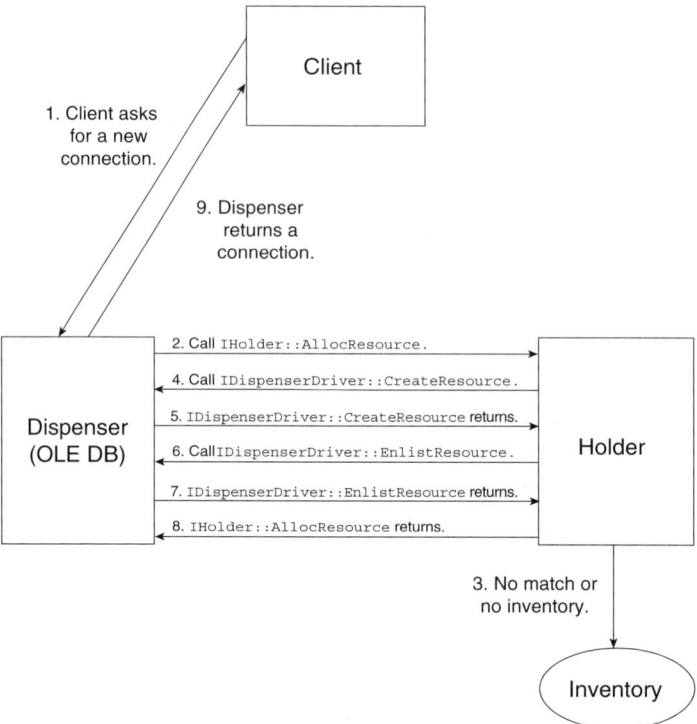

Figure 3–7   Dispenser: No match or no inventory, enlistment required

transaction (subject to the `TransactionAttribute` value) unless this behavior is overridden by setting `OLE DB Services` property in the connection string to turn off automatic enlistment. Connection pooling must be turned on to enable automatic enlistment. In the `SqlClient` data provider, you can specify `Enlist=false` in the connection string to turn off automatic enlistment. Note that automatic enlistment is not even attempted unless the class that is using the `Connection` derives from `ServicedComponent`, even though `Enlist=true` is `SqlConnection`'s default. For more information on the ramifications of using declarative distributed transactions, reference *Transactional COM+* by Tim Ewald (Addison-Wesley, 2001).

3.12   Permission Classes

Both the `SqlClient` and the `OleDb` data providers implement a typed `Permission` class and a `PermissionAttribute` attribute. These derive from common bases `DBDataPermission` and `DBDataPermissionAttribute`. They are used to integrate the data stack with the rest of the .NET code access security framework. Code access security in .NET defines a set of permissions that code must have to access sensitive resources. The permissions are affected by the location from which the code is loaded. For example, code loaded from a network share or over the Internet may have a much more restricted set of permissions than does code loaded from a local drive. The `Permission` class is useful for prohibiting untrusted code from accessing your database through .NET data providers.

Code access security policy is set either through a Microsoft Management Console snap-in or using the CASPOL command-line utility. In addition, you can set attributes on an assembly to prevent code from being loaded if it does not have the necessary permissions, or you can program security checks directly into user classes. For more information on code access security, refer to the February 2001 *MSDN* security briefs column on this topic by Keith Brown (see the Bibliography).

Both `SqlClientPermission` and `OleDbPermission` attributes can be used to specify the fact that a blank database password may or may not be allowed. In addition, `OleDbPermission` can restrict or grant access to a subset of OLE DB providers. Listing 3–33 shows an example of using these attributes on an `assembly`. In the example, the `assembly` will not even be loaded unless the permission to access SQL Server with a blank password has been granted to the code. In addition, the `assembly` may require access to the `SQLOLEDB` and `MSDAORA` OLE DB providers, but it will not fail to load if this access has not been granted.

Listing 3–33   Using the `Permission` attributes

```
[assembly: SqlClientPermission(
  SecurityAction.RequestMinimum,
  AllowBlankPassword=true)]
[assembly: OleDbPermission(
  SecurityAction.RequestOptional,
  Provider="sqloledb,msdaora")]
[assembly: OleDbPermission(
  SecurityAction.RequestOptional,
  AllowBlankPassword=true)]
```

3.12.1 Database Security

As long as we're on the topic of security and databases access, I must make an important point about developing database applications. Many sample programs use (and will continue to use) the SQL Server user `sa`, which stands for "system administrator." The Oracle `sys` and `system` accounts are approximately analogous.

You shouldn't use the database administrator account even when developing an application. In addition, application developers using a database with OS integrated security should not test the application while logged on to the Windows Administrator rights because this maps them to SQL Server `system administrator` by default. There are three reasons for this:

- Ordinary users of the application may not have permissions to perform operations that the administrator can perform. When such an application is distributed to real users, it will fail because of lack of database permissions.

- If applications connect to the database using administrator credentials, they will have the capability to do harm to the database and possibly the operating system.

- In SQL Server, each login account has a "default" database. The default database of the administrator is the master database. Because applications usually are not installed in the master database, a database *context switch* is required with every connection. This adversely affects performance.

A good rule of development is to define user IDs and roles that are analogous to the real users of the application and use them in testing. For production, when you're using SQL Server, the default database for these users should be the database in which the application is installed.

3.13 Where Are We?

You've covered the connection-oriented data provider model in detail and examined the two data providers—`System.Data.SqlClient` and `System.Data.OleDb`—that are part of the runtime. Next, you'll look at the relational `DataSet` class used as a disconnected data store.

In Chapter 8 you'll examine writing your own custom data provider and using custom (unsupported) OLE DB providers with the `OleDb` data provider.

Chapter 4

The **DataSet** Class: Sets of Relational Data

The DataSet class provides a disconnected cache of data from any source. The DataSet structure follows the relational data model.

4.1 **DataSets**

In this chapter, we begin our journey into the disconnected data access model by looking at the DataSet class. As described in Chapter 2, DataSet is a specialized collection class. It is the top-level object in the disconnected ADO.NET data access model. The DataSet class is built around relational data concepts, the CLR type system, and .NET collections. It can exchange data with both XML providers and data providers, or it can be manipulated directly in program code.

The DataSet class is meant to provide a cache of data outside the database that can be used in read-only mode, thereby preventing unnecessary round-trips to the database to fetch *lookup tables*—that is, tables of relatively constant information, such as interest rates, state names, or county names. My rule of thumb is this: If a programmer must submit a form signed by management in order to update a table's data, it is a lookup table.

DataSets also participate in a disconnected update pattern. A set of data is fetched from a database into a DataSet, the DataSet is updated offline, and changes in the DataSet are later written back to the database.

This chapter doesn't discuss either of these uses. To see a DataSet populated from a database, refer to Chapter 2 or Chapter 5. I defer to Chapter 5 the discussion of interoperability with data providers through the DataAdapter model. Although I touch on the XML aspects here, Chapter 7 investigates XML integration in more detail.

This chapter discusses `DataSet` as a standalone collection class along with related classes. `DataSet` and its supporting classes are so feature-rich (almost overengineered, according to detractors) that it takes a chapter to discuss all the standalone features before we go on to the interactions with databases. You can instantiate a `DataSet` and populate its collections with data from any source, much as you can an XML DOM model. Doing this provides the necessary background before proceeding to interactions between the `DataSet` and databases, and between the `DataSet` and `XmlDocument` and `XPathNavigator`.

4.1.1 `DataSet` as an In-memory Database

Because `DataSet` contains multiple tables and uses familiar relational terminology, it is often compared to an in-memory relational database. It's illustrative to compare the two. `DataSet` looks like an in-memory database for these reasons:

- `DataTables` contain `DataColumns` and `DataRows`. There is metadata only at the column level; in other words, each `DataColumn` has a single data type.
- `DataTables` can have a primary key as well as foreign keys, relationships, and unique constraints.
- A `DataSet` can be case-sensitive with respect to its table and column names as well as its data.
- Computed columns are supported.
- There are methods for composing multiple changes so that they all happen or none happen.

`DataSet` does not share these behaviors with a relational database:

- There is no concept of authentication or authorization.
- Only a subset of a SQL-like syntax is supported, and it is used only for selecting sets of data.
- There are no transaction isolation or locking semantics in a multiuser environment.
- Some of the properties of a `DataSet` relate directly to XML mappings.
- CLR types do not have an exact mapping to the data types defined by the SQL-92 or SQL-99 standard.

4.1.2 What Can You Do with a `DataSet`?

A `DataSet` can serve as an in-memory cache of complex data represented as a generic object model that works the same irrespective of the problem space. It can be conveniently described using both an extended relational format schema and the XML schema standard, XSD. Either the `DataSet` itself or a series of before and after images that constitute changes to rows can be marshaled or stored to disk in XML format. Multiple users can share a `DataSet` in a middle-tier scenario, subject to isolation and locking limitations just mentioned, although it is possible to layer locking and isolation in your own extension code. You can bind collections in a `DataSet` to either Windows Forms or Web Forms controls by using `DataSource` and related properties on the control.

`DataSet` contains advanced functionality that is useful in a generic caching model, including keeping track of multiple versions of the same row and associating an error with each row. Each major class in the hierarchy has a `PropertyCollection` (a specialized `Hashtable`) member variable that holds user-definable extended properties. A standard event model facilitates customization of updates composed with external data sources.

4.2 The `DataSet` Object Model

The object model begins with `DataSet` as the highest-level class and is collection-based. The `DataSet` hierarchy and its major collections are shown in Figure 4–1 (not all collections and classes are shown in the diagram). Here's a synopsis of the classes:

- `DataSet`: High-level container class
- `InternalDataCollectionBase`: Base for collection classes
- `Constraint` and `ConstraintCollection`: Data constraints to ensure table and inter-table consistency
- `DataColumn` and `DataColumnCollection`: Relational columns (*attribute* is the correct relational term, not to be confused with XML's attributes)
- `DataRelation` and `DataRelationCollection`: Relations between two tables to ensure data consistency
- `DataRow` and `DataRowCollection`: Relational tuples

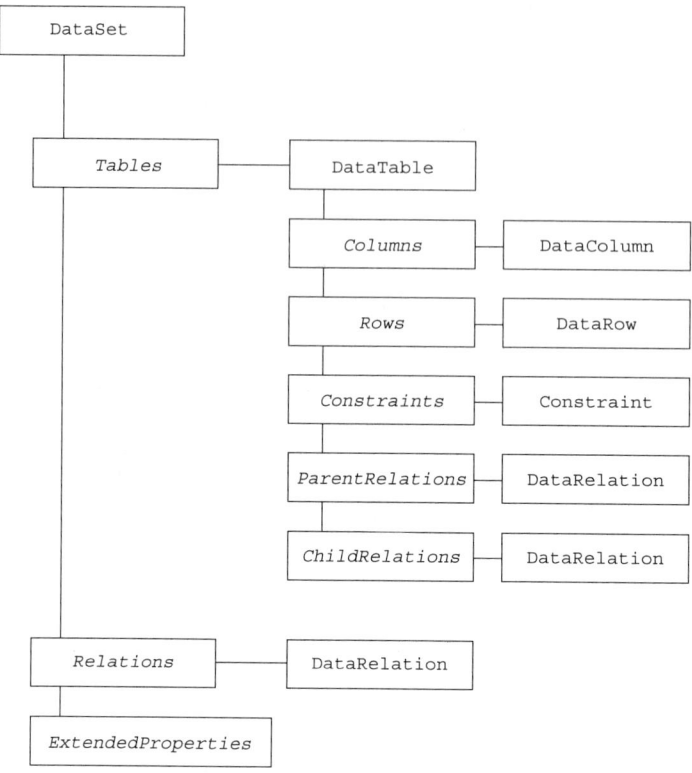

Figure 4–1 Collection classes in `DataSet`

- `DataTable` and `DataTableCollection`: Table with columns and rows
- `ForeignKeyConstraint`: Subclass of `Constraint`, ensures relational integrity
- `UniqueConstraint`: Subclass of `Constraint` that ensures columns are unique in a table
- `PropertyCollection`: Subclass of `Hashtable` (a property of `DataSet`, `DataTable`, and `DataColumn`); user-definable, extended properties
- `DataRowView`: Customizable view of any `DataRow`
- `DataView`: Customizable view of any `DataTable`
- `DataViewManager`: A property of the `DataSet` that keeps track of a collection of views on `DataSet`'s collection of `DataTable`s

- `DataViewSetting` and `DataViewSettingCollection`: Default settings on `DataViews` managed by `DataViewManager`
- `DataSysDescriptionAttribute`: An attribute consisting of descriptive text for display by designers

`DataViews` and their associated classes provide finding, sorting, and filtering in memory along with integration with databound controls and WYSIWYG programming tools. They are discussed in Chapter 6.

4.2.1 `DataColumns`, `DataRows`, and `DataTables`

Because `DataSet` contains a collection of `DataTables`, one way to populate an empty `DataSet` is to define `DataColumns` and add them to a `DataTable`. This approach manually populates a single `DataTable`'s schema. `DataTables` can be added to the `DataSet`'s `Tables` collection or can be used standalone. After the `DataTable`'s schema is defined, `DataRows` can be created and added. You can access individual column values of a `DataRow` in a `DataTable` as though the `DataTable` were a two-dimensional array.

The `DataColumn` class has a variety of constructors. The most commonly used constructors set the `ColumnName` and `DataType`. The default for `ColumnName` is a null string. The default for `DataType` is `System.String`. The `ColumnName` property must be unique within a `DataTable`. In theory, `DataType` can be any CLR type because the domain of data types is `System.Type`. In practice, there are some limitations. The documentation for `System.DataColumn.DataType` narrows the list of supported `DataTypes` to the following:

```
Boolean
Byte
Char
DateTime
Decimal
Double
Int16
Int32
```

```
Int64

SByte

Single

String

TimeSpan*

UInt16*

UInt32*

UInt64*
```

* Not supported by Visual Basic .NET

I discuss using other, nonrelational data types later in the chapter.

As in relational databases, DataColumns have the concept of nullability and default values. DataColumn.AllowDBNull specifies whether a column can contain an object of a specific CLR type, DBNull, and not whether the column can contain a null object reference. The System.DBNull class corresponds to the concept of a NULL value in a relational database and has a single static field, Value. AllowDBNull lets you set a DataColumn to System.DBNull.Value, and you can use an IsNull(n) on the DataRow class to determine whether the nth DataColumn contains a System.DB-Null.Value. The DataColumn.DefaultValue property specifies the default value. If no default value is specified and no value is set, the column's value will be DBNull.Value by default. If that column does not specify AllowDBNull, adding a DataRow with a DBNull.Value'd column will fail, as illustrated in Listing 4–1.

Listing 4–1 Using DBNull and default value with DataColumns

```
DataColumn[] col = new DataColumn[3];

// Default is DBNull
col[0] = new DataColumn("col0", typeof(String));
col[0].AllowDBNull = true;

// Default is "foo", DBNull is allowed
col[1] = new DataColumn("col1", typeof(String));
col[1].AllowDBNull = true;
col[1].DefaultValue = "foo";
```

```
// Default is DBNull, DBNull not allowed
// If this column is not set to a value
// adding the row will fail
col[2] = new DataColumn("col2", typeof(String));
col[2].AllowDBNull = false;
```

Most of the properties of `DataColumn` are similar to those in a relational database column, but because the `DataSet` model integrates with XML, `DataColumn` also contains some XML-specific properties. Relational properties include the `AutoIncrement` (identity) property and a `Unique` property. When a column is defined as `AutoIncrement=true`, its `DataType` is `Int32` by default; other integral `DataTypes` are permitted. `AutoIncrement` columns can specify `AutoIncrementSeed` and `AutoIncrementStep` values. Setting a `DataColumn`'s `Unique` property causes a `UniqueConstraint` to be added to the `DataTable`'s `Constraints` collection when that `DataColumn` is added to the `DataTable`. XML properties include `Namespace` and `Prefix` (that is, XML `namespace prefix`) as well as `ColumnMapping`. These properties are used when `DataSet` is serialized or deserialized to XML. In addition, `DataColumn` includes a `Caption` property that can be used with databound controls, and a property that specifies that the `DataColumn` is `ReadOnly`. Finally, there is a `PropertiesCollection` of user-defined `ExtendedProperties`, which can be used to store any column-specific property you can imagine—for example, an edit mask for use in graphical user interfaces.

Unless you derive from `DataColumn`, you can perform only a limited amount of domain checking in the `DataColumn` definition. For example, you can define a `DataColumn` as a `String` data type, but you cannot specify that it must contain only four characters (as you can with the SQL CHARACTER data type). You can set a maximum length (as in the SQL VARYING CHARACTER(4) data type) using `DataColumn`'s `MaxLength` property. You can specify an expression that does domain checking (using the `DataColumn.Expression` property), but the expression cannot contain a reference to the column itself. For example, you can specify an expression that ColumnA cannot be greater than ColumnB, but you cannot specify that ColumnA must have a value less than 20.

DataColumn expressions are similar to the concept of a computed column in SQL Server. Expressions can also be used to create aggregate columns. Unlike aggregates in relational databases, these are calculated when the column is referenced. Appendix B contains the complete syntax for the expression language. The expression can contain a discrete set of functions and can refer to other columns in the same row and even child rows. There is a simple conditional (IIF) as well. Listing 4–2 shows a computed column expression as well as an aggregate column.

Listing 4–2 Computed DataColumns

```
DataColumn cPrice;
DataColumn cTax;
DataColumn cTotal;
DataTable myTable = new DataTable ();

// Create the first column.
cPrice = new DataColumn();
cPrice.DataType = System.Type.GetType("System.Decimal");
cPrice.ColumnName = "price";
cPrice.DefaultValue = 50;

// Create the second, calculated, column.
cTax = new DataColumn();
cTax.DataType = System.Type.GetType("System.Decimal");
cTax.ColumnName = "tax";
cTax.Expression = "price * 0.0862";

// Create third column.
cTotal = new DataColumn();
cTotal.DataType = System.Type.GetType("System.Decimal");
cTotal.ColumnName = "total";
cTotal.Expression = "price + tax";

// Add columns to DataTable.
myTable.Columns.Add(cPrice);
myTable.Columns.Add(cTax);
myTable.Columns.Add(cTotal);
```

4.2.2 DataTable and Its Uses

To be usable, DataColumns must be added to a DataTable. A single DataColumn cannot be added to multiple DataTables. The DataColumn.Table property names the table that a DataColumn belongs to. The DataTable class encapsulates a standard rectangular table containing columns and rows. The most common constructor contains a string with the `DataTable` name. After a `DataTable` has been instantiated, you can add `DataColumns` to it. `DataTable` uses a standard collection of type `DataColumnCollection`. You can add `DataColumns` to this collection one at a time through `DataColumn-Collection`'s `Add` method, or you can add an array of `DataColumns` en masse using `DataColumnCollection.AddRange`. In addition, `DataColumnCollection.Add` has a convenience overload that takes analogous parameters to the `DataColumn` constructor so that the `DataColumn` is defined and added to the array in a single statement. These alternatives are shown in Listing 4–3.

Listing 4–3 Adding `DataColumns` to `DataTables`

```
DataTable t = new DataTable();

DataColumn col = new DataColumn();
col.ColumnName = "foo";
col.DataType = typeof(Int32);
t.Columns.Add(col);

t.Columns.Add(
    new DataColumn("bar", typeof(Int32)));

DataTable t2 = new DataTable("mytablename");
DataColumn[] cols = new DataColumn[2];

cols[0] = new DataColumn(
    "col0", typeof(String));
cols[1] = new DataColumn(
    "col1", typeof(String));
t2.Columns.AddRange(cols);
```

Much like `DataColumn`, the `DataTable` class has a user-defined `ExtendedProperties` collection. A good use for this might be to store the creation date of the table, a version number, or the date on which the `DataTable` might be scheduled for refreshing if it represents a table in the database.

`DataTable` is a useful standalone entity, much like the ADO `Recordset`. You've already seen two uses of it in Chapter 3; both the schema information about a resultset (`IDataReader.GetSchemaTable`) and the database metadata returned from the information schema (`OleDbConnection.GetOleDbSchema-Table`) return a `DataTable`. You'll see many more uses in later chapters.

In addition to its use as a standalone entity, a `DataTable` can be a member of `DataSet`'s `Tables Collection` (type `DataTableCollection`). This is where we'll be using it most often. `DataTable` also contains a member called `DefaultView` that is used with complex databound controls, such as `ListBox`.

`DataTable` has a protected constructor that takes `SerializationInfo` and `StreamingContext` instances as parameters. This is required because `DataTable` implements custom `Serialization` and can be remoted using `System.Runtime.Serialization`. Chapter 7 discusses remoting `DataSets` and `DataTables`.

4.2.3 `DataRows`

For now, you'll use `DataTable` standalone, but first you must populate it with some rows. `DataTable` contains a collection (type `DataRowCollection`) of `DataRows`. You cannot create a `DataRow` by using `new`; instead, you must create it associated with a `DataTable` so that the `DataRow` knows what its shape is (i.e., what `DataColumns` it contains). You create a `DataRow` by calling `DataTable.NewRow`. This method creates a `DataRow` having the correct number and type of `DataColumns` but does *not* add it to the `DataTable`'s `Rows` collection. To do that, you must fill in the required fields with data and then call `DataTable.Rows.Add` to add it to the table. There is an overload of `DataRow.Add` that takes an array of objects that are the column values. However, you can add only a single `DataRow` at a time. After a `DataRow` has been created with `DataTable.NewRow` and even before it is added to `DataTable.Rows`, its `Table` property refers to the `DataTable` it belongs to.

If you have a column that is defined as an `AutoIncrement` column, you can specify its value in a new row, and this overrides the generated auto-increment value. Setting it directly to a `null` object will cause an exception. However, if you use the form of `DataRow.Add` that takes an object array, you can specify the `AutoIncrement` column using a `null` object as a placeholder in the array. This is demonstrated in Listing 4–4.

Listing 4–4 Adding to a table with an `AutoIncrement` column

```
DataTable t = new DataTable("foo");

// Column 0 of Table t is AutoIncrement
DataColumn[] cols = new DataColumn[3];
cols[0] = new DataColumn(
          "col0", typeof(Int32));
cols[0].AutoIncrement = true;
cols[0].AutoIncrementSeed = 1;
cols[1] = new DataColumn(
          "col1", typeof(String));
cols[2] = new DataColumn(
          "col3", typeof(Int32));
t.Columns.AddRange(cols);

DataRow[] r = new DataRow[4];

// this works and generates the identity
t.Rows.Add(new Object[3] {null, "fred", 1});

// leaving out column 0 generates
// the correct identity
r[0] = t.NewRow();
r[0][1] = "bob";
r[0][2] = 42;
t.Rows.Add(r[0]);

// this sets the column to the value
// DBNull, if it's a nullable column
r[1] = t.NewRow();
r[1][0] = DBNull.Value;
r[1][1] = "ethel";
r[1][2] = 15;
t.Rows.Add(r[1]);

// this sets the column to the value 5
r[2] = t.NewRow();
r[2][0] = 5;
r[2][1] = "sam";
r[2][2] = 41;
t.Rows.Add(r[2]);

r[3] = t.NewRow();
// this fails at the next line
```

```
r[3][0] = null;
r[3][1] = "bob";
r[3][2] = 42;
t.Rows.Add(r[3]);
```

Now let's look at two examples of the process of creating and populating a `DataTable`. The first one adds each item in the most direct, clear manner, and the other one uses as few statements as possible.

Using the most direct manner is a seven-step process:

1. Create a `DataTable` using its constructor.
2. Create each `DataColumn` and initialize its properties.
3. Add each `DataColumn` to the `DataTable`.
4. Create a new `DataRow` by using `DataTable.NewRow`.
5. Fill in the fields of each column in the `DataRow`.
6. Add the `DataRow` to the `DataTable`'s `Rows` collection.
7. Repeat steps 4–6 to taste.

This process is shown in Listing 4–5. You can also use the direct manner with arrays, as shown in Listing 4–6. To use the fewest statements, use the overloads of `DataColumnCollection.Add` and `DataTable.Rows.Add`.

Listing 4–5   Filling the `DataSet` programmatically

```
DataSet           ds = new DataSet();
DataTable  tab = new DataTable("MyTableName");
DataColumn col1 = new DataColumn(
   "col1", typeof(Int32));
DataColumn col2 = new DataColumn(
   "col2", typeof(string));

tab.Columns.Add(col1);
tab.Columns.Add(col2);
ds.Tables.Add(tab);

DataRow r = tab.NewRow();
r[0] = 0;
r[1] = "Niels";
tab.Rows.Add(r);

foreach (DataTable t in ds.Tables)
```

```
Console.WriteLine(
    "Table " + t.TableName + " is in dataset");
```

Listing 4–6   Using an array of objects

```
DataSet   ds = new DataSet();
DataTable  tab = new DataTable("MyTableName");

tab.Columns.Add("col1", typeof(Int32));
tab.Columns.Add("col2", typeof(string));
ds.Tables.Add(tab);

// this works unless there is an identity column
tab.Rows.Add(new Object[] {1, "Bill"});
tab.Rows.Add(new Object[] {2, "Steve"});

foreach (DataTable t in ds.Tables)
  Console.WriteLine(
    "Table " + t.TableName + " is in dataset");
```

4.2.4   Keys, Relations, and Constraints

Now that you've seen the basics of columns, rows, and tables, let's move on to some of the advanced relational data concepts in the model.

As in a relational database, you can define one or more columns to serve as a DataTable's primary key. Having a primary key is not a requirement, but it is required for some advanced functions used in merging DataSets. A primary key requires uniqueness, but adding a Unique constraint to a DataColumn or setting DataColumn.Unique=true does not make it a primary key. Setting a single column as the PrimaryKey results in the AllowDBNull property being set to false, but setting the Unique property does not set AllowDBNull to false. Because PrimaryKey is a property of DataTable, it is not an instance of a class in its own right but is accessed through a setter/getter pair. The value of this property consists of an array of DataColumn objects. Even if the PrimaryKey is a single column, an array of one must be used. Listing 4–7 illustrates setting up a PrimaryKey.

Listing 4–7   Defining a primary key

```
DataTable t = new DataTable("atable");

t.Columns.Add("id", typeof(int));
t.Columns.Add("name", typeof(string));
```

```
// must have an array
DataColumn[] c = new DataColumn[1];
c[0] = t.Columns["id"];
t.PrimaryKey = c;
```

A `DataSet` contains a `Constraints` property that consists of a `ConstraintCollection` of type `DataConstraint` instances. `Constraint` is an abstract base class that has two concrete subclasses: `ForeignKeyConstraint` and `UniqueConstraint`. A `UniqueConstraint` subclass corresponds to the SQL-92 concept of uniqueness. One `ForeignKeyRelation` describes the "child" half of a parent-child relationship between two `DataTable`s.

`UniqueConstraint` is a standalone class that has five overloaded constructors that permit variations of parameters. These parameters can be a single `DataColumn`, a `DataColumn` array, a constraint name, and a Boolean that indicates whether this `UniqueConstraint` represents the `PrimaryKey` of a `DataTable`. The `UniqueConstraint.Table` property names the `DataTable` the columns belong to. Because `UniqueConstraint` is a standalone class, you can use three mechanisms to create it. As shown in Listing 4–8, setting a `DataTable`'s `PrimaryKey` property defines a `UniqueConstraint` as a result. Setting a `DataColumn`'s `Unique` property to `true` will also result in a `UniqueConstraint` when the `DataColumn` is added to a `DataTable`. If the `DataColumn` is already part of a `DataTable`, the `UniqueConstraint` is added to the `DataTable`'s `Constraints` collection. This is shown in Listing 4–9. In addition, because a `UniqueConstraint` is a standalone class, it can be defined over a `DataColumn` or `DataColumn` array before the `DataColumns` are associated with any `DataTable`. When the `DataColumns` are added to the `DataTable`'s `Columns` collections, the `UniqueConstraints` are also added to the `DataTable`'s `Constraints` collection.

Listing 4–8 Keys and constraints

```
DataTable t = new DataTable("atable");
t.Columns.Add("id", typeof(int));
t.Columns.Add("name", typeof(string));

DataColumn[] c = new DataColumn[1];
```

```
c[0] = t.Columns["id"];
t.PrimaryKey = c;

// it adds a unique constraint
Console.WriteLine(
  "constraint count is {0}", t.Constraints.Count);
// column marked as Unique, prints "True"
Console.WriteLine(t.Columns["id"].Unique);
```

Listing 4–9 Creating a constraint by using `Unique`

```
t.Columns["name"].Unique = true;
// constraint added to collection
Console.WriteLine(
  "constraint count is {0}", t.Constraints.Count);
```

A `DataRelation` is a parent-child relationship between two `DataTables`, based on a `PrimaryKey/ForeignKey` pair. This means that, for every child table row, the column values in the child table must exist in a related parent. The `PrimaryKey` in the parent is specified along with the `ForeignKey` in the child. Strictly speaking, the column in the parent table need not be a primary key, but it must be `Unique`. If the column is defined as `PrimaryKey` or `Unique`, the `Relation` creation succeeds and a `UniqueConstraint` is added for the related column in the parent, as shown in Listing 4–10. A `ForeignKeyConstraint` is also added by default. From this point forward, both the `Unique` and the `ForeignKey` constraints are enforced when rows are added, unless `DataSet.EnforceConstraints` is set to `false`. This is usually done temporarily—for example, during a merge of two `DataSets` or to facilitate adding multiple child rows at once—as shown in Listing 4–11. Also, an overload of the `DataRelationsCollection.Add` method lets you create `Relations` without creating the corresponding `Constraints`.

Listing 4–10 Defining a DataRelation

```
DataTable parent = new DataTable("atable");
parent.Columns.Add("id", typeof(int));
parent.Columns.Add("name", typeof(string));

DataTable child = new DataTable("achild");
child.Columns.Add("id", typeof(int));
child.Columns.Add("tid", typeof(int));
child.Columns.Add("name", typeof(string));
```

```
// can I add a relation without a primary key?
DataSet ds = new DataSet();
ds.Tables.Add(parent);
ds.Tables.Add(child);

// yes
ds.Relations.Add(parent.Columns["id"],
                 child.Columns["tid"]);
```

Listing 4–11   Relaxing constraints

```
// add parent rows...
parent.Rows.Add(new Object[2] {1, "bob"});
parent.Rows.Add(new Object[2] {2, "steve"});

// set to allow child without parent
ds.EnforceConstraints = false;

// this works even through no parent with id=4
child.Rows.Add(new Object[3] {1,4,"noparent"});

// add parent, then set constraints back
parent.Rows.Add(new Object[2] {4, "fred"});
ds.EnforceConstraints = true;
```

A `DataRelation` can be defined only between `DataTables` that belong to the same `DataSet`. The `DataRelation` can be used in `DataColumn` expressions through the `Child` keyword. Because `DataRelation` not only defines which tables are involved but also identifies parent and child, a given relation appears in the following:

- The `DataSet`'s `Relations` collection
- The child `DataTable`'s `ParentRelations` collection
- The parent `DataTable`'s `ChildRelations` collection

This is shown in Listing 4–12. Note also that when a `DataRelation` is added to a `DataSet`, a `ForeignKeyConstraint` is also added to the child `DataTable` as a result.

Listing 4–12   Counting relations

```
ds.Relations.Add(parent.Columns["id"],
                 child.Columns["tid"]);
```

```
// all these display the value '1'
Console.WriteLine(
  "{0} relations in DataSet", ds.Relations.Count);
Console.WriteLine(
  "{0} parent relations", parent.ChildRelations.Count);
Console.WriteLine(
  "{0} child relations", child.ParentRelations.Count);
```

As an example, consider the `Customer-Order-LineItem` relationships. Each `Customer` has zero-to-N `Orders`, and each `Order` has one-to-N `LineItems`. The `CustomerID` (`Unique` in the parent) appears also in the `Order` row, where it is a foreign key. An `OrderID` (`Unique` in the parent) appears in the `LineItem`. The cardinality is the number of possible children for a given parent. Common relationships are one-to-one (one child per parent), zero-or-one-to-many (many children), and many-to-many (many parents, many children). As in relational databases, the `DataRelations` do not permit specification of cardinality, which is usually enforced manually by rules. In relational databases and among `DataTables`, many-to-many relationships are usually expressed as a pair of zero-or-one-to-many relationships through a join table.

4.2.5 Navigating through Relationships: Select and Find

Not only do parent-child relationships enable enforcement of unique and foreign key integrity constraints, but also they can be used to permit navigation through levels of a hierarchy. Each `DataTable` contains properties that are collections of `ParentRelations` and `ChildRelations`; the shape of the hierarchy can be determined by inspection of these. The fact that a relationship exists does not indicate cardinality, however, and not every parent row is guaranteed to have corresponding child rows. The `DataRow` class contains a method that allows you to get the collection or individual parent rows (`DataRow.GetParentRow/GetParentRows`) for a given child or to get a collection of children for a given parent (`DataRow.GetChildRows`). This arrangement permits navigation and processing through hierarchical or CODASYL structures, as shown in Listings 4–13 and 4–14. Also, a corresponding `SetParentRow` method allows you to set up the relationship without specifying the corresponding column in the child row.

Listing 4–13 Getting `Child` rows

```
DataTable parent;
// Initialize and fill
// parent and child DataTables

DataRow[] arrRows;

// allows multiple child relations
foreach(
  DataRelation rel in parent.ChildRelations)
{
    foreach(DataRow row in parent.Rows)
    {
       arrRows = row.GetChildRows(rel);
       for (int i=0;i<arrRows.Length;i++)
       {
        // DL/I Get Next Within Parent
        // print row...
       }
    }
}
```

Listing 4–14 Navigating hierarchies

```
void Navigation()
{
DataTable parent = null;
// IMDS navigation through set
DataRow[] arrRows;

DataRelation rel = parent.ChildRelations[0];
arrRows = parent.Rows[0].GetChildRows(rel);
int j=0;
if (arrRows.Length>0)
  while (this.getNext(arrRows, rel, j) !=
         parent.Rows[0])
  {
    //process row..
    j++;
  }
}

DataRow getNext(DataRow[] r,
                DataRelation rel,
                int curr_pos)
```

```
{
if (curr_pos<r.Length)
  return r[curr_pos];
else
  return r[0].GetParentRow(rel);
}
```

Similar in concept to a SQL SELECT statement, DataTable's Select method uses a subset of SQL and returns a collection of DataRows. The Select method uses filter expression syntax, which is syntactically the same as the DataColumn's expression syntax. This syntax, discussed further in Chapter 6, can be used to sort and filter in a DataView used within a GUI control. When you're using Select, the matching behavior, as well as sorting and filtering, is affected by the DataSet's CaseSensitive property. DataTable contains a Compute method that can be used to compute aggregate values on its set of DataRows. Listing 4–15 shows examples of using Select and Compute.

Listing 4–15 Using Select and Compute
```
DataSet myDataSet;
// Initializing DataSet elided...

// Presumes a DataTable named Orders
// has a column named "Total."
DataTable myTable;
myTable = myDataSet.Tables["Orders"];

// Select all Fred's orders
// Sorted by (order) Total
DataRow[] arrRows;
arrRows = myTable.Select(
  "SalesName = 'Fred' ", "Total DESC");

// Total Fred's orders.
// must be an object variable.
object objSum;
objSum = myTable.Compute(
  "Sum(Total)", "SalesName = 'Fred' ");
```

Using the Contains method, you can search a DataRowCollection to determine whether a DataRow matching the primary key exists. If it does, you can retrieve it using the Find method. Find is usually used by consumers; Contains is used internally in the `DataSet` object model. You'll learn more about sorting later, but note that the `DataRowCollection` must be sorted for `Find` to work.

4.2.6 Adding, Retrieving, Changing, and Deleting Rows

As in a relational database, after the `DataTable` and `DataColumns` are created, `DataRows` can be added, deleted, or updated. Similarly, constraints and `DataColumn` types are enforced while changing rows. Unlike a relational database, however, `DataSet` and `DataTable` do not use SQL syntax to perform row maintenance, instead using direct program code affecting the `Rows` collection of a specific table. You've seen a few of the ways that you can add `DataRows`, so it's instructive to reiterate that `DataRows` are shaped when you use `DataTable.NewRow` but are added to the collection only when `DataTable.Rows.Add` is called. The following syntax combines both steps in a single operation:

```
tab.Rows.Add(new object[2] = {1, "norm"});
```

`DataTable` can be treated as a two-dimensional array. You can retrieve data values by using array syntax or by specifying a `Row` index and a `DataColumn` name using C# indexer syntax (`DataRows` do not have names). Two different ways are shown in Listing 4–16. `DataTables` can also be updated using either syntax, as shown in Listing 4–17.

Listing 4–16   Accessing columns

```
DataSet ds;
// Initializing DataSet elided...

// First DataTable is named "authors"
// Second DataColumn is named "au_lname"

// Access row 3 au_fname by names
// Access row 3 au_lname by ordinals
Console.WriteLine("Third author name is " +
    ds.Tables["authors"].Rows[2]["au_fname"] + " " +
    ds.Tables[0].Rows[2][1]);
```

Listing 4–17   Updating columns

```
// First DataTable is named "authors"
// Second DataColumn is named "au_fname"
```

```
// Third DataColumn (ordinal 2) is last name

ds.Tables["authors"].Rows[2]["au_fname"] = "Bob";
ds.Tables["authors"].Rows[2][2] = "Jones";
```

Rows are deleted using the `Rows[n].Delete` syntax. Row deletions do not leave a "hole" in the array; rather, they are live, affecting array position immediately. This means that the first code example in Listing 4–18 deletes only half of the rows in the array. The alternative method must be used to delete all the rows.

Listing 4–18 Deleting rows

```
DataTable t = new DataTable("atable");
t.Columns.Add("id", typeof(int));
t.Columns.Add("name", typeof(string));

t.Rows.Add(new Object[2] {1, "one"});
t.Rows.Add(new Object[2] {2, "two"});
t.Rows.Add(new Object[2] {3, "three"});
t.Rows.Add(new Object[2] {4, "four"});

// this deletes half of the rows
for (int i=0;i<t.Rows.Count;i++)
{
    t.Rows[i].Delete();
    Console.WriteLine("deleted row {0}", i);
}

// this works...
int count = t.Rows.Count;
for (int i=0;i<count;i++)
{
    t.Rows[0].Delete();
}
```

`DataSet` follows the relational model in that the order of rows in a table is irrelevant; rows are not sorted by primary key or otherwise. Each `DataRow` has a (changeable) item number in the `Rows` collection, however, and it is possible to manipulate the position in the `Collection` where a new `DataRow` is added. `DataRowCollection.InsertAt` allows you to insert a new `DataRow` at a certain position in the `Collection`, as shown in Listing 4–19.

Listing 4–19   Inserting at a particular position

```
DataTable t = new DataTable("atable");
t.Columns.Add("id", typeof(int));
t.Columns.Add("name", typeof(string));

t.Rows.Add(new Object[2] {1, "one"});
t.Rows.Add(new Object[2] {2, "two"});
t.Rows.Add(new Object[2] {3, "three"});
t.Rows.Add(new Object[2] {4, "four"});

DataRowCollection rcol = t.Rows;
DataRow r = t.NewRow();
r["id"] = 8;
r["name"] = "eight";
rcol.InsertAt(r, 2);

for (int i=0;i<rcol.Count;i++)
    Console.WriteLine(rcol[i]["id"]);
```

In addition to the usual INSERT, UPDATE, and DELETE methods (actually the equivalent methods on the DataRowCollection), DataTable lets you load data through a series of methods—BeginLoadData, LoadDataRow, and EndLoadData—that is a hybrid of INSERT and UPDATE. The LoadDataRow method takes an array of values and attempts to find a DataRow with a matching primary key. If no DataRow exists with a matching primary key, the row is added; if the row already exists, it is updated using the values in the array. Maintaining indexes, enforcement of constraints, and notification events are turned off while data is being loaded. EndLoadData controls whether changes to existing rows should be accepted (committed) immediately, something I discuss later in the chapter. A DataRow can also be imported into a new DataTable using the DataTable.ImportRow method. Listing 4–20 shows an example of loading and importing rows.

Listing 4–20   Using LoadDataRow and ImportDataRow

```
DataTable t = new DataTable("atable");
t.Columns.Add("id", typeof(int));
t.Columns.Add("name", typeof(string));

DataColumn[] c = new DataColumn[1];
c[0] = t.Columns["id"];
```

```
      t.PrimaryKey = c;

      // add rows and commit
      t.Rows.Add(new Object[2] {1, "one"});
      t.Rows.Add(new Object[2] {2, "two"});
      t.Rows.Add(new Object[2] {3, "three"});
      t.Rows.Add(new Object[2] {4, "four"});
      t.AcceptChanges();

      t.BeginLoadData();

      t.LoadDataRow(
        new Object[2] {2, "too"}, false);
      t.LoadDataRow(
        new Object[2] {2, "deux"}, true);
      t.LoadDataRow(
        new Object[2] {3, "trois"}, true);
      t.LoadDataRow(
        new Object[2] {8, "eight"}, true);
      t.EndLoadData();

      for (int i=0;i<t.Rows.Count;i++)
      {
      // writes 1, one
      //        2, deux
      //        3, trois
      //        4, four
      //        8, eight
        Console.WriteLine("row {0} is {1}, {2}",
          i, t.Rows[i]["id"], t.Rows[i]["name"]);
      }

      DataTable t2 = new DataTable("t2");
      t2.Columns.Add("id", typeof(int));
      t2.Columns.Add("name", typeof(string));
      t2.ImportRow(t.Rows[2]);

      Console.WriteLine("table t2 has {0} row",
          t2.Rows.Count);
      Console.WriteLine("first row is {0}, {1}",
          t2.Rows[0]["id"], t2.Rows[0]["name"]);
```

You can copy entire DataTables to other DataTables using the Data-Table.Copy and DataTable.Clone methods. Using Copy copies all the

DataRows as well as the structure. Clone copies only the structure. Listing 4–21 demonstrates the difference. Table t2 does not have any rows after this series of operations, but it does have constraints. Table t3 has both constraints and data.

Listing 4–21 Using Copy and Clone

```
DataTable t = new DataTable("atable");
t.Columns.Add("id", typeof(int));
t.Columns.Add("name", typeof(string));
t.Columns["id"].Unique = true;

t.Rows.Add(new Object[2] {1, "one"});
t.Rows.Add(new Object[2] {2, "two"});
t.Rows.Add(new Object[2] {3, "three"});
t.Rows.Add(new Object[2] {4, "four"});

// copies only metadata
DataTable t2 = t.Clone();

// copies metadata and data
DataTable t3 = t.Copy();

Console.WriteLine("table t has {0} rows",
                t.Rows.Count);
Console.WriteLine("table t2 has {0} rows",
                t2.Rows.Count);
Console.WriteLine("table t3 has {0} rows",
                t3.Rows.Count);

Console.WriteLine("table t has {0} constraints",
                t.Constraints.Count);
Console.WriteLine("table t2 has {0} constraints",
                t2.Constraints.Count);
Console.WriteLine("table t3 has {0} constraints",
                t3.Constraints.Count);
```

4.2.7 Combining Changes

Although DataSet cannot ensure all the properties of transactions (it has no durable transaction log or locking mechanism), it can compose multiple updates so that they are atomic and consistent. This means that a set of changes can be composed so that they all occur or none occurs (the property of atomicity) and that, within a set of changes, integrity rules will not be allowed to be broken. As Listing 4–22 shows, however, even though all the changes taken as a whole must not violate integrity rules, intermediate states where inconsistency exists are allowed.

Listing 4–22 Editing DataRows

```
DataTable t = new DataTable("atable");
t.Columns.Add("id", typeof(int));
t.Columns.Add("tid", typeof(int));
t.Columns.Add("name", typeof(string));

// composite primary key
DataColumn[] c = new DataColumn[2];
c[0] = t.Columns["id"];
c[1] = t.Columns["tid"];
t.PrimaryKey = c;

t.Rows.Add(new Object[3] {1, 1, "one"});
t.Rows.Add(new Object[3] {2, 1, "two"});
t.Rows.Add(new Object[3] {3, 1, "three"});
t.Rows.Add(new Object[3] {4, 1, "four"});
t.AcceptChanges();

// edit the second row
t.Rows[1].BeginEdit();

// change the key of row "two" to 1,1
// this would cause an integrity constraint here
t.Rows[1][0] = 1;
// now it won't
t.Rows[1][1] = 99;

t.Rows[1].EndEdit();
t.Rows[1].AcceptChanges();
```

The DataRow's BeginEdit method notifies the internal workings of the DataSet to temporarily suspend enforcement of referential and other integrity rules because multiple changes may be made that leave the DataSet in a consistent state at the end. BeginEdit must be called on every DataRow that participates in a multiple-change scenario. Calling BeginEdit puts a DataRow into edit mode. Calling either CancelEdit or EndEdit ends edit mode. Referential and other constraints are not applicable to rows that are in edit mode. `Can-celEdit` rolls back the changes for a single `DataRow`. The `EndEdit` method does not "accept" the changes but turns on referential and other constraints. Calling `EndEdit` causes an exception if constraints such as `Unique` or `Read-Only` are broken.

In addition to canceling edits on a specific `DataRow`, you can accept or roll back a series of changes on a `DataRow`, `DataTable`, or `DataSet` basis. To do this, you use `AcceptChanges` or `RejectChanges`. The chosen method accepts or rejects all the changes en masse and can result in intra- or inter-`DataTable` constraint checking, in addition to the `DataRow` checking mentioned earlier. `AcceptChanges` and `RejectChanges` affect `DataRow` states and `DataRow` versions, which are described in more detail later.

4.2.8 Merging `DataSets`

You can use `DataSet.Merge` to directly merge in changes or new information from another `DataSet`. Or you can use it to merge in changes from a database by re-querying all or part of the database into a second `DataSet` and then calling `Merge`. Chapter 5 talks more about merging changes from a database.

There are six overloads of `Merge` but really only three specific configurable behaviors. You can merge `DataSet` A with `DataSet` B, with a `DataTable`, or with an array of `Rows`. When you merge two `DataSets`, the one that you call the `Merge` method on is known as the *target* (or *current*) database. The `DataSet` that is the first parameter is called the *source*. One set of overloads permits you to specify whether the changes to the target `DataSet` are preserved after the merge completes. Figure 4–2 shows an example of a simple merge operation, including the before and after images of the `DataSet`.

In general, if the target `DataTable` has a primary key, one of two things happens: `DataRows` that match by primary key overwrite the existing `DataRow` in the target, or `DataRows` that have no match in the target `DataTable` are added to the target `DataTable`. If the target `DataTable` does not have a primary key, all rows in the source are added to the target as new rows.

A final parameter permits you to specify what happens when schemas in the source and target `DataSets` conflict. The choices are Add, Ignore, or Error. By

CustID	CustName	Age
00001	Bob Smith	45
00002	Bill Jones	34
00003	Sally Walker	23

dsSource

CustID	CustName
10023	Meg Fleming
12345	Bill Kidd
13444	Tom Liu

dsTarget

OrderID	CustID	OrderDate
2387	10023	2000-01-01
9872	10023	2000-05-19
2357	13444	2001-02-12

```
dsTarget.Merge(dsSource);
```

CustID	CustName	Age
00001	Bob Smith	45
00002	Bill Jones	34
00003	Sally Walker	23
10023	Meg Fleming	null
12345	Bill Kidd	null
13444	Tom Liu	null

dsTarget

OrderID	CustID	OrderDate
2387	10023	2000-01-01
9872	10023	2000-05-19
2357	13444	2001-02-12

Figure 4–2 Merging DataSets

"conflict" I mean that DataTable A in DataSet A may have Columns foo1, foo2, and foo3, but the same-named DataTable in DataSet B might have an additional column foo4. The default is for foo4 to be added to the DataTable in the target DataSet.

A MergeFailed event can be raised when the target and source tables have a DataColumn with differing data type. MergeFailed can also be raised when the target and source tables each have primary keys, but on different columns. DataRow constraints (and missing schema mappings) will also throw their events at the time of a merge. Constraints are checked during `Merge` only after all the data has been merged. This might affect the granularity of the reconciliation logic that you implement.

4.2.9 `DataRow` States and Versions

Each `DataRow` has a `RowState` property. This property represents the state of the `DataRow` with respect to its `DataTable`'s `Rows` collection. As a simple example, remember that when a `DataRow` is created with `DataTable.NewRow`, it is not yet associated with the `DataTable`; this is accomplished using `Data-Table.Rows.Add`. Before it is added to the `DataRows` collection, this `DataRow`'s `State` property is `Da-taRowState.Detached`. Table 4–1 shows the possible values for `DataRowState`.

A `DataRow`'s state is sensitive to whether or not `AcceptChanges` has been called. The new values of a `DataRow` can be seen by all readers (a violation of the isolation portion of the ACID properties) before `AcceptChanges` is called, but the change is not really final until `AcceptChanges` is called. This arrangement is useful when the `DataSet` is acting as a cache for tables in a database, as you will see in Chapter 5.

Table 4–1 `DataRowState` values

DataRowState Value	Meaning
Added	The row has been added to a `DataRowCollection`, and `AcceptChanges` has not been called.
Deleted	The row was deleted using the `Delete` method of the `DataRow`.
Detached	The row has been created but is not part of any `DataRowCollection`. A `DataRow` is in this state immediately after it has been created and before it is added to a collection, or if it has been removed from a collection.
Modified	The row has been modified and `AcceptChanges` has not been called.
Unchanged	The row has not changed since `AcceptChanges` was last called.

Because only a call to `AcceptChanges` finalizes a series of changes, multiple *versions* of a single `DataRow` are kept in the `DataSet` object model. These versions are related to, but are not the same as, the `DataRow.State` property. The four `DataRow` versions possible are `Current`, `Default`, `Original`, and `Proposed`, and they relate to `DataRow` editing and to `DataRow`, `DataTable`, and `DataSet` `AcceptChanges` as follows:

1. After calling the `DataRow` object's `BeginEdit` method, if you change the value, the `Current` and `Proposed` values become available.

2. After calling the `DataRow` object's `CancelEdit` method, the `Proposed` value is deleted.

3. After calling the `DataRow` object's `EndEdit` method, the `Proposed` value becomes the `Current` value.

4. After calling the `DataRow` object's `AcceptChanges` method, the `Proposed` value becomes the `Current` value; the `Original` value persists.

5. After calling the `DataTable` object's `AcceptChanges` method, the `Original` value becomes identical to the `Current` value.

6. After calling the `DataRow` object's `RejectChanges` method, and the version becomes `Current`.

Listing 4–23 shows an example of the interaction between collection changing operations, `RowState`s, and `RowVersion`s. If you're doing something such as updating databases from a cache, it is useful to use a specific `RowVersion` (original versus proposed) if such a version exists. Attempting to access a nonexistent version will throw an exception, so the `DataRow.HasVersion` method allows you to determine whether a certain `DataRowVersion` exists for a specific `DataRow`. A getter exists for a `DataRow`'s `Item` property (that is, the indexers by ordinal or name) that lets you get data values of a specific `DataRowVersion`. In addition, `GetParentRows` and `GetChildRows` have overloads that accept a `DataRowVersion`.

Listing 4–23 `DataRowState`s and `DataRowVersion`s

```
public void versions()
{
  DataTable t = new DataTable("atable");
  t.Columns.Add("id", typeof(int));
  t.Columns.Add("name", typeof(string));
```

```
// row r is detached
DataRow r = t.NewRow();
Console.WriteLine(r.RowState);
checkversion(r);
r[0] = 4;
r[1] = "four";
Console.WriteLine(r.RowState);
checkversion(r);

t.Rows.Add(r);
// now it is "added"
Console.WriteLine(r.RowState);
checkversion(r);

t.AcceptChanges();
// now it is "unchanged"
Console.WriteLine(r.RowState);
checkversion(r);

r.BeginEdit();
r[1] = "newvalue";
Console.WriteLine(r.RowState);
checkversion(r);
r.EndEdit();

// now it is "modified"
Console.WriteLine("EndEdit called");
Console.WriteLine(r.RowState);
checkversion(r);

// this or t.AcceptChanges
r.AcceptChanges();
// now it is "unchanged" again
Console.WriteLine(r.RowState);
checkversion(r);

r.Delete();
// now it is "deleted"
Console.WriteLine(r.RowState);
checkversion(r);

r.AcceptChanges();
// back to detached
Console.WriteLine(r.RowState);
checkversion(r);
```

```
}

void checkversion(DataRow r)
{
  if (r.HasVersion(DataRowVersion.Default))
    Console.WriteLine("   has Default");
  if (r.HasVersion(DataRowVersion.Original))
    Console.WriteLine("   has Original");
  if (r.HasVersion(DataRowVersion.Proposed))
    Console.WriteLine("   has Proposed");
  if (r.HasVersion(DataRowVersion.Current))
    Console.WriteLine("   has Current");
}
```

Listing 4–23 produces this output:

```
Detached
    has Default
    has Proposed
Detached
    has Default
    has Proposed
Added
    has Default
    has Current
Unchanged
    has Default
    has Original
    has Current
Unchanged
    has Default
    has Original
    has Proposed
    has Current
EndEdit called
Modified
    has Default
    has Original
    has Current
Unchanged
    has Default
    has Original
    has Current
Deleted
    has Original
Detached
```

When you're loading data rows using `BeginLoadData` and `LoadDataRow`, rows that match existing rows cause an update rather than a duplicate row exception. When you're updating an existing row, a parameter of `LoadDataRow` indicates whether the change should be accepted immediately. Listing 4–24 shows how this parameter affects the `DataRowVersion`.

Listing 4–24 Using `LoadDataRow` and `RowVersions`

```
DataTable t = new DataTable("atable");
t.Columns.Add("id", typeof(int));
t.Columns.Add("name", typeof(string));

DataColumn[] c = new DataColumn[1];
c[0] = t.Columns["id"];
t.PrimaryKey = c;

t.Rows.Add(new Object[2] {1, "one"});
t.Rows.Add(new Object[2] {2, "two"});
t.AcceptChanges();

t.BeginLoadData();

t.LoadDataRow(new Object[2] {2, "too"}, false);

// Original != Current
Console.WriteLine(
  "row 1: is {0}, {1}",
  t.Rows[1]["id"],
  t.Rows[1]["name",DataRowVersion.Original]);
Console.WriteLine(
  "row 1: is {0}, {1}",
  t.Rows[1]["id"],
  t.Rows[1]["name",DataRowVersion.Current]);

// Calls AcceptChanges on replace row 1
t.LoadDataRow(new Object[2] {2, "deux"}, true);

// Original == Current
Console.WriteLine(
  "row 1: is {0}, {1}",
  t.Rows[1]["id"],
  t.Rows[1]["name",DataRowVersion.Original]);
Console.WriteLine(
```

```
        "row 1: is {0}, {1}",
        t.Rows[1]["id"],
        t.Rows[1]["name",DataRowVersion.Current]);

    t.EndLoadData();
```

As discussed in Chapter 5, `DataRowVersion`s are used mostly for updating a database from the `DataSet` (cache). `DataRowState`s are used to filter certain operations on sets of rows to select pending changes.

4.2.10   Rules and Relationships

When changes are applied to the primary keys of tables that contain child relationships, or when parent rows are deleted, you must determine what action should be taken with respect to the corresponding child rows. The SQL-99 standard defines five actions to take when such a primary key of a parent is updated or the row deleted:

- No action: The child rows remain the same, becoming orphaned.
- Restrict: An exception is thrown.
- Set null: Child rows have their foreign key field(s) set to database `NULL`.
- Set default: Child rows have their foreign key field(s) set to the `Data-Column`'s default value.
- Cascade: The children are updated or deleted to stay in sync with the parent.

This policy is enforced on a `DataSet`-wide basis by setting the `DataSet.EnforceConstraints` property to `true`. Then you have some choices to make. You implement the choice using `DeleteRule`, `UpdateRule`, and `AcceptRejectRule`, which are properties of the foreign key constraint (as with a relational database). `DeleteRule` and `UpdateRule` determine what happens (when `EndEdit` is called on the parent) when a delete or update is performed on the primary key of a parent table. You have a choice of everything except for restricting the update/delete, which you must do using events discussed later in this chapter. Listing 4–25 shows examples. When you use `UpdateRule=Cascade`, parent rows should be updated before the corresponding child rows are.

Listing 4–25 Setting cascading updates

```
DataTable t = new DataTable("atable");
t.Columns.Add("id", typeof(int));
t.Columns.Add("name", typeof(string));
t.Columns[0].AllowDBNull = false;

DataTable t2 = new DataTable("achild");
t2.Columns.Add("id", typeof(int));
t2.Columns.Add("tid", typeof(int));
t2.Columns.Add("name", typeof(string));

t2.Columns[0].DefaultValue = 1;

DataSet ds = new DataSet();
ds.Tables.Add(t);
ds.Tables.Add(t2);

// add constraints and relations
ds.Relations.Add(t.Columns["id"], t2.Columns["id"]);
DataRelation rel = ds.Relations[0];

// add data
t.Rows.Add(new Object[2] {1, "bob"});
t.Rows.Add(new Object[2] {2, "steve"});
t.AcceptChanges();

// children of bob
t2.Rows.Add(new Object[3] {1,1, "fred"});
t2.Rows.Add(new Object[3] {1,2, "sam"});
t2.Rows.Add(new Object[3] {1,3, "buddy"});
// children of steve
t2.Rows.Add(new Object[3] {2,4, "mary"});
t2.Rows.Add(new Object[3] {2,5, "alice"});
t2.Rows.Add(new Object[3] {2,6, "judy"});
t2.AcceptChanges();

rel.ChildKeyConstraint.UpdateRule =
  Rule.SetDefault;
rel.ChildKeyConstraint.AcceptRejectRule =
  AcceptRejectRule.Cascade;

// change steve to 99
t.Rows[1][0] = 99;
```

```
// steve's child change to default (1)
t.AcceptChanges();
```

When `AcceptChanges` or `RejectChanges` is called on the `DataRow`, `DataTable`, or `DataSet` and an integrity error occurs here, rather than at the time of the update or delete, the `ForeignKey.AcceptRejectRule` specifies that either no action occurs or cascade occurs at this time.

4.2.11 Error Handling

Any of the operations that change data in a `DataSet`, `DataTable`, `DataRow`, or `DataColumn` can cause an exception. The `DataSet` object model throws a series of typed exceptions that are derived from (or are) `DataException`; these are listed in Table 4–2. Each of these typed exceptions also provides a useful error message and can be caught either as the typed exception, `DataException`, or any other subclass.

Table 4–2 Errors thrown by the `DataSet` classes

Exception	Thrown By	When
`ConstraintExcep-tion`	`DataRow.EndEdit` `DataRowCollection.Add`	Violates relation constraint Violates unique column in row constraint
`DataException`	—	Base class

`DeletedRowInaces-sibleException`	`DataRow.BeginEdit`
	`DataRow.Item`
	`DataRow.Delete`
		`DataRow` has already been deleted

`DuplicateName-Exception`	`New DataTable`
	`New DataColumn`
	`New DataRelation`
	`New DataConstraint`
		When adding to collection

`InRowChanging-EventException`	`DataRow.EndEdit`	`RowChanging`

(continues)

Table 4–2 Errors thrown by the `DataSet` classes (Continued)

Exception	Thrown By	When

`InvalidConstraint-`
`Exception`
	`DataRelationCollec-`
	`tion.Add`
	`DataRowCollection.Clear`
	`DataRow.GetParentRow`
		Incorrectly attempting to create or access a relation

`InvalidExpression-` `Exception`	`DataColumn.Expression`	When setting expression

`MissingPrimary-`
`KeyException`
	`DataRowCollection.Con-`
	`tains`
	`DataRowCollection.Find`
		When using a method that requires a primary key to work successfully

`NoNullAllowed-` `Exception`	`DataRow.Column` setter `DataTables.Rows.Add`	Column is `DBNull` and `AllowDBNull` is `false`
`ReadOnlyException`	`DataRow.Column` setter	Column is read-only

`RowNotInTable-`
`Exception`
	`DataRow.AcceptChanges`
	`DataRow.GetChildRows`
	`DataRow.GetParentRow`
	`DataRow.GetParentRows`
	`DataRow.RejectChanges`
	`DataRow.SetParentRows`
		When row has already been deleted

`StrongTypingExcep-` `tion`	`DataRow.Column` getter	Strongly typed `DataSet` only, when setting `DBNull`
`SyntaxErrorExcep-` `tion`	`DataColumn.Expression` setter	When expression contains syntax error
`VersionNotFoundEx-` `ception`	`DataRow` getter with version	Version has been deleted or does not exist

When a `DataException` is thrown, the action that caused the exception is not performed. For example, if you attempt to set to `DBNull` a column that does not allow `DBNull`, it will throw a `NoNullAllowedException`. When you examine the value of the column, the value has not changed, as shown in Listing 4–26. Note that you can't retrieve any information about the specific column, row, or table from this exception. A more common occurrence is that the column, row, or table in error violates a logical, rather than a referential, constraint. In this case, you can set the column (incorrectly) and would like to mark the column, row, and table as containing user-defined errors. You use error descriptions, rather than throw Exceptions, for this case.

Listing 4–26   Causing a DataException

```
DataTable t;
// initialization of DataTable t elided...

try
{
  // column zero does not allow DBNull
  // attempt to set DBNull
  t.Rows[0][0] = DBNull.Value;
}
catch (Exception e)
{
  // This is a NoNullAllowedException
  Console.WriteLine("Error of type {0}", e.GetType());
  // Source is System.Data
  Console.WriteLine(e.Source);
  // Column contains old value
  Console.WriteLine(t.Rows[0][0]);
}
```

Errors are associated with DataColumns in DataRows. The DataColumn class itself does not contain an error as a property, but the DataRow contains a method called GetColumnError that takes a DataColumn, column ordinal, or column name and returns an error description string. These error descriptions can be set to custom values with SetColumnError. The DataRow.GetColumnsInError method returns an array of DataColumn instances for the columns containing errors in that DataRow. In addition, the DataRow itself has a RowError property, which can be set with a custom string on a per-row basis. DataRow.ClearError clears all the columns' error descriptions and the RowError property as well.

Errors on `DataRows` also bubble up to `DataTable` and `DataSet`. The bubbling is somewhat symmetric. `DataRow` has a `HasErrors` property that returns `true` or `false`. `GetColumnsInError` returns an array of `DataColumn` instances that contain errors, and `GetColumnError` returns the error message for a specific column. The corresponding `DataTable` has a similar `HasErrors` property and a way to get rows in error through `DataTable.GetErrors`, returning an array of `DataRows`. The `DataSet` has a corresponding `HasErrors` property. Listing 4–27 shows an example of getting error information. Errors can be cleared on a per-row basis by using `DataRow.ClearError`.

Listing 4–27   Processing errors

```
DataSet ds = new DataSet();
DataTable t = ds.Tables[0];
DataRow r = t.Rows[0];
// Initialization elided...

// bad value set by user
r[0] = 999;

// business rule
if ((int)r[0] > 500)
{
  t.Rows[0].SetColumnError(
    0, "Can't be greater than 500");
  t.Rows[0].RowError = "Invalid ID";
}

// process errors
DataColumn[] errCols = r.GetColumnsInError();
if (errCols.Length != 0)
{
  Console.WriteLine("Row error is {0}", r.RowError);
  for (int x=0;x<errCols.Length;x++)
    Console.WriteLine("Column {0} has error {1}",
      errCols[x].ColumnName,
        r.GetColumnError(errCols[x].Ordinal));
}

// these all print true
Console.WriteLine("row[0] HasErrors = {0}",
  t.Rows[0].HasErrors);
```

```
Console.WriteLine("table HasErrors = {0}",
   t.HasErrors);
Console.WriteLine("DataSet.HasErrors = {0}",
   ds.HasErrors);
```

`DataSet` improves on the ADO `Recordset` in that, when you're marshaling a `DataSet`, errors are also marshaled, on a per-`DataRow` basis. You'll read more about this in Chapter 7.

4.2.12 Events

One problem that I breezed past in the preceding section is you can't know which `DataColumn` or `DataRow` caused the exception simply by looking at the information in `DataException`. However, `DataSet` and `DataTable` have a rich event model that enables you to get the kind of information you need for this type of error reporting, as well as other types of change tracking. For example, suppose you want to render changed columns in a different color or alternative icon; catching events will do the trick. However, programs that don't need such granular change tracking can choose to ignore the events.

Table 4–3 shows the events exposed on `DataTable`. Notice that each change triggers a "before" and "after" event so that the data can be inspected and changed before the action takes place. Although there are six events, there are only two types of `EventArgs`: `DataColumnChangeEventArgs` and `DataRowChangeEventArgs`.

Table 4–3   Events exposed by `DataTable`

Event	Description
`ColumnChanged`	Occurs when a value has been inserted successfully into a column
`ColumnChanging`	Occurs when a value has been submitted for a column
`RowChanged`	Occurs after a row in the table has been edited successfully
`RowChanging`	Occurs when a `DataRow` is changing
`RowDeleted`	Occurs after a row in the table has been deleted
`RowDeleting`	Occurs when a row in the table is marked for deletion

Listing 4–28 presents a program that handles all six events and prints the information that goes with each one. The program performs a series of operations and then calls `DataTable.RejectChanges`, performs the same series of operations, and calls `AcceptChanges`.

Listing 4–28   Sample program that handles `DataTable` events

```
using System;
using System.Data;

namespace Chapter4_Events
{
    /// <summary>
    /// Summary description for Class1.
    /// </summary>
    class Class1
    {
      DataSet ds = new DataSet();
      DataTable t = new DataTable("tabname");

      static void Main(string[] args)
      {
        Class1 c = new Class1();
        c.instanceMain();

      }

      protected void T_Changing(object sender,
        DataRowChangeEventArgs e)
      {
        if (e.Row.RowState == DataRowState.Deleted)
          Console.WriteLine("Row Changing: Action {0}, State {1}",
            e.Action,  e.Row.RowState);
        else
         Console.WriteLine("Row Changing: {0} id = {1}, State {2}",
            e.Action, e.Row[0], e.Row.RowState);
      }

      protected void T_Changed(object sender,
        DataRowChangeEventArgs e)
      {
        if (e.Row.RowState == DataRowState.Detached)
          Console.WriteLine("Row Changed: Action {0}, State {1}",
            e.Action,  e.Row.RowState);
```

```
    else
    Console.WriteLine("Row Changed: {0} id = {1}, State {2}",
        e.Action, e.Row[0], e.Row.RowState);
}

protected void T_Deleting(object sender,
    DataRowChangeEventArgs e)
{
 Console.WriteLine("Row Deleting: {0} id = {1}, State {2}",
        e.Action, e.Row[0], e.Row.RowState);
}

protected void T_Deleted(object sender,
    DataRowChangeEventArgs e)
{
    Console.WriteLine("Row Deleted: Action {0}, State {1}",
        e.Action, e.Row.RowState);
}

protected void C_Changing(object sender,
    DataColumnChangeEventArgs e)
{
    Console.WriteLine("Column {0} changing to {1}",
        e.Column.ColumnName, e.ProposedValue);
}

protected void C_Changed(object sender,
    DataColumnChangeEventArgs e)
{
    Console.WriteLine("Column {0} changed to {1}",
        e.Column.ColumnName, e.ProposedValue);
}

void instanceMain()
{
    maketables();
    t.RowChanging +=
        new DataRowChangeEventHandler(T_Changing);
    t.RowChanged +=
        new DataRowChangeEventHandler(T_Changed);
    t.RowDeleting +=
        new DataRowChangeEventHandler(T_Deleting);
    t.RowDeleted +=
        new DataRowChangeEventHandler(T_Deleted);
```

```
      t.ColumnChanging +=
        new DataColumnChangeEventHandler(C_Changing);
      t.ColumnChanged +=
        new DataColumnChangeEventHandler(C_Changed);

      rollback();
      accept();

    }

    void rollback()
    {
      // column and row events
      t.Rows[0]["name"] = "one";

      // column and row events
      t.Rows[1]["name"] = "deux";

      t.Rows[2].BeginEdit();
      // column events
      t.Rows[2]["name"] = "trois";
      // nothing
      t.Rows[2].CancelEdit();

      t.Rows[2].BeginEdit();
      // column events
      t.Rows[2]["name"] = "drei";
      // row events
      t.Rows[2].EndEdit();

      // column and row events
      t.Rows[3].Delete();

      t.Rows.Add(new Object[2] {8, "eight"});
      Console.WriteLine("===========");

      t.RejectChanges();
    }


    void accept()
    {
      t.Rows[0]["name"] = "one";
      t.Rows[1]["name"] = "deux";
```

```
        t.Rows[2].BeginEdit();
        t.Rows[2]["name"] = "trois";
        t.Rows[2].CancelEdit();
        t.Rows[2].BeginEdit();
        t.Rows[2]["name"] = "drei";
        t.Rows[2].EndEdit();
        t.Rows[3].Delete();

        t.Rows.Add(new Object[2] {8, "eight"});
        Console.WriteLine("===========");

        t.AcceptChanges();
    }

    void maketables()
    {
        t.Columns.Add("id", typeof(int));
        t.Columns.Add("name", typeof(string));

        t.Rows.Add(new Object[2] {1, "one"});
        t.Rows.Add(new Object[2] {2, "two"});
        t.Rows.Add(new Object[2] {3, "three"});
        t.Rows.Add(new Object[2] {4, "four"});

        t.AcceptChanges();
    }
  }
}
```

The output (except for the redundant change series) is as follows:

```
The Changes:
============
Column name changing to one
Column name changed to one
Row Changing: Change id = 1, State Unchanged
Row Changed: Change id = 1, State Modified
Column name changing to deux
Column name changed to deux
Row Changing: Change id = 2, State Unchanged
Row Changed: Change id = 2, State Modified
Column name changing to trois
Column name changed to trois
Column name changing to drei
Column name changed to drei
Row Changing: Change id = 3, State Unchanged
```

```
Row Changed: Change id = 3, State Modified
Row Deleting: Delete id = 4, State Unchanged
Row Deleted: Action Delete, State Deleted
Row Changing: Add id = 8, State Detached
Row Changed: Add id = 8, State Added
===========
RejectChanges
===========
Row Changing: Rollback id = 1, State Modified
Row Changed: Rollback id = 1, State Unchanged
Row Changing: Rollback id = 2, State Modified
Row Changed: Rollback id = 2, State Unchanged
Row Changing: Rollback id = 3, State Modified
Row Changed: Rollback id = 3, State Unchanged
Row Changing: Action Rollback, State Deleted
Row Changed: Rollback id = 4, State Unchanged
Row Changing: Rollback id = 8, State Added
Row Changed: Action Rollback, State Detached
===========
CommitChanges
===========
Row Changing: Commit id = 1, State Modified
Row Changed: Commit id = 1, State Unchanged
Row Changing: Commit id = 2, State Modified
Row Changed: Commit id = 2, State Unchanged
Row Changing: Commit id = 3, State Modified
Row Changed: Commit id = 3, State Unchanged
Row Changing: Action Commit, State Deleted
Row Changed: Action Commit, State Detached
Row Changing: Commit id = 8, State Added
Row Changed: Commit id = 8, State Unchanged
```

There are a few interesting points to be made concerning the output:

- If the new values are the same as the old values (as in the "one" row), the events are still fired.

- Column events are fired immediately, whether or not the row is in edit mode. Row events are fired when EndEdit is called, but not when CancelEdit is called.

- A single row version is available with all events except deleted events.

- Although you can find out whether other versions of the same row exist in the event, you can't get these RowVersions directly. Instead, you must get a reference to the `Table` and use, for example, `Data-Table.Select` or `DataTable.DefaultView.Find` to find the `Row`.

- Deleted rows that have been committed are not null but rather are in a detached state. You can't access their columns without calling `BeginEdit`.

- Detached "new" rows (to be added) have state that is available during the event.

You must be very careful referencing rows because otherwise this program can throw some esoteric exceptions. For example, attempting to refer to a deleted, committed, or detached row produces a `DeletedRowInaccessibleException`. And regarding the `DataTable`'s events, you cannot filter the events—that is, receive only events of a certain state. The only way to turn off events is to shut off the event handler completely. Finally, the `DataSet` itself exposes a single `Merge-Failed` error that is thrown when conflicts occur during a `Merge` operation.

4.2.13 `DataSet`s and Nonrelational Types

As discussed previously, in theory, the `DataType` of a `DataColumn` can be any CLR data type because the domain of data types is the CLR's `System.Type`. This is a big departure from the relational model, which has no support for multivalued types. Strictly speaking, however, there is no support in `DataSet` for types other than the few simple data types listed in the beginning of this chapter. Because `DataSet` has this flexibility and because it is used to support such nonrelational types as SQL Server's `SQL_VARIANT` (as you'll see in Chapter 5), let's explore this a little further now.

CLR types include multivalued types such as `Arrays` and `Objects`, and the CLR supports type inheritance. The fact that `DataSet` can contain columns of type `Object` means that each column can contain a different type. For example, a column could contain `Person` types and also contain not only `Person` objects but also derived types such as `Student` (a subclass of `Person`). This is similar (but not the same as) the multivalue set in a CODASYL database discussed in Chapter 1, with the limitation that all types must derive from a common base. For example, there is no way to specify that a `DataColumn` must contain only `Person` or `Animal` objects, unless they derive from a common base and are the only classes that do. In theory (and perhaps someday in practice), Data-Column could also be used with an object database. This flexibility in typing means that DataSet can map to almost all types of data stores.

I present two examples: one that uses a DataColumn of type Person, and another that uses a DataColumn of type DataTable. Listing 4–29 shows the use of the Person instance as a DataColumn value. A DataColumn of type DataTable (or, strictly speaking, a discrete strongly typed subclass of Data-Table) would be equivalent to TABLE columns in Oracle 8 or in a traditional hierarchical database, such as Unisys's DMS III. Listing 4–30 shows the use of an embedded DataTable as a DataColumn.

Listing 4–29 Using objects with DataSet

```
public class Person
{
  public String name;
  public int age;

  public Person(String n, int a)
  {
    name = n;
    age = a;
  }
}

// use it
DataTable t = new DataTable("people");
DataColumn[] col = new DataColumn[2];

col[0] = new DataColumn("OID");
col[1] = new DataColumn("PersonCol");

col[0].DataType = typeof(Int32);

// this type isn't directly supported
col[1].DataType = typeof(Person);

t.Columns.AddRange(col);

Person[] p = new Person[3];
p[0] = new Person("Curley", 25);
p[1] = new Person("Larry", 32);
```

```
  p[2] = new Person("Moe", 35);

  for (int i=0; i<3;i++)
  {
    DataRow r = t.NewRow();
    r[0] = i+1;
    r[1] = p[i];
    t.Rows.Add(r);
  }

  // who's in the database?
  foreach (DataRow row in t.Rows)
  {
    Person person = (Person)row[1];
    Console.WriteLine("{0} is {1} years old",
      person.name, person.age);
  }
```

Listing 4–30 Embedded `DataTables`

```
  // DataTable to be used as a column
  DataTable t = new DataTable();
  // ... initialization of DataTable t elided

  // Base table
  DataTable pt = new DataTable("base");
  DataColumn[] pcol = new DataColumn[2];

  pcol[0] = new DataColumn("oid");
  pcol[0].DataType = typeof(Guid);

  // DataColumn of type DataTable
  pcol[1] = new DataColumn("embedded");
  pcol[1].DataType = typeof(DataTable);

  pt.Columns.AddRange(pcol);

  // populate it
  DataRow[] pr = new DataRow[2];
  pr[0] = pt.NewRow();
  pr[0][0] = Guid.NewGuid();
  pr[0][1] = t;
  pt.Rows.Add(pr[0]);

  pr[1] = pt.NewRow();
```

```
pr[1][0] = Guid.NewGuid();
pr[1][1] = t;
pt.Rows.Add(pr[1]);

// fetch data
for (int i=0;i<pt.Rows.Count;i++)
  for (int j=0;j<pt.Columns.Count;j++)
  {
    Console.WriteLine("{0}: {1}",
      pt.Columns[j].ColumnName, pt.Rows[i][j]);
    if (pt.Rows[i][j].GetType() == typeof(DataTable))
    {
      Console.WriteLine("***Embedded Table***");
      DataTable ct = (DataTable)pt.Rows[i][j];
      for (int ci=0;ci<ct.Rows.Count;ci++)
        for (int cj=0;cj<ct.Columns.Count;cj++)
          Console.WriteLine("{0}: {1}",
            ct.Columns[cj].ColumnName,
            ct.Rows[ci][cj]);
    }
  }
```

This code does only simple operations: defining the columns, putting data in, and immediately getting data out. Because these types are not directly supported by `DataTable`, the `Copy` mechanism isn't supported. In addition, there are problems with sorting, filtering, and comparing columns of this type, as well as marshaling and persisting them in XML format. Later chapters explore these problems (and possible solutions), but at this point, seeing how to define a nonrelational `DataColumn` in a `DataTable` helps to solidify the issues in dealing with nonrelational data in a relational world.

4.3 Defining an Information Schema

As you've seen throughout this chapter, `DataSet` is very similar to an in-memory relational database. In fact, it's so similar that I end this chapter by discussing a way to produce the "standard" SQL-99 information schema views from a `DataSet`. You remember that the SQL-99 (and before it, SQL-92) information schema is simply a standard way for a database to expose metadata about its objects. The standard information schema defines views that enumerate what it considers to be standard database objects, such as tables, columns, stored procedures, and so on, and standard information that could be exposed about them. Chapter 3 shows how this information is retrieved by the `OleDb` data provider (using `Connection.GetSchemaTable`) and the `SqlClient` data provider (using the `INFORMATION_SCHEMA` views directly). Following are the information schema views we'll expose from `DataSet`.

- `TABLES`: tables in the catalog
- `COLUMNS`: columns in the catalog
- `REFERENTIAL_CONSTRAINTS`
- `TABLE_CONSTRAINTS`: primary key, foreign key, and unique constraints
- `KEY_COLUMN_USAGE`: key columns in constraints
- `CONSTRAINT_TABLE_USAGE`: tables in constraints
- `CONSTRAINT_COLUMN_USAGE`: columns in constraints

`Tables` and `Columns` map easily to the `DataTables` contained in a `DataSet` and to the `DataColumns` within specific `DataTables`. Many of the properties of the `DataColumn`—such as `MaxLength`, `AllowDBNulls`, and `DefaultValue`—have almost exact mappings in the information schema. Because `DataSet` exposes keys and constraints, including `PrimaryKey` and `ForeignKey` constraints, the other six information schema tables relate to them. `RELATIONAL_CONSTRAINTS` is the most straightforward, mapping directly to the `DataTable`'s `Constraints` collection. Table constraints include primary keys and unique columns in a `DataTable` as well as `ForeignKeys`, which are easy to derive from the constraints. The table, column, and key usage schema tables are derived from the relationships and keys, and they are usually used in a relational database to keep track of participation in constraints as a check against inadvertent deletion of these database objects.

We could go a lot further with this. Some column expressions are similar to either SQL `DOMAINS` (which restrict the value space of a column) or `CHECK_CONSTRAINTS`. Finally, `DataViews` are similar to database `VIEWS` but in most ways are more restrictive because they can contain columns only from a single `DataTable`. If the nonrelational user-defined types (UDTs) that you looked at in the preceding section were permitted, another large subset of the information schema would be permitted in our model. As it was, we could have defined the `DATA_TYPES` supported by `DataColumn` in the information schema's

TYPE_INFO view. The information schema views that we've implemented provide a large enough subset to bring home the point that the DataSet class is quite similar to an in-memory relational database in structure. As a means to try it out, the GetInformationSchema sample that appears on the book's Web site contains a sample DataSet with constraints.

4.4 Where Are We?

You've spent most of this chapter going through the use of DataSet and related classes as part of a standalone, in-memory object model that represents relational data. This chapter prepares you for what is to come. In the next three chapters you'll be using DataSet with relational databases, XML data, and graphical user interfaces. This chapter allows you to identify what DataSet adds and helps you to determine when to use it as opposed to the direct streaming and command model discussed in Chapter 3.

Chapter 5

`DataAdapters`: Synchronizing Databases and Datasets

To synchronize operations between a database and the `DataSet` class, you use the `DataAdapter` class.

5.1 Optimistic Concurrency

Chapter 4 explores the `DataSet` type and explains how this type lets you manage multiple tables using relational structures and constraints in memory. Although `DataSet` can be used as a standalone class, one of its uses is to facilitate using disconnected updates with other data sources such as databases. Disconnected fetching and updating use the classes described in the connected model in Chapter 3.

In general, updates to databases consist of inserts, updates, and deletes of individual rows or sets of rows. They can usually be done in three ways:

- Discrete SQL or other command statements are executed.

- A row is retrieved from the database and presented to the user for updating. That user has exclusive access to the row (or exclusive updating capability), which typically is enforced by means of locking the row. This method is called *pessimistic concurrency*.

- A row or set of rows is presented to the user in an updatable manner but not locked. This is known as *optimistic concurrency*.

Optimistic concurrency brings with it the problem of conflict resolution at update time. For example, suppose a data entry clerk is presented with a screen of unlocked data and a series of changes—say, address and credit information—to enter. After about 10 changes, the clerk presses the Accept Edits button because accepting changes requires a trip to the database and is potentially time-consuming. What should the program do if no one has updated nine of the rows, but a single update fails due to a concurrency violation? The choices are as follows:

- Roll back all the information, making the clerk enter the offending data again. At this point there may be another concurrency violation, and the batch of changes may never be accepted.

- Accept all the changes, possibly writing over someone else's changes.

- Accept only the changes that cause no concurrency violations, and roll the others back (in my experience, the most used path). Then what is the clerk to do about the change he is making? He does a refresh and sees whether the situation has changed with respect to the update.

It is said that long response times and the possible distribution of processing (resulting in distributed transactions, further lengthening response times) make optimistic concurrency untenable, especially in a Web-based application. This is certainly true in a business-to-business application or manufacturing resource planning (MRP) system—where applying compensating actions after a failure might be preferable to transactions—but in most Web applications concurrency is more applicable than in other types of applications. The reason? In a customer-oriented Web-based application, there are no data entry clerks. Customers do their own data entry. It is highly unlikely (although not impossible) that a customer would be updating personal information from two Web browsers simultaneously. For Web applications, then, optimistic concurrency in updates still makes sense.

This chapter focuses on optimistic concurrency using `DataSet` as the means of storing the data the user has fetched and is busily working on. To fill `DataSet` and send updates through it back to the database, you'll use a .NET class called `DataAdapter`. You can hand-code SQL or other update commands, or you can use the `CommandBuilder` class to build them automatically based on database metadata. You'll use an event-delegate model to gain fine-grained control and feedback through interception.

5.2 `DataAdapter` Classes

The `DataAdapter` class contains four `Command` instances as member variables. It uses `SelectCommand` to move data from the database to `DataSet` and uses `InsertCommand`, `UpdateCommand`, and `DeleteCommand` to flush updates made to the `DataSet` back to the database. Figure 5–1 shows the classes that participate in `DataSet` interactions when you use the `SqlClient` data provider.

Both the `SqlClient` provider and the `OleDb` provider implement `Data-Adapter`s derived from a common base class, `DbDataAdapter`. Most custom providers, such as the ODBC data provider, also use this base class. `System.Data.Common` contains an abstract implementation of the `DataAdapter` and `DbDataAdapter` base classes. `DbDataAdapter` derives from `Data-Adapter` and adds the four `Command` members referred to earlier. `Data-Adapter` exposes its functionality through an `IDataAdapter` interface. The `DbDataAdapter` class implements the `IDbDataAdapter` interface, which derives from `IDataAdapter`. The data providers add a few customizations, but if you're striving for data-provider-independent code you should use the interfaces. Figure 5–2 shows the interface and class inheritance hierarchies.

5.3 Populating a `DataSet` from a Managed Provider

You use the `Fill` method of `IDataAdapter` to fill tables in `DataSet` by executing a specified command on the database and using the resultset. `Fill` uses

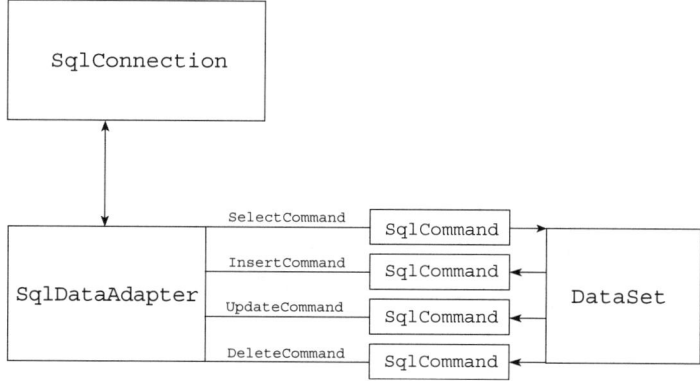

Figure 5–1 `DataAdapter` **Model for** `SqlClient`

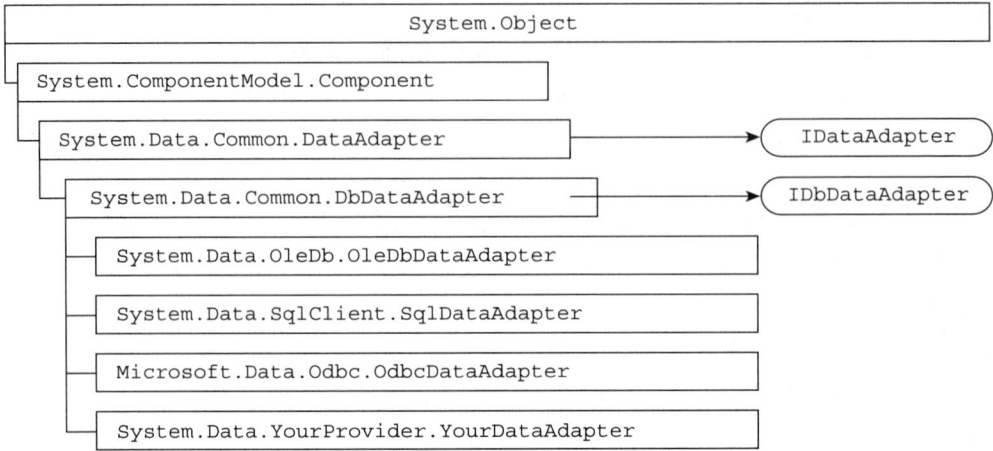

Figure 5–2 `DataAdapter` **class and interface hierarchy**

the `SelectCommand` member of `IDbDataAdapter`. An often-used constructor overload of a typed `DataAdapter`—such as `SqlDataAdapter` or `OleDb-DataAdapter`—takes a command string and connection string as parameters and creates the correct type of `Connection` class and `Command` class, populating the `SelectCommand`. If the `Connection` is not open when `Fill` is called, `Fill` automatically opens it, automatically closes it when finished, and returns. If the `Connection` is already open when `Fill` is called, it remains open after `Fill` returns. This process is demonstrated in Listing 5–1.

Listing 5–1   Filling `DataSet` from `DataAdapter`

```
SqlDataAdapter da = new SqlDataAdapter(
  "select * from authors",
  "server=localhost;uid=sa;database=pubs");

DataSet ds = new DataSet();

// connection not open here
// opened and closed during Fill
da.Fill(ds, "authors");
// connection not open here

da.SelectCommand.Connection.Open();
```

```
da.SelectCommand.CommandText = "select * from jobs";
da.Fill(ds, "jobs");
// connection still open here
```

If the `Connection` is not closed when `Fill` completes, the data rows used to fill the `DataSet` may still be locked in the database. This is the only way to achieve pessimistic concurrency with `DataSet`. With SQL Server, the rows are locked if the `Connection` has an associated `Transaction` at isolation level `RepeatableRead` or `Serializable`. With Oracle, you can use SELECT FOR UPDATE in the `Command` to explicitly lock the rows using any supported transaction isolation level. Listings 5–2 and 5–3 show examples using this method with SQL Server and Oracle, respectively. Note that, because the rows are locked until the user (possibly remote) releases them, this scenario is not recommended. Because the connection must be kept open while the user is processing the data and because of the locking concerns, this technique is not usable in a Web application or in a highly scalable environment.

Listing 5–2   Pessimistic locking: SQL Server

```
DataSet ds = new DataSet();
SqlConnection conn = new SqlConnection(
    "server=localhost;uid=sa;database=pubs");
conn.Open();
SqlTransaction tx = conn.BeginTransaction(
    IsolationLevel.Serializable);

SqlCommand cmd = new SqlCommand(
    "select * from authors", conn, tx);
SqlDataAdapter da = new SqlDataAdapter(cmd);
da.Fill(ds, "authors");
// rows locked here

ds.Tables[0].Rows[1][2] = "Fred";

SqlCommandBuilder bld = new SqlCommandBuilder(da);
da.Update(ds, "authors");
tx.Commit();
// rows unlocked here
da.Dispose();
conn.Close();
```

Listing 5–3   Pessimistic locking: Oracle

```
DataSet ds = new DataSet();
OleDbConnection conn = new OleDbConnection(
  "provider=msdaora;data source=orcll;" +
  "user id=scott;password=tiger");
conn.Open();
OleDbTransaction tx = conn.BeginTransaction();

OleDbCommand cmd = new OleDbCommand(
  "select * from emp for update", conn, tx);
OleDbDataAdapter da = new OleDbDataAdapter(cmd);
da.Fill(ds, "emp");
// rows locked here

ds.Tables[0].Rows[9][2] = "CLERK";

OleDbCommandBuilder bld =
    new OleDbCommandBuilder(da);
da.Update(ds, "emp");
tx.Commit();
// rows unlocked here
da.Dispose();
conn.Close();
```

As shown in Listing 5–4, `IDataAdapter` has four public overloads of `Fill`. The string specified in the `Fill` method is the name to be given to the resulting `DataTable` in the `DataSet`; it does not need to correspond to the name of the table in the database. Also note that, if multiple tables are combined in a SQL `JOIN`, a single `DataTable` is produced in the `DataSet`. If the `DataTable` name is not specified in the `Fill` method, it defaults to `Table`. If multiple results are produced, `DataTable`s named `Table`, `Table1`, `Table2`, and so on are produced.

In addition to filling `DataTable`s in a `DataSet`, you can use `Fill` to specify a starting row number in the database resultset and the maximum number of rows to fill. The final overload fills a `DataTable` instance rather than a `DataSet`. All overloads of the `Fill` method return the number of rows actually added to the resulting table.

Listing 5–4   Overloads of `Fill`

```
public int Fill(DataSet)
public int Fill(DataTable)
// String = name of DataTable
public int Fill(DataSet, String)
```

```
// First Int32 = starting record
// First Int32 = max records
public int Fill(DataSet, Int32, Int32, String)
```

A specific `DataSet` instance is not associated with any data store. It is possible to mix data from different data providers, synthesized data, or XML inside a single `DataSet` instance. The `DataSet` does not keep track of the source of each `DataTable`. For example, a `DataTable` populated through the `SqlClient` data provider may be functionally indistinguishable from a similarly named `DataTable` populated through the `OleDbDataProvider` or from a synthesized `DataTable`.

As you saw in Chapter 4, changes made to `DataSet` are not realized until you call `AcceptChanges` on the appropriate `DataTable` or `DataSet`. By default, using `DataAdapter`'s `Fill` method populates `DataSet` and automatically calls `DataSet.AcceptChanges`. In some situations—for example, when you wish to populate a `DataSet` from multiple data stores and write back to a different data store—this is not the desired behavior. Because `AcceptChanges` was called, no rows are "newly changed" and nothing will be written back. `DataAdapter` has a property, `AcceptChangesDuringFill`, that accommodates these situations. If you want the resulting rows in the `DataSet` to appear newly added, set `AcceptChangesDuringFill` to `false` (the default is `true`).

5.3.1 Using `Fill` with Schema and Mapping Information

As you saw in Chapter 4, `DataTables` have a schema of their own. Similar to columns produced with data definition language (DDL) in a database, each `DataColumn`, when it is defined, contains a series of properties that you can use. You can populate this schema directly, either by defining `DataColumns` and `DataTables` using native `DataSet` methods or by loading an XML schema into the `DataSet`. When `DataAdapter.Fill` is called, if the schema is already defined, metadata from the database need not be required and will already be present in the `DataSet`, saving the database the trouble of producing it. You can also populate the `DataSet` schema through the `DataAdapter` by using `DataAdapter.FillSchema`.

When schema information is missing, the default behavior is to add it to the `DataTable`(s). This behavior is specified using the `MissingSchemaAction` property on `DataAdapter`. The following choices are available when schema mappings are missing:

- `Add` (the default): This adds the missing tables or columns silently.
- `AddWithKey`: This adds the missing tables or columns and additional key information.
- `Ignore`: This throws away the tables or columns in the resultsets that are not already defined in `DataSet`.
- `Error`: This throws a `SystemException`.

Listing 5–5 shows an example of an exception caused by specifying `Miss-ingSchemaAction=Error`. With most providers, `AddWithKey` gives you information similar to the information you get with `DataAdapter.FillSchema` but makes only a single round-trip to the underlying database to obtain both schema and data. As you saw in Chapter 3, resultsets returned by databases do not usually contain primary key information. `AddWithKey` returns much more additional schema information, although the exact amount is data-provider-specific and, with the `OleDb` data provider, OLE DB provider-specific. For example, when using the `SqlClient` data provider, `MissingSchemaAction.Add-WithKey` populates the `AutoIncrement` property but not `AutoIncrement-Seed` and `AutoIncrementStep`. Moreover, it does not populate the `Default` property with the database default value. `AddWithKey` is particularly useful when used with the `OleDb` data provider, which does not always return all schema information if a `SelectCommand` that generates multiple resultsets is issued. In this case, the `OleDb` data provider returns schema information only for the first resultset, and you must specify `AddWithKey` to get the schema information for the remaining results. An example is shown in Listing 5–6. Be careful: With some providers (such as Microsoft's OLE DB provider for Oracle), extra columns containing the key and other metadata may be added directly to the resultset (and to the `DataTable` produced).

Listing 5–5 Missing schema actions

```
try
{
  SqlDataAdapter da = new SqlDataAdapter(
    "select * from authors",
```

```
      "server=localhost;uid=sa;database=pubs");
    DataSet ds = new DataSet();

    // no schema, no tables
    da.MissingSchemaAction = MissingSchemaAction.Error;
    da.Fill(ds, "authors");
}
catch (Exception e)
{
    // this generates a SystemException,
    // no authors table.
    Console.WriteLine("Type: {0}, Message: {1}",
      e.GetType(), e.Message);
}

try
{
    SqlDataAdapter da = new SqlDataAdapter(
      "select * from authors",
      "server=localhost;uid=sa;database=pubs");
    DataSet ds = new DataSet();
    ds.Tables.Add(new DataTable("authors"));

    // this has a table but,
    // no column mappings
    da.MissingSchemaAction = MissingSchemaAction.Error;
    da.Fill(ds, "authors");
}
catch (Exception e)
{
    // this generates a SystemException
    // for the first column
    Console.WriteLine("Type: {0}, Message: {1}",
      e.GetType(), e.Message);
}
```

Listing 5–6 Returning metadata for multiple results

```
OleDbDataAdapter da = new OleDbDataAdapter(
         "select * from authors;select * from jobs",
         "provider=sqloledb;uid=sa;database=pubs");
DataSet ds = new DataSet();

// metadata for first table
da.Fill(ds);
```

```
// extra metadata for both tables
da.MissingSchemaAction =
    MissingSchemaAction.AddWithKey;
da.Fill(ds);
```

To accommodate the use of table and column names in the `DataSet` that differ from those in the database, the `DataAdapter` classes have a `TableMappings` property of type `DataTableMappingCollection`. The `DataTableMappingCollection`s are collections of `DataTableMapping` instances. Each `DataTableMapping` instance has a `ColumnMappings` property of type `DataColumnMappingCollection`. A `DataColumnMappingCollection` is a collection of `DataColumnMapping` instances. These relationships are shown in Figure 5–3. Implementations of the mapping classes and collections are provided in `System.Data.Common`, and these are used by both `SqlClient` and `OleDb` providers. Mappings can be specified through the array or left to default. Listing 5–7 shows the use of table and column mappings.

Listing 5–7   Using table and column mappings

```
SqlDataAdapter cmd = new SqlDataAdapter(
  "select * from authors",
  "server=localhost;uid=sa;database=pubs");
DataSet ds = new DataSet();

cmd.TableMappings.Add(
    "authors", "AllAuthors");
cmd.TableMappings[0].ColumnMappings.Add(
    "au_id", "AuthorID");

cmd.Fill(ds, "authors");

foreach (DataTable t in ds.Tables)
  Console.WriteLine("Table name is " + t);

foreach (DataColumn c in ds.Tables[0].Columns)
  Console.WriteLine("Column name is " + c);
```

You need not specify table and column mappings nor a schema before calling `Fill`. If they are not specified, or if the incoming data does not match the

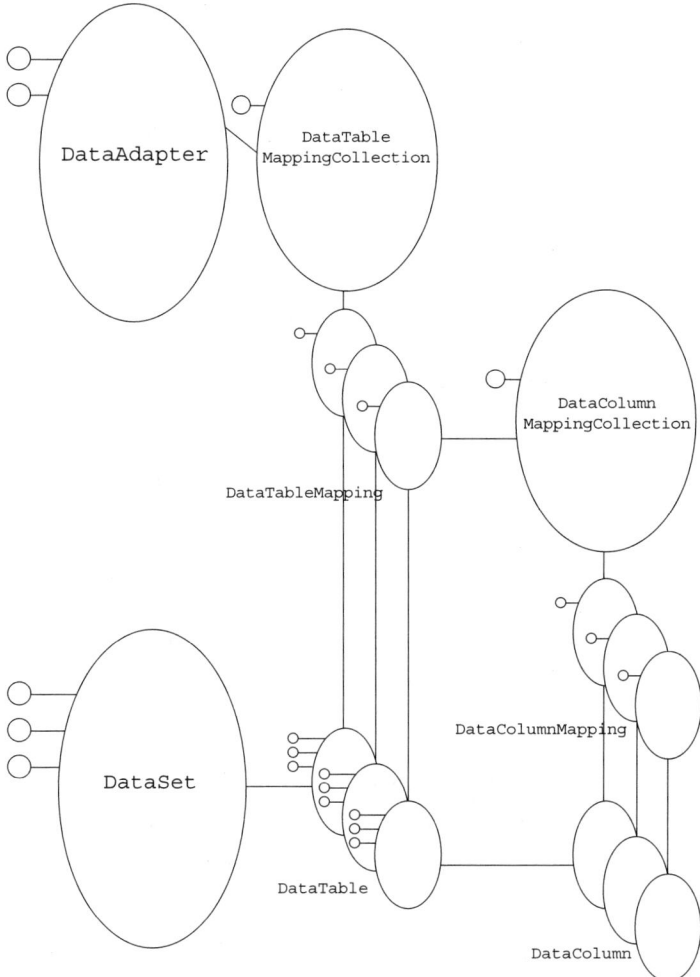

Figure 5–3 The `Mapping` classes in `DataSet`

`Schema` or `Mappings` provided, the results of `Fill` are determined by the `DataAdapter` properties `MissingMappingsAction` and `MissingSchemaAction`. If mappings are missing, the choices are `Passthrough` (the default), which uses the names from the data source; `Ignore`, which ignores the columns without mappings; and `Error`, which throws a `SystemException`.

One last additional item of metadata can be returned with `DataAdapter`. When you're using stored procedures or parameterized queries in `SelectCommand`, you can obtain the parameters by using the `DataAdapter.GetFillParameters` method. This returns a typed `ParametersCollection`. Listing 5–8 shows an example. Note that the parameters must already be set by the user before they can be retrieved using this method. This technique is useful when you don't know what the `DataAdapter`'s parameters are; perhaps the `DataAdapter` was passed to you, and you want to perform a parameterized update.

Listing 5–8   Getting the user's parameters

```
SqlDataAdapter da = new SqlDataAdapter(
  "select * from jobs where job_id > @jobid",
   "server=localhost;uid=sa;database=pubs");
DataSet ds = new DataSet();

da.SelectCommand.Parameters.Add(
  "@jobid", SqlDbType.TinyInt);
da.SelectCommand.Parameters[0].Value = 5;

da.Fill(ds, "jobs");
IDataParameter[] parms = da.GetFillParameters();
Console.WriteLine("user set {0} parms", parms.Length);
Console.WriteLine("parm0 value is {0}", parms[0].Value);
```

5.3.2   Error Handling during `DataAdapter.Fill`

During the execution of the `Fill` method, errors may arise. These are exposed by the `DbDataAdapter` base class by using a typed `FillError` event. The `FillError`-specific information is provided in the `FillErrorEventArgs` instance. Errors are caught by registering a `FillError` event handler with `DbDataAdapter` and are reported on a per-row basis. `FillErrorEventArgs` contains four properties, as shown in Listing 5–9.

Listing 5–9   The `FillErrorEventArgs` class

```
class FillErrorEventArgs : EventArgs
{
// should I continue?
public bool Continue {get; set;}
// which DataTable?
public DataTable DataTable {get;}
// what errors happened?
public Exception Errors {get; set;}
// array of row values for the error-causing row
public object[] Values {get;}
```

```
}
```

A common use for `FillErrorEventArgs` is to add logic to fix a row that would otherwise violate a `DataSet` constraint. Another use is to catch precision errors that occur with some data types. The most common error relates to `Decimal` data types with more than 28 digits of precision. Because the managed `System.Decimal` type permits only 28 digits of precision, a `System.OverflowException` will result. Database decimal values are often represented as having 38 digits of precision and can cause such errors if the actual value is that large. Listing 5–10 shows an example of using the `FillError` delegate. Note that you can also use a `FillError` delegate to catch `MissingSchemaError`s or `MissingMappingError`s that happen during `Fill`.

Listing 5–10   Handling errors on `Fill`

```
void doit()
{
  try
  {
    DataSet ds = new DataSet();
    ds.Tables.Add(new DataTable("emp"));

    // tinyint, too small for the values in this column
    ds.Tables[0].Columns.Add("empno", typeof(byte));

    OleDbDataAdapter da = new OleDbDataAdapter(
      "select * from emp",
      "provider=msdaora;data source=orcl1" +
      ";user id=scott;password=tiger");

    da.FillError += new FillErrorEventHandler(MyHandler);
    da.Fill(ds, "emp");
  }
  catch (Exception e)
  {
    Console.WriteLine(e.Message);
  }

}

public void MyHandler(
  object da, FillErrorEventArgs e)
{
```

```
    Console.WriteLine(e.Errors.Message);

    if (e.Errors.Message.StartsWith(
        "System.OverflowException"))
    {
      Console.WriteLine("value truncation has occurred");
      // if you want to ignore this error
      e.Continue = true;
    }
  }
```

5.4 How `DataAdapter.Fill` Works

After understanding what `DataAdapter.Fill` does in general, programmers invariably ask two questions: "What calls does it make to my data provider?" and, more directly, "What does it call inside my database?" These questions are an attempt to determine the overhead of using `DataAdapter.Fill` versus getting data through a `DataReader`, to determine whether to use one provider over another one, or even to determine whether to use a different data access API, such as ADO (classic) through COM interoperability. Because almost every data provider uses the same base classes (`DbDataAdapter` and `DataAdapter` in `System.Data.Common`), it is straightforward to determine which calls are made to the data provider. And because data providers can implement the data provider classes differently, and the underlying OLE DB provider or ODBC driver can implement the OLE DB interfaces or ODBC APIs differently, the question "What does it call inside my database?" cannot be answered specifically. It depends. In addition, as provider writers add functionality to the provider (or to the database) to enhance API functionality over time, the answer may change between data provider releases. With those caveats in mind, I attempt to answer the first question, and I use the `SqlClient` provider as an example to answer the second one. Chapter 8 talks about what the `OleDb` data provider does. It documents the procedure I used so that you can repeat the experiment going forward to new releases of ADO.NET.

IDataAdapter.Fill uses the underlying `Connection` and `Command` classes to retrieve the information. If the base class's implementation from `System.Data.Common` is used, it uses the underlying `DataReader` for fastest performance. As you can see by tracing through the data provider presented in Chapter 8, the implementation of `DataAdapter` in `System.Data.Common` uses `CommandBehavior.SequentialAccess` for ease in handling BLOB columns. Because `DataReader` can read only sequentially forward, BLOB columns must be read "inline"; there is no deferred fetch capability for them. The corresponding `DataReader`'s `GetSchemaTable` implementation is not called, so the extra metadata is not picked up.

A limited subset of metadata from the resultset is also propagated to the `DataSet`. Listing 5–11 shows how to fill a `DataTable` from a SQL statement using the `SqlClient` data provider, along with the corresponding `DataTable` properties produced. In addition to the subset of metadata that is fetched by default, metadata can be fetched separately by means of the `FillSchema` method. `FillSchema` has overloads similar to those of `Fill`, but it uses `CommandBehavior.SequentialAccess` or'd with `CommandBehavior.SchemaOnly` and `CommandBehavior.KeyInfo`. The returned information is used to populate the `DataTable` or `DataSet` specified by `FillSchema`.

Listing 5–12 shows the list of column properties that are populated by `FillSchema`. If key columns exist, the corresponding `PrimaryKey` constraint is populated in the `DataTable` columns. If there is no primary key constraint, but there is a column with a `UniqueConstraint`, this column is designated as the primary key. The information used by `FillSchema` is obtained by using the `DataReader`'s `GetSchemaTable`. Of course, this happens after the behavior of `Command.Execute` is changed so that it asks for more schema information than usual. When you're using commands that produce multiple resultsets, `FillSchema` gets schema information only for the first resultset. In this case, using `MissingSchemaAction.AddWithKey` is the preferred method. When you're using `FillSchema`, you can use either the `ColumnMappings` collection or the schema from the database, overwriting the `ColumnMappings`. You specify your choice in the second parameter to `FillSchema`, which is either `SchemaType.Mapped` or `SchemaType.Source`. Whether or not `FillSchema` or `MissingSchemaAction.FillWithKey` is used, inter-table properties, such as relationships, and metadata, such as foreign key constraints, are not propagated to the `DataSet`. There is an exception: When you're using hierarchical

OLE DB providers, such as the `MSDataShape` OLE DB provider, it does propagate relationships.

Listing 5–11 `DataColumn` **properties after** `DataAdapter.Fill` **is called**

```
SqlDataAdapter da = new SqlDataAdapter(
        "select * from jobs",
        "server=localhost;uid=sa;database=pubs");
DataSet ds = new DataSet();

da.Fill(ds, "jobs");

DataTable t = ds.Tables[0];
DataColumn[] kc = t.PrimaryKey;

// No primary key, though table actually has one
//
Console.WriteLine("{0} columns in key", kc.Length);

foreach (DataColumn c in t.Columns)
{
Console.WriteLine(c.AllowDBNull);    // always true
Console.WriteLine(c.AutoIncrement);  // always false
Console.WriteLine(c.ColumnName);     // correct
Console.WriteLine(c.DataType);       // correct
Console.WriteLine(c.DefaultValue);   // always empty
Console.WriteLine(c.Expression);     // always empty
Console.WriteLine(c.ExtendedProperties.Count); // 0
Console.WriteLine(c.MaxLength);      // always -1
Console.WriteLine(c.Ordinal);        // correct
Console.WriteLine(c.ReadOnly);       // always false
Console.WriteLine(c.Unique);         // always false
}
```

Listing 5–12 `DataColumn` **properties after** `DataAdapter.FillSchema` **is called**

```
SqlDataAdapter da = new SqlDataAdapter(
        "select * from jobs",
        "server=localhost;uid=sa;database=pubs");
DataSet ds = new DataSet();

da.FillSchema(ds, SchemaType.Source);

DataTable t = ds.Tables[0];
DataColumn[] kc = t.PrimaryKey;
```

```
// Correct primary key information
//
Console.WriteLine("{0} columns in key", kc.Length);

foreach (DataColumn c in t.Columns)
{
Console.WriteLine(c.AllowDBNull);      // correct
Console.WriteLine(c.AutoIncrement);    // correct
Console.WriteLine(c.ColumnName);       // correct
Console.WriteLine(c.DataType);         // correct
Console.WriteLine(c.DefaultValue);     // always empty
Console.WriteLine(c.Expression);       // always empty
Console.WriteLine(c.ExtendedProperties.Count); // 0
Console.WriteLine(c.MaxLength);        // correct
Console.WriteLine(c.Ordinal);          // correct
Console.WriteLine(c.ReadOnly);         // correct
Console.WriteLine(c.Unique);           // sometimes correct
}
```

If the `DataTable` already exists when `Fill` is called, the behavior depends on whether a primary key has been defined in the existing `DataTable`. If a primary key exists for the `DataTable`, the `Fill` method replaces the rows in the existing `DataTable`, matching by primary key. If no primary key exists in the `DataTable`, the new rows are appended to the existing `DataTable`.

Now let's look at what goes on behind the scenes in SQL Server. Again, because the implementation—both in the database and in the data provider—can change over time, depending on this behavior is similar to depending on the behavior of a private method in any .NET class—that is, risky. With the `SqlClient` provider, both `DataReader` and `DataAdapter` submit the same SQL command. For example, if your `CommandText` was `select * from jobs`, SQL Server would receive `exec sp_executesql N'select * from jobs'`. The system stored procedure `sp_executesql` is a convenient way to submit a command string to SQL Server, allowing for parameterization, which you'll look at in a moment. It takes a Unicode command string, which is executed. What is returned by SQL Server is a series of tabular data stream (TDS) packets of streaming mode (cursorless) output. (`SqlClient` contains its own TDS parser implemented in managed code.) The first packets are TDS *describe packets* that contain a limited set of metadata information about the following rows. This is reflected in the information contained in `DataReader.GetSche-maTable` and `DataTable`'s metadata. No information is returned about keys or about which underlying SQL Server tables produced the resultset.

There are two ways you can ask a data provider for extra metadata information. These do approximately the same thing in SQL Server. You can ask specifically for extra metadata by making a separate call to `SqlData-Adapter.FillSchema`. This call produces the following string in SQL Server:

```
"exec sp_executesql N' SET FMTONLY OFF;
SET NO_BROWSETABLE ON;
SET FMTONLY ON;
select * from jobs'"
```

If you change the `SqlDataAdapter`'s `MissingSchemaAction` from `Add` (the default) to `AddWithKey` and then call `SqlDataAdapter.Fill` in the original call, the following string is sent to SQL Server:

```
"exec sp_executesql N' SET FMTONLY OFF;
SET NO_BROWSETABLE ON;
select * from jobs'"
```

Effectively, you're using two SQL Server options: FMTONLY and NO_BROWSETABLE.

The FMTONLY option, as you might guess, tells SQL Server to return only the metadata and not the data itself. NO_BROWSETABLE is a bit more interesting. SQL Server lets you append a FOR BROWSE clause to SELECT statements. Usually, FOR BROWSE uses a temporary table to return keys, timestamps, and extra metadata that enables updating with optimistic concurrency. NO_BROWSETABLE, a variation on this theme, bypasses the temporary table, returning the extra metadata as part of the output stream. NO_BROWSETABLE is also used with both `MissingSchemaAction.AddWithKey` and `FillSchema` to retrieve extra metadata. NO_BROWSETABLE was also used by ADO and RDS for the same reason. Note that the difference in using `MissingSchemaAc-tion.AddWithKey` and using `FillSchema` is that `FillSchema` makes an extra round-trip just to get the metadata. On the other hand, filling the

`DataTable`'s schema "by hand" (that is, predefining the `DataTable` and `DataColumn` information) or doing without the extra metadata saves both the round-trip and the extra overhead of `NO_BROWSETABLE`.

5.5 ADO Integration in `OleDbDataAdapter`

Many programs written in ADO classic use commands to produce a `Recordset`. ADO `Recordset`s are most similar to ADO.NET's `DataTable`. Like a `DataTable`, an ADO `Recordset` can be produced from a database resultset or can be synthesized as data in a standalone class. As a conversion aid, the `OleDb` data provider exposes an overload of `Fill` that takes an ADO `Recordset` as input, rather than filling the `DataSet` through the `OleDbDataAdapter`'s `SelectCommand`.

In addition, ADO classic includes a `Record` class that is more lightweight and faster than using a `Recordset`. Think of the `Record` as a one-row `Recordset`. The `OleDbDataAdapter` method can also fill a `DataSet` from an ADO `Record` object using the same overload. When you call `Fill` with an ADO `Record` object, a `DataTable` containing a single `DataRow` is produced. Listing 5–13 shows an example of filling a `DataSet`'s `DataTable` from an ADO `Recordset` and `Record`.

Listing 5–13 Using `DataAdapter` with ADO `Recordset` and `Record`

```
DataSet ds = new DataSet();
ADODB.Recordset rs = new ADODB.Recordset();
rs.Open("select * from authors",
    "provider=sqloledb;uid=sa;database=pubs",
    CursorTypeEnum.adOpenForwardOnly,
    LockTypeEnum.adLockReadOnly, -1);

OleDbDataAdapter da = new OleDbDataAdapter();
da.Fill(ds, rs, "authors");

Console.WriteLine("{0} rows in authors table",
                  ds.Tables[0].Rows.Count);
// not needed, object is closed
//rs.Close();

ADODB.Record rec = new ADODB.Record();
rec.Open("select * from jobs where job_id = 10",
    "provider=sqloledb;uid=sa;database=pubs",
    ConnectModeEnum.adModeUnknown, // ignored by SQLOLEDB
```

```
RecordCreateOptionsEnum.adOpenIfExists, // also ignored
RecordOpenOptionsEnum.adOpenExecuteCommand, "", "");

da.Fill(ds, rec, "jobs");

Console.WriteLine("{0} rows in jobs table",
                  ds.Tables[1].Rows.Count);
// not needed, object is closed
//rec.Close();
```

Although `OleDbDataAdapter.Fill` can be used to populate a `DataSet`, there is no analogous method that fills an ADO object using a `DataSet` as input. Such code can be easily written and is available on the Web site for this book. Because the ADO `Recordset` is a functional subset of `DataTable`, the metadata in `DataTable` is more than sufficient to populate the `Recordset`. If only `Fill` is called, some pieces are missing from the `DataTable`. You can add them by using `MissingSchemaAction.AddWithKey` or calling `DataAdapter`'s `FillSchema` method.

5.6   Updating a Database through `DataAdapter`

The disconnected update pattern is a good choice when you have a single user per `DataSet`. The `DataSet` class supports this pattern of data access. Data is read into `DataSet` using `DataAdapter`. The `DataAdapter` class can sever the connection, and multiple updates can be made in disconnected mode. `DataSet` keeps a cache of these updates. The changes are visible immediately within `DataSet` itself but can be flushed back to a data store. Attempting to set a `DataColumn` to an incorrect value (for example, attempting to set a non-nullable column to `DB-Null.Value`) results in an error at column update time in `DataSet`, rather than when the change is flushed to a database. This means that by specifying constraints in the `DataSet` you can edit the data in disconnected mode.

By "the `DataSet` keeps a cache" I mean that, inside a `DataSet`, multiple versions of the same `DataRow` are available. They are specified by the `DataRowVersion` enumeration. `DataRows` originally inside the `DataSet` have a `DataRowVersion` of `DataRowVersion.Original`. When `BeginEdit` is called on a `DataRow`, the `DataRowVersion.Proposed` version becomes available, and changes are made to the `Proposed` version. When `EndEdit` is called, the

DataRowVersion.Proposed version of the row becomes the DataRow-Version.Current version. Whether EndEdit or CancelEdit is called, the DataRowVersion.Proposed version is deleted. When DataSet.AcceptChanges is called (it can be called at the DataRow, DataTable, or DataSet level), the changes are made to a DataRow in memory, and the Original and Current versions are synchronized.

DataAdapter is used to flush a set of changes back to the underlying data store, as shown in Listing 5–14. The data source that the changes are flushed to need not be the same data source that populated the DataSet originally, as long as the data types are the same and the appropriate UpdateCommand is used.

Listing 5–14   Updating through DataSet

```
SqlDataAdapter da = new SqlDataAdapter(
  "select * from authors",
  "server=localhost;uid=sa;database=pubs");
// command builder for default update commands
SqlCommandBuilder bld = new SqlCommandBuilder(da);
DataSet ds = new DataSet();
da.Fill(ds, "authors");

// update the fifth row, third column
ds.Tables[0].Rows[4][2] = "Bob";
// use the default update commands
da.Update(ds, "authors");
```

With optimistic concurrency, rows are not locked between the time they are read into DataSet and the time changes are flushed back to the database from DataSet. When changes are flushed back to the database, it is possible for someone else to have already changed the same row, causing your update to fail. DataAdapter checks for this by submitting the changes one row at a time and checking whether zero or one or more rows are affected. Zero rows affected means that there is a concurrency violation; one or more rows affected means that the update, insert, or delete was successful. DataSet accommodates reconciliation in this situation by keeping track of multiple copies of the same row. By using a specific DataRowVersion, you can deduce whether or not the row in the database has changed since you updated it and you can implement a conflict resolution strategy. These types of concurrency checking are most common when SQL is used:

- The changes will be flushed to the database as long as the row can be located by primary key.

- The changes will be flushed to the database as long as none of the columns updated by this user has been updated since the row was read.

- The changes will be flushed to the database as long as none of the columns in the entire row has been updated since the row was read.

- The changes will be flushed to the database as long as the row's timestamp column has not changed. The logic of this check is similar to that of the preceding case.

With databases such as SQL Server, the updates can be batched in client code and submitted as a single statement, although when you use `CommandBuilder` (discussed in the following section) the default `Command` does not do this. In the default case, updates are submitted one at a time, and the first update error results in an exception with the message "Concurrency error." This stops the series of updates unless the `DataAdapter`'s `ContinueUpdateOnError` property is set to `true`. Multiple updates can be transacted manually or by using declarative transactions through attributes. Transacted batches are not the default.

When `ContinueUpdateOnError` is set to `true`, an exception is not thrown when a concurrency error occurs. Instead, the `Update` method continues and attempts to update the rest of the rows involved. Error information is placed in the `RowError` property of the `DataRow`(s) involved, and the error can be examined after the `Update` completes. Listing 5–15 shows an example. Strategies to deal with the concurrency violation include presenting an error message to the user and canceling the change, or retrying the update based on new information retrieved from the database.

Listing 5–15   Using the `ContinueUpdateOnError` property

```
SqlDataAdapter da = new SqlDataAdapter(
  "select * from authors",
  "server=.;uid=sa;database=pubs");

/* stored procedure is:
 * create procedure DeleteAuthors(
 *   @au_id varchar(11))
 * as
 * delete authors from au_id = @au_id
```

```
  *
  */

da.DeleteCommand = new SqlCommand(
  "DeleteAuthors", da.SelectCommand.Connection);
da.DeleteCommand.CommandType =
  CommandType.StoredProcedure;

DataSet ds = new DataSet();
da.Fill(ds, "authors");

ds.Tables[0].Rows[4].Delete();
ds.Tables[0].Rows[5].Delete();

da.DeleteCommand.Parameters.Add(
  "@au_id",
  SqlDbType.VarChar, 11,
  "au_id");  // au_id is the source column
            // in the DataSet
da.DeleteCommand.Parameters[0].SourceVersion =
  DataRowVersion.Original;

// change value of the deleted row in the database here....
// this would normally cause a concurrency error
da.ContinueUpdateOnError = true;
da.Update(ds, "authors");

if (ds.Tables[0].HasErrors == true)
{
  DataRow[] dr = ds.Tables[0].GetErrors();
  Console.WriteLine("{0} rows not deleted", dr.Length);
}
```

In addition to flushing the cache to a database, you can apply or clear the cache manually. `DataSet.AcceptChanges` accepts all the `DataSet` changes en masse, and `AcceptChanges` can also be called on individual `DataTable`s or `DataRow`s. The `RejectChanges` method rolls back the `DataRow`, `DataTable`, or `DataSet` to the original state. `AcceptChanges` and `RejectChanges` happen in disconnected mode and are unrelated to database transactions. After `AcceptChanges` or `RejectChanges` is called, the rows affected are not flushed to the database the next time `Update` is called; instead, they are removed from the cache of pending rows.

5.6.1 The CommandBuilder Class

You can configure the flushing of changes to the database through the Update method by using the InsertCommand, UpdateCommand, and DeleteCommand objects of DataAdapter. Any command, including customized stored procedures, can be used. These commands are not auto-generated by the DataAdapter by default, and DataAdapter.Update will fail if the Commands do not exist when DataAdapter.Update is called. To provide an easy-to-use default mechanism by which the data provider can generate Commands from database metadata, data providers implement the CommandBuilder class.

SqlCommandBuilder and OleDbCommandBuilder use some of the same methods from a common class, CommandBuilder, in System.Data.Common. Microsoft's Odbc data provider also uses this class. To use a CommandBuilder, you simply instantiate it and fill in the member variable that indicates which DataAdapter it will generate Commands for. The most common way is to name a DataAdapter in the constructor, as shown in Listing 5–16.

Listing 5–16   Using CommandBuilder

```
SqlDataAdapter da = new SqlDataAdapter(
  "select * from jobs",
  "server=localhost;uid=sa;database=pubs");

// create a command builder over the DataAdapter
SqlCommandBuilder bld = new SqlCommandBuilder(da);
```

To use a CommandBuilder, you need not call any specific CommandBuilder methods in the program. When the DataAdapter property is set, CommandBuilder registers a RowUpdating event delegate and, when next you call DataAdapter.Update, generates command strings and parameters during this event. CommandBuilder does not populate the DataAdapter's InsertCommand, UpdateCommand, or DeleteCommand members at any time and does not overwrite (or override, at execution time) any commands that you have manually placed there. If you want to populate the DataAdapter's InsertCommand, UpdateCommand, or DeleteCommand members from CommandBuilder, you must call CommandBuilder.GetInsertCommand and friends, as shown in Listing 5–17.

Listing 5–17   Using `CommandBuilder` to populate `DataAdapter`

```
SqlDataAdapter da = new SqlDataAdapter(
    "select * from jobs",
    "server=localhost;uid=sa;database=pubs");

// create a command builder over the DataAdapter
SqlCommandBuilder bld = new SqlCommandBuilder(da);

// get the Commands
da.InsertCommand = bld.GetInsertCommand();
da.UpdateCommand = bld.GetUpdateCommand();
da.DeleteCommand = bld.GetDeleteCommand();
```

Notice that `CommandBuilder` actually collects metadata for building its commands only when you call `GetInsertCommand`, `GetUpdateCommand`, or `GetDeleteCommand` or when you call `DataAdapter.Update`. It does this based on the current value of `SelectCommand`. If `SelectCommand` is changed, you must call `CommandBuilder.RefreshSchema` to force `CommandBuilder` to rebuild the commands based on the new metadata in the new `SelectCommand`. This is shown in Listing 5–18.

Listing 5–18   Forcing `CommandBuilder` to rebuild commands

```
SqlDataAdapter da = new SqlDataAdapter(
    "select * from jobs",
    "server=localhost;uid=sa;database=pubs");

// create a command builder over the DataAdapter
SqlCommandBuilder bld = new SqlCommandBuilder(da);

// change the SelectCommand
da.SelectCommand.CommandText =
    "select * from employees";

// must force rebuild
bld.RefreshSchema();
```

`CommandBuilder`s generate update commands only on `DataTable`s that contain columns derived from a single database table. Currently, none of the `CommandBuilder`s supports building commands against a `SelectCommand` that contains a SQL `JOIN` statement. This table must contain a primary key or column that has the `Unique` attribute in the database. The column names and table name also cannot contain special characters, such as spaces and periods, although SQL multipart names using the period character as a delimiter are acceptable. You can work around this limitation with most special characters by setting CommandBuilder's QuotePrefix and QuoteSuffix, as shown in Listing 5–19.

Listing 5–19 Using table names containing spaces

```
SqlDataAdapter da = new SqlDataAdapter(
        "select * from [some table]",
        "server=;uid=sa;database=pubs");
DataSet ds = new DataSet();
da.Fill(ds);

SqlCommandBuilder bld = new SqlCommandBuilder(da);
bld.QuotePrefix = "[";
bld.QuoteSuffix = "]";

ds.Tables[0].Rows[0].Delete();

// if QuotePrefix and QuoteSuffix not set
// this Update would fail
da.Update(ds);
```

CommandBuilder generates parameterized updates if it is supported by the provider. Generated update commands update the database based on the premise that none of the columns in the entire row has been updated since the row was read. Listing 5–20 shows a sample update and the SQL statement produced by SqlCommandBuilder.

Listing 5–20 Update generated by SqlCommandBuilder

```
SqlDataAdapter da = new SqlDataAdapter(
  "select * from jobs where job_id > @jobid",
  "server=localhost;uid=sa;database=pubs");

// create a command builder over the DataAdapter
SqlCommandBuilder bld = new SqlCommandBuilder(da);

DataSet ds = new DataSet();

da.SelectCommand.Parameters.Add("@jobid", 10);
da.Fill(ds, "jobs");
```

```
// change from "old description" to "new description"
ds.Tables["jobs"].Rows[0][1] = "new description";
da.Update(ds, "jobs");

exec sp_executesql
N'UPDATE jobs SET job_desc = @p1 WHERE (
  (job_id = @p2) AND
  ((job_desc IS NULL AND @p3 IS NULL)
OR
  (job_desc = @p4)) AND
  ((min_lvl IS NULL AND @p5 IS NULL)
OR
  (min_lvl = @p6)) AND
  ((max_lvl IS NULL AND @p7 IS NULL)
OR
  (max_lvl = @p8)) )',

N'@p1 varchar(15),
@p2 smallint,
@p3 varchar(18),
@p4 varchar(18),
@p5 tinyint,
@p6 tinyint,
@p7 tinyint,
@p8 tinyint',

@p1 = 'new description',
@p2 = 11,
@p3 = 'old description',
@p4 = 'Operations Manager',
@p5 = 75,
@p6 = 75,
@p7 = 150,
@p8 = 150
```

I end this section with some comments about how CommandBuilders work by experimentation. As with my explanation of how DataAdapter.Fill works, this one is fraught with danger because CommandBuilder is a private class and implementation can change. Again, I use SqlCommandBuilder as an example, but because SqlCommandBuilder, OleDbCommandBuilder, and OdbcCommandBuilder contain an instance of System.Data.Common.CommandBuilder (they do not derive from a common base class), the others should work in a similar way. Chapter 8 explores what OLE DB providers must do to work properly with their CommandBuilder classes.

To use SqlCommandBuilder, you must ensure that the table contains a primary key. If the table contains a TIMESTAMP column but not a primary key, command generation will fail at Update time. If a primary key does not exist in the database, setting the PrimaryKey of the DataTable programmatically in the DataSet before or after it is populated will not make the update succeed. As with DataAdapter.Fill, the CommandBuilder always makes a single trip to the database to get table metadata using SET FMTONLY and SET NO_BROWSETABLE. If a database table has a timestamp column, this timestamp is not used. Deletes are the simplest and always use only the primary key. The Update statement, discussed earlier, always compares all the fields in a row to their original value.

Insert statements include all values except identity and timestamp columns. Actually, after the metadata is set into the DataTable, inserts exclude any DataColumn that has AutoIncrement=true, ReadOnly=true, RowVersion=true, or Hidden=true. Setting a DataColumn value to DBNull.Value results in NULL being sent to the database. Omitting the value of a field when inserting a DataRow also results in a NULL being sent to the database if CommandBuilder can determine that the column allows NULL values. If it is determined that the column does not support NULL values, an INSERT statement is composed with that column omitted. This allows database DEFAULT values to be inserted if you allow null to be inserted into the corresponding DataRow (i.e., the DataColumn's AllowDBNull property is set to true). Interestingly, setting a DefaultValue in the DataTable's DataColumn definition will result in the DataRow containing the default value (as a literal value, rather than using the SQL keyword DEFAULT), which is passed to the database.

As one last curious point of interest, if you set columns in the DataTable to the same value they had when they were fetched, CommandBuilder does not send an update command to the database. In addition, both SqlCommandBuilder and OleDbCommandBuilder take NULL values into consideration in generated update commands, both when changing values to NULL and when specifying values that are already NULL. In each case, the generated command takes into consideration the fact that the statement must specify IS NULL rather than "= NULL" according to the rules of SQL. CommandBuilder also is aware of TableMappings and ColumnMappings in the DataSet, and it updates using the DataTable's and DataColumn's (mapped) names from the DataSet but using the correct database table and column names in the generated commands. CommandBuilder doesn't work if you manually rename columns after the DataTable has been filled rather than use ColumnMappings.

During the development phase of a project, it is sometimes useful to automatically populate the Parameters collection of a Command based on database metadata that describe the parameters of a given stored procedure. This automatic population makes a round-trip to the database to determine the number and type of parameters, usually by querying the INFORMATION_SCHEMA.PARAMETERS view. The CommandBuilder class exposes this functionality through its DeriveParameters method. DeriveParameters can populate parameters for any correctly typed instance of a Command class, and not only the ones that would be automatically generated based on a DataSet's DataTable. Listing 5–21 shows an example of using DeriveParameters. Although this method is a convenient one to use during development or in programs that permit ad hoc invocation of arbitrary stored procedures, you should not use it in most production applications because of the performance penalty incurred by the extra database round-trip.

Listing 5–21 Using `DeriveParameters` with a stored procedure

```
SqlConnection conn = new SqlConnection(
    "server=.;uid=sa;database=pubs");
// DeleteAuthors is a stored procedure
SqlCommand cmd = new SqlCommand(
    "DeleteAuthors", conn);
cmd.CommandType = CommandType.StoredProcedure;

// the connection must be open for this to work
conn.Open();

// get the parameter information
SqlCommandBuilder bld = new SqlCommandBuilder();
SqlCommandBuilder.DeriveParameters(cmd);
```

```
// print parameter info
foreach (SqlParameter p in cmd.Parameters)
{
Console.WriteLine(
  "parm name is {0}", p.ParameterName);
Console.WriteLine(
  "parm type is {0}", p.SqlDbType.ToString());
Console.WriteLine(
  "parm length is {0}", p.Size);
}
```

5.6.2 Coding Update Logic Directly

The InsertCommand, UpdateCommand, and DeleteCommand members of DataSet are completely customizable. As shown in Listing 5–22, you specify a parameterized statement or stored procedure and then select which version of the row is to be used in the parameter. You can use custom update commands to flush the cache to a different table from the one that originally produced it or to enable inserts, updates, and deletes of multiple tables from a single DataRow update.

Listing 5–22   Specifying row version

```
// set the delete command's parameter
da.DeleteCommand.CommandText =
  "update customers set del_flag = 'D' " +
  "where custid = @CUSTID";

// add the parameter based on original name
da.DeleteCommand.Parameters.Add(
  new SqlParameter(
            "@CUSTID",
            SqlDbType.VarChar,
            6,
            ParameterDirection.Input,
            true,
            0,0,
            "",
            DataRowVersion.Original,
            "CustId"));
```

The default behavior of `DataAdapter.Update` is to invoke an insert, update, or delete command, as specified in the `DataAdapter`'s `Command` members, for each row changed. It is possible for a `Command` to return output parameters (in the case of a stored procedure) or a resultset or both. `Command` classes contain a member variable, `UpdatedRowSource`, that affects how (and whether) this output information is used to refresh the `DataRow` in the `DataSet`. The choices are as follows:

- `None`: No information is changed in the `DataSet` by the results of the `Command`.

- `Output parameters`: This maps output parameters to the updated `DataRow`.

- `FirstReturnedRecord`: This maps the column values in the first record returned in a resultset to the updated `DataRow`.

- `Both`: This maps output parameters and the column values in the first record returned in a resultset. This is the default.

This technique is effective only when you use parameterized commands or when the stored procedure contains an extra SELECT statement to select the newly updated row. Each `Parameter` in a `Command`'s `Parameters` collection can specify a `SourceColumn` and a `SourceVersion`. The `SourceColumn` parameter in this method call refers to a `DataColumn` in the `DataTable` being updated. This `SourceColumn` must map back to an actual `DataColumn` in the `DataTable`, or else a `SystemException` will occur. The only time this need not be specified is if `MissingMappingAction = Passthrough` and the name of the `Parameter` or resultset column is the same as the name in the `DataTable`.

When coding your own update commands, you can implement optimistic concurrency by any of the means discussed here. Because `CommandBuilder` already implements the method that compares all the row values, I present implementations of two of the other three versions. This will also help in solidifying the `UpdatedRowSource` and `Parameter` choices discussed earlier. We'll also try to specify generalized commands inline rather than catch the update events and construct each command on-the-fly. The latter technique is discussed in a few pages.

Listing 5–23 shows a simple optimistic update that updates all the columns based on your cached value of the row, whether or not you have updated each column. This technique writes over any changes made by others to the row; it's a "last writer wins" implementation. Note that, although you would like to change only the value of the columns you have changed in the data row, this is not possible. That's because each row to be updated might have different columns that are changed. This is an immediate drawback of hard-coding an update command.

Listing 5–23 Simple hand-generated update command

```
try
{
  SqlDataAdapter da = new SqlDataAdapter(
    "select * from jobs",
    "server=localhost;uid=sa;database=pubs");

  DataSet ds = new DataSet();
  da.Fill(ds, "jobs");

  ds.Tables[0].Rows[0][1] = "Vice Chairman";

  // generate update command - overwrite all columns
  // check concurrency by key only
  SqlCommand updatecmd = new SqlCommand();
  updatecmd.Connection = da.SelectCommand.Connection;

  updatecmd.CommandText = "update jobs set " +
    "job_desc = @newdesc, " +
    "min_lvl = @newmin, " +
    "max_lvl = @newmax" +
    " where job_id = @jobid";
  // add parms
  SqlParameter[] parms = new SqlParameter[4];
  parms[0] = new SqlParameter(
            "@newdesc", SqlDbType.VarChar, 50);
  parms[1] = new SqlParameter(
            "@newmin", SqlDbType.TinyInt);
  parms[2] = new SqlParameter(
            "@newmax", SqlDbType.TinyInt);
  parms[3] = new SqlParameter(
            "@jobid", SqlDbType.SmallInt);

  int i;
```

```
for (i=0;i<4;i++)
  updatecmd.Parameters.Add(parms[i]);

for (i=0;i<3;i++)
{
  parms[i].SourceVersion = DataRowVersion.Current;
  parms[i].SourceColumn =
    ds.Tables[0].Columns[i+1].ColumnName;
}

// we want original column for key
parms[3].SourceVersion = DataRowVersion.Original;
parms[3].SourceColumn = "job_id";

da.UpdateCommand = updatecmd;
da.Update(ds, "jobs");
}
catch (Exception e)
{
  Console.WriteLine("Type: {0}, Message: {1}",
    e.GetType(), e.Message);
}
```

The last version uses a single timestamp column, rather than all the column values, to ensure that no one has changed the row since you fetched it. This logic is similar to that of the command generated by `CommandBuilder` except that it is shorter and executes faster on the database. Note that you still must change every column value, as in the preceding example. Listing 5–24 shows the use of a timestamp with SQL Server.

Listing 5–24   Using a timestamp to construct an update command
```
/* SQL Server table definition
create table tabwithts (
id int primary key,
name varchar(11) not null,
age int not null,
ts timestamp)
*/

// update starts here...
SqlDataAdapter da = new SqlDataAdapter(
    "select * from tabwithts",
```

```
    "server=localhost;uid=sa;database=pubs");

DataSet ds = new DataSet();
da.Fill(ds, "tabwithts");
ds.Tables[0].Rows[0][1] = "Grand Wazoo";

// generate update command for all columns
// check concurrency by timestamp
SqlCommand updatecmd = new SqlCommand();
updatecmd.Connection = da.SelectCommand.Connection;

updatecmd.CommandText = "update tabwithts set " +
  "name = @newname, " +
  "age = @newage " +
  "where id = @oldid and ts = @oldts";

// add parms
SqlParameter[] parms = new SqlParameter[4];
parms[0] = new SqlParameter(
  "@newname", SqlDbType.VarChar, 11);
parms[1] = new SqlParameter("@newage", SqlDbType.Int);
parms[2] = new SqlParameter("@oldid", SqlDbType.Int);
parms[3] = new SqlParameter("@oldts", SqlDbType.Binary);

int i;
for (i=0;i<4;i++)
    updatecmd.Parameters.Add(parms[i]);

for (i=0;i<2;i++)
{
  parms[i].SourceVersion = DataRowVersion.Current;
  parms[i].SourceColumn =
      ds.Tables[0].Columns[i+1].ColumnName;
}

// we want original column for key and timestamp
parms[2].SourceVersion = DataRowVersion.Original;
parms[2].SourceColumn = "id";
parms[3].SourceVersion = DataRowVersion.Original;
parms[3].SourceColumn = "ts";

da.UpdateCommand = updatecmd;
da.Update(ds, "tabwithts");
```

You haven't yet set `UpdatedRowSource` to any value other than `None` because you didn't want to retrieve anything from the UPDATE command. You'd always want to do this when you're INSERTing a row with an identity column. Listing 5–25 shows a simple example of using a stored procedure to do this. The stored procedure simply retrieves the identity column for you and passes it back in an output parameter. You must use `UpdateRowSource.Output-Parameters`, and I've directly specified it rather than rely on `Both`, which is the default and would also work.

Listing 5–25 Using `InsertCommand` to retrieve an identity column

```
/* SQL Server stored procedure for INSERT
create procedure insert_job
(
@jobdesc varchar(50),
@minlvl tinyint,
@maxlvl tinyint,
@jobid   smallint output
)
as
insert jobs values(@jobdesc, @minlvl, @maxlvl)
select @jobid = @@identity
*/

// code to use it...
SqlDataAdapter da = new SqlDataAdapter(
  "select * from jobs",
  "server=localhost;uid=sa;database=pubs");

DataSet ds = new DataSet();
da.Fill(ds, "jobs");

ds.Tables["jobs"].Rows.Add(
  new Object[4] {null, "New Job", 20, 30});

SqlCommand insertcmd = new SqlCommand();
insertcmd.Connection =
  da.SelectCommand.Connection;

insertcmd.CommandText = "insert_job";
insertcmd.CommandType =
  CommandType.StoredProcedure;

SqlParameter[] parms = new SqlParameter[4];
```

```
parms[0] = new SqlParameter(
  "@jobdesc", SqlDbType.VarChar, 50);
parms[1] = new SqlParameter(
  "@minlvl", SqlDbType.TinyInt);
parms[2] = new SqlParameter(
  "@maxlvl", SqlDbType.TinyInt);
parms[3] = new SqlParameter(
  "@jobid", SqlDbType.SmallInt);

int i;
for (i=0;i<4;i++)
    insertcmd.Parameters.Add(parms[i]);

for (i=0;i<3;i++)
{
  parms[i].SourceVersion = DataRowVersion.Current;
  parms[i].SourceColumn =
    ds.Tables[0].Columns[i+1].ColumnName;
}

parms[3].SourceVersion = DataRowVersion.Current;
parms[3].SourceColumn = "job_id";
parms[3].Direction = ParameterDirection.Output;

insertcmd.UpdatedRowSource =
  UpdateRowSource.OutputParameters;
da.InsertCommand = insertcmd;
da.Update(ds, "jobs");

// Get the job_id for the last row added.
DataRow r = ds.Tables[0].Rows[ds.Tables[0].Rows.Count-1];
Console.WriteLine("added job_id {0}", r["job_id"]);
```

5.7 How Update Works

Calling the DbDataAdapter.Update method triggers a series of steps to update the database with changes made to the object specified (DataTable, on a per-row basis). The sequence of events is as follows:

1. The values in the DataRow are moved to the parameter values.

2. The OnRowUpdating event is raised.

3. The command executes.

4. If the command is set to `FirstReturnedRecord`, then the first returned result is placed in the `DataRow`.

5. If there are output parameters, they are placed in the `DataRow`.

6. The `OnRowUpdated` event is raised.

7. `AcceptChanges` is called.

5.7.1 Controlling Updates

The `DataAdapter.Update` method, when applied to a `DataSet`, applies inserts, updates, and deletes in a predefined order. Sometimes, when rows from multiple tables are inserted or updated, this may not be the order that you want. For example, if you update or insert a `DataRow` containing the "parent" of a parent-child relationship, the change to the parent should occur in the database before any of the changes to the children. You have fine-grained control over the `Update` process in at least three ways.

First, the granularity of `Update` is controlled by the overload that is used. `Update` can be called on an array of `DataRow`s (obviously including a single `DataRow`), a single `DataTable` (either directly or by naming the `DataTable` in a `DataSet`), or an entire `DataSet`. If you wish to define actions to take place in a specific order, this is a usable (but labor-intensive) method.

You can check for the appropriate `RowVersion` using `HasVersion` to arrange groups of database actions—for example, all INSERTS, followed by all UPDATES. Listing 5–26 demonstrates how to use `HasVersion` to group INSERTS before UPDATES.

Listing 5–26 Using versions to change the order of INSERTS

```
DataSet ds;
SqlDataAdapter da;
// Initialization elided..

// Later...
// Go through all rows looking
// for rows with the correct version
// Update these first.
// Added rows don't have an Original version
DataRow[] nr = new DataRow[1];
foreach (DataRow r in ds.Tables[0].Rows)
   if (!r.HasVersion(DataRowVersion.Original))
```

```
  {
    nr[0] = r;
    da.Update(nr);
  }

// Now update the rest...
da.Update(ds, "jobs");
```

You can use the event model to catch and control updates. You can use it before the update—for example, to affect the update command—or afterward to control execution in case one update of a batch fails.

Groups of updates can also be composed within a database transaction by establishing a `Connection`, calling `Connection.BeginTransaction`, and using the `Connection` instance (and associated `Transaction`) in the `DataAdapter`'s `Constructor`.

5.8 The `DataSet` Event Model

The `DataTable` class has an event model that permits you to catch inserts, updates, and deletes when they occur in the `DataTable`. The `DataRowChanged` delegate is used for this. You can cancel inserts, change columns, or tag each `DataRow` with a row-specific error message through the `RowError` class. This process, discussed in Chapter 4, occurs inside the `DataSet` before an attempt is made to update the database.

You can further customize the update process by using the event model in `DataAdapter`. When `DataAdapter.Update` is called, `RowUpdating` and `RowUpdated` events are fired for each `DataRow` that has changes. You can catch `RowUpdating` events and refine, change, or cancel the updates on a per-`DataRow` basis. As shown in Listing 5–27, you can use this method for simple editing at update time or for enforcing business rules.

Listing 5–27 Using a `RowUpdating` handler
```
public static void MyHandler(
     object adapter,SqlRowUpdatingEventArgs e)
{
if (e.StatementType == StatementType.Update)
        {
        // Set Command Text and Type
```

```
e.Command.CommandText =
    "Insert into DeletedCustomers (CustId)" +
    " values(@CustId)";
e.Command.CommandType = CommandType.Text;

// Set up Parameter
e.Command.Parameters.Clear();
e.Command.Parameters.Add(
    new SqlParameter("@CustId",SqlDbType.Int,4 ));

// Set Parameter Value from DataRow
e.Command.Parameters["@CustId"].Value =
    e.Row["CustId",DataRowVersion.Original];
    }
}
```

One good use for `RowUpdated` event delegates is to examine the results returned from individual update statements. Usually, a single error in a batch of database updates stops the batch at that point. Although you can override this by setting the `DataAdapter`'s `ContinueUpdateOnError` property to `true`, you can gain finer granularity by catching the `RowUpdated` event. If `RowUpdated` indicates an error, the error can be retained but the batch allowed to continue. Listing 5–28 shows how to implement this by setting the `Update-Status` to `UpdateStatus.SkipCurrentRow`. You can decide whether to set this status on a row-by-row basis. Another use for `UpdateStatus.SkipCurrentRow` is to prevent `AcceptChanges` from being called on a specific row when you're performing an insert that contains an identity or autonumber column. The column's value may have been determined during the insert and may now differ from the original value in `DataSet`.

Listing 5–28 Turning off errors during a batch

```
public static void MyUpdateMethod()
{
SqlDataAdapter da = new SqlDataAdapter();

//.... hook up RowUpdated event handler
da.RowUpdated += new SqlRowUpdatedEventHandler( MyHandler );
}

public static void MyHandler(
```

```
                object adapter,SqlRowUpdatedEventArgs e)
{
    // depending on type of statement...
    switch(e.StatementType)
    {
        case StatementType.Delete:
            // catch an error
            // do something and turn off the error
            if (e.Status ==
UpdateStatus.ErrorsOccurred)
            {
             e.Status = UpdateStatus.SkipCurrentRow;
            }
            break;
    }
}
```

You can use `RowUpdating` events to construct SQL UPDATE commands that implement concurrency checking based on changes in only the columns changed in the data row. Like `CommandBuilder`, the event handler would intercept the update and construct a custom UPDATE statement for each row updated. The statement constructed would be different in that only the changed columns and the primary key columns would be included in the SQL WHERE clause. This code is available on this book's Web site.

5.8.1 Refreshing `DataSet` Using `Update` and `Merge`

When working with a cache of data in disconnected mode, you might want to use the easiest way possible (and the least expensive on the database) to refresh the data every so often. In addition, after updating a row you may want to refresh the individual row you just updated. This is especially useful if there are business rules in stored procedures or calculated values that might change based on your update or other users' updates. The `DataAdapter` and `DataSet` model gives you two ways to refresh your data.

When updating individual rows through `DataAdapter`, you can use update batches or stored procedures that contain SQL to select the row immediately after you have updated it. This gives you a granular refresh mechanism. Using `Command.UpdatedRowSource`, you map the data in the first row returned to the row that you just updated. Listing 5–29 shows an alternative version of the stored procedure; this version returns the entire row when a row with an identity column is inserted. Note that the default behavior of `UpdatedRowSource` is to map both the stored procedure output parameter and the first row if a `CommandBuilder` is not used. If a `CommandBuilder` is used, the default is to map nothing (value `UpdatedRowSource.None`).

Listing 5–29 Returning an entire row after an update

```
/* SQL Server stored proc
create procedure insert_job2
(
@jobdesc varchar(50),
@minlvl tinyint,
@maxlvl tinyint
)
as
insert jobs values(@jobdesc, @minlvl, @maxlvl)
select * from jobs where job_id = @@identity
*/

//...use it
SqlDataAdapter da;
SqlCommand insertcmd;
DataSet ds;

insertcmd.UpdatedRowSource =
  UpdateRowSource.FirstReturnedRecord;
da.InsertCommand = insertcmd;
da.Update(ds, "jobs");

DataRow r =
  ds.Tables[0].Rows[ds.Tables[0].Rows.Count-1];
Console.WriteLine("added job_id {0}", r["job_id"]);
```

If you need to refresh an entire `DataTable` when the `DataSet` contains multiple data tables or need to refresh only portions of a `DataTable`, one way is to use `DataSet.Merge`. You can obtain a refreshed copy of a single table or portions of it and merge the changes on the middle tier or client. One of the most common uses for `DataSet.Merge` is to refresh a portion of a `DataSet` after an update. This approach is especially useful when you make the update on the middle tier using a `DataSet` containing only changed rows from a "master" `DataSet` on the client. You produce such a `DataSet` by calling `DataSet.GetChanges`. When the changes have been made and any optimistic concurrency issues are taken care of, you can marshal the changes-only `DataSet` back to the client and merge the changed rows back into the original `DataSet`. Listing 5–30 shows an example of this technique. If the cache is shared by more than one user and further changes may have been made in the interim, you can keep the interim changes by using `DataSet.Merge` and specifying `PreserveChanges=True`.

Listing 5–30 Using a merge to write back changes

```
SqlDataAdapter da;
// Initialize DataAdapter elided..

DataSet ds1 = new DataSet("target");
DataSet ds2;

da.Fill(ds1, "jobs");

// change something here
ds1.Tables[0].Rows[6]["min_lvl"] = 130;
ds1.Tables[0].Rows[7]["min_lvl"] = 130;

// get changes and update from ds2
ds2 = ds1.GetChanges();
da.Update(ds2, "jobs");

// merge final changes back into ds1
ds1.Merge(ds2, false);
ds1.AcceptChanges();
```

5.9 Writing General Customized Commands

Because the `CommandBuilder` provided in `System.Data.Common` has only a single concurrency behavior, it would be nice to be able to reuse the command generating functionality in this class to build custom `CommandBuilder` classes that derive from `System.Data.Common.CommandBuilder`. Unfortunately, this class is currently private and sealed, making the code unavailable for reuse. `Command-Builder`'s `CommandText` is not available until you call `DataAdapter.Update`; however, you can also retrieve it by using `CommandBuilder`'s `GetInsertCommand`, `GetUpdateCommand`, or `GetDeleteCommand` method. It is relatively straightforward to implement custom command patterns in your own delegates or to refine the pregenerated commands. Let's look at a couple of examples.

5.9.1 The ADOX `CommandBuilder`

This method lets you define a table that doesn't exist in the database. ADOX is an extension to ADO to build data definition language statements based on a programmatic API. OLE DB and ADO programmers who have gotten used to using OLE DB's `ITableDefiniton` and ADOX for convenience have missed the equivalent functionality in the .NET data access stack. Microsoft has announced that a future version of ADO.NET will contain similar functionality, but for now, you can roll your own.

For defining tables and primary keys, it is fairly easy to do. First, determine whether the table that you're going to update already exists in the database: Either perform a `SELECT` statement and catch the "table does not exist" error, or catch errors in the `RowUpdated` event. Then, using the properties from the `DataTable` to be updated, construct a DDL statement using `ColumnProperties` and simple data type mappings. This technique allows you to use `DataAdapter.Update` to add rows to a table from the `DataSet` whether or not it already exists.

5.9.2 Building a Batch `Update Command`

Programmers who do a large batch of disconnected updates can realize a significant performance gain when executing multiple SQL statements in a single batch. When you use `DataAdapter`'s `Update` method, each updated row constitutes a separate round-trip to the database. Although you could construct a long batch of SQL programmatically in code, it is convenient to reuse the statements created by the .NET `CommandBuilders` classes.

To do this, you intercept the `RowUpdatingEvent` and concatenate the update commands and `Parameters` collections. The way in which the batching is implemented means that you must cancel each command (by using the `RowUpdatingEventArgs.Status` field) except the last one in the list. But how do you know which `Command` is the last one? You can determine this by using an instance variable that contains the number of rows to be updated. The total number of rows to be updated is the rows that can be obtained using the `DataViewRowState` and filtering through `DataViews`. Follow these steps:

1. Use a `DataViewRowState` of `Added` to obtain the number of rows to be added.
2. Use a `DataViewRowState` of `ModifiedOriginal` to obtain the number of rows to be updated.
3. Use a `DataViewRowState` of `Deleted` to obtain the number of rows to be deleted.

Another technique for counting rows to be updated is to use the version of the `DataTable.Select` method that takes a `DataViewRowState` parameter. The code for a batch update is available on the book's Web site.

5.10 `DataSet`s and Nonrelational Data Types Revisited

In Chapter 4, you learned about using nonrelational data types, such as `Object`, with `DataSet`. There I note that `DataColumn` supports only a certain subset of data types. `Object` is not among them, although you can define and use a `DataColumn` of type `Object` (or `Person`) with only minor difficulties. In this chapter you've started using `DataSet` with nonrelational types by virtue of using `SqlDataAdapter`, which supports SQL Server's `SQL_VARIANT` type. The data type mappings in Appendix A map this data type to the CLR type `Object`.

The `SQL_VARIANT` data type was added to SQL Server to support the use of OLE DB providers such as the Exchange OLE DB Provider, which exposes heterogeneous hierarchies and heterogeneous data types in a single column. Listing 5–31 shows the use of the `SQL_VARIANT` data type with the `SqlClient` provider. Note that, although `SQL_VARIANT` implies multiple pieces of information (actual data type and actual value), you cannot get these pieces separately. In addition to the nonrelational `SQL_VARIANT`, SQL Server exposes some data types that are not explicitly supported by `DataColumn`, such as `SqlDbType.Timestamp` and `SqlDbType.Guid`.

Listing 5–31 Using a nonrelational data type

```
/* Create a table with a nonrelational data type
   SQL_VARIANT is a multivalued type
create table nonrel (
 id int primary key,
 name varchar(11),
 varcol sql_variant)
```

```
insert into nonrel values(1, 'bob', 'astring')
insert into nonrel values(2, 'fred', 42)
*/

// ...use it
SqlDataAdapter da = new SqlDataAdapter(
    "select * from nonrel",
    "server=localhost;uid=sa;database=pubs");
SqlCommandBuilder bld = new SqlCommandBuilder(da);
DataSet ds = new DataSet();

da.Fill(ds);

// data type is "Object"
Console.WriteLine("col2 datatype is " +
  ds.Tables[0].Columns[2].DataType);


ds.Tables[0].Rows[1][2] = "anotherstring";
da.Update(ds);

// updated correctly
Console.WriteLine("row 1, column 2 = " +
  ds.Tables[0].Rows[1][2]);
```

Using a nonrelational data type in this context depends more on the capabilities of the data provider or OLE DB provider than on any special capabilities of `DataSet`. Both the fetch (`Fill`) and the update (`Update`) particulars are controlled by the data provider. You'll look at this topic more in reference to `DataSet` as we go on. For now, this means that nonrelational data types are usable only if support for them is built into the underlying `DataAdapter`.

5.11   Should You Use `DataSet` or `DataReader`?

A contentious issue among programmers is when to use `DataReader` and when to use `DataAdapter` and `DataSet`. As almost always, the answer is, "It depends." Let's look at the consequences of using each and the situations in which you might prefer one or the other. Again, we'll use SQL Server as the sample data store.

`DataReader` is a lightweight stream of data that can be read into an array. `DataTable` simply provides the array and captures the TDS describe packets to populate the data type. As discussed earlier in this chapter, neither one lets you preallocate the array because the number of rows that will be returned (at least in the case of SQL Server) is unknown when a SELECT statement returns. It is not known until after you've read all the rows. You've also seen that `SqlDataAdapter` and `SqlData-Reader` make exactly the same calls to the database. `SqlDataAdapter` actually uses the lightweight `CommandBehavior.SequentialAccess`. Because the data is being streamed forward, you can't defer the fetching of a BLOB column using `SqlDataReader` or `SqlDataAdapter`; you can either read the data or skip it.

`SqlDataReader` permits you to read one row of data at a time (modulo TDS buffering), do some processing, and throw the row away (or write over it with the next row), saving memory on the middle tier or client. In a middle-tier situation, doing middle-tier processing while reading—with an open connection to the database—is potentially wasting a precious shared resource: database connections. On the other hand, retrieving an array of rows into `DataTable` when you could process them one at a time is potentially wasting a different precious shared resource: memory on the middle tier. Because the point of a middle-tier or client-server architecture is to balance processing on the database and outside the database, if `DataTables` are relatively small the improvement in database throughput may offset middle-tier memory usage.

As opposed to `DataReader` classes that are optimized by the provider writer, `DataSet` is a collection class that you can optimize if you know where to look. `DataTable` has a `MinimumCapacity` property that you can use to optimize performance if you know that a large number of rows will be fetched. By default, `DataTable` allocates space for 25 rows, and subsequent allocations would use time. In addition, if you do not use all the facilities of `DataSet`—such as `Relations`, marshaling, and XML integration—using the more lightweight `DataTable` as a standalone object may better suit your needs.

It has been postulated that using `SqlDataReader` allows you to quickly spin through a resultset and extract only pieces of data of interest, something that's analogous to using a Simple API for XML (SAX) parser to parse a large XML document rather than read it into a DOM. Although this technique may be a good choice when you're using XML, with a database such subsetting should be done in the SELECT using the database engine. Fetching a lot of data from a database, only to throw most of it away on the client, is wasteful of database and network resources. It's best to SELECT only what you need.

If you're going to fetch data quickly and use it quickly, there is no need to replicate the relational model of data access in the middle tier using a DataSet. Setting it up costs overhead that you may not need. In addition, if you're going to copy it quickly into Web Forms components for a single use (as discussed in Chapter 6), there is no need to make an extra copy of the data. If the DataSet is directly bound to a Windows Forms form or DataGrid control, however, the story is completely different because the DataSet is directly updatable. Finally, when multiple users can use data in a cache or you can use multiple views of the same data, using DataSet makes perfect sense.

5.12 Where Are We?

After learning how DataSet can be used as a standalone, relational cache, you've gone on in this chapter to investigate a method for using DataSet with a data-provider-specific DataAdapter to implement disconnected database caching and updating based on optimistic concurrency. You've gone through several optimistic update scenarios and common solutions, including that provided by default through the CommandBuilder class. Although DataSet is relational, the exact semantics of using it with a database (relational or nonrelational) is based on how the data provider's DataAdapter class is implemented, especially in mapping database data types to CLR types in DataSet.

You'll go on from here to look at two types of data access in .NET: binding data to graphical user interface components and using data access with XML, a format used in .NET for data access, data representation, and marshaling.

Chapter 6

Data Binding: ADO.NET and Graphical User Interfaces

One of ADO.NET's design goals is ease of use with graphical user interfaces. The model contains built-in binding to ASP.NET controls.

6.1 Windows Forms and Web Forms

The previous chapters have discussed issuing commands to a database, retrieving data from a database, caching the data using `DataSet`, passing the data around, and updating the database when the data is changed by a client. This chapter completes the picture by discussing how to present data to the user. The .NET framework supports two presentation mechanisms:

- Windows Forms provide a graphical rendering of local data using the Windows operating system user interface and controls such as list boxes and radio buttons. This mechanism has the highest fidelity—that is, the output looks like a Windows program and follows the Windows style guidelines. Windows Forms classes live in `System.Windows.Forms`.

- Web Forms is a form paradigm that is similar in appearance to Windows Forms to the programmer but renders HTML instead of windows and buttons. The HTML is then sent over the wire to a browser. The data classes exist only in Web server processes, and only an HTML representation of the data is sent to the client. The Web Forms classes live in `System.Web.UI` and its associated namespaces. Web Forms are part of ASP.NET.

Figure 6–1 compares the two approaches. Although the location of the controls in the geography of the application is different, the controls and data binding mechanisms are similar.

6.2 Patterns of Data Presentation

The ADO.NET infrastructure supports the most commonly used methods of data presentation without the need to write custom code. *Single-record* presentation

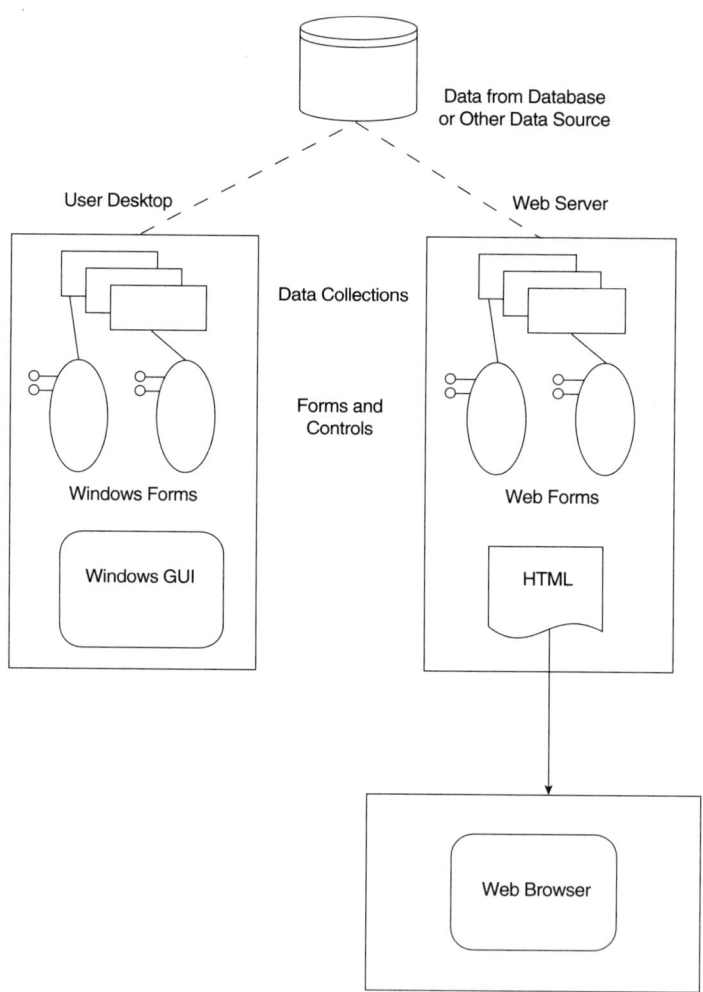

Figure 6–1 Comparison of Windows Forms and Web Forms

displays one record of data at a time. A single record might contain data from more than one table or even more than one data store. Data can be locked, pessimistically or optimistically, while being presented. You implement insert, update, and delete using discrete SQL statements. With the ADO.Net infrastructure and single-record presentation, you can, for example, display user account information on a Web page or a PC screen using approximately the same code.

Scrolling-rowset presentation displays data in a grid. User changes to rows are sent to the database a single row at a time when the user changes the selection from the changed row to some other row. This approach is suited mainly to desktop DBMS, where the data is owned by a single user and located on that user's desktop. Optimistic locking or file locking (in which a user locks the entire database) is typically used.

A compromise exists between the single record and scrolling rowset styles. This is called *batch optimistic concurrency*. The user can be presented with a grid of unlocked, updatable data. A single update does not flush to the data store. When the user finishes, updates are implemented through a single batch of SQL statements. The application must resolve any conflicts that occur when the update attempts to change a record that has been updated since the application read it.

ADO.NET provides direct support for different presentation styles. It supports discrete SQL statements through the data provider's `Command` object, including parameterized queries and multiple results. Support for scrollable, updatable rowsets is not provided through support of server cursors, as in other data access APIs. (In fact, this model is deprecated, and server cursor support must be implemented through custom data providers.) Instead, ADO.NET exposes cursor-like functionality through `DataSet`, used with pessimistic or optimistic concurrency and, as you'll see in Chapter 7, in `XPathNavigator`. Support for the compromise is provided by `DataAdapter` used in conjunction with `DataSet`. The latter two models are facilitated by generalization in the data binding architecture.

6.3 Using Databound Controls

Both Windows Forms and ASP.NET Web Forms support a data binding architecture. As in past APIs, such as the OLE DB data control architecture, data binding is defined as part of the control architecture in .NET. The major data binding improvement is an increase in the number of classes that can bind data. In Visual Basic 6, for example, a `DataSource` property must point to an actual data access component, usually a `Recordset`; in .NET data binding, any data can be used. Using `DataTable` (the .NET equivalent of `Recordset`) is certainly permitted, but simpler classes (such as arrays) are also supported. The other major change is that when you use the disconnected model, .NET disallows "live" database updates and the locking they imply. In ADO.NET there is no direct updating of a database through `DataTables` or `DataSets`. Instead, you must use `DataAdapter` (or a `Command` class) to flush the update to the database after the fact.

Live database updates work best with a local file-based data store, such as Microsoft Access. In this approach, the graphical user interface is considered an extension of the database file, and updates are immediate. Although .NET Web Forms and Windows Forms permit databound controls, there is no mechanism in the .NET class libraries to accommodate binding of data directly to a database. Using the Jet DAO access API or ADO through COM interoperability may accommodate this, but that is not covered here. Instead, this chapter focuses on *databound* controls, which bind discrete data items or sets of data that exist outside the database. This technique is illustrated in Figure 6–2. For most applications and most databases, disallowing live, connected updates is a good thing. Live cursors take up database resources on a per-user basis. The disconnected model scales better because connections are short-lived and the amount of time spent in the database, using its resources, is reduced. Because database resource utilization is reduced, more users can be accommodated at a time.

Both Windows Forms and Web Forms expose a form-based model in which the data is bound to subclasses of a `Control` class. Both Windows Forms and Web Forms have a class called `Control`, but `System.Windows.Forms.Control` is different from `System.Web.UI.Control`. Both the `Form` class in Windows Forms and the `Page` class in Web Forms are subclasses of their corresponding `Control` class.

The Windows Forms `Control` class has a `BindingContext` property. `BindingContext` manages a `BindingManagerBase` for the Form's child controls that have binding properties. This `BindingManagerBase` helps to keep the controls synchronized when the underlying data source changes—for

ESSENTIAL ADO.NET

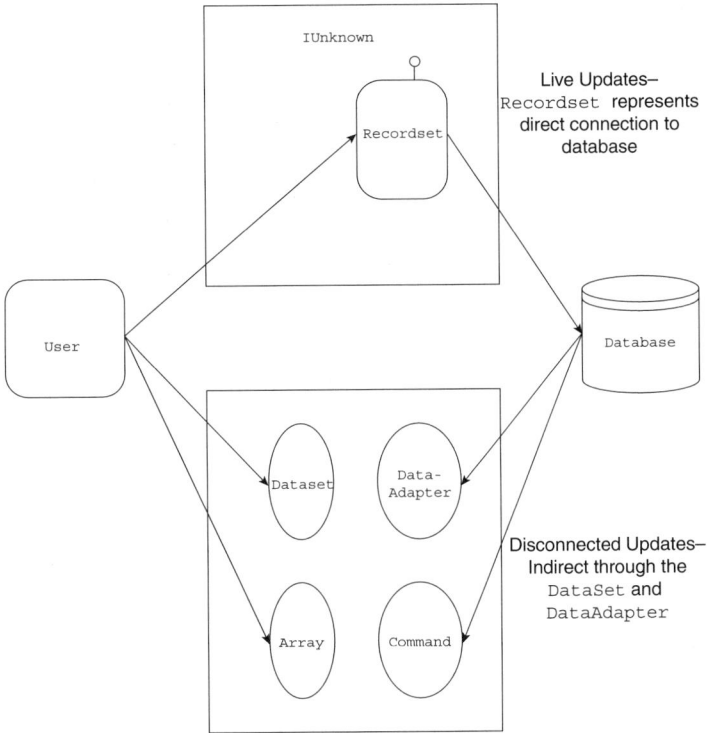

Figure 6–2 Live updating versus disconnected updates

example, when you move to the next row. Windows Forms defines two types of data binding: simple data binding and complex data binding. A control is bound to a single `BindingContext` and a single column value in a row—for example, a text box that is bound to the author name (`au_lname`) of the current row—by a simple data binding. A control is bound to a column value over a collection of rows—for example, a list box that is bound to a collection of author names—by a complex data binding. In Windows Forms, data binding that does not flush its changes back to its source is a one-way binding. A data binding that does flush its changes back to its source is a two-way binding. Obviously, you can't use two-way control binding with a `DataReader` class because there is no way to directly write the changes back. In Windows Forms, column values from a data source can be bound to any property on the form and not only the designated `DataSource` property.

The Web Forms `Page` class's `Render` method is used to render HTML for an entire Web page. A `Control`'s `Render` method iterates through its collection of child controls, calling `Render` on each one. When a Web Forms control's `Render` method is called, it renders HTML. Web Forms uses declarative binding syntax for variables as well as data- and list-based binding syntax, which is similar to Windows Forms' complex data binding. Although this appears similar to Windows Forms on the surface, there is no equivalent to Windows Forms simple data binding—which occurs on the client in the Web Forms architecture—because there is no concept of "live data" on the eventual Web client, not even through the read-only `DataReader`. Web Forms is a Web server-only architecture. The rest of this chapter concentrates on the Web Forms controls and rendering because a subset of the concepts is parallel.

6.3.1 Web Forms Data Binding Types

Web Forms adds a variation on the declarative scripting syntax known as *declarative data binding*. Data binding in Web Forms or (classic) ASP pages has always been possible by means of the following declarative binding syntax:

```
<!-- language = VBscript -->
Author ID: <% =rsAuthors.Fields("au_id") %>
First Name: <% = rsAuthors.Fields("au_fname") %>
Last Name: <% = rsAuthors.Fields("au_lname") %>
```

With this code, binding takes place at the time the page is rendered. When you're using ASP's `printf`-style functionality, the presentation is easy to predict; the page renders from top to bottom. You must ensure that the data variable is filled in when you get to the point in the page where it is used, however, and that causes problems if the page has server-side includes.

With this syntax, the Web Forms model ensures that data binding is taking place during page rendering, but there needs to be a way to codify more exactly when data binding is taking place. In ASP.NET, the declarative style has been retained, with an extension:

```
<!-- language = VB.NET -->
Author ID: <%# dtAuthors("au_id") %>
First Name: <%# dtAuthors("au_fname") %>
Last Name: <%# dtAuthors("au_lname") %>
```

This code indicates that your data will be bound when you explicitly call `DataBind`. With this syntax, you can bind to any object instance's state variables and not just data exposed by ADO.NET. You can call `DataBind` at any time, on any subclass of `System.Web.UI.Control`, although the typical usage suggested by the documentation is to call it on the `Page` class. Because ASP.NET encapsulates everything (even raw HTML) as a subclass of `System.Web.UI.Control`, this gives you complete control over when data binding occurs. In addition, because the ASP.NET `Page` class is also a subclass of `System.Web.UI.Control` and because calling `DataBind` on a `Control` always results in `DataBind` being called on that control's children, data binding semantics can be as fine-grained or coarse-grained as you like. Declarative binding syntax also does evaluation, letting you use portions of an ASP.NET page (controls) with expressions in addition to simple variables.

Set-based data binding, like complex data binding in Windows forms, is the concept of binding a single control having multiple "rows," such as a grid or combo box, to a set of data. This works well with the scrolling-rowset presentation style when you're using `DataGrid`. Combo boxes populated with set-based data binding can be used as a data prompting and editing feature. The list contains an enumeration of the items that are valid values from which a user often can choose. The data that is used in this binding is exposed in a subset of ASP.NET Web Forms `Controls` (both `WebControls` and `HtmlControls`) through `DataSource`, `DataMember`, and related properties. .NET data binding extends the traditional data binding concept by permitting binding to any object that implements `IEnumerable` in addition to sets of data from a data provider. This means that simple enumerable types such as `Array`, `ArrayList`, and `Hashtable` can be bound. Listing 6–1 shows a simple example of using a list-bound control (see the next paragraph) with `SqlDataReader`.

Listing 6–1   List box bound to `SqlDataReader`
```
<script language="C#" runat=server>
void Page_Load(Object sender, EventArgs e)
{

SqlConnection conn = new SqlConnection(
  "server=localhost;uid=sa;database=pubs");
```

```
SqlCommand cmd = new SqlCommand(
    "select * from authors", conn);
conn.Open();
SqlDataReader rdr = cmd.ExecuteReader();

listbox1.DataSource = rdr;
listbox1.DataTextField = "au_id";
DataBind();
conn.Close();

}
</script>
<form runat=server>
<asp:ListBox id="listbox1" runat=server />
</form>
```

IEnumerable is a simple interface that consists of a single method, GetEnumerator, which returns an IEnumerator interface implemented by a separate Enumerator class. The IEnumerator interface consists of two methods—MoveNext and Reset—and a read-only property, Current, which fetches the current instance. Enumerators enable the foreach syntax in C# (For each in VB.NET) and are mostly boilerplate code over an array-like collection. In data binding scenarios, the Control iterates through the collection items by calling MoveNext. Because any IEnumerator will suffice, controls that use this interface are sometimes known as *listbound* controls. Listing 6–2 shows a simple example of using a listbound control with a simple array.

Listing 6–2   Data binding to an array

```
<script language="C#" runat=server>
void Page_Load(Object sender, EventArgs e)
{
String[] numbers = new String[4]
    {"one", "two", "three", "four"};

listbox1.DataSource = numbers;
DataBind();
}
</script>
<form runat=server>
<asp:ListBox id="listbox1" runat=server />
</form>
```

Following are some of the items that can be bound to listbound controls:

- `Array`
- `ArrayList`
- `HashTable`
- `Queue`
- `SortedList`
- `Stack`
- `StringCollection`
- `DataView`
- `DataTable`
- `DataSet`
- `SqlDataReader`
- `OleDbDataReader`

6.3.2 Anatomy of Databound Control Types

This section presents a brief overview of the ASP.NET controls that support data binding or list binding, the details of that support, and the properties that apply to data. It doesn't discuss how ASP.NET works internally nor present the HTML generation features of ASP.NET controls in great detail; instead, I focus on how they integrate with ADO.NET. For more detail about ASP.NET, see the book *Essential ASP.NET*, by Fritz Onion (see the Bibliography).

ASP.NET exposes two sets of controls. `HtmlControls` (in `System.Web.UI.HtmlControls`) are a thin layer on top of the generic HTML forms and controls as defined in the HTML 2.0 specification (RFC 1866). `WebControls` (in `System.Web.UI.WebControls`) are more complex. They generate HTML and, for clients that support it, stylesheets and client-side JavaScript. Both types of controls generate HTML on the server side for rendering on any Web browser. Even when `WebControls` are used to generate pure HTML, they present a more consistent programmer paradigm than do the controls specified in the HTML 2.0 standard, especially for those programmers who have worked with Visual Basic Forms, Microsoft Foundation Classes, or .NET Windows forms. `WebControls` are also more efficient in that they require fewer Web server round-trips if up-level browsers are used and no more round-trips than ordinary Web pages if down-level browsers are used. Both `HtmlControls` and `WebControls` (as well as the ASP.NET `Page` object, which encapsulates an HTML page) inherit from `System.Web.UI.Control`, which defines methods through which controls render HTML or XML text and also cause their child controls to render. Figure 6–3 shows an overview of the class hierarchy of `HtmlControls` classes. `WebControls` are shown in Figure 6–4.

The following subset of controls supports data binding:

- `HtmlSelect`
- `CheckBoxList`
- `DataGrid`
- `DataList`
- `Repeater`
- `DropDownList`

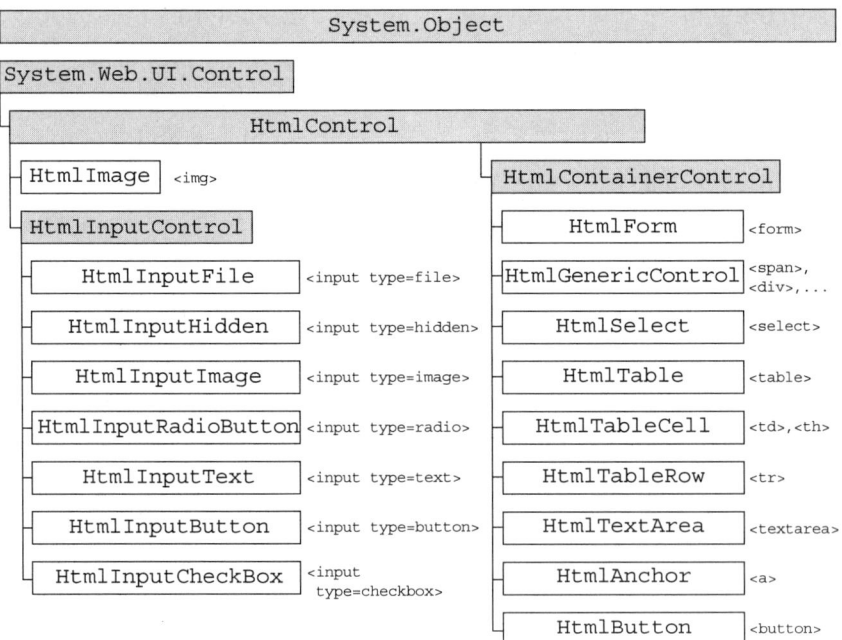

Figure 6–3 `HtmlControls` **class hierarchy**

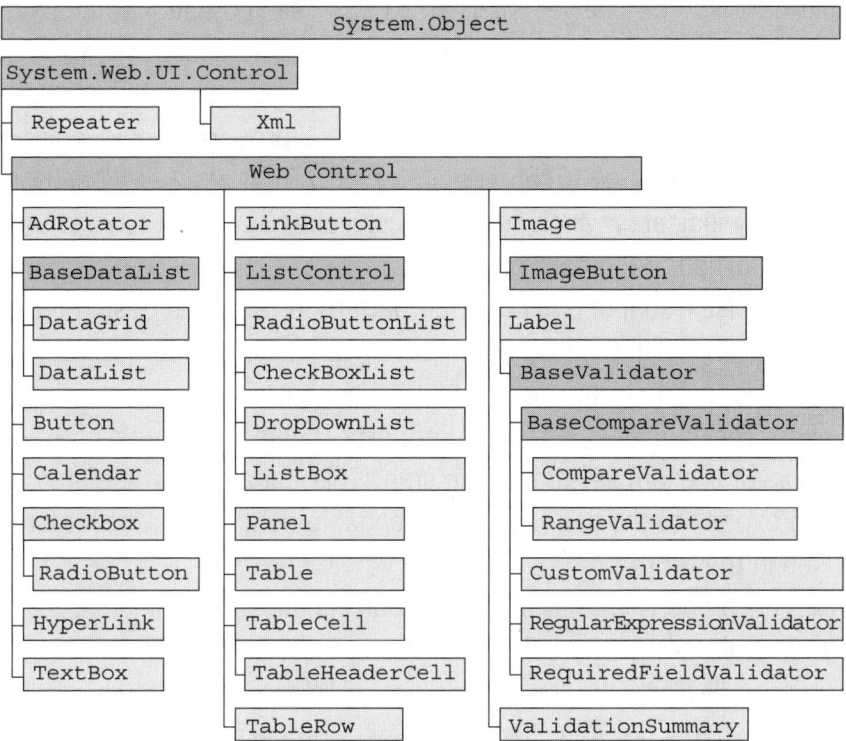

Figure 6–4 `WebControls` **class hierarchy**

- `ComboBox`
- `ListBox`
- `RadioButtonList`

This list shows only the controls shipped as part of the .NET base class library; third-party controls will soon become available. Microsoft has already released some additional controls to the Web.

Let's start with the simplest data binding. The only `HtmlControl` that supports data binding is the `HtmlSelect` control class. This control renders a simple selection (dropdown) list. It exposes only four properties related to data binding: `DataSource`, `DataMember`, `DataTextField`, and `DataValue-Field`. The `DataSource` property indicates which class provides the data for the control; any class that implements `IEnumerable` or `ICollection` will do.

For simple data source classes such as `Array`, all you need to specify is the `DataSource` property. The `DataMember` property is useful when the `DataSource` contains more than one possible source. For example, a `DataSet` can contain multiple `DataTables`; the `DataSource` property would point to the `DataSet`, and `DataMember` can specify which `DataTable`. The `DataTextField` property indicates which field in a multifield `DataSource` is to be bound to the visible portion of the control.

Finally, ASP.NET supports a common pattern in relational design for a table that relates an `ID` column and a `Description` column. You use `DataTextField` to choose the value displayed in the control—for example, the `Description`. The `DataValueField` property is used to choose the value of the selection—for example, the `ID` column. This capability is useful in a dropdown list to expose to the user an understandable description; the underlying ID is then used in the program.

The `Value` property of `HtmlSelect` contains the values—that is, the `DataValueField` values—for the selected items in the control. You use `SelectedIndex` as an index into the `Items` collection to retrieve `DataTextField`. If `DataValueField` is not specified, the `Value` property is equal to the `Items`' `SelectedIndex`. This common pattern in list-based classes is shown in Listing 6–3. If `HtmlSelect` allows multiple selections, `SelectedIndex` points to the first selection; you must iterate through the `Items` collection, checking the `Selected` property of each `Item`.

Listing 6–3   Using `HtmlSelect`

```
// ASP.NET control declarations omitted...
// Here are variable declarations
HtmlSelect jobs_select;
Label whichjob;
Button Button1;

private void Page_Load(
  object sender, System.EventArgs e)
{
if (!Page.IsPostBack)
 {
   SqlConnection conn = new SqlConnection(
     "server=localhost;uid=sa;database=pubs");
```

```csharp
    SqlCommand cmd = new SqlCommand(
      "select * from jobs", conn);
    conn.Open();
    SqlDataReader rdr = cmd.ExecuteReader();

    jobs_select.DataSource = rdr;

    // description field
    jobs_select.DataTextField = "job_desc";
    // value field
    jobs_select.DataValueField = "job_id";

    DataBind();
    conn.Close();
  }
}

private void Button1_Click(
    object sender, System.EventArgs e)
{
whichjob.Text = "Selected Job id = " +
    jobs_select.Value + " " +
    jobs_select.Items[jobs_select.SelectedIndex];
}
```

Now let's look at the `WebControls`. The `WebControls` namespace contains a series of controls that represent groups of items, such as check boxes. These inherit a common abstract base class, `ListControl`, and include the following:

- `CheckBoxList`: an array of check boxes
- `RadioButtonList`: an array of mutually exclusive radio buttons
- `ListBox`: a simple list in which all the items can be seen at the same time
- `DropDownList`: a selection box, like `HtmlSelect`

Each of these items exposes `DataSource`, `DataMember`, `DataText-Field`, and `DataValueField`, as in the `HtmlSelect` control. In addition, these classes support another property, `DataTextFormatString`, which contains a formatting string to specify how you want the visible data to appear. You may want the display field to be formatted a little differently than it is in the data source—for example, using commas, dollar signs, and decimal points. To summarize:

- `DataTextField` names the field that appears in the list (the `Description` field in the preceding example).
- `DataTextFormatString` allows you to control how it is formatted.
- `DataValueField` names the field whose value will be used when you read the chosen item.

Listing 6–4 shows an example of using `DataListFormatString` with the `ListBox` control. Note that `ListControl` exposes its values through a `SelectedItem` property that contains `Value` and `Text` properties. This means that item handling is consistent throughout all the controls that inherit from it.

Listing 6–4 Using the `DataFormatString` property

```
// ASP control declarations not here...
// Here are variable declarations
ListBox emp_select;
Label whichsal;
Button Button1;

private void Page_Load(
  object sender, System.EventArgs e)
{
 if (!Page.IsPostBack)
  {
  OleDbConnection conn = new OleDbConnection(
     "provider=msdaora;user id=scott;" +
     "password=tiger;data source=orcll");
  OleDbCommand cmd = new OleDbCommand(
    "select ename, sal from emp order by sal", conn);
  conn.Open();
  OleDbDataReader rdr = cmd.ExecuteReader();

  emp_select.DataSource = rdr;
  emp_select.DataTextField = "sal";
  emp_select.DataValueField = "ename";
  // format as currency
  emp_select.DataTextFormatString = "{0:C}";
  DataBind();
  conn.Close();
  }
```

```
  }

  private void Button1_Click(
    object sender, System.EventArgs e)
  {
    whichsal.Text = "Employee " +
      emp_select.SelectedItem.Value +
      " earns " +
      emp_select.SelectedItem.Text;
  }
```

The `Repeater` control is used to render items in a flexible layout in which individual items can have any style you like. `Repeater` renders its list of items using a set of user-definable templates that control the appearance of the header, footer, separator, and items. A series of templates describes the appearance of each item. Figure 6–5 shows a sample `Repeater`.

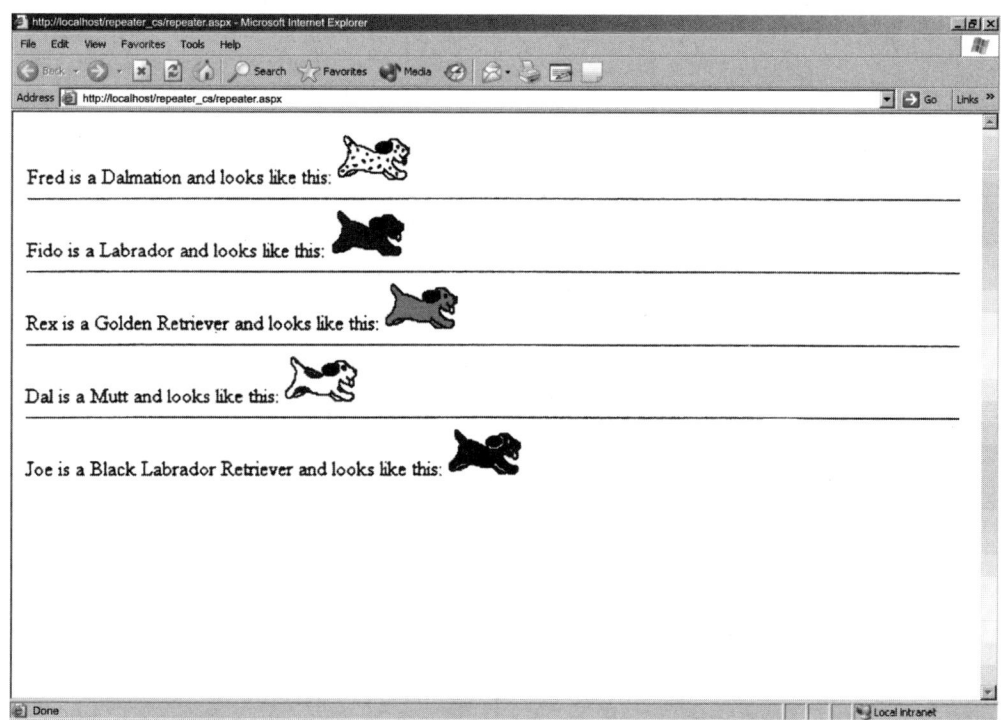

Figure 6–5   Result of a `Repeater` control

Repeater inherits directly from the Control class and contains only a DataSource and a DataMember. If the DataSource is a DataView or DataReader, each item in a Repeater is a single row. Although any or all of the columns can be used in the data binding expression, presentation is at the row level and not the column level. When the user clicks on a specific item, the item value can be retrieved. Listing 6–5 shows the sample code and template that produced the repeater in Figure 6–4. The code uses a utility class, System.Web.UI.DataBinder, that exposes a static method, Eval. This method uses reflection to parse and evaluate a data binding expression, avoiding casting. There is also an overload of Eval that uses a format string.

Listing 6–5   Code for the Repeater control

```
protected void Page_Load(Object src, EventArgs e)
{
SqlConnection conn = new SqlConnection(
  "server=localhost;uid=sa;pwd=;database=Test");
SqlDataAdapter da =
  new SqlDataAdapter("select * from Dogs", conn);

try
{
  DataSet ds = new DataSet();
  da.Fill(ds, "Dogs");

  rp1.DataSource = ds.Tables["Dogs"].DefaultView;
}
    catch (Exception ex)
    { Response.Write(ex.ToString()); }

    DataBind();
}

<asp:Repeater id="rp1" runat=server>
  <ItemTemplate>
    <%# DataBinder.Eval(Container.DataItem, "Name") %> is a
    <%# DataBinder.Eval(Container.DataItem, "Breed") %>
    and looks like this:
    <asp:Image runat=server
        ImageUrl=
    <%# DataBinder.Eval(Container.DataItem, "Image") %> />
  </ItemTemplate>
```

```
<SeparatorTemplate>
  <hr/>
</SeparatorTemplate>
</asp:Repeater>
```

The two remaining controls—`DataList` and `DataGrid`—are the only ones that deal with multiple columns and rows. These complex controls allow updating in place. In these controls, data binding policy is critical, and we'll return to them after we've discussed binding policies and `DataView`s.

6.3.3 Binding to a `DataReader`

The two data classes for which support of `IEnumerable` is most useful are `DataReader` and `DataView`. Because both `OleDbDataReader` and `SqlDataReader` implement `IEnumerable`, they can be bound to listbound controls. Both classes use the same underlying `Enumerator` class, `System.Data.Common.DbEnumerator`, which has a constructor that takes an `IDataReader` reference. This class calls `IDataReader.Read` when `Move-Next` is called and, because `DataReader` can only read forward, throws an `InvalidOperation-Exception` when `Reset` is called. Listing 6–6 shows the use of `SqlDataReader` with an ASP.NET `DataGrid`.

Listing 6–6   Binding a `DataGrid` to a `SqlDataReader`

```
<script language=C# runat=server>
protected void Page_Load(Object src,EventArgs e)
{
  SqlConnection conn = new SqlConnection(
    "server=localhost;uid=sa;database=pubs");
  SqlCommand cmd = new SqlCommand(
    "select * from authors", conn);
  SqlDataReader rdr = cmd.ExecuteReader();
  gd1.DataSource = rdr;
  DataBind();
}
</script>
<body>
<asp:DataGrid id="gd1" runat="server" />
</body>
</html>
```

Because `DataReader` uses a forward-only mechanism to get its data, after the data is consumed you must obtain it again to bind it to another control. `IEnumerable` simply calls `Read` to spin through the resultset each time. For example, if you bind `DataReader` to two list-based controls on the same page, you must obtain two sets of data, one for each control. That usually means two trips to the database. Even if `DataReader` could remain open while `DataBind` is being executed, there is no way to reset `DataReader` to reuse the same results. `DataReader` is most useful when you're using a single databound control—for example, a `Repeater`, `DataList`, or `DataGrid`.

If your form has many controls, each bound to a `DataReader`, a separate `DataReader` (and database connection) is required for each one. Note that you cannot bind a single `DataReader` to multiple controls by using different columns as `DataTextValues`. For example, the code in Listing 6–7 would result in one of the list boxes being empty. Unless the `Control` is subclassed to do its connection opening and closing inside a specific control's `DataBind` code, then instead of opening before `Page.DataBind` and closing after `Page.DataBind` (as does the code in Listing 6–6), all the connections stay open during the entirety of the `DataBind` call, thus defeating connection pooling.

Listing 6–7 `DataReader` **cannot bind to two controls**

```
SqlConnection conn = new SqlConnection(
        "server=localhost;uid=sa;database=pubs");
SqlCommand cmd = new SqlCommand(
        "select au_id, au_fname from authors", conn);
conn.Open();
SqlDataReader rdr = cmd.ExecuteReader();
listbox1.DataSource = rdr;
listbox1.DataTextField = "au_id";

listbox2.DataSource = rdr;
listbox2.DataTextField = "au_fname";

DataBind();
// listbox1 is full here
// but listbox2 is empty

conn.Close();
```

It is technically possible to use a single connection with a command that returns multiple resultsets. If you call `DataBind` individually on each control and advance `DataReader` to `NextResult` between calls, a single control will be bound to each resultset, as shown in Listing 6–8. Note that this is a fragile solution if you need to add another control. That's because the `Page`'s `DataBind` is not being called, and you must bind the new control individually. If you need to add a new result, you must remember that the order of calls to `DataBind` is critical.

Listing 6–8   Data binding using multiple results

```
SqlConnection conn = new SqlConnection(
        "server=localhost;uid=sa;database=pubs");
SqlCommand cmd = new SqlCommand(
        "select au_id, au_fname from authors;" +
    "select au_id, au_lname from authors", conn);
conn.Open();
SqlDataReader rdr = cmd.ExecuteReader();
listbox1.DataSource = rdr;
listbox1.DataTextField = "au_fname";
listbox1.DataBind();

rdr.NextResult();

listbox2.DataSource = rdr;
listbox2.DataTextField = "au_lname";
listbox2.DataBind();
// both are bound at this point

conn.Close();
```

6.4   Data Binding with `DataSets`

You can bind `DataSets` and `DataTables` directly using the `DataSource` and `DataMember` fields. When you use `DataSet` and do not specify a `DataMember` field, the first `DataTable` (`DataSet.Tables[0]`) is used by default. `DataSets` are preferable to `DataReaders` when you're using multiple controls to bind to the same data because you need obtain only a single copy of the data. In addition, the `DataSet` can be retained in memory, typically in an ASP.NET `Session` variable if it is user-specific, or in an ASP.NET `Application` variable or the ASP.NET Cache class if it is application-global. If this results in overuse of memory in the ASP.NET worker process, you can persist and retrieve the DataSet from disk in XML format if that is more efficient than getting it from the database. Listing 6–9 shows an example of using a DataSet with a multiple-results SQL statement and a single call to DataBind.

Listing 6–9 Data binding using multiple results

```
DataSet ds = new DataSet();
SqlDataAdapter da = new SqlDataAdapter(
        "select au_id, au_fname from authors" +
      "select au_id, au_lname from authors",
        "server=localhost;uid=sa;database=pubs");

// gets Table1 and Table2 by default, can be renamed
da.Fill(ds);
// data connection closed here

listbox1.DataSource = ds;
listbox1.DataMember = "Table1";
listbox1.DataTextField = "au_fname";

listbox2.DataSource = ds;
listbox1.DataMember = "Table2";
listbox2.DataTextField = "au_lname";

// bind them all
DataBind();
```

Notice the trade-off in the simplest case, without caching the DataSet. The DataSet is less efficient for these reasons:

- An extra copy of the data is thrown away when the DataSet goes out of scope.

- Nondeterministic destruction exacerbates the memory usage problem. On the other hand, the ASP.NET Page class itself is not recycled in any way, and ASP.NET can recycle its worker process based on memory usage.

- It is slower to fill a DataTable in a DataSet and then fill a ListBox than it is to fill the ListBox through a DataReader.

The `DataSet` is more efficient for these reasons:

- You can use a single `SELECT` statement to populate multiple controls easily.

- You can easily use a multiple-results SQL statement to populate multiple controls.

- The SQL Server connection is usually open for less time.

- When multiple results are not usable, you can use multiple SQL Server connections, but only one of them will be open at a time, making the application more scalable.

- You can use multiple related tables (with their relationships if these are defined) in `DataSet` for ease in coding master-detail forms.

Whether to use `DataSet` or `DataReader` is a difficult decision based on the trade-offs. What may turn the decision toward using `DataSet` is that it can be cached rather than being thrown away with each use. But what kinds of data can be cached effectively? Most database-based applications contain a large number of lookup tables. They are often used in dropdown list boxes to make databound forms user-friendly and as a rudimentary type of validation (users must select a choice that appears on the list). If your list box is completely static—holding, for example, a list of countries and states—you should either hard-code the data into the ASP.NET template page or generate the page offline on a schedule. Databases need not be queried at all, and `DataSet`s need not be cached. But if the data is user-specific—for example, a user's stock portfolio—you can cache it using the `Session` class. Highly dynamic data, such as hospital records, cannot be cached at all. Data that changes infrequently but at unscheduled times—such as a new term-of-greeting that's displayed in a combo box—is an excellent candidate for caching. Because ASP.NET has a programmable `Cache` class, in addition to the `Session` and `Application` objects, infrequently changed data can trigger a `Cache Item` invalidation, and refresh will occur the next time the item is referenced.

Managing a cache is usually more difficult than managing a database, and most programmers use only the simplest caching because of the problems of managing complex schemes. With ASP.NET this need not be the case; caching support is built-in, and caching can ease the database's workload in these situations.

Sometimes you have data that you want to cache and reuse, but it must be presented in a different order in each use, or you might find it useful to obtain a subset of the data. Do you need two copies of the data? No. Enter the `Data-View`.

6.5 `DataViews` and Common Transformations

A `DataView` is a view of a `DataTable` with a settable sort order and filtering criteria. Each `DataTable` contains a property that points to the `DefaultView`. You can set the properties of the `DefaultView` as well as create additional `DataViews` over the same `DataTable`. This capability is useful for exposing the same data in multiple formats without the overhead of multiple copies.

The following properties of `DataView` are settable:

- `Sort`: a string specifying sort order.
- `RowFilter`: a filter based on row values.
- `RowStateFilter`: a filter based on added, deleted, modified, or current rows.
- `ApplyDefaultSort`: a property that applies a default sort order based on primary key. `ApplyDefaultSort` works only if the `Sort` property is `null` or an empty string.

Although the `DataTable`'s property is named `DefaultView`, changing `DefaultView`'s settings does not alter the way the data is presented when accessed directly through `DataTable`—for example, in a console application. When you fill `DataTable` programmatically or by using `DataAdapter.Fill`, the rows appear in the order in which they were inserted in the table or retrieved from the database. If you set properties on `DefaultView`, the ordering or filtering changes only if the data is accessed through the view, as illustrated in Listing 6–10. You can also use `DataView`'s `Find` method to find a particular `DataRow` or an array of `DataRows` by sort key, as shown in Chapter 2. For the `Find` method to work, you must set a sort key by either setting the `Sort` property or setting `ApplyDefaultSort` to `true`.

Listing 6–10 Using `DefaultView`

```
SqlDataAdapter da = new SqlDataAdapter(
  "select * from authors",
```

```
    "server=.;uid=sa;database=pubs");

  DataSet ds = new DataSet();
  da.Fill(ds, "authors");

  // default table order
  for (int i=0;i<ds.Tables[0].Rows.Count;i++)
    Console.WriteLine(
      "au_id = " +
      ds.Tables[0].Rows[i]["au_id"]);

  // set sort order on the DefaultView
  ds.Tables[0].DefaultView.Sort = "au_id desc";

  // list the table, same order as above
  for (int i=0;i<ds.Tables[0].Rows.Count;i++)
    Console.WriteLine(
      "au_id = " +
      ds.Tables[0].Rows[i]["au_id"]);

  // list the view, in descending order
  for (int i=0;i<ds.Tables[0].DefaultView.Count;i++)
    Console.WriteLine(
      "au_id = " +
      ds.Tables[0].DefaultView[i].Row["au_id"]);
```

In a Web Forms application, when you bind a control such as a `DataGrid` or a `DataRepeater` to a `DataTable`, the `DataGrid` is actually bound to the `DataTable`'s `DefaultView`. This may be misleading in light of the different behaviors of the `DataTable` and its `DefaultView` when you're using console applications.

The `DataView` class is ideally suited for data binding. It implements `IEnumerable`, as well as `ICollection` and `IList`, and that allows indexing into the collection. A `DataGrid` paging control pages faster if it uses `IList` as its index implementation. Listing 6–11 shows an example of using `DataView`s to bind two variations of the same `DataTable`. This example is similar to functionality used often in Web pages: the ability to show an employee list sorted by first or last name. In this case the `DataView` serves its purpose well because there is only one copy of the data in memory. You could also implement this same sorting for a single list by using `DataView`'s `Sort` property.

Listing 6–11   Using two views of the same `DataTable`

```
protected void Page_Load(Object src, EventArgs e)
{
ListBox lb1, lb2;

SqlConnection conn =new SqlConnection(
  "server=localhost;uid=sa;pwd=;database=pubs");
SqlDataAdapter da = new SqlDataAdapter(
 "select au_id, au_fname, au_lname, " +
 "au_fname + ' ' + au_lname as full_name " +
 "from Authors", conn);

 DataSet ds = new DataSet();
 da.Fill(ds, "Authors");

 DataView view1 = new DataView(ds.Tables["Authors"]);
 view1.Sort = "au_fname";
 lb1.DataSource = view1;
 lb1.DataTextField = "full_name";
 lb1.DataValueField = "au_id";

 DataView view2 = new DataView(ds.Tables["Authors"]);
 view2.Sort = "au_lname";
 lb2.DataSource = view2;
 lb2.DataTextField = "full_name";
 lb2.DataValueField = "au_id";
 DataBind();
 }
```

You can set `DataView` to allow or disallow editing and updates to the underlying `DataTable` through the `DataView`. This does not affect whether changes are permitted to the `DataTable` directly. This behavior can be set individually for `Inserts`, `Updates`, and `Deletes` through the `AllowNew`, `AllowUpdate`, and `AllowDelete` properties of `DataView`, as shown in Listing 6–12.

Listing 6–12   Restricting editing through `DataView`

```
DataSet ds;
DataGrid DataGrid1;
// Fill DataSet..elided

DataView dv = ds.Tables[0].DefaultView;
dv.Sort = "desc";
```

```
// Only allow editing existing rows
// No inserts or deletes
dv.AllowEdit = true;
dv.AllowDelete = false;
dv.AllowNew = false;
DataGrid1.DataSource = dv;
```

`DataView` contains a collection of `Items`, and you can access the underlying `DataRow` information through the collection, as shown in Listing 6–13. As with `DataRows`, the `BeginEdit`, `EndEdit`, and `CancelEdit` methods are called on the view. You can use `DataView`'s `ListChanged` event to determine whether the view has been updated due to changes in the underlying table.

Listing 6–13   Reading through a `DataView`'s `Items`
```
DataSet ds;
SqlDataReader da;
// Initialization elided...

DataViewSetting dvs =
    ds.DefaultViewManager.DataViewSettings["jobs"];
dvs.ApplyDefaultSort = false;
dvs.Sort = "job_desc";

da.Fill(ds, "jobs");

DataView dv = ds.Tables[0].DefaultView;

// read the items (rows) in the DataView
for (int i=0;i<dv.Count;i++)
  Console.WriteLine("description = {0}", dv[i]["job_desc"]);
```

`DataRows` in a `DataView` can be filtered by `RowState` and by value. Filtering by `RowState` can be used to show or toggle between before and after images of a `DataView`'s rows, as shown in Listing 6–14. Filtering data by value uses a SQL-like syntax, which is applied via a `RowFilter` property. Filters can be arbitrarily complex and can be based on multiple columns and parent-child relationships. The results of filtering are affected by the `CaseSensitive` property of the `DataSet` that contains the `DataView`. The definition of the filtering expression language is identical to that of the `DataColumn` expression language shown in Appendix B. You can sort in a `DataView` based on one or more columns, and each column can be sorted in ascending or descending order. Listing 6–15 shows an example of sorting and filtering by value.

Listing 6–14 Filtering using `DataRowState` in `DataViews`

```
int ShowChanges(DataSet ds, bool showcurrent)
{
  DataView dv = ds.Tables[0].DefaultView;
  if (showcurrent == true)
    dv.RowStateFilter = DataViewRowState.ModifiedCurrent;
  else
    dv.RowStateFilter = DataViewRowState.ModifiedOriginal;
}
```

Listing 6–15 Sorting and filtering by value

```
int SortFilter(DataSet ds, string exp, bool sortasc)
{
  DataView dv = ds.Tables[0].DefaultView;

  dv.Filter = exp;
  if (sortasc == true)
    dv.Sort = "lastname ASC";
  else
    dv.Sort = "lastname DESC";
}
```

The `DataViewManager` class contains a collection of `DataViewSettings` for `DataTables` in a `DataSet`, and each `DataViewManager` instance must be associated with a `DataSet`. In addition to maintaining the collection, `DataViewManager` has a method that can be used to create a `DataView`; each `DataView` contains a reference to its `DataViewManager` (which can be `null`) as a member. `DataSet` also contains a reference to `DefaultViewManager`, which can keep a collection of the `DefaultView` settings of each table in the `DataSet`. This means that, in addition to setting `Sort`, `Filter`, and other properties on a specific `DataView` or a `DataTable`'s `DefaultView`, you can set it by creating a `DataViewSetting` on a `DataViewManager`. Listing 6–16 shows an example of how to create `DataViewSettings`.

Listing 6–16 Modifying `DefaultView`

```
DataSet ds = new DataSet();

SqlDataAdapter da = new SqlDataAdapter(
  "select * from jobs",
  "server=localhost;uid=sa;database=pubs");

da.TableMappings.Add("jobs", "jobs");
da.TableMappings[0].ColumnMappings.Add(
 "job_id", "jobid");
da.TableMappings[0].ColumnMappings.Add(
 "job_desc", "desc");
da.TableMappings[0].ColumnMappings.Add(
 "min_lvl", "minlvl");
da.TableMappings[0].ColumnMappings.Add(
 "max_lvl", "maxlvl");

ds.Tables.Add("jobs");
ds.Tables[0].Columns.Add("jobid", typeof(short));
ds.Tables[0].Columns.Add("desc", typeof(String));
ds.Tables[0].Columns.Add("minlvl", typeof(byte));
ds.Tables[0].Columns.Add("maxlvl", typeof(byte));

// Either of these will have the same effect
//ds.Tables["jobs"].DefaultView.Sort = "desc";

// This has the same effect
DataViewSetting dvs =
    ds.DefaultViewManager.DataViewSettings["jobs"];
dvs.ApplyDefaultSort = false;
dvs.Sort = "desc ASC";

// Either data binding will work
//DataGrid1.DataSource = ds.Tables[0].DefaultView;
DataGrid1.DataSource = ds.Tables[0];
```

When views share a common `DataViewManager`, you can use the `DataRowView.CreateChildView` method to obtain a `DataView` over a set of child rows based on a `DataRelation`. Whereas `DataRow.GetChildRows` will get all the child rows in the order in which they appear in `DataTable`, `DataRowView.CreateChildView` produces a `DataView` of child rows based on the `DataViewSettings` for the child `DataTable` in the `DataViewManager`. Listing 6–17 shows an example.

Listing 6–17 Using `DataViewManager`

```
SqlDataAdapter da = new SqlDataAdapter(
  "select * from authors;select * from titleauthor",
  "server=localhost;uid=sa;database=pubs");
DataSet ds = new DataSet();

da.Fill(ds);
ds.Tables[0].TableName = "authors";
ds.Tables[1].TableName = "titleauthor";

ds.Relations.Add(
  ds.Tables[0].Columns["au_id"],
  ds.Tables[1].Columns["au_id"]);
ds.Relations[0].RelationName = "foo";

System.Data.DataViewManager dvm = ds.DefaultViewManager;

// Add sort settings for each table
dvm.DataViewSettings["authors"].Sort =
  "au_id DESC";
dvm.DataViewSettings["titleauthor"].Sort =
  "title_id DESC";

DataView v = ds.Tables[0].DefaultView;

// parent table sort by ViewSetting
for (int i=0;i<v.Count;i++)
{
  DataRowView r = ds.Tables[0].DefaultView[i];
  Console.WriteLine("Author " + r[0]);

  // get child rows through DataRow
  // does NOT sort by ViewSetting of child table
  DataRow[] cr =
    r.Row.GetChildRows(ds.Relations[0]);

  for (int j=0;j<cr.Length;j++)
  {
    Console.WriteLine(
      "author id = " + cr[j]["au_id"]);
    Console.WriteLine(
      "title id = " + cr[j]["title_id"]);
  }
```

```
// DataViewRow.CreateChildView
// DOES sort by ViewSetting of child table
DataView cv =
  r.CreateChildView(ds.Relations[0]);

for (int k=0;k<cv.Count;k++)
{
  Console.WriteLine(
    "author id = " + cv[k]["au_id"]);
  Console.WriteLine(
    "title id = " + cv[k]["title_id"]);
}
}
```

You can bind `DataViewManager` as a `DataSource` to the Windows Forms `DataGrid`. Attempting to bind it to the Web Forms `DataGrid` will cause an exception. You can also bind `DataViewManager` to a pair of `DataGrids` representing parent and child `DataTables` in a Windows Forms application, and if you use a special syntax (`Tablename.Relationname`) for the `DataMember`, not only is the "child grid" kept in sync with the parent grid, but also the sort order of both parent and child (according to the `DataViewSettingCollection`) is maintained. Listing 6–18 shows an example. The `DataGrid` control handles this synchronization using the relation name as a parameter to `DataViewRow.CreateChildView`. Although the Web Forms `DataGrid` does not directly expose `DataViewManager` as a `DataSource`, you can program parent-child grids that behave in a similar manner by using `CreateChildView` directly. The DataFormWizards for both Windows Forms and Web Forms write code that exposes this behavior, as you'll see.

Listing 6–18 `DataViewManager` and parent-child grids

```
public class Form1 : System.Windows.Forms.Form
{

System.Windows.Forms.DataGrid dgParent;
System.Windows.Forms.DataGrid dgChild;

private void Form1_Load(object sender, System.EventArgs e)
{
SqlDataAdapter da = new SqlDataAdapter(
  "select * from authors;select * from titleauthor",
```

```
    "server=.;uid=sa;database=pubs");

    DataSet ds = new DataSet();
    da.Fill(ds, "authors");
    ds.Tables[1].TableName = "titleauth";

    ds.Relations.Add(
        ds.Tables[0].Columns["au_id"],
        ds.Tables[1].Columns["au_id"]);
    ds.Relations[0].RelationName = "authors_titleauthor";

    DataViewManager dvm = ds.DefaultViewManager;
    dvm.DataViewSettings["authors"].Sort = "au_id";
    dvm.DataViewSettings["titleauth"].Sort = "title_id desc";

    dgParent.DataSource = ds.DefaultViewManager;
    dgChild.DataSource = ds.DefaultViewManager;

    dgParent.DataMember = "authors";
    dgChild.DataMember = "authors.authors_titleauthor";
    }
    }
```

6.6   Table and Column Mappings

DataTables and DataColumns in a DataSet are assigned default names when Fill is called. These names usually correspond to the names in the SQL SELECT command. By using DataTableMappingCollection, you can apply a collection of names before calling Fill. For example, the table named authors in the database can be mapped to Addison-Wesley Authors in the DataSet. When the Addison-Wesley Authors DataTable is specified in the Fill statement as the table name, the Command with CommandText select * from authors produces the specified table.

Each DataTableMapping in the DataSet's DataTableMappingCollection contains a collection of DataColumnMappings. This collection can map individual columns by name or position in the SELECT statement. You can use position in the SELECT for columns that do not have names (such as calculated columns), but it is always better to specify a column alias to ensure the correct mapping. One problem with the last name/first name DataView solution shown earlier is that you must select an extra column from SQL Server to combine the first and last names. If you want to do this in client-side code, remember that you can shape `DataTable` before filling it from `DataAdapter`. If you define `DataTable` first, you can define a computed column to accommodate this value. Because `ListBox` doesn't know the difference between synthesized data and data retrieved from a database, the computed column can be used as a `DataTextValue` property, as shown in Listing 6–19.

Listing 6–19 Two views with a computed column

```
SqlConnection conn =new SqlConnection(
  "server=localhost;uid=sa;pwd=;database=pubs");
SqlDataAdapter da = new SqlDataAdapter(
 "select au_id, au_fname, au_lname, " +
 "au_fname + ' ' + au_lname as full_name " +
 "from Authors", conn);
DataSet ds = new DataSet();

DataTable t = new DataTable("Authors");
t.Columns.Add("au_id", typeof(String));
t.Columns.Add("au_fname", typeof(String));
t.Columns.Add("au_lname", typeof(String));
t.Columns.Add("full_name", typeof(String));
t.Columns[3].Expression =
  "au_fname + Convert(' ', 'System.String')" +
  " au_lname";
ds.Tables.Add(t);
da.Fill(ds, "Authors");
```

In addition to mappings, the overall structure of a `DataSet` instance can be defined by creating a schema. You create the schema either by direct creation of the underlying objects (`DataTables`, `DataColumns`, `DataRelations`, and so on) or by reading an XML schema through the `ReadXmlSchema` method. If the schema is not specified before `IDbDataAdapter.Fill` or `DataSet.ReadXml` is called, the schema will be either inferred or read from the underlying `DataReader`, as discussed in Chapter 5.

You can define behaviors that specify actions to be taken when the table or column mappings do not match when `Fill` is called. You specify these actions on `DataAdapter`. The choices are as follows:

- `Passthrough`: This creates a mapping based on the column name. Table names default to `Table`, `Table1`, and so on.

- `Ignore`: This means that columns or tables that do not have mappings will not be added to `DataSet`.

- **Error:** A `SystemException` will be thrown for unmapped columns and tables. You can catch these in your `FillErrorEvent` delegate or through normal exception handling.

Note that `MissingMappingAction` is unrelated to `MissingSchema-Action`, which is discussed in Chapter 7. It is possible to have an item in the `DataSet`'s schema without having a mapping for it, and vice versa.

Table and column mappings and `DataViews` are especially useful when you use them in conjunction with complex controls that render two-dimensional data, such as the list controls.

Now that you've seen how to control the behavior of these data sources, let's look at binding these complex controls.

6.7 Editable List Controls: `DataList` and `DataGrid`

The most complex controls in `System.Web.UI.WebControls` are those that derive from `System.Web.UI.WebControls.BaseDataList`. This includes `DataGrid` and `DataList`. Both render rows and columns, and, although `DataList` is, for the most part, a simplified version of `DataGrid`, each has unique features. Each controls its appearance through a set of templates and styles. Each uses complex data binding, based on lists and in-place editing. More than one template can be databound in a single control. Each implements its in-place editing by a series of events and delegates. Each control contains a `DataSource` and a `DataMember` property as well as a `DataKeyField` and a `DataKeys` property that lets you retrieve a key—or keys, in the case of a multi-column composite key—when updating. `DataLists` and `DataGrids` are said to "respond" to a series of "Commands" such as `ItemCommand` and `EditCom-mand`; these are not related to a data provider's `Command` class.

6.7.1 DataList

Seven templates can be used to control the appearance of a `DataList`:

- `Header`
- `Footer`
- `Separator`
- `Item`

- `AlternatingItem`
- `SelectedItem`
- `EditItem`

The last four can be databound and are typically bound to the same data item using data evaluation expressions. `DataList`'s uniqueness is you can define layout behaviors through the `RepeatDirection` and `RepeatLayout` properties. Listing 6–20 shows sample `DataList` code, and the resulting `DataList` is shown in Figure 6–6.

Listing 6–20 Declarative code for a `DataList`

```
<%@ Page %>
<%@ Import Namespace="System.Data" %>
<%@ Import Namespace="System.Data.SqlClient" %>


<html>
```

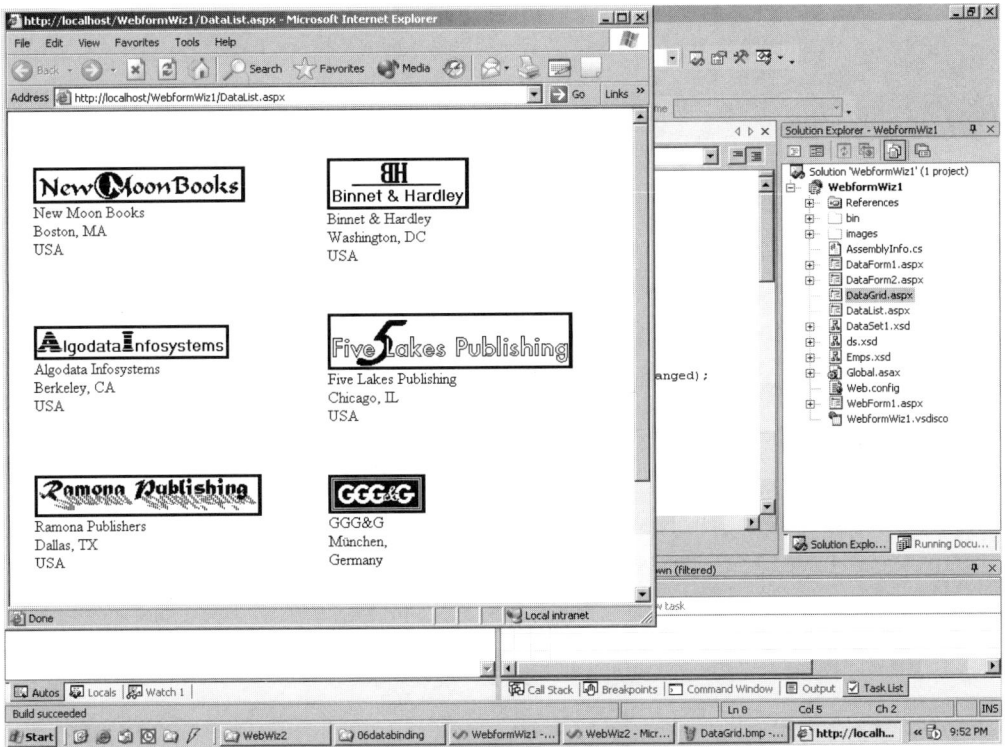

Figure 6–6 `DataList` **resulting from Listing 6–20**

```
<script language="C#" runat="server">
protected void Page_Load(Object src, EventArgs e)
{
  SqlConnection conn = new SqlConnection(
    "server=localhost;uid=sa;pwd=;database=pubs");
  SqlDataAdapter da =
    new SqlDataAdapter(
    "set concat_null_yields_null off;" +
    "select 'images/logo' + pub_id + '.bmp' as lurl," +
    "pub_id, pub_name," +
    "city + ', ' + state as addr, country " +
    "from publishers",
    conn);

  try
  {
    DataSet ds = new DataSet();
    da.Fill(ds, "Pubs");

    dl1.DataSource = ds.Tables["Pubs"].DefaultView;
  }
  catch (Exception ex)
  { Response.Write(ex.ToString()); }

  DataBind();
}

</script>

<body>
<asp:DataList id="dl1" runat=server RepeatColumns=2
    RepeatDirection=Horizontal>
  <ItemTemplate>
    <div style="padding:15,15,15,15">
    <br/>
    <asp:Image runat=server  BorderWidth=3
      ImageUrl=<%# DataBinder.Eval(
      Container.DataItem, "lurl") %> /><br/>
    <%# DataBinder.Eval(
      Container.DataItem, "pub_name") %><br/>
    <%# DataBinder.Eval(
      Container.DataItem, "addr") %><br/>
    <%# DataBinder.Eval(
      Container.DataItem, "country") %>
```

```
      </div>
    </ItemTemplate>
  </asp:DataList>
  </body>
  </html>
```

The `DataList` responds to a command with a number of server-side events that can be used to implement selection and editing. `OnEditCommand` is called when a cell transitions to edit mode. Edit mode enables update, delete, and cancel commands through a series of buttons. `OnItemCreated` is called when an item is created, and `OnDataBoundCreated` when an item is databound. Whenever a button is pressed, `OnItemCommand` is called. You can find the source of the command in the `DataListComandEventArgs CommandSource` property and can use this information to process your own custom command in this event handler. When responding to any of these events, you are expected to repopulate your data by calling `DataBind`. If your data is not cached, it must also be fetched each time.

Because `DataList` does not implement any subsetting of the data, all the data must be fetched at once. To assist in building SQL commands that update or delete database rows corresponding to `DataList` items, you set the `DataKeyField` or `DataKeyCollection` property with the column or columns that can be used as a primary key. `DataSet` updating is not automatic in the control; you must implement your own commands to update `DataSet` or use your own `SqlCommand` instances to update the database directly.

6.7.2 `DataGrid`

As far as data access is concerned, `DataGrid` is the most complex control. Layout is always in a rectangular grid format, but the data grid lets you customize its appearance using styles and templates. You can bind all the columns exposed by your `DataSource` (the default), or you can use a series of `BoundColumns` through templates. To expose button controls to start row editing operations, you use a column of type `ButtonColumn`. The control also supports `Hyperlink-Columns`, control-defined `EditCommands`, and user-defined `Commands`. Using a template, you can even bind a `DropDownList` or custom control to a column. Listing 6–21 shows the code for a sample editable `DataGrid` bound to a `DataSet`, and Figure 6–7 shows the result. `DataGrid` supports editing and paging and is so flexible and customizable that an entire chapter could be written on its intricacies. This chapter sticks to data binding issues.

Listing 6–21   Declarative code for a `DataGrid`

```
<%@ Page %>
<%@ Import Namespace="System.Data" %>
<%@ Import Namespace="System.Data.SqlClient" %>
<html>
<script language="C#" runat="server">
protected void Page_Load(Object src,EventArgs e)
{
  // event handling code deleted for clarity

  SqlDataAdapter da = new SqlDataAdapter(
    "select id as ID, name as Name, " +
    "age as Age from employees, " +
    "server=localhost;uid=sa;database=pubs");
  DataSet ds = new DataSet();

  da.MissingSchemaAction = MissingSchemaAction.AddWithKey;
  da.Fill(ds, "Employees");

  gd1.DataSource = ds;
  gd1.DataMember = "Employees";
  gd1.DataKeyField = "ID";
  DataBind();
}
</script>
<body>

<form id="Form1" method="post" runat="server">
<asp:DataGrid id="gd1" runat="server"
   BorderColor="White" BorderStyle="Ridge"
   CellSpacing="1" BorderWidth="2px" BackColor="White"
   CellPadding="3" GridLines="None" AllowPaging="True">

 <!-- Styles -->
 <SelectedItemStyle Font-Bold="True" ForeColor="White"
    BackColor="#9471DE" />
 <ItemStyle ForeColor="Black" BackColor="#DEDFDE" />
 <HeaderStyle Font-Bold="True" ForeColor="#E7E7FF"
    BackColor="#4A3C8C" />
 <FooterStyle ForeColor="Black" BackColor="#C6C3C6" />
```

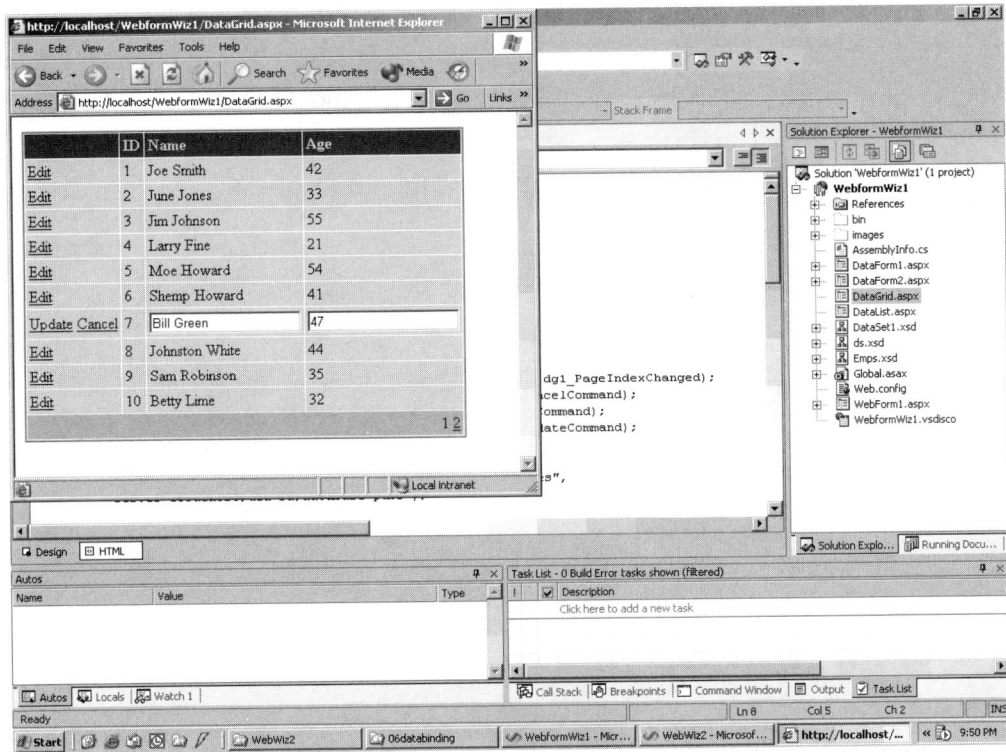

Figure 6–7   Screen produced by code in Listing 6–21

```
<!-- Command Column -->
<Columns>
  <asp:EditCommandColumn ButtonType="LinkButton"
      UpdateText="Update" CancelText="Cancel"
      EditText="Edit" />
  </Columns>
<PagerStyle HorizontalAlign="Right" ForeColor="Black"
    BackColor="#C6C3C6" Mode="NumericPages" />

</asp:DataGrid>
</form>
</body>
</html>
```

For updating, you use the same set of events and delegates as with `Data-List`. Only a single row can be edited at a time. Updating is "manual"; you must write data access code in the event handlers. In addition to the built-in grid commands such as `OnUpdateCommand` and `OnDeleteCommand`, you can define your own custom commands, as in `DataList`. Listing 6–22 shows how you would implement an `UpdateCommand` delegate and use an ordinary `SqlCommand` to access the `SelectedItem` and update the database.

Listing 6–22   Updating `DataGrid`

```
DataGrid gd1;

public void gd1_Update(Object sender,
              DataGridCommandEventArgs E)
{
  String updateCmd =
    "UPDATE Employees " +
    "SET Name = @vName, Age = @vAge where ID=@vId";
  SqlConnection conn = new SqlConnection(
    "server=.;uid=sa;database=people");
  SqlCommand cmd = new SqlCommand(updateCmd, conn);

  cmd.Parameters.Add(new SqlParameter(
                  "@vId", SqlDbType.Int));
  SqlParameter param = new SqlParameter(
                  "@vName", SqlDbType.VarChar);
  param.Size = 50;
  cmd.Parameters.Add(param);
  cmd.Parameters.Add(new SqlParameter(
                  "@vAge", SqlDbType.Int));

  cmd.Parameters["@vId"].Value =
    gd1.DataKeys[(int)E.Item.ItemIndex];
  cmd.Parameters["@vName"].Value =
    ((TextBox)E.Item.Cells[2].Controls[0]).Text;
  cmd.Parameters["@vAge"].Value =
    ((TextBox)E.Item.Cells[3].Controls[0]).Text;

  cmd.Connection.Open();

  cmd.ExecuteNonQuery();
  gd1.EditItemIndex = -1;
  cmd.Connection.Close();
  DataBind();
}
```

To support data access optimization, `DataGrid` implements *paging* (a next/previous/number page button in various styles). The built-in paging mechanism requires that all the data be available and that the total number of rows be known when you perform data binding.

You can also implement custom paging. This doesn't mean that the appearance of the paging buttons changes but rather that the grid behaves differently when `DataBind` is called. With custom paging, you initialize the `Virtual-ItemCount` property of `DataGrid` to the approximate total number of rows. When `DataBind` is called, the only items that you are responsible for making available are the items on a specific page, the *current* page. During the `Page-IndexChangedEvent`, the `DataGridPageChangedEventArgs` parameter contains the current page index. From this and `PageSize`, you can calculate the starting row and number of rows to be refreshed. These rows can be prepopulated or demand-populated. If, for example, you were refreshing the entire `DataSource` each time by calling `DataAdapter.Fill`, you could use the overload of `Fill` that takes a starting row number and the number of rows to fetch into the `DataTable`, and then fetch only subsets of the `DataTable` when necessary.

If your database provides a mechanism to SELECT a subset of rows—as with SQL Server SELECT TOP N functionality or Oracle's ROWNUM—this technique can greatly optimize your data access. You can use variations of SQL call sequences that mimic this functionality. Listing 6–23 shows an example of a `PageIndex-ChangedEvent` delegate and the corresponding calls to fetch the data.

Listing 6–23 Custom pager with `DataSet`

```
int start_rownum=0;
DataGrid ItemsGrid;

ICollection GetData()
{
DataSet ds = new DataSet();
SqlDataAdapter da = new SqlDataAdapter(
  "select * from jobs",
  "server=localhost;uid=sa;database=pubs");

da.Fill(ds, start_rownum,
```

```
      start_rownum + ItemsGrid.PageSize, "subset");

    return ds.Tables["subset"].DefaultView;
  }

  void Page_Change(Object sender,
    DataGridPageChangedEventArgs e)
  {
    ItemsGrid.CurrentPageIndex = e.NewPageIndex;
    start_rownum =
      ItemsGrid.CurrentPageIndex * ItemsGrid.PageSize;
    GetData();
    DataBind();
  }
```

As a final feature, `DataGrid` implements sorting by exposing a `LinkBut-`
`ton` as a header of each column. When the `LinkButton` is pressed, `OnSort-`
`Command` is fired. In this command, you can extract the `SortExpression` and
set the `DataView.Sort` property accordingly, as shown in Listing 6–24.

Listing 6–24   Sorting in `DataGrid`

```
  void Sort_Grid(
    Object sender, DataGridSortCommandEventArgs e)
  {
    String sortBy = e.SortExpression.ToString();
    ItemsGrid.DataSource = GetData(sortBy);
    ItemsGrid.DataBind();
  }

  ICollection GetData(String sortBy)
  {
  DataSet ds;
  // Initialize DataSet...

  if (sortBy != null)
    ds.Tables["mytbl"].DefaultView.Sort = sortBy;

  return ds.Tables["mytbl"].DefaultView;
  }
```

As with all ASP.NET databound controls, you do not have to refresh `Data-`
`Grid`'s data on postback events. *Postbacks* consist of sending the data back to
the server to accommodate changes that the user has made on the client. You

make the data available during postback events by storing it in `ViewState`, a hidden field that is sent to the client with every page. With most controls, this step has little effect, but it does mean that the data in `DataGrid` is sent twice: once as an HTML table, and a second time in `ViewState`. Depending on the amount of data in the grid, the overhead could be significant.

When you're using the built-in editing, sorting, and paging with `DataGrid`, remember that `DataBind` must be called when any of these activities is performed. Calling `DataBind` always requires that `DataSource` be re-created or retrieved from cache, whether the `DataSource` is an array, `DataReader`, or `DataSet`.

6.8   Nonrelational Data and `DataViews`

`DataViews` do not work well with nonrelational `DataTables`—that is, `Data-Tables` that contain object data types or multivalued data. This is not surprising because the `Sort` and `Filter` syntax used in `DataViews` mimics SQL syntax defined in SQL-92. SQL-99 extends SQL to provide for embedded tables and object data types (user-defined types). To reference attributes of user-defined types, SQL-99 specifies that observer functions must be available. To update such types, you use mutator functions. Listing 6–25 presents an example of using a user-defined type in a SQL table definition and retrieving it through the mutator functions exposed by the database. (Note: No "mainstream" database exposes this functionality, and no database currently supports the entire SQL-99 spec.)

Listing 6–25   Mutator functions in SQL-99

```
/* create user-defined type */
CREATE TYPE book AS
 title char(50),
 retail_price decimal(7,2),
 wholesale_price decimal(7,2),
 instock boolean

/* book_isbn is a unique object identifier (OID) */
CREATE TABLE BOOKS (
  book_obj book,
  book_isbn varchar(11))
```

```
/* use it in a SQL-expression */
SELECT book_obj.title(),
       book_obj, retail_price()
WHERE book.obj.instock = 1
```

Observers and mutators in user-defined types are similar in concept to getters and setters in CLR types, and they could be represented this way. For your filtering language to be usable with user-defined types and the extended SQL syntax, you would have to support the dot notation variant to refer to embedded tables or object properties. Instead, for these tables to be used by `DataViews` and `Column Expressions` in ADO.NET, you must represent these tables as parent-child relationships. ADO.NET exposes special `CHILD` and `PARENT` keywords to support this.

6.9 Integrating Visual Studio

In general, if you're performing well-known rather than ad hoc operations, performance will improve if you provide as much information as possible at design time. When using `DataSet`, you can avoid having to rely on `MissingSchemaAction` and `MissingMappingAction` by predefining `DataSet` schema and mappings. You should provide custom stored procedures to be used with `DataAdapter.Update` rather than relying on the default `Commands` generated by the `CommandBuilder` classes or obtaining stored procedure parameters with `CommandBuilder.DeriveParameters`. Obtaining database metadata at runtime usually involves extra round-trips and may not be as accurate as design-time specification, depending on the capabilities of the data provider. Although obtaining metadata at design time does not provide the flexibility of loose coupling, it is almost always faster.

Visual Studio supports the design of data-based applications by reading existing metadata and permitting overrides at design time. Mapping data to Web Forms and Windows Forms is exposed by libraries known as *designers*. The interfaces used by the designers are public, so custom data providers can hook in to the environment.

6.9.1 Server Explorer and Data Toolbox

A Server Explorer window in Visual Studio allows you to connect to SQL Server databases and view and edit database metadata, subject to security constraints. SQL Server stored-procedure debugging is integrated into the environment; you can debug into a stored procedure from program code. A Data Connections item in Server Explorer lets you configure connection information using the standard OLE DB connection prompt (shown in Figure 6–8) and store sets of database connection information for future use. When the OLE DB provider for SQL Server is chosen (the default), a `SqlConnection` is generated; otherwise, an `OleDbConnection` is generated. At this writing, the `Odbc` data provider is not integrated into Server Explorer—that is, an ODBC connection can be used to

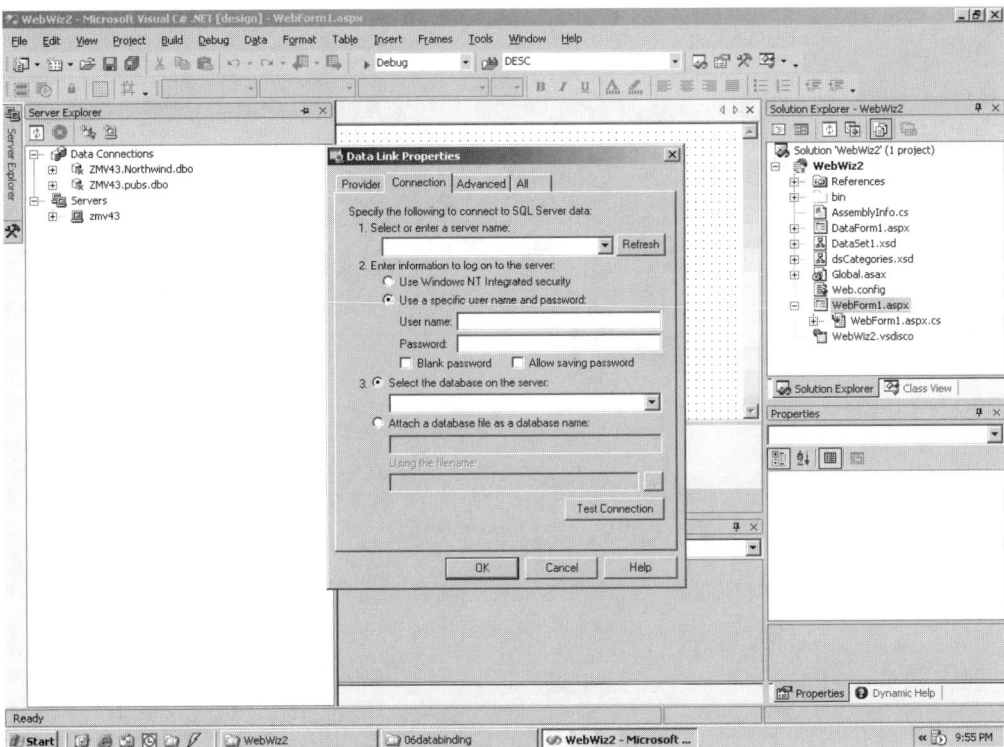

Figure 6–8   Connection prompt in Server Explorer

browse a data source, but the connection strings produced cannot be used to produce a typed instance of `OdbcConnection` for use with the designers.

The Visual Studio toolbox contains a Data tab that allows you to drag a typed `Connection`, `Command`, or `DataAdapter` as well as a `DataSet` or `DataView` onto a form. You can also drag a `Connection` from Server Explorer's Data Connection item, and the connection parameters will be preconfigured.

In `Connection`'s property window, you can configure the `ConnectionString` property visually; if you don't select a Data Connection from Server Explorer's list, you are prompted for a new connection. In `Command`'s property window, if the `CommandType` is `CommandType.Text`, you can invoke a visual Query Builder (shown in Figure 6–9) to set the `CommandText` property. When stored procedures or parameterized queries are specified, the `Command`.

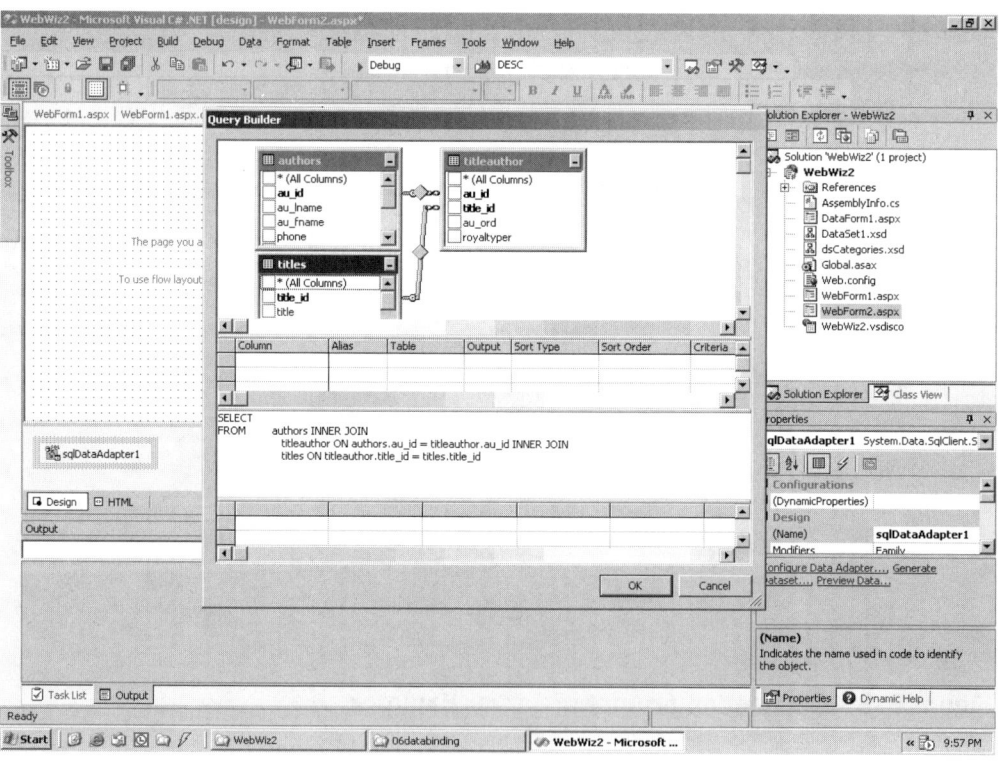

Figure 6–9   SQL Query Builder

ESSENTIAL ADO.NET

`Parameters` collection can be filled in automatically. A graphical interface is also available for specification of `Parameter` information.

When you drag a `DataAdapter` onto a form or choose Configure Data-Adapter, you can use a wizard-like series of panels to configure its properties. First, you select a connection. You then configure the `DataAdapter`'s `Select-Command` by choosing to use SQL statements, create new stored procedures, or use existing stored procedures.

If you choose to use SQL statements, you can enter them manually or use Query Builder. Choosing Create New Stored Procedure creates a stored procedure from the (single) SQL statement you specify. You have the option of generating simple `INSERT`, `UPDATE`, and `DELETE` statements or stored procedures based on the `SELECT` statement. In either case, parameterized statements are generated, with the corresponding parameters collection.

If you choose Use Existing Stored Procedures, you're presented with a series of list boxes and can choose stored procedures to use with `DataAdapter`'s `Insert-Command`, `UpdateCommand`, `DeleteCommand`, and `SelectCommand`.

Two additional options are Use Optimistic Concurrency and Refresh the DataSet. Choosing optimistic concurrency is reflected in the phrasing of the `UPDATE` and `DE-LETE` statements, as discussed in Chapter 5. With optimistic concurrency, the `UP-DATE` and `DELETE` statements will fail if any of the column values has changed since the row was read. Clearing the optimistic concurrency option results in `UPDATE` or `DELETE` statements that depend only on the primary key. Choosing to refresh the `DataSet` appends a statement that returns the affected row.

All the automatic configuration options work best when you're using the `SqlClient` data provider. With the `OleDb` data provider, your mileage may vary depending on the capabilities of the underlying OLE DB provider.

Selecting the `TableMappingsCollection` property of `DataAdapter` presents you with a visual method of mapping tables and columns to `Data-Tables` and `DataColumns` in `DataSet`. If a `DataSet` is added to your project, you can use its configuration information to "suggest" mappings.

When dragging a `DataSet` onto a form, you can configure it as a typed or untyped `DataSet`. Typed `DataSet` schemas are based on an XSD schema, which you can code by hand or by using Visual Studio's schema designer. Typed

`DataSet`s are discussed in Chapter 7. When using an untyped `DataSet`, you can visually specify the `DataSet`'s `DataTables` (and, in this designer, `Data-Columns`) as well as the `Relations` collection.

6.10 Controls and Data Forms

Some of the controls in Windows Forms and Web Forms contain a Property Builder, a graphical interface for specifying the control properties. The most elaborate Property Builder is the one used by the Web Forms `DataGrid`, shown in Figure 6–10. In addition to specifying the `DataSource` and `DataMember`, you can map data columns in `DataSet` to columns in the grid. Other controls contain less elaborate builders.

Data Form Wizards, which exist for both Windows Forms and Web Forms, let you produce a starter form in which columns are bound to individual controls (simple

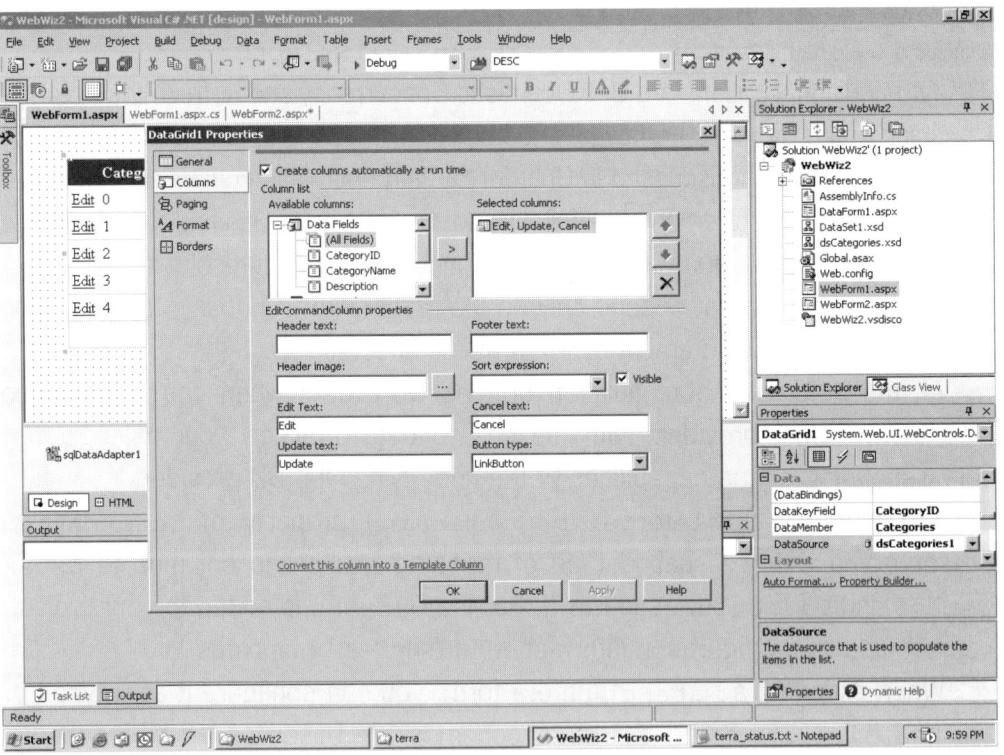

Figure 6–10 `DataGrid` **Property Builder**

data binding) or `DataSets` that are bound to a `DataGrid`. In addition, both wizards let you produce code for coordinated parent-child grids based on table relationships, as described earlier. The `DataGrid` produced is shown in Figure 6–11.

6.11 Where Are We?

You've seen the internals of the ADO.NET data presentation paradigms. You've explored how Windows Forms and Web Forms expose somewhat analogous programming paradigms for graphical user interfaces but produce either Windows GUI items or HTML. You've also learned how to use `DataReaderS`, `DataViewS`, expressions, and any class that implements `IEnumerable` to bind to Web Forms, and how the new data binding strategy makes data binding more flexible.

So far, your trip through data access has focused on a strict relational view of the world, both when you're using data providers and when you're using the

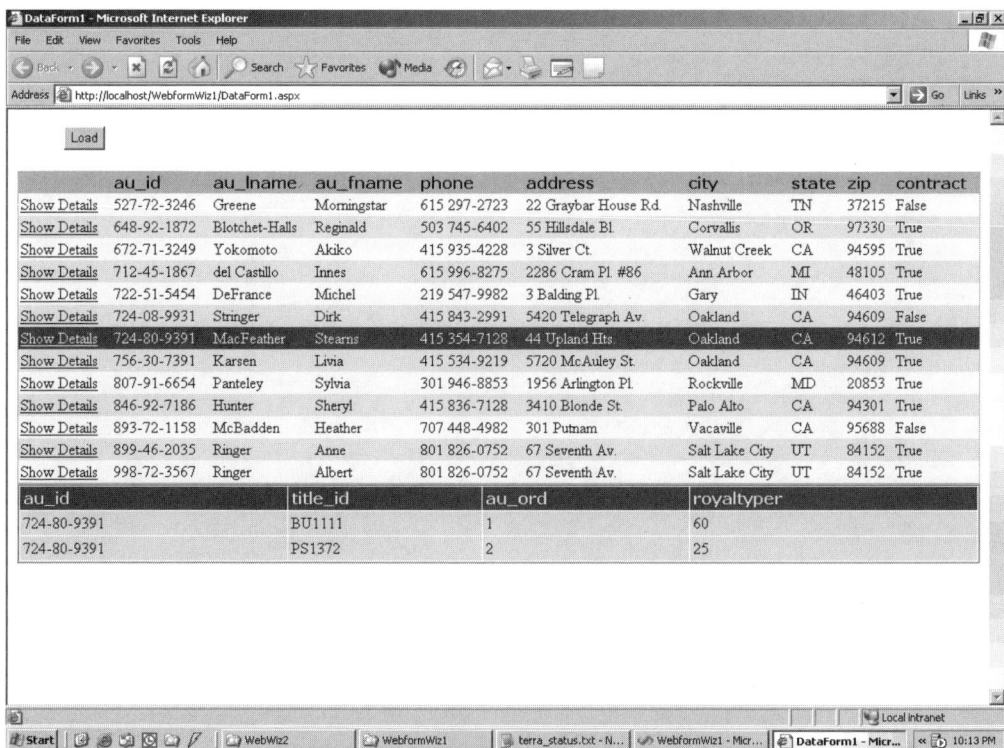

Figure 6–11   `DataGrid` **produced by the Data Form Wizard**

`DataSet` class. I've talked about nonrelational data along the way, but now you're going to expand your data access horizons to include XML, which can represent and provide an access path to nonrelational as well as relational data. Next, you'll see how XML fits into the picture.

Chapter 7

XML and Data Access Integration

The `DataSet` class interoperates with XML schema and data. The `XmlData-Document` combines `XmlDocument` and `DataSet` functionality.

7.1 XML and Traditional Data Access

The preceding chapters have talked about the data access stack mostly as it relates to traditional data access and relational data. Each time, I've mentioned nonrelational data (homogeneous and heterogeneous hierarchies and semistructured data) almost as an afterthought, or to illustrate that it would be a stretch to support it by using the classes in `System.Data`. But a wide variety of data can be represented in a nonrelational way. Here are a few examples.

- LDAP readable directories, such as Active Directory, contain multivalued attributes. This violates relational theory's first normal form.

- Each item in the NT file system is either a directory or a file. This is an example of a heterogeneous hierarchy. A related case is the reading of data from an Exchange store. Not only are contacts in the Contacts folder structured differently from mail messages in the Inbox, but also each mail message can contain 0–N attachments. The attachments can also vary in data format. Exchange—or other IMAP (Internet Mail Access Protocol) mail systems—can also expose hierarchical folders. All these data structures are analogous to the multiset in IDMS.

- Screen scraping from HTML or XML pages consists of reading through a combination of text and tags and extracting only the data you need—for example, the number in the third column of the fourth row of an HTML table and the contents of the third `<h3>` tag. This is an example of semistructured data.

There are ways to approximate each different data type—with the possible exception of semistructured data—by using a variation of a relational concept. Sometimes, however, you need to present the data in an alternative, nonrelational format. For example, suppose you're managing an electronic student registration form that contains data that affects the value of 15 different normalized relational tables. In addition, the form may contain information, such as a request for low-fat, vegetarian meals, that has no correlation in the relational schema. You may want to store the information in the request into multiple tables and reproduce the original request on demand. This might require that you retain additional information or even the entire request in its original form. It might also be nice if the information could be transmitted in a platform-independent, universally recognized format. Enter XML.

7.2 XML and ADO.NET

One of the most useful features of ADO.NET is its integration with portions of the managed XML data stack. Traditional data access and XML data access have the following integration points:

- The `DataSet` class integrates with the XML stack in schema, data, and serialization features.
- The XML schema compiler lets you generate typed `DataSet` subclasses.
- You can mix nonrelational XML data and the relational `DataSet` through the `XmlDataDocument` class and do XPath queries on this data using `DataDocumentXPathNavigator` class.
- ADO.NET supports SQL Server 2000 XML integration features, both in the `SqlClient` data provider and in an add-on product called SQLXML. The latter product features a series of `SqlXml` managed data classes and lets you update SQL Server via updategram or DiffGram format.

These features, although unrelated in some aspects, work to complete the picture of support of nonrelational as well as relational data in ADO.NET, and direct support of XML for marshaling and interoperability. Let's look first at integration in the `System.Data.DataSet` class and its support for XML.

7.2.1 Defining a `DataSet`'s Schema

In many ways, the ADO.NET `DataSet` class mimics a relational database. Each `DataSet` instance contains a schema—the set of tables, columns, and relationships—as does a relational database. You can define the schema of an ADO.NET `DataSet` instance in at least four ways:

- Use the `DataSet` APIs directly to create `DataTables`, `DataColumns`, and `DataRelations`. This approach is similar in concept to using DDL in relational databases.

- Infer the schema using database metadata through a `DataAdapter` class. Using `DataAdapter.Fill` creates tables and columns matching the metadata from `DataAdapter`'s `SelectCommand`. For this to work, `DataAdapter`'s `MissingSchemaAction` property must be set to `Add` or `AddWithKey`.

- Define the desired `DataSet` schema using XSD (XML Schema Definition language), and use `DataSet.ReadXmlSchema` to load the schema definition into the `DataSet`. The schema may not use nonrelational data definition styles, or else `ReadXmlSchema` will throw an error.

- Use `DataSet.InferXmlSchema`. The `DataSet` class will use a set of schema inference rules to infer a `DataSet` schema from a single XML document.

You can also define `DataSet`'s schema incrementally by using a combination of these methods, as shown in Figure 7–1. Note that in each case the result is the same: `DataSet` contains a set of tables, columns, constraints, and relationships that comply with relational rules.

`DataSet` is not aware of the source of the schema, and therefore any method of defining the schema works as well as any other. For example, let's define a simple schema that includes a customers table, an orders table, and a one-to-many relationship between customers and orders. Listing 7–1 uses the four schema-definition methods to accomplish this. Note that, when using `DataSet` or `DataAdapter`, you need additional code to set up the relationship, whereas in the case of XML schema or document inference, this information may be available in the schema or exemplar document.

Figure 7–1 Ways to fill the DataSet's schema

Listing 7–1 Ways to create a DataSet schema

```
DataSet ds1, ds2, ds3, ds4;

// Use DataSet APIs
ds1 = new DataSet();
ds1.Tables.Add("Customers");
ds1.Tables[0].Columns.Add("custid", typeof(int));
ds1.Tables[0].Columns.Add("custname", typeof(String));
ds1.Tables.Add("Orders");
ds1.Tables[1].Columns.Add("custid", typeof(int));
ds1.Tables[1].Columns.Add("orderid", typeof(int));
ds1.Relations.Add(
  ds1.Tables["Customers"].Columns["custid"],
  ds1.Tables["Orders"].Columns["custid"]);

// Create schema from SQL resultset metadata
ds2 = new DataSet();
SqlDataAdapter da = new SqlDataAdapter(
  "select * from customers;select * from orders",
  "server=localhost;uid=sa;database=northwind");
da.FillSchema(ds2, SchemaType.Source);
ds2.Tables[0].TableName = "Customers";
ds2.Tables[1].TableName = "Orders";
ds2.Relations.Add(
  ds2.Tables["Customers"].Columns["customerid"],
```

```
    ds2.Tables["Orders"].Columns["customerid"]);

    // Read schema from a file
    // Contains customers and orders
    ds3 = new DataSet();
    ds3.ReadXmlSchema(
      @"c:\xml_schemas\customers.xsd");

    // Infer schema from exemplar document
    // Contains customers and orders
    ds4 = new DataSet();
    ds4.InferXmlSchema(
      @"c:\xml_documents\customers.xml",
      null);
```

Past Microsoft (and other) APIs let you map XML to relational data but require that you specify the XML in a special format. ADO classic, for example, requires the XML to be specified in the format used by ADO's XML support. Some XML support systems require manual coding for each case, based on the programmer's knowledge of the underlying structure and the underlying types of all the elements or attributes involved. Some systems use a document type definition to specify type, but because the DTD is designed around XML's original use as a document markup language it is largely type-ignorant in the traditional programming sense, and the programmer still must know each type that is not `string`.

ADO classic's XML support uses a Microsoft-specific predecessor of XSD schemas; it's known as XDR (XML Data Reduced). XDR's type system is limited. Simple types are based loosely on OLE DB types, and there is no notion of type derivation, precluding the use of the object-oriented concepts of inheritance and polymorphism. .NET object persistence and `DataSet` take full advantage of XSD's improvements in these areas. This "object-relational" mapping layer includes two main classes: `System.Data.DataSet`'s XML support and `System.Xml.XmlDataDocument`, a class that represents a hybrid of the DOM/`DataSet` model. Unlike the ADO `Recordset`, which can consume and produce a single XML format based on a single schema style, `DataSet` can read and write XML corresponding to almost any schema.

Because XSD supports complex user-defined types as well as type derivation by extension and restriction, using XSD to define types supports a schema-based representation of objects and facilitates a natural mapping to object-based data stores, such as object databases. The hierarchical nature of XML makes this a natural for mapping to homogeneous hierarchies and databases such as IMS. Adding support for navigation and multisets brings CODASYL and object-relational data into the picture. Of course, data can also be stored in files using XML's native serialization format.

Using the XML native serialization format, which is defined in the XML 1.0 and Namespaces recommendations, is arguably a specialization of the object database case, although it enables standards compliance and a measure of code similarity to other platforms using the same object models to access serialized documents. In addition, including `DataSet` in the mix enables codifying of a set of default rules for mapping XML to relational databases. The relational structure of any Infoset can be defined directly using an XML schema for mapping, and it can also be inferred by using a rule-based approach. You can use relations to map XML hierarchies to multiple relational tables. As you've seen, you can map columns to either attributes or subelements of a particular element.

XML schema definition language is more flexible than the rules of a relational database. This means that when you load a `DataSet` via an XSD schema, you use a simple set of rules to map the XSD schema to a relational schema:

- `ComplexTypes` are mapped to `DataTables`.
- Nested `ComplexTypes` are mapped to related `DataTables`.
- `Key` or `Unique` constraints are mapped to `UniqueConstraints`.
- `KeyRefs` are mapped to `ForeignKeyConstraints`.

Schema inference is the attempt to deduce a schema from a single exemplar document. Because a single document is used, this technique is more error-prone than simply supplying the schema, and using a predefined schema should always be preferred over schema inference. When you attempt to infer a nonrelational XSD schema into `DataSet` format, it is either coerced into a relational schema (as in Listing 7–2) or you receive an error (as in Listing 7–3). Just as the schema compiler (`XSD.exe`) can infer an XSD schema for an XML document, `DataSet` uses a set of schema inference rules to infer a relational schema for an XML document. The complete set of rules is described in Appendix C. The

`DataSet.InferSchema` method permits you to specify as an optional parameter, a set of namespaces that will be excluded from schema inference.

Listing 7–2 Schema coercion to relational

```
<!-- This results in a table with three columns -->
<root>
  <document>
     <name>Bob</name>
     <address>111 Any St</address>
  </document>
  <document>
     <name>Bird</name>
     <livesin>tree</livesin>
  </document>
</root>
```

Listing 7–3 Attempt to infer a nonrelational schema

```
// Attempt to infer a schema from this document
/*
<book>
<chapter>
<title>Testing your <noun>typewriter</noun></title>
<p>The quick brown <noun>fox</noun> jumps over
the lazy <noun>dog</noun></p>
</chapter>
</book>
*/
DataSet ds = new DataSet();
ds.InferXmlSchema(
  @"c:\xml_documents\semistruct.xml",
  null);

// produces error:
// System.ArgumentException,
// The same table (noun) cannot be the child
// table in two nested relations.
```

Methods that read XML data in .NET usually have the same four overloads. You can read or write XML schema using `Stream`, `String`, `TextReader`, or `XmlReader`. The XML methods in `DataSet` follow the same pattern, as shown in Listing 7–4. The `ReadXmlSchema` method can read the schema in either XDR format or XSD (XML Schema Definition language) format. `InferXmlSchema` can exclude a set of namespaces from the schema inference process; there is no way to do this with `ReadXmlSchema`.

Listing 7–4 Overloads of `ReadXmlSchema`

```
public class DataSet
{
  // ... other methods omitted
  public void ReadXmlSchema(Stream stream);
  public void ReadXmlSchema(string);
  public void ReadXmlSchema(TextReader reader);
  public void ReadXmlSchema(xmlReader reader);
}
```

`DataSet` also exposes symmetric `WriteXmlSchema` methods. `WriteXmlSchema` uses a hard-coded algorithm to write schemas (see "Writing XML Schemas from `DataSet`" later in this chapter). You can also obtain schema information by using `GetXmlSchema`, which returns the XML schema as a string.

7.2.2 Refining `DataSet`'s XML Schema

You can further refine `DataSet`'s XML schema by using the properties of `Data-Column`, `DataTable`, and `DataSet` that relate to XML. Properties that are useful for setting the schema include `Namespace`, `Prefix`, `ColumnMapping`, and `DataSet`'s `DataRelations` collection. Listing 7–5 shows an example of changing the XML schema for `DataSet`. The default namespace for `DataSet` and its underlying `DataColumns` and `DataTables` is no namespace.

Listing 7–5 Changing a schema using column mappings

```
SqlDataAdapter da = new SqlDataAdapter(
    "select * from authors",
    "server=localhost;uid=sa;database=pubs");
DataSet ds = new DataSet();

da.TableMappings.Add("authors", "AllAuthors");
da.TableMappings[0].ColumnMappings.Add("au_id","AuthorID");

da.Fill(ds, "authors");
ds.Tables[0].Namespace = "http://www.develop.com/dmauth";
ds.Tables[0].Prefix = "dmauth";
ds.WriteXmlSchema("myauthors.xsd");
```

XML data can take the form of elements, attributes, or element text. The default in `DataSet` is elements, but you can override it by specifying an XML schema or by using the `InferXmlSchema` method. For those `DataSet`s that do not populate their schema from XML, it can be specified by using `DataColumn`'s `ColumnMapping` property. `ColumnMapping` choices are `MappingType.Element`, `Attribute`, `SimpleText`, or `Hidden`. The latter indicates that this column will not be serialized when `DataSet` is serialized as XML. Listing 7–6 shows the results of using the XML properties of `DataSet`.

Listing 7–6 Using namespace, prefix, and mappings

```
// This code:

DataSet ds = new DataSet();
SqlDataAdapter da = new SqlDataAdapter(
  "select top 2 * from jobs",
  "server=localhost;uid=sa;database=pubs");
da.Fill(ds);
DataTable t = ds.Tables[0];
t.Columns[1].Namespace = "http://www.develop.com";
t.Columns[1].Prefix = "DM";
t.Columns[2].ColumnMapping = MappingType.Attribute;
ds.WriteXml(@"c:\xml_documents\dmjobs.xml");

// Produces this document:

<?xml version="1.0" standalone="yes"?>
<NewDataSet>
  <Table min_lvl="10">
    <job_id>1</job_id>
    <DM:job_desc
     xmlns:DM="http://www.develop.com">
    Vice Chairman</DM:job_desc>
    <max_lvl>10</max_lvl>
  </Table>
  <Table min_lvl="200">
    <job_id>2</job_id>
    <DM:job_desc
     xmlns:DM="http://www.develop.com">
    Grand Poobah</DM:job_desc>
    <max_lvl>250</max_lvl>
  </Table>
</NewDataSet>
```

When you write a DataSet containing multiple DataTables in XML format, each DataTable is an immediate child of the root element, as shown in Listings 7–7 and 7–8.

Listing 7–7 Data relations and XML

```
SqlDataAdapter da = new SqlDataAdapter(
  "select au_id, au_fname, au_lname from authors;" +
  "select au_id, title_id from titleauthor",
  "server=localhost;uid=sa;database=pubs");
DataSet ds = new DataSet();
da.Fill(ds, "foo");
ds.Tables[0].TableName = "authors";
ds.Tables[1].TableName = "titleauthor";

// non-nested relation
ds.Relations.Add(ds.Tables[0].Columns["au_id"],
  ds.Tables[1].Columns["au_id"]);
ds.Relations[0].Nested = false;
ds.WriteXml("myfile.xml");
```

Listing 7–8 With Nested=false (default)

```xml
<?xml version="1.0" standalone="yes"?>
<NewDataSet>
  <authors>
    <au_id>213-46-8915</au_id>
    <au_fname>Bob</au_fname>
    <au_lname>Green</au_lname>
  </authors>
  <authors>
    <au_id>472-27-2349</au_id>
    <au_fname>Burt</au_fname>
    <au_lname>Gringlesby</au_lname>
  </authors>
  <titleauthor>
    <au_id>213-46-8915</au_id>
    <title_id>BU1032</title_id>
  </titleauthor>
  <titleauthor>
    <au_id>213-46-8915</au_id>
    <title_id>BU2075</title_id>
  </titleauthor>
  <titleauthor>
    <au_id>486-29-1786</au_id>
```

ESSENTIAL ADO.NET

```
      <title_id>PS7777</title_id>
    </titleauthor>
  </NewDataSet>
```

To produce hierarchical XML from multiple `DataTables`, you must define a `DataRelation` between them, and the `DataRelation`'s `Nested` property must be set to `true`. This is illustrated in Listing 7–9.

Listing 7–9   With `Nested=true`

```
  <NewDataSet>
    <authors>
      <au_id>213-46-8915</au_id>
      <titleauthor>
        <au_id>213-46-8915</au_id>
        <title_id>BU1032</title_id>
      </titleauthor>
      <titleauthor>
        <au_id>213-46-8915</au_id>
        <title_id>BU2075</title_id>
      </titleauthor>
      <au_fname>Bob</au_fname>
      <au_lname>Green</au_lname>
    </authors>
    <authors>
      <au_id>472-27-2349</au_id>
      <titleauthor>
        <au_id>472-27-2349</au_id>
        <title_id>TC7777</title_id>
      </titleauthor>
      <au_fname>Burt</au_fname>
      <au_lname>Gringlesby</au_lname>
    </authors>
  </NewDataSet>
```

7.2.3   Reading XML into `DataSet`

XML document data can be read into `DataSet` just as data from `DataAdapter` can, using one of the overloads of `DataSet.ReadXml`. There are the usual four overloads: `String`, `Stream`, `TextReader`, and `XmlReader`. To refine the process, you can use another set of overloads via a second `XmlReadMode` parameter. There is also a set of mostly symmetric `WriteXml` methods.

There are two ways to read and write the contents of `DataSet`. The default is to read or write all the current values in `DataSet` that are not specified as `DataColumn.ColumnMapping = MappingType.Hidden`. An example is shown earlier in Listing 7–6. A second format, known as DiffGram, includes all the current rows, before images for those rows that you have changed since the last time you called `AcceptChanges`, and a set of error elements that contains errors for specific rows. Listing 7–10 shows the general layout of a DiffGram.

Listing 7–10   General format of a DiffGram

```
<?xml version="1.0"?>
<diffgr:diffgram
 xmlns:msdata="urn:schemas-microsoft-com:xml-msdata"
 xmlns:diffgr="urn:schemas-microsoft-com:xml-diffgram-v1"
 xmlns:xsd="http://www.w3.org/2001/XMLSchema">

   <DataInstance>
   </DataInstance>

  <diffgr:before>
  </diffgr:before>

  <diffgr:errors>
  </diffgr:errors>
</diffgr:diffgram>
```

The DiffGram format adds annotations from the namespace `urn:schemas-microsoft-com:xml-diffgram-v1` to the XML output. The most important annotation is the `id` attribute, which is used to tie before images and errors to specific rows. Listing 7–11 shows a typical DiffGram. DiffGrams are discussed further in "Writing XML Data from `DataSet`" later in this chapter.

Listing 7–11   A DiffGram in which both rows have been changed

```
<?xml version="1.0" standalone="yes"?>
<diffgr:diffgram
 xmlns:msdata="urn:schemas-microsoft-com:xml-msdata"
 xmlns:diffgr="urn:schemas-microsoft-com:xml-diffgram-v1">
  <NewDataSet>
    <Table diffgr:id="Table1" msdata:rowOrder="0"
           diffgr:hasChanges="modified">
      <job_id>1</job_id>
      <job_desc>Different value</job_desc>
```

```
        <min_lvl>10</min_lvl>
        <max_lvl>10</max_lvl>
      </Table>
      <Table diffgr:id="Table2" msdata:rowOrder="1"
            diffgr:hasChanges="modified">
        <job_id>2</job_id>
        <job_desc>Different value</job_desc>
        <min_lvl>200</min_lvl>
        <max_lvl>250</max_lvl>
      </Table>
    </NewDataSet>
    <diffgr:before>
      <Table diffgr:id="Table1" msdata:rowOrder="0">
        <job_id>1</job_id>
        <job_desc>Vice Chairman</job_desc>
        <min_lvl>10</min_lvl>
        <max_lvl>10</max_lvl>
      </Table>
      <Table diffgr:id="Table2" msdata:rowOrder="1">
        <job_id>2</job_id>
        <job_desc>Grand Poobah</job_desc>
        <min_lvl>200</min_lvl>
        <max_lvl>250</max_lvl>
      </Table>
    </diffgr:before>
  </diffgr:diffgram>
```

When you read an XML document into a `DataSet` using `ReadXml`, you might have a document with an *embedded* schema (one that is contained in the same file or stream as the document) or a document that contains only the data. In addition, you can use `ReadXml` to read from a document that contains a Diff-Gram or a "normal" XML document. `XmlReadMode` specifies how the `ReadXml` method works. The following `XmlReadModes` are affected by the existence of a schema:

- `InferSchema`: Ignores an inline schema and infers the schema from the data. If tables already exist in the `DataSet` but have incompatible properties, an error is thrown. If the `DataSet`'s existing schema overlaps, tables or columns will be added.

- `IgnoreSchema`: Uses only the `DataSet`'s existing schema. Data in the XML input that does not match the existing schema is thrown away.

- `ReadSchema`: Uses the inline schema if one exists. If tables with the same name already exist in the `DataSet`'s schema, an exception is thrown.

- `DiffGram`: Applies the changes assuming DiffGram format as input. If the input is in DiffGram format, this works in the same way as the `DataSet.Merge` method. If the XML input is not in DiffGram format, this works the same as `IgnoreSchema`.

If the `XmlReadMode` is not specified, the default is `XmlReadMode.Auto`, which works as follows:

- If the XML input is a DiffGram, it is read as a DiffGram, possibly populating multiple `RowVersion`s in the `DataSet`.

- If the input is not in DiffGram format and if the `DataSet` already has a schema or there is an inline schema, `ReadSchema` is used.

- If no schema exists in the `DataSet` or inline, `InferSchema` is used.

Schemas used by `ReadXml` can be in either XDR or XSD format. Either XDR or XSD format can use inline schemas. XSD can also use the `xsi:SchemaLocation` attribute to specify the schema location.

Filling the `DataSet` by using `ReadXml` works differently than filling the `DataSet` using `DataAdapter.Fill`. When you use `DataAdapter`, by default, changes are implicitly accepted when `Fill` is finished; you can override this by setting `DataAdapter`'s `AcceptChangesDuringFill` property. Calling `RejectChanges` immediately after calling `Fill` has no effect. When `ReadXml` is used, the changes are not accepted until `AcceptChanges` is explicitly called. The reasoning behind this behavior is that `ReadXml` can be used to read rows into the `DataSet`, and these rows can be used to update a database through a `DataAdapter`, as shown in Listing 7–12. If `AcceptChanges` were implicit, attempting to update a database in this way would fail because the rows in the `DataSet` would be marked as original rows only. Calling `RejectChanges` after using `ReadXml` rolls back any rows added but leaves the schema intact, as shown in Listing 7–13.

Listing 7–12 Changes are not accepted during `ReadXml`

```
DataSet ds = new  DataSet();
SqlDataAdapter da = new SqlDataAdapter(
```

```
  "select * from jobs",
   "server=localhost;uid=sa;database=pubs");
SqlCommandBuilder bld = new SqlCommandBuilder(da);

da.MissingSchemaAction = MissingSchemaAction.AddWithKey;
da.Fill(ds, "jobs");

ds.ReadXml(@"c:\xml_documents\more_jobs.xml");

// adds jobs in more_jobs.xml to database
da.Update(ds, "jobs");
```

Listing 7–13 Calling `RejectChanges` deletes rows added by `ReadXml`

```
SqlDataAdapter da = new SqlDataAdapter(
   "select * from jobs",
   "server=localhost;uid=sa;database=pubs");
DataSet ds = new DataSet();
da.Fill(ds);
// 15 rows here
Console.WriteLine("{0} rows in table 0",
   ds.Tables[0].Rows.Count);
ds.RejectChanges();
// still 15 rows here
Console.WriteLine("{0} rows in table 0",
   ds.Tables[0].Rows.Count);

DataSet ds2 = new DataSet();
ds2.ReadXml(@"c:\xml_documents\jobs.xml");
// 15 rows here
Console.WriteLine("{0} rows in table 0",
   ds2.Tables[0].Rows.Count);
ds2.RejectChanges();
// table still exists but 0 rows
Console.WriteLine("{0} rows in table 0",
   ds2.Tables[0].Rows.Count);
```

The DiffGram format works differently from "ordinary" XML, no matter which `XmlReadMode` is specified. With any of the `XmlReadMode`s, if the table or tables that the DiffGram refers to do not already exist in the `DataSet`'s schema, `ReadXml` results in a `System.Data.DataException` being thrown. In addition, you must be very careful when mixing DiffGrams with `DataSet`s that are filled using `DataSet.Fill`. If all the metadata (such as `PrimaryKey` or `Unique` constraint) is not present when the DiffGram is read, the `DataSet` may contain duplicate rows, and the resulting call to `DataAdapter.Update` may fail or produce the wrong results. For best results when using `DataAdapter` to update a database, always retrieve the metadata by specifying `MissingSchemaAction.AddWithKey` or explicitly calling `DataAdapter.FillSchema`. The rule is to remember that using `XmlReadMode.DiffGram` acts like `DataSet.Merge`.

7.2.4 Writing XML Schemas from `DataSet`

When you write XML from `DataSet`, you have similar options as when reading XML. The instructions for writing the XML data and schema are specified as properties of `DataSet` and related classes, so the process is straightforward. `WriteXmlSchema` has the same four overloads as `ReadXmlSchema`; it can write to `Stream`, `String`, `TextWriter`, or `XmlWriter`. In contrast to reading, `WriteXmlSchema` does not allow a choice of schema format; only XSD schemas are supported. The schemas written reflect the `Namespace` and `Prefix` properties of the `DataSet`, `DataTables`, and `DataColumns` as well as the `DataRelation`'s `Nested` property and the `DataColumn`'s `ColumnMapping`. Although the schema is a full-fidelity XML schema, it does reflect the relational nature of the `DataTables` in the `DataSet`. In addition, the `DataSet`'s schema contains annotations from a Microsoft-specific namespace, making XML documents that use the schema load faster into the `DataSet` than those that don't use the schema.

Let's look at a sample `DataSet` containing two `DataTables` and a primary-foreign key relationship between them. The code that produced this `DataSet` is shown in Listing 7–14.

Listing 7–14   Code to produce an XML schema

```
SqlConnection conn = new SqlConnection(
  "server=(local);uid=sa;pwd=;database=pubs");
SqlDataAdapter da = new SqlDataAdapter(
  "select * from authors;select * from titleauthor",
  conn);

da.TableMappings.Add("Table", "authors");
da.TableMappings.Add("Table1", "titleauthors");
```

```
DataSet ds = new DataSet("OneMany");
da.MissingSchemaAction =
  MissingSchemaAction.AddWithKey;
da.Fill(ds);
ds.Relations.Add(
  "au_ta",
  ds.Tables[0].Columns["au_id"],
  ds.Tables[1].Columns["au_id"],
  true);
ds.Relations[0].Nested = true;
ds.WriteXmlSchema("one_to_many.xsd");
```

Listing 7–15 shows the schema produced by calling `DataSet.WriteXml-Schema`. Examining the schema in detail elucidates the relationship between relational data and XML. The most interesting point is that the schema is nonrelational! Although both the `authors` and the `titleauthors DataTables` are represented as `xsd:ComplexType`, the `titleauthors` table is represented as a nested `xsd:ComplexType`, an embedded member of `authors`. This representation is more similar to an object-oriented, embedded table view than to a relational view, where the tables are not hierarchical. This schema does not allow a "child" type without an existing parent, something that is consistent with the primary-foreign key constraint in a relational database.

Listing 7–15   Schema produced by the code in Listing 7–14

```
<?xml version="1.0" standalone="yes"?>
<xsd:schema id="OneMany" targetNamespace=""
    xmlns="" xmlns:xsd="http://www.w3.org/2001/XMLSchema"
    xmlns:msdata="urn:schemas-microsoft-com:xml-msdata">
  <xsd:element name="OneMany" msdata:IsDataSet="true">
    <xsd:complexType>
      <xsd:choice maxOccurs="unbounded">
        <xsd:element name="authors">
          <xsd:complexType>
            <xsd:sequence>
              <xsd:element name="au_id"
                           type="xsd:string" />
              <xsd:element name="au_lname"
                           type="xsd:string" />
              <xsd:element name="au_fname"
                           type="xsd:string" />
              <xsd:element name="phone"
```

```xml
                              type="xsd:string" />
              <xsd:element name="address"
                           type="xsd:string"
                           minOccurs="0" />
              <xsd:element name="city"
                           type="xsd:string"
                           minOccurs="0" />
              <xsd:element name="state"
                           type="xsd:string"
                           minOccurs="0" />
              <xsd:element name="zip"
                           type="xsd:string"
                           minOccurs="0" />
              <xsd:element name="contract"
                           type="xsd:boolean" />
              <xsd:element name="titleauthors"
                           minOccurs="0"
                           maxOccurs="unbounded">
              <xsd:complexType>
                <xsd:sequence>
                  <xsd:element name="au_id"
                               type="xsd:string" />
                  <xsd:element name="title_id"
                               type="xsd:string" />
                  <xsd:element name="au_ord"
                               type="xsd:unsignedByte"
                               minOccurs="0" />
                  <xsd:element name="royaltyper"
                               type="xsd:int"
                               minOccurs="0" />
                </xsd:sequence>
              </xsd:complexType>
              </xsd:element>
            </xsd:sequence>
          </xsd:complexType>
        </xsd:element>
      </xsd:choice>
    </xsd:complexType>
    <xsd:unique name="titleauthors_Constraint1"
     msdata:ConstraintName="Constraint1"
     msdata:PrimaryKey="true">
      <xsd:selector xpath=".//titleauthors" />
      <xsd:field xpath="au_id" />
      <xsd:field xpath="title_id" />
```

```
      </xsd:unique>
      <xsd:unique name="Constraint1"
                  msdata:PrimaryKey="true">
        <xsd:selector xpath=".//authors" />
        <xsd:field xpath="au_id" />
      </xsd:unique>
      <xsd:keyref name="au_ta"
                  refer="Constraint1"
                  msdata:IsNested="true">
        <xsd:selector xpath=".//titleauthors" />
        <xsd:field xpath="au_id" />
      </xsd:keyref>
    </xsd:element>
  </xsd:schema>
```

Because the code does not specify otherwise, all `DataColumns` are represented as elements. This results in `DataColumns` that can be NULL, using the `minOccurs="0"` facet in the schema. NULL values will be represented, not by empty elements but instead by the element's absence in the data. This distinguishes a NULL value from an empty string, as in relational databases. Both the `authors` and the `titleauthors` primary keys are represented by the `xsd:unique` production. The relationship between the two tables is represented by an `xsd:keyref` production. Note that the `xsd:key` production is not used to indicate that the unique fields are primary keys. Instead, this is indicated by a Microsoft-specific annotation.

7.2.5 Microsoft-Specific Annotations

The `urn:schemas-microsoft-com:xml-msdata` namespace annotations used in the `DataSet`'s schema are the most controversial part of the schema, although they are in complete compliance with the schema recommendation document. XML purists argue that they are a "hack" and should not be included in an XML schema at all. Another opinion is that they are convenience features that can be safely ignored by systems that do not support .NET `DataSets`. The truth falls somewhere in between.

Let's look at some of these annotations. The first annotation, `msdata:Is-DataSet="true"`, appears on the element that will become the `DataSet`. Although it may appear at first that there should be a `DataSet xsd:ComplexType`, it is impossible because `DataSet` is a generic container. The number of `DataTable`, `DataColumn`, and `DataRelation` items can vary with each instance, although each `DataSet` instance can be precisely described. The `msdata:IsDataSet` annotation assists in deserialization for systems that support such a container; other systems can safely ignore it, although the resulting structure graph will not have `DataSet` semantics, such as the ability to dynamically add a `DataTable`.

The `msdata:ConstraintName="Constraint1"` annotation is an interesting way to specify a relational constraint. It combines with the `"name"` attribute of the `authors` table `PrimaryKey` and the `"refer"` attribute of the `xsd:keyref` production to define a relationship. This definition is nonstandard and outside the realm of XSD, but it is a compliant schema element. Using the annotation that results in using `msdata:PrimaryKey="true"` on an `xsd:unique` production instead of the `xsd:key` production is not technically the best way to describe the key in XML schemas, but it does permit the `DataSet` to have primary-foreign key relationships using unique fields that are not primary keys. Because `DataSet` allows this, using the `PrimaryKey` production simplifies deserialization.

The last annotation, `msdata:IsNested="true"`, allows `DataSet` to serialize hierarchical XML when the relationship is not actually a nested table hierarchy. This is a convenience feature for XML processors that "prefer" a hierarchical representation.

Using Microsoft-specific annotations to coerce relational data into different shapes is a step you can take toward bridging the gap between relational and other data representations. This step is necessary because strict relational is a simplification of the rich set of data representations possible in XML. I discuss this issue further in Chapter 10.

7.2.6   Writing XML Data from `DataSet`

XML data can be written from `DataSet` in a variety of formats. Each format reflects the `Prefixes`, `Namespaces`, `Relations`, and `ColumnMappings` and can be validated using the schema that would be written using `WriteXmlSchema` against the same `DataSet`. The `DataSet.WriteXml` method has two series of the same four overloads as `DataSet.ReadXml`; the second parameter is the

`XmlWriteMode` enumeration. The `XmlWriteMode` is a simple enumeration; a `DataSet` can be written with or without the corresponding XSD schema. In addition, it can be written as DiffGram format.

DiffGram format is an XML representation of an entire `DataSet` with extra rows that correspond to pending changes. Listing 7–16 shows an example that adds, deletes, and changes rows in an existing `DataSet`, along with the Diff-Gram produced. Note that this code uses annotations from the `msdata` prefixed namespace and that the DiffGram itself comes from a new namespace (`urn:schemas-microsoft-com:xml-diffgram-v1`). The `msdata` annotation is used to define the order in which the rows occur in the `DataSet`. Everything else is defined in the DiffGram's namespace. The DiffGram assigns each row a unique ID composed of the `TableName` and an ordinal, in this case `Table1X`, where `Table1` is the `TableName` and `X` is the unique-ifier. The DiffGram consists of a set of current rows in the `DataSet` followed by a set of rows contained within a `diffgram:before` element. Changes are represented by `before` images and the `diffgram:hasChanges` attribute. Changed rows have a `before` and `current` row, and each has a `hasChanges="modified"` attribute. Inserted rows appear in the `current` set of rows only and have a `hasChanges="inserted"` attribute. Deleted rows appear in the `before` section only and are marked with `hasChanges="deleted"`. From this format, an entire `DataSet` of rows and changes is represented. A DiffGram can be persisted with or without schema.

Listing 7–16 DiffGram produced after making changes

```
//
// This code:

DataSet ds = new DataSet();
SqlDataAdapter da = new SqlDataAdapter(
  "select * from jobs",
  "server=localhost;uid=sa;database=pubs");

da.MissingSchemaAction = MissingSchemaAction.AddWithKey;
da.Fill(ds);

ds.Tables[0].Rows[1][1] = "newer description";
ds.Tables[0].Rows[2].Delete();
```

```
ds.Tables[0].Rows.Add(
  new object[4] { null, "new row", 40, 40 });

ds.WriteXml(@"c:\xml_documents\writeDiffGram.xml",
  XmlWriteMode.DiffGram);

<!-- produces this DiffGram -->
<?xml version="1.0" standalone="yes"?>
<diffgr:diffgram
 xmlns:msdata="urn:schemas-microsoft-com:xml-msdata"
 xmlns:diffgr="urn:schemas-microsoft-com:xml-diffgram-v1"
>
  <NewDataSet>
    <Table diffgr:id="Table1" msdata:rowOrder="0">
      <job_id>1</job_id>
      <job_desc>Vice Chairman</job_desc>
      <min_lvl>10</min_lvl>
      <max_lvl>10</max_lvl>
    </Table>
    <Table diffgr:id="Table2" msdata:rowOrder="1"
           diffgr:hasChanges="modified">
      <job_id>2</job_id>
      <job_desc>newer description</job_desc>
      <min_lvl>200</min_lvl>
      <max_lvl>250</max_lvl>
    </Table>
    <Table diffgr:id="Table4" msdata:rowOrder="3">
      <job_id>4</job_id>
      <job_desc>Chief Financial Officier</job_desc>
      <min_lvl>175</min_lvl>
      <max_lvl>250</max_lvl>
    </Table>
    <Table diffgr:id="Table5" msdata:rowOrder="4">
      <job_id>5</job_id>
      <job_desc>Publisher</job_desc>
      <min_lvl>150</min_lvl>
      <max_lvl>250</max_lvl>
    </Table>
    <Table diffgr:id="Table6" msdata:rowOrder="5">
      <job_id>6</job_id>
      <job_desc>Managing Editor</job_desc>
      <min_lvl>140</min_lvl>
      <max_lvl>225</max_lvl>
    </Table>
```

```
    <!-- some rows (6-14) deleted from diagram here... -->
    <Table diffgr:id="Table16" msdata:rowOrder="15"
            diffgr:hasChanges="inserted">
      <job_id>0</job_id>
      <job_desc>new row</job_desc>
      <min_lvl>40</min_lvl>
      <max_lvl>40</max_lvl>
    </Table>
  </NewDataSet>
  <diffgr:before>
    <Table diffgr:id="Table2" msdata:rowOrder="1">
      <job_id>2</job_id>
      <job_desc>zzz</job_desc>
      <min_lvl>200</min_lvl>
      <max_lvl>250</max_lvl>
    </Table>
    <Table diffgr:id="Table3" msdata:rowOrder="2">
      <job_id>3</job_id>
      <job_desc>Business Operations Manager</job_desc>
      <min_lvl>175</min_lvl>
      <max_lvl>225</max_lvl>
    </Table>
  </diffgr:before>
</diffgr:diffgram>
```

Finally, you can produce a second `DataSet` consisting only of changes and then write the changes as a DiffGram. This technique is useful when you're marshaling changes because the entire `DataSet` need not be passed across the wire. To implement this, you use `DataSet`'s `GetChanges` method. Listing 7–17 shows an example of the code and resulting DiffGram.

Listing 7–17 Using `GetChanges` and DiffGrams

```
//
// This code

DataSet ds = new DataSet();
SqlDataAdapter da = new SqlDataAdapter(
  "select * from jobs",
  "server=localhost;uid=sa;database=pubs");
da.MissingSchemaAction = MissingSchemaAction.AddWithKey;
da.Fill(ds);

ds.Tables[0].Rows[1][1] = "newer description";
```

```
ds.Tables[0].Rows[2].Delete();
ds.Tables[0].Rows.Add(
  new object[4] { null, "new row", 40, 40 });

DataSet ds2 = new DataSet();
ds2 = ds.GetChanges();
ds2.WriteXml(
 "c:\\xml_documents\\writeDiffGramChanges.xml",
 XmlWriteMode.DiffGram);

<!-- produces this DiffGram -->
<?xml version="1.0" standalone="yes"?>
<diffgr:diffgram
 xmlns:msdata="urn:schemas-microsoft-com:xml-msdata"
 xmlns:diffgr="urn:schemas-microsoft-com:xml-diffgram-v1"
>
  <NewDataSet>
    <Table diffgr:id="Table1" msdata:rowOrder="0"
           diffgr:hasChanges="modified">
      <job_id>2</job_id>
      <job_desc>newer description</job_desc>
      <min_lvl>200</min_lvl>
      <max_lvl>250</max_lvl>
    </Table>
    <Table diffgr:id="Table3" msdata:rowOrder="2"
           diffgr:hasChanges="inserted">
      <job_id>0</job_id>
      <job_desc>new row</job_desc>
     <min_lvl>40</min_lvl>
      <max_lvl>40</max_lvl>
    </Table>
  </NewDataSet>
  <diffgr:before>
    <Table diffgr:id="Table1" msdata:rowOrder="0">
      <job_id>2</job_id>
      <job_desc>zzz</job_desc>
      <min_lvl>200</min_lvl>
      <max_lvl>250</max_lvl>
    </Table>
    <Table diffgr:id="Table2" msdata:rowOrder="1">
      <job_id>3</job_id>
      <job_desc>Business Operations Manager</job_desc>
      <min_lvl>175</min_lvl>
      <max_lvl>225</max_lvl>
```

```
    </Table>
  </diffgr:before>
</diffgr:diffgram>
```

After you have produced a `DataSet` as a result of using `GetChanges`, you can persist it as a DiffGram (current and changed rows) or as a normal XML document (current rows only). You can also use `GetChanges` to get the rows that have a certain `RowState`, such as only `Added` rows. Listing 7–18 shows the use of `GetChanges` to marshal changes made on the client tier back to a middle tier, where they are used in an update. Note that, although all data is always marshaled in XML format, only changed data is sent across the wire, thereby cutting down on network traffic. Finally, the changed rows are returned to the client to refresh the client's copy of the `DataSet`.

Listing 7–18 Round-trip update; only changes are marshaled in XML format

```
// 1. middle tier
DataSet ds = new DataSet();
SqlDataAdapter da = new SqlDataAdapter(
   "select * from jobs",
   "server=localhost;uid=sa;database=pubs");

da.MissingSchemaAction = MissingSchemaAction.AddWithKey;
da.Fill(ds);
// 2. pass to client here

ds.Tables[0].Rows[1][1] = "newer description";
ds.Tables[0].Rows[14].Delete();
ds.Tables[0].Rows.Add(
  new object[4] { null, "new row", 40, 40 });

DataSet ds2 = new DataSet();
ds2 = ds.GetChanges();
// 3. pass ds2 back to middle tier here
// just pass back the changes

SqlCommandBuilder bld = new SqlCommandBuilder(da);
da.InsertCommand = bld.GetInsertCommand();
da.UpdateCommand = bld.GetUpdateCommand();
da.DeleteCommand = bld.GetDeleteCommand();

// make sure we get the identity column on insert
```

```
da.InsertCommand.CommandText +=
  ";select * from jobs where job_id = @@identity";
da.InsertCommand.UpdatedRowSource =
  UpdateRowSource.FirstReturnedRecord;

// update on middle tier using changes only.
// refresh with most current rows
// this is only needed for insert,
// update has most current rows
da.Update(ds2);
// 4. pass changes only back to client

// client now contains latest changes
ds.Merge(ds2);
```

7.3 Serialization, Marshaling, and `DataSet`

Rather than use a binary format by default, as in ADO classic, the `DataSet` default is XML serialization and marshaling. This means that you can populate `DataSet` from non-Microsoft data sources, and the data is consumable from non-Microsoft platforms. Because `DataSet` marshals as an XML document, it is natively supported without transformation by Web Services.

The .NET platform includes two libraries that serialize and deserialize classes in XML format:

- `System.Runtime.Serialization` is used for marshaling in .NET implementations.

- `System.Xml.Serialization` is used in Web Services to support unlike implementations.

`DataSet` is compatible with both of them.

`System.Runtime.Serialization` serializes .NET classes using two formatters included in the .NET framework: the Binary formatter and the SOAP formatter. The Binary formatter uses a .NET-specific format and protocol to optimize size by reducing the number of bytes transmitted. The SOAP formatter uses an XML-based format and the Simple Object Access Protocol. The standardization of SOAP details is in progress under the auspices of the W3C XML-SP committee. `System.Runtime.Serialization.SoapFormatter` uses SOAP 1.1 as its format. SOAP 1.1 is currently a W3C note; an updated version

(SOAP 1.2) has been released. The SOAP formatter is CLR type-centric. It can serialize any CLR type to SOAP format but cannot serialize any arbitrary XML; some XML types cannot be processed, and others are serialized differently from the expected XSD-defined format. For example, arrays are serialized according to SOAP section 5, which is not consistent with XSD schemas.

`System.Xml.Serialization` is XML-centric in its approach. It can serialize any XML simple or complex type that can be represented in an XML schema, but it may not be able to serialize all CLR types with 100 percent fidelity. It is used in the `System.Web.Services` library for greatest compatibility with unlike platforms. The inability of CLR serialization to serialize all schema types, and the inability of `XML.Serialization` to handle all CLR types, is not a deficiency of the implementation; rather, it's a result of the inherent difference between the schema type system and the CLR type system.

To indicate support for serialization using `System.Runtime.Serialization`, the class must mark itself with the `[Serializable]` attribute. Classes that use the `[Serializable]` attribute can either accept the system's default serialization mechanism or implement `ISerializable` in a class-specific manner. Listing 7–19 shows how to use the `[Serializable]` attribute and implement a custom version of `ISerializable`.

Listing 7–19   A class that implements `ISerializable`

```
[Serializable]
public class Foo : ISerializable
{
  public int x, y;
  public Foo() {}

  internal Foo(SerializationInfo si,
            StreamingContext context)
  {
      //Restore our values.
      x = si.GetInt32("i");
      y = si.GetInt32("j");
  }

  public void GetObjectData(SerializationInfo si,
                      StreamingContext context)
  {
```

```
        //Add our three scalar values;
        si.AddValue("x", x);
        si.AddValue("y", y);

        Type t = this.GetType();
        si.AddValue("TypeObj", t);
    }
}
```

Note that implementing `ISerializable` requires two things: implementing the `GetObjectData` method to fill in the `SerializationInfo` property bag, and implementing a constructor that takes the `SerializationInfo` and `StreamingContext` parameters. Custom serialization methods can be implemented to optimize serialization based on the `StreamingContext`. The `DataSet` class implements a custom version of `ISerializable`.

XML schema-centric serialization is controlled by the `XmlSerializer` class in the `System.Xml.Serialization` namespace. This class can generate custom `XmlSerializationReader`/`XmlSerializationWriter` pairs on a per-type basis. By default, `XmlSerializer` uses a one-to-one CLR-class-to-XML-complex-type mapping. Classes can customize the exact serialization by decorating their class declarations with a series of CLR attributes from the `System.Xml.Serialization` namespace. `DataSet` uses a custom mechanism to interact with `XmlSerializer`.

`DataSet` supports both `System.Runtime.Serialization` and `System.Xml.Serialization`. It supports each one through its implementations of `ReadXmlSchema`/`ReadXml` and `WriteXmlSchema`/`WriteXml`. When `System.Runtime.Serialization` is used, `GetObjectData` uses the `WriteXmlSchema` and `WriteXml` methods directly. In addition, `DataSet` has the appropriate constructor for custom serialization and invokes `ReadXmlSchema` and `ReadXml` to populate itself from `SerializationInfo`. There are no optimizations for different streaming contexts; `DataSet` is marshaled by value even across `appdomain` boundaries.

`DataSet` supports custom XML-centric serialization by implementing a special interface, `IXmlSerializable`. Currently it is the only class in the base class libraries to implement this interface. `IXmlSerializable` has three methods—`ReadXml`, `WriteXml`, and `GetSchema`—which are implemented in

DataSet by calling the appropriate Read or WriteXml and Read or WriteXmlSchema, just as in System.Runtime.Serialization.

If you want to use complex types as DataColumns, it is useful to know exactly how DataSet is serialized. When DataSet is serialized, WriteXml calls XmlDataTreeWriter, which eventually writes each row with an XmlDataRowWriter. Then XmlDataRowWriter calls DataColumn.ObjectToXml on every column. DataColumn.ObjectToXml calls only System.Data.Common.DataStorage.ObjectToXml. The System.Data.Common.DataStorage class has a static method called CreateStorage. It creates Storage classes for any of the concrete types it supports—that is, it calls the constructor on the concrete classes: System.Data.Common.XXXStorage.

A final storage class is called ObjectStorage. Any class that is not directly supported by DataSet will use the ObjectStorage class. This is important when you think back to the example in Chapter 4 that stores Object types in DataSet.

Every DataColumn value in a DataTable is represented as XML by calling its ToString method. It is rehydrated from XML by using a constructor that takes a single string as input. Therefore, to use arbitrary objects as DataColumn types, they must have a ToString method that renders their value as XML and a single string constructor. This is a difficult design decision because a method (ToString) that may produce string output for reports must be reserved for XML, but the decision must be tempered by the fact that a complex type usually cannot be represented as a single string. Listing 7–20 illustrates this type of object using the Person class from Chapter 4.

Listing 7–20 Producing correct XML with the Person class

```
public class Person
{
  public String name;
  public int age;

  public Person(String serstr)
    {
      Person p;
      XmlSerializer ser = new XmlSerializer(typeof(Person));
      p = (Person)ser.Deserialize(new StringReader(serstr));
```

```
            this.age = p.age;
            this.name = p.name;
        }

    public override string ToString()
        {
            String s;
            StringBuilder mysb =
                new StringBuilder();
            StringWriter myStringWriter =
                new StringWriter(mysb);
            XmlSerializer ser = new XmlSerializer(this.GetType());
                ser.Serialize(myStringWriter, this);

            s = myStringWriter.ToString();
            return s;
        }
    }
```

To use an embedded `DataTable` in a `DataColumn`, as you did in Chapter 4, you must override the `DataTable`'s implementation of these two methods. Unfortunately, the `DataTable` has a single string constructor, and to implement this constructor in such a way changes the semantics of the base class and is suboptimal. SQL Server's `UNIQUEIDENTIFIER` class is an example of using this pair of methods to map to `System.Guid`, which has the appropriate constructor and `ToString` method to be correctly marshaled as a column inside `DataSet`. The `DataSet` class implements two additional public methods—`ShouldSerializeTables` and `ShouldSerializeRelations`—to allow `Serialization` to work with subclasses, such as strongly typed `DataSets`.

7.4 Typed `DataSets`

One of the functions performed by `XSD.exe`, the XML schema generation tool, is to generate a *typed* `DataSet` from an XSD schema. This functionality is also available in Visual Studio as a menu item and context menu entry on an existing "`DataAdapter` object." What exactly is a typed `DataSet`?

A typed `DataSet` is a subclass of `System.Data.DataSet` in which the tables that exist in the `DataSet` are derived by reading the XSD schema information. The difference between a typed `DataSet` and an "ordinary" `DataSet` is that the `DataRows`, `DataTables`, and other items are available as strong types; that is, rather than refer to `DataSet.Tables[0]` or `DataSet.Tables["customers"]`, you code against a strongly typed `DataTable` named, for example, `MyDataSet.Customers`. Typed `DataSets` have the advantage that the strongly typed variable names can be checked at compile time rather than causing errors at runtime. A short example will illustrate this concept.

Suppose you have a `DataSet` that should contain a table named `customers`. It should have columns named `custid` and `custname`. You can refer to the table and the columns by ordinal or by name. As shown in Listing 7–21, the data is loosely typed when referred to by ordinal or name, meaning that the compiler cannot guarantee that you've spelled the column name correctly or used the correct ordinal. The problem is that the error informing you of this occurs at runtime rather than at compile time. If the `DataSet` items were strongly typed, misspelling the column name or using the wrong ordinal would be prevented because the code simply would not compile.

Listing 7–21 Referring to `DataTables` and `Columns`

```
DataSet ds = new DataSet();
// some action to load the DataSet...

// this will fail if second table does not exist
String name = ds.Tables[1].TableName;
// this will fail if the table is named customers
DataTable t = ds.Tables["customesr"];

// This will fail if the DataRow r has fewer than 5 columns
// or if column 5 is a String data type
DataRow r;
int value = (int)r[4];
// This will fail if there is a column named "custname"
String value = r["custnam"].ToString();
```

This does not solve every problem; mismatches can still occur if the database schema changes between the time the typed `DataSet` was generated and runtime. But because the structure of the `DataSet` is built into the names, the compiler can catch the misspellings. The examples in Listing 7–22 illustrate this.

Listing 7–22 Strong typing in `DataSet`

```
// this fails at compile time if the name of
// the table should be "customers"
DataTable t = MyDataSet.Customesr;

// so does this, should be custname
String value = MyDataSet.Customers[0].custnam;
```

The easiest way to generate a typed `DataSet` corresponding to an existing database resultset is through Visual Studio or `XSD.exe`, using an existing table, stored procedure, SQL statement, or in the case of `XSD.exe`, an XML schema. In Visual Studio, you can create a typed `DataSet` from any `DataAdapter` object that has been dropped on a form, as shown in Figure 7–2. The Visual Studio designer instantiates the `DataAdapter`, calls `FillSchema` internally, and feeds the results into a code generator (you can produce typed `DataSets` in C# or VB.NET).

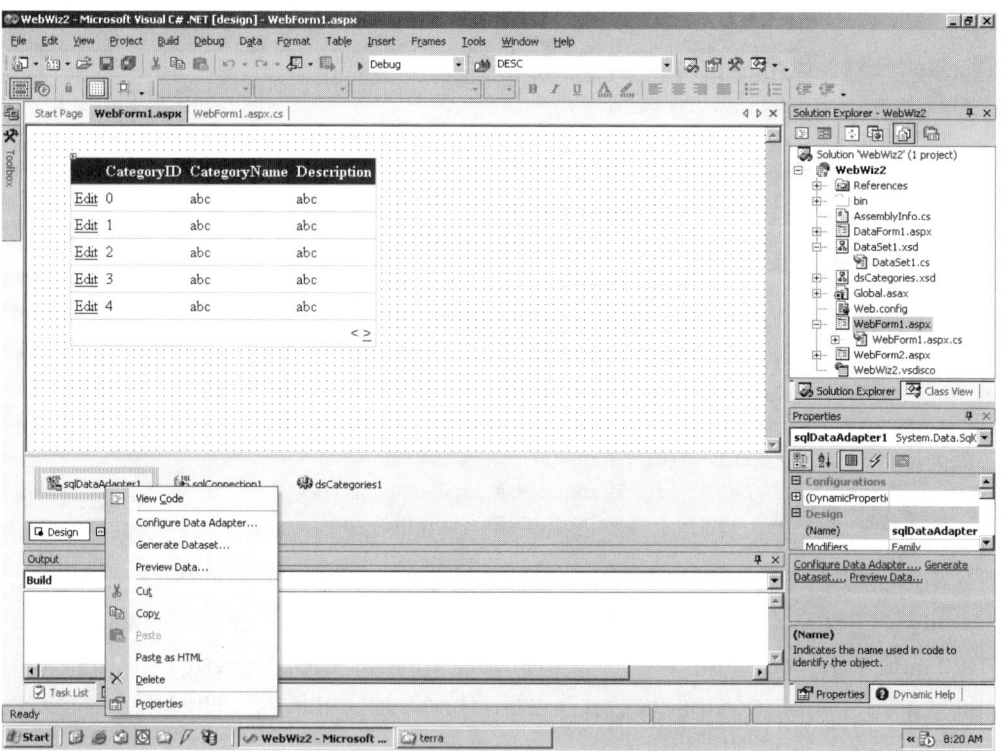

Figure 7–2 Generating a typed `DataSet` in Visual Studio

ESSENTIAL ADO.NET

The manual equivalent of this is to `Fill` a `DataSet`, save the schema with `DataSet.WriteXmlSchema`, and then use the schema as input into `XSD.exe`. For example, let's generate a typed `DataSet` for the simple one-table case shown in Listing 7–23 and see what we get.

Listing 7–23 Producing input for a typed `DataSet`

```
SqlDataAdapter da = new SqlDataAdapter(
   "select * from jobs",
   "server=localhost;uid=sa;database=pubs");

// name the DataSet MyDS
DataSet ds = new DataSet("MyDS");

// name the table MyTable
da.Fill(ds, "MyTable");

ds.WriteXmlSchema("myschema.xsd");
```

Listing 7–24 shows the complete source code for the sample typed `DataSet`.

Listing 7–24 A typed `DataSet` subclass generated by `XSD.exe`

```
//
// This source code was auto-generated by xsd
//
using System;
using System.Data;
using System.Xml;
using System.Runtime.Serialization;


[Serializable()]
[System.ComponentModel.DesignerCategoryAttribute("code")]
[System.Diagnostics.DebuggerStepThrough()]
[System.ComponentModel.ToolboxItem(true)]
public class JobsDS : DataSet {

  private jobsDataTable tablejobs;

    public JobsDS() {
        this.InitClass();
        System.ComponentModel.CollectionChangeEventHandler
          schemaChangedHandler = new
          System.ComponentModel.CollectionChangeEventHandler(
```

```
                        this.SchemaChanged);
                this.Tables.CollectionChanged += schemaChangedHandler;
                this.Relations.CollectionChanged += schemaChangedHandler;
            }

        protected JobsDS(SerializationInfo info, StreamingContext context) {
                string strSchema = ((string)(info.GetValue("XmlSchema",
                  typeof(string)))));
                if ((strSchema != null)) {
                    DataSet ds = new DataSet();
                    ds.ReadXmlSchema(new XmlTextReader(new
                        System.IO.StringReader(strSchema)));
                    if ((ds.Tables["jobs"] != null)) {
                    this.Tables.Add(new jobsDataTable(ds.Tables["jobs"]));
                    }
                    this.DataSetName = ds.DataSetName;
                    this.Prefix = ds.Prefix;
                    this.Namespace = ds.Namespace;
                    this.Locale = ds.Locale;
                    this.CaseSensitive = ds.CaseSensitive;
                    this.EnforceConstraints = ds.EnforceConstraints;
                  this.Merge(ds, false, System.Data.MissingSchemaAction.Add);
                    this.InitVars();
                }
                else {
                    this.InitClass();
                }
                this.GetSerializationData(info, context);
                System.ComponentModel.CollectionChangeEventHandler
                  schemaChangedHandler = new
                    System.ComponentModel.CollectionChangeEventHandler(
                        this.SchemaChanged);
                this.Tables.CollectionChanged += schemaChangedHandler;
                this.Relations.CollectionChanged += schemaChangedHandler;
            }

        [System.ComponentModel.Browsable(false)]
        [System.ComponentModel.DesignerSerializationVisibilityAttribute(
         System.ComponentModel.DesignerSerializationVisibility.Content)]
        public jobsDataTable jobs {
            get {
                return this.tablejobs;
            }
        }
```

```
public override DataSet Clone() {
    JobsDS cln = ((JobsDS)(base.Clone()));
    cln.InitVars();
    return cln;
}

protected override bool ShouldSerializeTables() {
    return false;
}

protected override bool ShouldSerializeRelations() {
    return false;
}

protected override void ReadXmlSerializable(XmlReader reader)
{
    this.Reset();
    DataSet ds = new DataSet();
    ds.ReadXml(reader);
    if ((ds.Tables["jobs"] != null)) {
        this.Tables.Add(new jobsDataTable(ds.Tables["jobs"]));
    }
    this.DataSetName = ds.DataSetName;
    this.Prefix = ds.Prefix;
    this.Namespace = ds.Namespace;
    this.Locale = ds.Locale;
    this.CaseSensitive = ds.CaseSensitive;
    this.EnforceConstraints = ds.EnforceConstraints;
    this.Merge(ds, false, System.Data.MissingSchemaAction.Add);
    this.InitVars();
}

protected override System.Xml.Schema.XmlSchema
  GetSchemaSerializable() {
    System.IO.MemoryStream stream = new System.IO.MemoryStream();
    this.WriteXmlSchema(new XmlTextWriter(stream, null));
    stream.Position = 0;
    return System.Xml.Schema.XmlSchema.Read(new
        XmlTextReader(stream), null);
}

internal void InitVars() {
    this.tablejobs = ((jobsDataTable)(this.Tables["jobs"]));
```

```csharp
            if ((this.tablejobs != null)) {
                this.tablejobs.InitVars();
            }
        }

        private void InitClass() {
            this.DataSetName = "JobsDS";
            this.Prefix = "";
            this.Namespace = "";
            this.Locale = new System.Globalization.CultureInfo
                ("en-US");
            this.CaseSensitive = false;
            this.EnforceConstraints = true;
            this.tablejobs = new jobsDataTable();
            this.Tables.Add(this.tablejobs);
        }

        private bool ShouldSerializejobs() {
            return false;
        }

        private void SchemaChanged(object sender,
         System.ComponentModel.CollectionChangeEventArgs e) {
            if ((e.Action ==
         System.ComponentModel.CollectionChangeAction.Remove)) {
                this.InitVars();
            }
        }

    public delegate void jobsRowChangeEventHandler(object sender,
        jobsRowChangeEvent e);

    [System.Diagnostics.DebuggerStepThrough()]
    public class jobsDataTable : DataTable,
                    System.Collections.IEnumerable {

        private DataColumn columnjob_id;

        private DataColumn columnjob_desc;

        private DataColumn columnmin_lvl;

        private DataColumn columnmax_lvl;
```

```csharp
internal jobsDataTable() :
        base("jobs") {
    this.InitClass();
}


internal jobsDataTable(DataTable table) :
        base(table.TableName) {
    if ((table.CaseSensitive != table.DataSet.CaseSensitive)) {
        this.CaseSensitive = table.CaseSensitive;
    }
    if ((table.Locale.ToString() !=
        table.DataSet.Locale.ToString())) {
        this.Locale = table.Locale;
    }
    if ((table.Namespace != table.DataSet.Namespace)) {
        this.Namespace = table.Namespace;
    }
    this.Prefix = table.Prefix;
    this.MinimumCapacity = table.MinimumCapacity;
    this.DisplayExpression = table.DisplayExpression;
}


[System.ComponentModel.Browsable(false)]
public int Count {
    get {
        return this.Rows.Count;
    }
}


internal DataColumn job_idColumn _
    get {
        return this.columnjob_id;
    }
}


internal DataColumn job_descColumn {
        return this.columnjob_desc;
    }
}


internal DataColumn min_lvlColumn {
    get {
        return this.columnmin_lvl;
    }
```

```
        }

        internal DataColumn max_lvlColumn {
            get {
                return this.columnmax_lvl;
            }
        }

        public jobsRow this[int index] {
            get {
                return ((jobsRow)(this.Rows[index]));
            }
        }

        public event jobsRowChangeEventHandler jobsRowChanged;

        public event jobsRowChangeEventHandler jobsRowChanging;

        public event jobsRowChangeEventHandler jobsRowDeleted;

        public event jobsRowChangeEventHandler jobsRowDeleting;

        public void AddjobsRow(jobsRow row)
            this.Rows.Add(row);
        }

        public jobsRow AddjobsRow(string job_desc, System.Byte min_lvl,
            System.Byte max_lvl) {
            jobsRow rowjobsRow = ((jobsRow)(this.NewRow()));
            rowjobsRow.ItemArray = new object[] {
                    null,
                    job_desc,
                    min_lvl,
                    max_lvl};
            this.Rows.Add(rowjobsRow);
            return rowjobsRow;
        }

        public jobsRow FindByjob_id(short job_id) {
            return ((jobsRow)(this.Rows.Find(new object[] {
                    job_id})));
        }

        public System.Collections.IEnumerator GetEnumerator() {
```

```
        return this.Rows.GetEnumerator();
}

public override DataTable Clone()
  jobsDataTable cln = ((jobsDataTable)(base.Clone()));
    cln.InitVars();
    return cln;
}

protected override DataTable CreateInstance() {
    return new jobsDataTable();
}

internal void InitVars() {
    this.columnjob_id = this.Columns["job_id"];
    this.columnjob_desc = this.Columns["job_desc"];
    this.columnmin_lvl = this.Columns["min_lvl"];
    this.columnmax_lvl = this.Columns["max_lvl"];
}

private void InitClass() {
    this.columnjob_id = new DataColumn("job_id", typeof(short),
        null, System.Data.MappingType.Element);
    this.Columns.Add(this.columnjob_id);
    this.columnjob_desc = new DataColumn("job_desc",
        typeof(string), null, System.Data.MappingType.Element);
    this.Columns.Add(this.columnjob_desc);
    this.columnmin_lvl = new DataColumn("min_lvl",
        typeof(System.Byte), null,
        System.Data.MappingType.Element);
    this.Columns.Add(this.columnmin_lvl);
    this.columnmax_lvl = new DataColumn("max_lvl",
        typeof(System.Byte), null,
        System.Data.MappingType.Element);
    this.Columns.Add(this.columnmax_lvl);
    this.Constraints.Add(new UniqueConstraint
        ("Constraint1", new DataColumn[] {this.columnjob_id}, true));
    this.columnjob_id.AutoIncrement = true;
    this.columnjob_id.AllowDBNull = false;
    this.columnjob_id.ReadOnly = true;
    this.columnjob_id.Unique = true;
    this.columnjob_desc.AllowDBNull = false;
    this.columnjob_desc.MaxLength = 50;
    this.columnmin_lvl.AllowDBNull = false;
```

```csharp
            this.columnmax_lvl.AllowDBNull = false;
    }

    public jobsRow NewjobsRow() {
        return ((jobsRow)(this.NewRow()));
    }

    protected override DataRow NewRowFromBuilder(
      DataRowBuilder builder) {
        return new jobsRow(builder);
    }

    protected override System.Type GetRowType() {
        return typeof(jobsRow);
    }

    protected override void OnRowChanged(
      DataRowChangeEventArgs e)
    {
        base.OnRowChanged(e);
        if ((this.jobsRowChanged != null)) {
            this.jobsRowChanged(this,
                new jobsRowChangeEvent(
                    ((jobsRow)(e.Row)), e.Action));
        }
    }

    protected override void OnRowChanging(DataRowChangeEventArgs e)
    {
        base.OnRowChanging(e);
        if ((this.jobsRowChanging != null)) {
            this.jobsRowChanging(this,
                new jobsRowChangeEvent(
                    ((jobsRow)(e.Row)), e.Action));
        }
    }

    protected override void OnRowDeleted(DataRowChangeEventArgs e) {
        base.OnRowDeleted(e);
        if ((this.jobsRowDeleted != null)) {
            this.jobsRowDeleted(this,
                new jobsRowChangeEvent(
                    ((jobsRow)(e.Row)), e.Action));
        }
```

```
        }

    protected override void OnRowDeleting(DataRowChangeEventArgs e)
        base.OnRowDeleting(e);
        if ((this.jobsRowDeleting != null)) {
            this.jobsRowDeleting(this,
                new jobsRowChangeEvent(
                    ((jobsRow)(e.Row)), e.Action));
        }
    }

    public void RemovejobsRow(jobsRow row) {
        this.Rows.Remove(row);
    }
}

[System.Diagnostics.DebuggerStepThrough()]
public class jobsRow : DataRow _par
    private jobsDataTable tablejobs;

    internal jobsRow(DataRowBuilder rb) : base(rb) {
        this.tablejobs = ((jobsDataTable)(this.Table));
    }

    public short job_id {
        get {
            return ((short)(this[this.tablejobs.job_idColumn]));
        }
        set {
            this[this.tablejobs.job_idColumn] = value;
        }
    }

    public string job_desc {
        get {
            return ((string)(this[this.tablejobs.job_descColumn]));
        }
        set {
            this[this.tablejobs.job_descColumn] = value;
        }
    }

    public System.Byte min_lvl
```

```csharp
            get {
              return ((System.Byte)
                (this[this.tablejobs.min_lvlColumn]));
            }
            set {
                this[this.tablejobs.min_lvlColumn] = value;
            }
        }

        public System.Byte max_lvl
            get {
                return ((System.Byte)
                  (this[this.tablejobs.max_lvlColumn]));
            }
            set {
                this[this.tablejobs.max_lvlColumn] = value;
            }
        }
    }

    [System.Diagnostics.DebuggerStepThrough()]
    public class jobsRowChangeEvent : EventArgs {

        private jobsRow eventRow;

        private DataRowAction eventAction;

        public jobsRowChangeEvent(jobsRow row, DataRowAction action) {
            this.eventRow = row;
            this.eventAction = action;
        }

        public jobsRow Row {
            get {
                return this.eventRow;
            }
        }

        public DataRowAction Action {
            get {
                return this.eventAction;
            }
        }
    }
}
```

The typed `DataSet` accomplishes strong typing by generating a class `MyDS`, which derives from `DataSet` (1). The name of the subclass of the `DataSet` class is equal to `DataSet.DataSetName` in the original `DataSet` that produced the XML schema. Four public nested classes are exposed:

- `MyDS.MyTabDataTable:DataTable, IEnumerable`
- `MyDS.MyTabRow:DataRow`
- `MyDS.MyTabRowChangeEvent:EventArgs`
- `MyDS.MyTabRowChangeEventHandler`

where

- `MyDS` is the `DataSet.DataSetName`
- `MyTab` is the `DataTable.TableName`
- `MyTabRow` is `DataTable.TableName + Row`

`MyDS.MyTabDataTable` has a series of private `DataColumn` members; one data member per column is the table or resultset. There are getters for these, but they are marked `internal` because you are not allowed to add or delete `DataColumns` at runtime. There are also four typed delegates for `Changing`, `Changed`, `Deleting`, and `Deleted` rows.

The typed `DataTable` has the following methods:

- An `Indexer` for `Rows` and a `GetEnumerator` method.
- Two add methods, both called `AddMyTabRow` but each used a little differently. `AddMyTabRow(row)`, which takes a `Row`, is used with `New-MyTabRow`, an empty typed row. `AddMyTabRow(n1,n2,n3)` takes N parms, where N is the number of columns in the table and `MyTab` is a placeholder. For example, if the table name were equal to `Jobs`, the method name would be `AddJobsRow`.
- `RemoveMyTabRow`, a delete method.

The `DataColumns` are created and added to the `DataTable` in the `DataTable`'s `InitClass` method. If metadata is available, it is also filled in at that time. If there is a primary key or unique column, there is a method called `FindBykeycolname` that uses the primary key as input.

The `MyDSRow` class exposes columns as public properties. If the column is nullable, there are two predefined helper functions—`IsColumnnameNull` and `SetColumnnameNull`—where `Columnname` is a placeholder for the name of the column.

To delete a `DataRow` provided by strongly typed `DataSets`, you would use the convenience method `DataRowCollection.Remove` rather than `Data-Row.Delete`. But the two methods have different semantics. The difference between the two is that calling `DataRowCollection.Remove` is the same as calling `DataRow.Delete` followed by `AcceptChanges`. If you use `Remove` and then use the `DataSet` to update a database through a `DataAdapter`, the rows that you deleted in the `DataSet` using `Remove` will not be deleted in the database. If this is the desired behavior, you should use `DataRow.Delete` instead of the convenience `RemoveMyTabRow` method.

A strongly typed `DataSet` can also contain more than one table. If you have tables with parent-child relationships—specified by the existence of a `DataRelation` in the `DataSet`'s `Relations` collection—some additional information and methods are generated. When the `DataSet` contains a `Relation`, the following things happen:

- The `PrimaryKey` property is added to `DataColumn` properties for the parent table, a `ForeignKeyConstraint` is added for the child table, and `DataRelation` is added. If the `DataSet`'s `Nested` property was set in the original schema, it is preserved in the typed `DataSet`.

- `ChildTabRow` has a property of type `ParentTabRow`. A property's `get` method calls `GetParentRow`, and the setter calls `SetParent`.

- `ParentRow` has a method, `GetChildTabRow`, that returns an array of typed child rows by calling `GetChildRows`.

where

- `ParentTab` is the `DataTable.TableName` of the parent table.
- `ChildTab` is the `DataTable.TableName` of the child table.

Finally, the strongly typed `DataSet` has certain methods and a property that are related to XML persistence. These override the `DataSet`'s methods.

- A protected constructor takes a `SerializationInfo` info and a `StreamingContext` context. This constructor calls `InitClass` before calling `GetSerializationData`. This is a requirement when you implement `ISerializable`.

- `ReadXmlSerializable` simply calls the base class's `ReadXml` method.

- `GetSchemaSerializable` calls `WriteXmlSchema` to write the schema to an `XmlTextWriter`. Then it reads it back into a `System.Xml.Schema.XmlSchema`. This is similar to the code in the base class (`DataSet`).

- The properties `ShouldSerializeTables` and `ShouldSerialize-Relations`, and an additional property called `ShouldSerial-ize[MyTable]`, return `false`.

The example in Listing 7–25 uses every method of a one-`DataTable` typed `DataSet` and a hierarchical typed `DataSet` with a parent-child relationship. Typed `DataSets` can also be used as ordinary `DataSets`, with a corresponding loss of compile-type syntax checking.

Listing 7–25 Using a Typed `DataSet`

```
using System;
using System.Data;
using System.Data.SqlClient;

namespace UseDataSet
{
  class Class1
  {
    static void Main(string[] args)
      {
        Class1 c = new Class1();
        c.instanceMain();
      }

    void instanceMain()
      {
        UseJobsWithDBMS();
        UseJobsDS();
        UseAuTitleDS();
      }
```

```
void UseJobsWithDBMS()
{
  try
  {
    JobsDS j = new JobsDS();
    SqlDataAdapter da = new SqlDataAdapter(
      "select * from jobs",
      "server=localhost;uid=sa;database=pubs");

    SqlCommandBuilder bld = new SqlCommandBuilder(da);
    da.Fill(j.jobs);
    Console.WriteLine(j.jobs.Rows.Count);

    JobsDS.jobsRow found_row = j.jobs.FindByjob_id(156);
    Console.WriteLine(j.jobs.Rows.Count);

    //j.jobs.RemovejobsRow(found_row);
    found_row.Delete();
    Console.WriteLine(j.jobs.Rows.Count);
    da.Update(j.jobs);
  }
  catch (Exception e)
  {
    Console.WriteLine(e.Message);
  }
}

protected void T_Changing(object sender,
  JobsDS.jobsRowChangeEvent e)
{
  if (e.Row.RowState == DataRowState.Deleted)
    Console.WriteLine("Row Changing: Action {0}, State {1}",
      e.Action,  e.Row.RowState);
  else
    Console.WriteLine("Row Changing: {0} id = {1}, State {2}",
      e.Action, e.Row[0], e.Row.RowState);
}

protected void T_Changed(object sender,
  JobsDS.jobsRowChangeEvent e)
{
  if (e.Row.RowState == DataRowState.Detached)
    Console.WriteLine("Row Changed: Action {0}, State {1}",
```

```
            e.Action,  e.Row.RowState);
    else
     Console.WriteLine("Row Changed: {0} id = {1}, State {2}",
        e.Action, e.Row[0], e.Row.RowState);
}

protected void T_Deleting(object sender,
   JobsDS.jobsRowChangeEvent e)
{
 Console.WriteLine("Row Deleting: {0} id = {1}, State {2}",
     e.Action, e.Row[0], e.Row.RowState);
}

protected void T_Deleted(object sender,
   JobsDS.jobsRowChangeEvent e)
{
   Console.WriteLine("Row Deleted: Action {0}, State {1}",
     e.Action, e.Row.RowState);
}

void UseJobsDS()
{
   // 1. One public class JobsDS
   // 2. Four public nested classes:
   //     JobsDS.jobsDataTable;
   //     JobsDS.jobsRow;
   //     JobsDS.jobsRowChangeEvent;
   //     JobsDS.jobsRowChangeEventHandler;

   // Generates one named high-level type
   // the DataSet
   JobsDS j = new JobsDS();
 Console.WriteLine(j.DataSetName);

   // event handlers
   j.jobs.jobsRowChanging +=
     new JobsDS.jobsRowChangeEventHandler(T_Changing);
   j.jobs.jobsRowChanged +=
     new JobsDS.jobsRowChangeEventHandler(T_Changed);
   j.jobs.jobsRowDeleting +=
     new JobsDS.jobsRowChangeEventHandler(T_Deleting);
   j.jobs.jobsRowDeleted +=
     new JobsDS.jobsRowChangeEventHandler(T_Deleted);
```

```
// The DataSet has a single new property named "jobs"
// It's also a public nested class
JobsDS.jobsDataTable t = j.jobs;
Console.WriteLine(j.jobs.TableName);

// add a row
//j.jobs.AddjobsRow(99, "new job", 20, 20);

// when you have metadata, it's smarter about this
// you can't add the identity column
j.jobs.AddjobsRow("new job", 20, 20);

// or add a row
// through the jobsRow public nested class
JobsDS.jobsRow r = j.jobs.NewjobsRow();

// convenience columns
//r.job_id = 100;
r.job_desc = "job 100";
r.max_lvl = 90;
r.min_lvl = 89;

j.jobs.AddjobsRow(r);

// convenience IsNull functions
// only if it can be null
//if (r.Isjob_descNull() == true)
//   Console.WriteLine("desc is null");

// and SetNull functions
//r.Setjob_idNull();

// jobs exposes a public property Count == table.Rows.Count
Console.WriteLine("row count is " + j.jobs.Count);

// convenience find function
JobsDS.jobsRow found_row = j.jobs.FindByjob_id(1)
Console.WriteLine(j.jobs.Rows.Count);

// strongly typed
//j.jobs.RemovejobsRow(r);
j.jobs.RemovejobsRow(found_row);
Console.WriteLine(j.jobs.Rows.Count);
```

```
          // 4 DataColumns as members.
          //j.jobs.job_idColumn;
          //j.jobs.job_descColumn;
          //j.jobs.max_lvlColumn;
          //j.jobs.min_lvlColumn;
          if (j.jobs.job_idColumn.ReadOnly == true)
            Console.WriteLine("its read only");
          Console.WriteLine(j.jobs[0].job_desc);

          // change the first column
          // this would fail, column is readonly
          //j.jobs[0].job_id = 98;
          j.jobs[0].job_desc = "new description";
          j.AcceptChanges();

          j.WriteXmlSchema("theschema.xsd");
          j.WriteXml("thedocument.xml");

          JobsDS j2 = new JobsDS();

          // fails, the typed DataSet already contains the typed
table.
          //j2.ReadXmlSchema("jobsds.xsd");
          j2.ReadXml("jobsds.xml");
      }

      void UseAuTitleDS()
      {
        try
        {
          SqlDataAdapter da = new SqlDataAdapter(
            "select * from authors;select * from titleauthor",
            "server=localhost;uid=sa;database=pubs");

          AuTitleDS om = new AuTitleDS();

          // we still must map these because the
          // mapping is on the DataAdapter
          da.TableMappings.Add("Table", "authors");
          da.TableMappings.Add("Table1", "titleauthors");
          da.Fill(om);
          Console.WriteLine("{0} tables", om.Tables.Count);

          AuTitleDS.authorsRow r = om.authors[0];
```

```
        // get array of children
        AuTitleDS.titleauthorsRow[] cr = r.GettitleauthorsRows();
        foreach (AuTitleDS.titleauthorsRow tr in cr)
        {
          Console.WriteLine("author {0}, title {1}",
                          tr.au_id, tr.title_id);
          AuTitleDS.authorsRow ar = tr.authorsRow;
          Console.WriteLine("author {0} is the parent", ar.au_id);
        }
      }
      catch (Exception e)
      {
        Console.WriteLine(e.Message);
      }
    }
  }
}
```

Although strongly typed `DataSets` are produced using the names in the schema, you can refine the naming process by using certain schema annotations. These attributes are specified on the element declaration that equates to the table. The annotations are as follows:

- `typedName`: Name of an object referring to a row
- `typedPlural`: Name of an object referring to a table
- `typedParent`: Name of a parent object in a parent-child relationship
- `typedChild`: Name of a child object in a parent-child relationship

There is also an annotation, `nullValue,` that refers to special handling in a strongly typed `DataSet` when the value in the underlying table is `DBNull`.

7.5 The `XmlDataDocument` Class

Having come at the problem of data representation from the point of view of the data storage mechanism—that is, the relational database—we've thus far represented the in-memory object model as though it, too, were a relational database. Chapter 2 touches on the XML Infoset as a different abstraction for data, and you looked at the XML DOM, one of its in-memory data representations. The classes that are used in the relational model parallel those in a relational database; you have a `DataSet` consisting of `DataTables`, `DataColumns`, `DataRows`, and `DataRe-`

lations. You even have a mechanism—DataView—to filter and sort Data-Tables in memory. The filtering mechanism uses a language similar to SQL.

In the DOM model, XmlDocuments consist of XmlNodes. The XmlDocument can use the XML query language, XPath, to produce either single nodes or nodesets. You can also transform an entire XmlDocument using the XSLT transformation language, producing XML, HTML, or any other format of text output. The .NET class that encapsulates this function is XslTransform. You can traverse the XmlDocument structure either sequentially or using a navigation paradigm. Navigation is represented by a series of classes that implement the XPathNavigator interface. XPathNavigator is optimized for XPath queries; its queries can return XPathNodeIterator or scalar values.

Sometimes it would be useful to integrate these two models—for example, to update a portion of a DOM document based on data in a relational database, or to query a DataSet using XPath as though it were a DOM. The class that lets you treat data as though it were both a DOM and a DataSet, exposing updatability but maintaining consistency in each model, is XmlDataDocument.

The XmlDataDocument class works around the limitation of the strict relational model by enabling partial mapping on DataSet. The DataSet class (and its underlying XML format) works only with homogeneous rowsets or hierarchies, in which all rows contain the same number of columns in the same order. When you attempt to map a document in which columns are missing in rows of the same type, as in Listing 7–26, the XmlRead function compensates by mapping every combination of columns, and setting the ones that do not exist in any level of hierarchy to DBNull.Value.

Listing 7–26 Missing columns in rows

```
<root>
  <document>
     <name>Bob</name>
     <address>111 Any St</address>
  </document>
  <document>
     <name>Bird</name>
     <livesin>tree</livesin>
  </document>
</root>
```

The XML Infoset has no limitation to homogeneous data. When data is semi-structured or contains mixed content (elements and text nodes mixed), as in Listing 7–27, coercing the data into a relational model will not work. An error, "The same table (noun) cannot be the child table in two nested relations.," is produced in this case. You can still integrate, at least partially, XML data that is shaped differently; you use the `DataSet` through the `XmlDataDocument` class. In addition, you can preserve white space and maintain element order in the `XmlDocument`, but when such a document is mapped to a `DataSet`, these extra representation semantics may be lost. XML comments and processing instructions will also be lost in the `DataSet` representation.

Listing 7–27   A document containing mixed content

```
<book>
<chapter>
<title>Testing your <noun>typewriter</noun></title>
<p>The quick brown <noun>fox</noun> jumps over
the lazy <noun>dog</noun></p>
</chapter>
</book>
```

7.5.1 `XmlDataDocuments` and `DataSets`

As shown in Figure 7–3, an `XmlDataDocument` is an `XmlDocument`. That's because `XmlDataDocument` extends `XmlDocument` and contains a `DataSet` as a member.

Data can be loaded into an `XmlDataDocument` through either the `DataSet` interfaces or the `XmlDocument` interfaces. You can import the relational part of the XML document into `DataSet` by using an explicit or implied mapping schema, as shown in Listing 7–28. Whether changes are made through `DataSet` or through `XmlDataDocument`, the changed values are reflected in both objects. The full-fidelity XML is always available through the `XmlDataDocument`.

Listing 7–28   Loading a `DataSet` through the `XmlDataDocument`

```
XmlDataDocument datadoc = new XmlDataDocument();
datadoc.DataSet.ReadXmlSchema("c:\\authors.xsd");
datadoc.Load ("c:\\authors.xml");

DataSet ds = datadoc.DataSet;
```

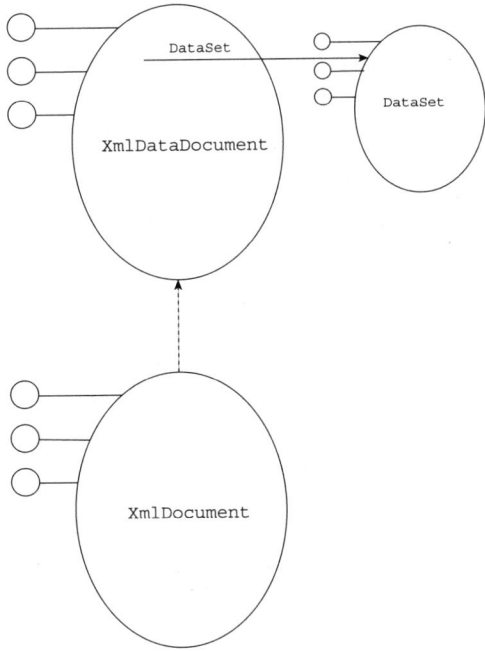

Figure 7–3 `XmlDataDocument` **and related classes**

```
// use DataSet as usual
foreach (DataTable t in ds.Tables)
  Console.WriteLine(
    "Table " + t.TableName + " is in dataset");
```

In addition to the DOM-style navigation supported by `XmlDocument`, the `XmlDataDocument` adds methods to let you get an `Element` from a `DataRow` or a `DataRow` from an `Element`. Listing 7–29 shows an example.

Listing 7–29 Using `GetElementFromRow`
```
XmlDataDocument datadoc = new XmlDataDocument();

datadoc.DataSet.ReadXmlSchema(
  "c:\\xml_schemas\\cust_orders.xsd");

datadoc.Load(new XmlTextReader(
  "http://localhost/northwind/template/modeauto1.xml"));

XmlElement e = datadoc.GetElementFromRow(
    datadoc.DataSet.Tables[0].Rows[2]);
```

```
Console.WriteLine(e.InnerXml);
```

You can create an `XmlDataDocument` using a prepopulated `DataSet`, as shown in Listing 7–30. Any data in the `DataSet` is used to construct a DOM representation. This DOM is exactly the same as the XML document that would be serialized using `DataSet.WriteXml`. The only difference, a trivial one, is that `DataSet.WriteXml` writes an XML directive at the beginning and `XmlDocument.Save` does not.

Listing 7–30 Creating an `XmlDataDocument` from a `DataSet`

```
DataSet ds = new DataSet();

// load the DataSet
SqlDataAdapter da = new SqlDataAdapter(
        "select * from authors;select * from titleauthor",
        "server=localhost;database=pubs;uid=sa");
da.MissingSchemaAction = MissingSchemaAction.AddWithKey;
da.Fill(ds);

// tweak the DataSet schema
ds.Tables[0].TableName = "authors";
ds.Tables[1].TableName = "titleauthor";
ds.Relations.Add(
   ds.Tables[0].Columns["au_id"],
   ds.Tables[1].Columns["au_id"]);
ds.Relations[0].Nested = true;

XmlDataDocument dd = new XmlDataDocument(ds);

// write the document
dd.Save("c:\\temp\\xmldoc.xml");
// write the dataset
dd.DataSet.WriteXml("c:\\temp\\dataset.xml");
```

An `XmlDataDocument` can also be populated by an XML document through its `Load` method, as shown in Listing 7–31. What makes `XmlDataDocument` unique is that you can load an entire XML document by using `XmlDataDocument.Load`, but the `DataSet` member contains only the tables that existed in the `DataSet`'s schema at the time that you called `Load`. Removing the `ReadXmlSchema` line in Listing 7–31 results in a complete document in the

DOM, but a `DataSet` that, when serialized, contains only an empty root element. Reading a schema that contains only authors will result in a complete DOM and a `DataSet` containing only authors. Attempting to use an "embedded schema plus document"–style XML document produced by using `DataSet.WriteXml` with `XmlWriteMode.WriteSchema`, or using an XSD inline schema recognized with the `XmlValidatingReader`, works to load the document, but this schema is not used to populate the `DataSet`; the `DataSet` contains no data.

Listing 7–31 Loading an `XmlDataDocument` from a document

```
XmlDataDocument dd = new XmlDataDocument();

dd.DataSet.ReadXmlSchema(
    "c:\\xml_schemas\\au_title.xsd");
dd.Load("c:\\xml_documents\\au_title.xml");

// write the document
dd.Save("c:\\temp\\xmldoc.xml");
// write the dataset
dd.DataSet.WriteXml("c:\\temp\\dataset.xml");
```

Here are a few rules to keep in mind when you're using `XmlDataDocument`:

- The mapping of `Document` to `DataSet` (using `XmlDataDocument.DataSet.ReadXmlSchema` or other means) must already be in place when you load the XML document using `XmlDataDocument.Load`.

- Each named piece of data represented in the XML schema can be a child of only one element. In general, this means that an XML schema cannot use global `xsd:element` elements.

- Tables cannot be added to the schema mapping after a document is loaded.

- Documents cannot be loaded after data has been loaded, either through `XmlDataDocument.Load` or by a `DataAdapter`.

You can use `XmlDataDocument` to coerce mixed content and other semi-structured data into a somewhat relational form. This technique could help you use the nonrelational document that you looked at in the beginning of this section. The relational schema must be defined so that each simple element type appears unambiguously in any table. Using the "Testing Your Typewriter" document in Listing 7–27 as an example, you cannot map the document so that `noun` elements appear under both `title` elements and `p` elements, as you saw earlier. Neither can you use a schema that maps `noun` under only `title` or only `p` elements. When you try to use a `DataSet` schema with `noun` only as a child of `p` (hoping to map only nouns that appear in paragraphs), you receive the error "`SetParentRow` requires a child row whose table is "p", but the specified row's `Table` is `title`." The way to map all `noun` elements is to use a schema in which `noun` is not a child of any other element. This produces a single `noun` table containing `noun` elements from (`title`)s and (p)aragraphs.

Another possible use for `XmlDataDocument` is to merge new data from a relational database into an existing XML document. This works, but with the limitations noted earlier. Consider a `DataSet` schema containing authors and rows from a nonrectangular document. You would first try to load both documents into the `XmlDataDocument`, but a second document cannot be loaded when the `XmlDataDocument` already contains data. The code in Listing 7–32 fails when trying to load the second document.

Listing 7–32   Merging data with `XmlDataDocument`; this fails

```
try
{
  XmlDataDocument dd = new XmlDataDocument();

  // schema contains authors and document
  dd.DataSet.ReadXmlSchema(@"c:\xml_schemas\au_nonr.xsd");

  // this document contains document
  dd.Load(@"c:\xml_documents\nonrect.xml");

  // this document contains authors
  // this fails
  dd.Load(@"c:\xml_documents\authors_doc.xml");

  foreach (DataTable t in dd.DataSet.Tables)
    Console.WriteLine("table {0} contains {1} rows",
      t.TableName, t.Rows.Count);
}
catch (Exception e)
{
```

```
  Console.WriteLine(e.Message);
}
```

Attempting to populate the `DataSet` with a `DataAdapter` after a document has been loaded produces partial success. The code in Listing 7–33 produces a `DataSet` containing two tables, but a document containing only the data originally loaded by calling `XmlDataDocument.Load`.

Listing 7–33 Merging documents with `XmlDataDocument`; this doesn't synchronize

```
try
{
  XmlDataDocument dd = new XmlDataDocument();

  // schema contains authors and document
  dd.DataSet.ReadXmlSchema(@"c:\xml_schemas\au_nonr.xsd");

  // this document contains document
  dd.Load(@"c:\xml_documents\nonrect.xml");

  // add authors
  SqlDataAdapter da = new SqlDataAdapter(
    "select * from authors",
    "server=localhost;uid=sa;database=pubs");

  da.Fill(dd.DataSet, "authors");

  // both appear in the DataSet
  foreach (DataTable t in dd.DataSet.Tables)
    Console.WriteLine("Table {0} contains {1} rows",
      t.TableName, t.Rows.Count);

  // no authors in the document
  dd.Save(@"c:\temp\au_nonr.xml");
}
catch (Exception e)
{
  Console.WriteLine(e.Message);
}
```

The correct way to accomplish a merge of two documents is to use two `DataSet`s and the `DataSet.Merge` method. The second `DataSet` can be either standalone or part of an XmlDataDocument, as shown in Listing 7–34. If data is merged into a DataDocument's DataSet, however, the schema for both tables must be loaded when the original document is loaded or else an error message will result during DataSet.Merge.

Listing 7–34 Merging documents with XmlDataDocument; this works

```
XmlDataDocument dd = new XmlDataDocument();

// schema contains authors and document
dd.DataSet.ReadXmlSchema(@"c:\xml_schemas\au_nonr.xsd");

// this document contains document
dd.Load(@"c:\xml_documents\nonrect.xml");

// 1. either of these will work

// add authors
SqlDataAdapter da = new SqlDataAdapter(
  "select * from authors",
  "server=localhost;uid=sa;database=pubs");

DataSet ds = new DataSet();
da.Fill(ds, "authors");
dd.DataSet.Merge(ds);

// 2. either of these will work
XmlDataDocument dd2 = new XmlDataDocument();
dd2.DataSet.ReadXmlSchema(@"c:\xml_schemas\au_nonr.xsd");

// add authors
dd2.Load(@"c:\xml_documents\authors_doc.xml");
dd.DataSet.Merge(dd2.DataSet);

// both appear in the DataSet
foreach (DataTable t in dd.DataSet.Tables)
  Console.WriteLine("Table {0} contains {1} rows",
    t.TableName, t.Rows.Count);

// both in the document
dd.Save(@"c:\temp\au_nonr.xml");
}
```

```
  catch (Exception e)
  {
    Console.WriteLine(e.Message);
  }
```

7.5.2 `XmlDataDocument` and `DataDocumentXPathNavigator`

An additional advantage of using `XmlDataDocument` is that you can query the
resulting object model using either the SQL-like syntax of `DataView` filters or
the XPath query language. `DataView` filters produce sets of rows and have simple support for parent-child relationships via the `CHILD` keyword. XPath is a
more full-featured query language that can produce sets of nodes or scalar values. You can use XPath directly via the `SelectSingleNode` and `SelectNode`
methods that `XmlDataDocument` inherits from `XmlDocument`. The `XPath-`
`Navigator` class also lets you use precompiled XPath queries. Resultsets from
XPath queries are exposed as `XPathNodeIterator`s. You can use `XPath-`
`Navigator`s in input to the XSLT transformation process exposed through the
`XslTransform` class. You can also use `XPathNavigator`s to update nodes
in their source document, using the presence of an `IHasXMLNode` interface on
a result node and using `IHasXMLNode.GetNode` to get the underlying (updatable) `XmlNode`.

  `DataDocumentXPathNavigator` is a private subclass of `XPathNaviga-`
`tor` that provides cursor-based navigation of the "XML view" of the data in an
`XmlDataDocument`. As with the `XPathNavigator` returned by `XmlDocu-`
`ment.CreateNavigator`, multiple navigators can maintain multiple currency
positions; in addition, a `DataDocumentXPathNavigator`'s position in the
`XmlDocument` is synchronized with its position in the `DataSet`. Programs that
depend on positional navigation under classic ADO's client cursor engine or
`DataShape` provider can be migrated to this model. Listing 7–35 shows an example of using `XPathNavigator` with `XmlDataDocument`.

Listing 7–35 Using `XPathNavigator`

```
XmlDataDocument datadoc = new XmlDataDocument();

datadoc.Load(new XmlTextReader(
  "http://localhost/nwind/template/modeauto1.xml"));
```

```
XPathNavigator nav = datadoc.CreateNavigator();
XPathNodeIterator i = nav.Select("//customer");
Console.WriteLine(
  "there are {0} customers", i.Count);
```

A final example, Listing 7–36, combines all the XmlDataDocument features shown so far. A DataSet is created from multiple results obtained from a SQL Server database. An XmlDataDocument and an XPathNavigator are created over the DataSet. Using the XPathNavigator, an XPath query returns a set of nodes in the parent (contract columns in the authors table) based on criteria in the children. The resulting XPathNodeIterator is used to update the XmlDocument nodes. Because the XmlDocument stays synchronized with the DataSet, the rows are then updated using a DataAdapter.

Listing 7–36   Updating through an XPathNavigator

```
DataSet ds = new DataSet("au_info");

// load the DataSet
SqlDataAdapter da = new SqlDataAdapter(
  "select * from authors;select * from titleauthor",
  "server=localhost;database=pubs;uid=sa");
da.MissingSchemaAction = MissingSchemaAction.AddWithKey;
da.Fill(ds);

// tweak the DataSet schema
ds.Tables[0].TableName = "authors";
ds.Tables[1].TableName = "titleauthor";
ds.Relations.Add(
  ds.Tables[0].Columns["au_id"],
  ds.Tables[1].Columns["au_id"]);
ds.Relations[0].Nested = true;

XmlDataDocument dd = new XmlDataDocument(ds);
// This must be set to false
// to edit through the XmlDocument nodes
dd.DataSet.EnforceConstraints = false;
XPathNavigator nav = dd.CreateNavigator();

// get the "contract" column (node)
// for all authors with a royalty percentage < 30%
XPathNodeIterator i = nav.Select(
```

```
    "/au_info/authors/contract[../titleauthor/royaltyper<30]");
while (i.MoveNext() == true)
{
    XmlNode node = ((IHasXmlNode)i.Current).GetNode();
    node.InnerText = "false";
}

SqlCommandBuilder bld = new SqlCommandBuilder(da);
da.Update(dd.DataSet, "authors");
```

7.6 Why Databases and XML?

Relational databases are good for storing data in a controlled, administered manner. They have built-in support for fast concurrent access and optimized set-based query capabilities. However, the protocol and packet formats are database-specific. XML is an almost universally supported method for passing data around. It is supported by heterogeneous architectures; for example, a big-endian Sun workstation can easily parse an XML document created on a little-endian Intel architecture machine. Given that each XML document must have a single root element, it must be somewhat hierarchical by default.

Some database servers have built-in XML features, and the underlying APIs also have built-in integration features. An ASP application can facilitate the sending and receiving of SQL results over HTTP and the formatting of output as XML, optionally adding stylesheets.

A rectangular resultset can easily be stored in XML format for transmission to any platform. Because an XML document can be a hierarchical representation of a complete graph of data, there must be a method to decompose this data when it is stored into the database. Conversely, to serve an XML document as output, it is often useful to compose information from two or more tables into a hierarchy.

7.6.1 XML as a Distinct Type

Object-relational databases and extensions to relational databases let you use an XML document as a distinct type. To do this, you use an XML DataBlade in Informix 9, or an XML Extender in DB2 6.0 and later.

When you use XML as a distinct type, you store the entire XML document as a CLOB column. Special user-defined functions, schemas, tables, and API extensions allow optimization of the XML type. For example, when a DB2 database is defined as XML `Extender`-aware, an XML `distinct` type is added at the database level. This equates to a CLOB. In addition, a series of user-defined functions (UDFs) and stored procedures is added to the database. These database objects take care of the addition and maintenance of the XML user-defined type (UDT) and keep optional tables of information (called *sidetables*) up-to-date when new XML column instances are added.

7.6.2 Document Composition and Decomposition

XML documents are *organic* types, meaning that they most closely represent a graph of objects in an ODBMS or a network DBMS. You can decompose the information contained in a document into multiple relational tables. Document decomposition can serve to reduce database round-trips because you can pass in the entire document at once and parse it into multiple relational tables.

Going the other way, when you need to present data as an XML document, composition of multiple tables is required. The easiest approach is to use extensions to SQL that know how to produce an XML hierarchy based on the individual tables in a join. Some databases provide extension functions that enable document decomposition. Special logic in stored procedures can be used to store extra data that is provided in the document but does not correspond to a specific relational table.

Document composition is often combined with services provided by APIs and XSLT stylesheets to enable direct output of XML-based HTTP pages and XML-based input formatting through Web browsers. This strategy is used by XML for SQL Server's Internet Services API (ISAPI) application and Oracle's XTK (XML toolkit).

7.7 SQL Server, XML, and Managed Data Access

SQL Server 2000 and the ensuing Web-released extensions, called SQLXML, have many kinds of support for XML. This topic could take an entire book by itself. Almost all the support is available through ADO.NET. First, let's enumerate them and then go over how each one is supported in ADO.NET.

7.7.1 The FOR XML Keyword

SQL Server added a FOR XML keyword to the SQL SELECT statement. This keyword can produce XML in four formats: RAW, AUTO, NESTED, and EXPLICIT. The AUTO, NESTED, and EXPLICIT formats can produce hierarchical nested XML output and attribute-normal or element-normal form. Listing 7–37 shows examples of using SELECT ... FOR XML and the results obtained.

Listing 7–37   Using SQL Server's FOR XML syntax

```
-- 1. raw mode:
-- this query:
SELECT Customers.CustomerID, Orders.OrderID
FROM Customers, Orders
WHERE Customers.CustomerID = Orders.CustomerID
ORDER BY Customers.CustomerID
FOR XML RAW

-- produces this XML output document fragment
  <row CustomerID="ALFKI" OrderID="10643" />
  <row CustomerID="ALFKI" OrderID="10692" />
  <row CustomerID="ALFKI" OrderID="10703" />
  <row CustomerID="ALFKI" OrderID="10835" />
  <row CustomerID="ANATR" OrderID="10308" />

-- 2. auto mode
-- this query:
SELECT Customers.CustomerID, Orders.OrderID
FROM Customers, Orders
WHERE Customers.CustomerID = Orders.CustomerID
ORDER BY Customers.CustomerID
FOR XML AUTO

-- produces the following XML document fragment
  <Customers CustomerID="ALFKI">
    <Orders OrderID="10643" />
    <Orders OrderID="10692" />
    <Orders OrderID="10702" />
    <Orders OrderID="10835" />
  </Customers>
  <Customers CustomerID="ANATR">
    <Orders OrderID="10308" />
  </Customers>
```

```
-- 3. explicit mode
-- this query:
SELECT            1 as Tag, NULL as Parent,
  Customers.CustomerID as [Customer!1!CustomerID],
  NULL as [Order!2!OrderID]
FROM              Customers
UNION ALL
SELECT            2, 1,
                  Customers.CustomerID,
                  Orders.OrderID
FROM              Customers, Orders
WHERE Customers.CustomerID = Orders.CustomerID
ORDER BY [Customer!1!CustomerID]
FOR XML EXPLICIT

-- produces this output document fragment
<Customer CustomerID="ALFKI">
   <Order OrderID="10643"/>
   <Order OrderID="10692"/>
   <Order OrderID="10702"/>
</Customer>
```

7.7.2 OpenXML

SQL Server 2000 can decompose XML passed in to a stored procedure using a user-defined function, OpenXML. This technique uses the normal stored procedure mechanism, so I don't discuss it further.

7.7.3 The SQLOLEDB Provider

The SQLOLEDB provider (that is, the native OLE DB provider for SQL Server) accepts two new query dialects: XPath and MSSQLXML. MSSQLXML consists of XPath or SQL queries surrounded by XML wrapper elements. Because SQL Server does not support XPath directly, XPath support requires an XML mapping schema that maps an XML view of a single SQL Server database. Multiple tables and relationships are supported in mapping schemas. The SQLOLEDB provider also supports streamed input and output. An XSLT transform can automatically be run on the output stream by means of a property on the XML query.

7.7.4 The `SqlXml` Managed Classes

The `SqlXml` set of managed classes, which provide some functionality similar to an ADO.NET data provider, encapsulate all the XML support in the OLE DB provider, listed earlier. We'll talk a lot more about this one.

7.7.5 The SQLXML Web Application

An ISAPI application exposes the ability to obtain an XML result through the HTTP protocol. The URL endpoint exposed can accommodate MSSQLXML templates in files, direct queries, and HTTP POST requests. This functionality works by calling the OLE DB provider from within the ISAPI application.

7.7.6 Updategrams

An update to the OLE DB provider accepts an XML dialect called *updategrams*. This functionality works either directly through the provider or through the ISAPI application. Several dialects of updategram are supported. Listing 7–38 shows a sample updategram document. Updategrams are similar in concept to ADO.NET DiffGrams.

Listing 7–38 Updategram formats

```
<DocumentElement
  xmlns:msdata="urn:schemas-microsoft-com:xml-msdata"
  xmlns:sql="urn:schemas-microsoft-com:xml-sql">
 <sql:ssync>
 <!-- Deleted -->

<sql:before>
    <Teachers sql:id="1">
       <ID>0</ID>
       <Name>Mr Apple</Name>
    </Teachers>
 </sql:before>
 <sql:after></sql:after>

 <!-- Unchanged -->

<sql:before>
    <Teachers sql:id="2">
       <ID>1</ID>
```

```
        <Name>Mrs Blue</Name>
      </Teachers>
    </sql:before>
    <sql:after>
    <Teachers sql:id="2"></Teachers>
    </sql:after>

    <!-- New -->

    <sql:before></sql:before>
    <sql:after>
      <Courses sql:id="7">
        <ID>6</ID>
        <Name>Home Ec 200</Name>
        </Courses>
        </sql:after>

    <!-- Modified -->

      <sql:before>
      <Students sql:id="1">
        <ID>0</ID>
        <Name>Abe</Name>
      </Students>
      </sql:before>
      <sql:after>
      <Students sql:id="1">
        <ID>0</ID>
        <Name>Abby</Name>
      </Students>
      </sql:after>

      <!-- Removed -->

      <sql:before>
        <Students sql:id="2"></Students>
        </sql:before>
        <sql:after>
        </sql:after>
    </sql:ssync>
  </DocumentElement>
```

7.7.7 FOR XML in the SQLXMLOLEDB Provider

A new OLE DB provider, SQLXMLOLEDB, allows the same processing of FOR XML output as the SQLOLEDB provider. The difference is that the FOR XML processing and conversion to XML occur on the client rather than inside SQL Server. This arrangement lets you optimize data transmission because data is transmitted using SQL Server's TDS protocol rather than XML. Because this client-side processing is exposed as an OLE DB service provider, it is possible that it may support providers other than SQLOLEDB in the future.

7.7.8 Bulk Loading

Bulk loading of XML to SQL Server is provided in SQLXML Web release 1. Because this is a COM interface available in .NET only through interoperability, I don't discuss this one further.

7.7.9 Future Support

Future plans for integration of SQL Server and XML include using SOAP as an output protocol (SQLXML3.0) and support of the relatively new XQuery language in addition to SQL and XPath.

7.8 Using SQLXML and .NET

Now let's look at some of these techniques in detail. The SqlClient data provider supports ExecuteXmlReader, a provider-specific method on the Sql-Command class. Rather than provide a SqlDataReader to process the result of a SQL query, ExecuteXmlReader produces an XmlReader, which can be used to directly consume the results of a SELECT ... FOR XML query. The XmlReader might be used directly—for example, to serialize the resulting document to a Stream for transmission to a BizTalk server. The document could be serialized to disk by using an XmlTextReader. It could be read directly into the DataSet by using the DataSet's ReadXml method. Listing 7–39 shows an example. The interesting point of ExecuteXmlReader is that, if you use a FOR XML query that produces nested hierarchies of XML output (AUTO or EXPLICIT mode), it takes only a single SELECT statement to produce multiple Data-Tables with the appropriate DataRelations in the DataSet.

Listing 7–39   Using SQLXML through ExecuteXmlReader

```
SqlConnection conn = new SqlConnection(
  "server=.;uid=sa;database=pubs");
SqlCommand cmd = new SqlCommand(
  "select * from authors for xml auto, xmldata",
  conn);
conn.Open();

XmlTextReader rdr;
rdr = (XmlTextReader)cmd.ExecuteXmlReader();

DataSet ds = new DataSet();
ds.ReadXml(rdr,
   XmlReadMode.Fragment);
```

When using ExecuteXmlReader to obtain an XmlReader followed by DataSet.ReadXml to populate a DataSet, you must take certain precautions because the XML produced by SQL Server does not contain a root element. To obtain all the XML nodes, you must use XmlReadMode.XmlFragment, a special XmlReadMode. In addition, you must either prepopulate the DataSet's schema with information that matches the incoming fragment or use the XML-DATA keyword in your SQL statement to prepend an XDR schema to your fragment. This XDR format schema will prepopulate the DataSet schema, as illustrated in Listing 7–40.

Listing 7–40   Using SQLXML through ExecuteXmlReader

```
// 1. This produces no rows
SqlConnection conn = new SqlConnection(
  "server=.;uid=sa;database=pubs");
SqlCommand cmd = new SqlCommand(
  "select * from authors for xml auto",
  conn);
conn.Open();

DataSet ds = new DataSet();
ds.ReadXml(
   (XmlTextReader)cmd.ExecuteXmlReader(),
   XmlReadMode.Fragment);

// 2. This produces 23 rows
SqlConnection conn = new SqlConnection(
```

```
    "server=.;uid=sa;database=pubs");
SqlCommand cmd = new SqlCommand(
    "select * from authors for xml auto, xmldata",
    conn);
conn.Open();

DataSet ds = new DataSet();
ds.ReadXml(
    (XmlTextReader)cmd.ExecuteXmlReader(),
    XmlReadMode.Fragment);

// 3. This produces 23 rows, 2 columns
//    because two columns are mapped
//

SqlConnection conn = new SqlConnection(
    "server=.;uid=sa;database=pubs");
SqlCommand cmd = new SqlCommand(
    "select * from authors for xml auto",
    conn);
conn.Open();

DataSet ds = new DataSet();

DataTable t = new DataTable("authors");
ds.Tables.Add(t);
t.Columns.Add("au_id", typeof(String));
t.Columns.Add("au_fname", typeof(String));

// "for xml" columns are attributes by default
for (int i=0; i<t.Columns.Count; i++)
    t.Columns[i].ColumnMapping =
      MappingType.Attribute;

ds.ReadXml(
    (XmlTextReader)cmd.ExecuteXmlReader(),
    XmlReadMode.Fragment);
```

SQL Server's XML ISAPI application can also be used as an endpoint to produce an `XmlTextReader`. You can then use this `XmlTextReader` to populate the `DataSet`, as shown in Listing 7–41. This method can be executed from any machine that supports .NET. No SQL Server client software need be installed because only ordinary XML is being produced.

Listing 7–41   Using SQL Server 2000's ISAPI application

```
DataSet ds = new DataSet();
XmlTextReader rdr = new XmlTextReader(
    "http://localhost/northwind/template/modeauto1.xml");

ds.ReadXml(rdr);
```

Updategrams are supported by the OLE DB provider or ISAPI application, and although they are similar to DiffGrams, DiffGrams could be used with SQL Server 2000's ISAPI application. (SQLXML Web release 2 adds support for DiffGrams in the ISAPI application.) The updategram format is fairly straightforward and can be created most easily from the information in an updated `DataSet`. This book's Web site contains an example of creating updategrams from a `DataSet` programmatically. Updategrams and DiffGram are especially useful for composing inserts, updates, and deletes to multiple SQL Server tables in a single round-trip to SQL Server.

Although SQL Server's ability to understand MSSQLXML and XPath queries and to use streaming input and output is part of the OLE DB provider, this functionality uses recent extensions to the OLE DB specification introduced in OLE DB version 2.6. The `OleDb` data provider supports most of the "base" OLE DB specification, but it does not support these extensions at all. Instead of adding these extensions to the `OleDb` data provider (they were used only by `SQLOLEDB`), Microsoft released a new set of `SqlXml` managed data classes as part of the SQLXML Release 2 Web release. These classes not only add support for the `SQLOLEDB` 2.6 extensions (by wrapping the original OLE DB code) but also support client-side transformation.

The `SqlXml` data provider does not implement a `Connection` class, implementing only `Command`, `Parameters`/`Parameter`, and `Adapter`. The special `Adapter` class, `SqlXmlAdapter`, does not derive from `System.Data.Common.DbDataAdapter`. You use the provider to execute a `FOR XML` query by creating a `SqlXmlCommand` and using one of its methods. Three methods of `SqlXmlCommand` produce XML output. `ExecuteStream` produces a new `System.IO.Stream` instance containing the results, as demonstrated in Listing 7–42.

Listing 7–42 Using `SqlXml`'s `ExecuteStream`

```
Stream s;
SqlXmlParameter p;
// note that provider keyword is required
SqlXmlCommand cmd = new SqlXmlCommand(
  "provider=sqloledb;server=localhost;" +
  "uid=sa;database=pubs");
cmd.CommandText =
 "select * from authors where au_lname = ?" +
 " For XML Auto";

p = cmd.CreateParameter();
p.Value = "Ringer";
s = cmd.ExecuteStream();
StreamReader sw = new StreamReader(s);
Console.WriteLine(sw.ReadToEnd());
```

`ExecuteToStream` populates an existing instance of `System.IO.Stream` rather than produce a new one, as shown in Listing 7–43. `SqlXmlCommand` also implements the `ExecuteNonQuery` and `ExecuteXmlReader` methods, which work the same as the corresponding methods in `SqlClient`, adding support for the MSSQLXML and XPath dialects.

Listing 7–43 Using `ExecuteToStream`

```
SqlXmlParameter p;
SqlXmlCommand cmd = new SqlXmlCommand(
  "provider=sqloledb;server=localhost;" +
  "uid=sa;database=pubs");
cmd.CommandText =
 "select * from authors where au_lname = ?" +
 " For XML Auto";

MemoryStream ms = new MemoryStream();
StreamReader sr = new StreamReader(ms);
p = cmd.CreateParameter();
p.Value = "Ringer";
cmd.ExecuteToStream(ms);
ms.Position = 0;
Console.WriteLine(sr.ReadToEnd());
```

`SqlXml` exposes all the extra functionality on the `Command` object that permits using streamed input, using MSSQLXML and XPath queries, specifying XML mapping schemas for XPath queries, adding XML root elements, and post-processing through an XSL stylesheet. All these are exposed as properties of `SqlXmlCommand`. For example, Listing 7–44 shows how to use an XPath query and XML mapping schema to execute a command on SQL Server and fetch the results.

Listing 7–44   Using an XPath query with `SqlXml`

```
Stream strm;
SqlXmlCommand cmd = new SqlXmlCommand(
  "provider=sqloledb;uid=sa;server=localhost;" +
  "database=northwind");
cmd.CommandText = "Emp";
cmd.CommandType = SqlXmlCommandType.XPath;
cmd.RootTag = "ROOT";
cmd.SchemaPath = "c:\\xml_mappings\\MySchema.xml";
strm = cmd.ExecuteStream();
StreamReader sr = new StreamReader(strm);
Console.WriteLine(sr.ReadToEnd());

<!-- this is MySchema.xml -->
<xsd:schema xmlns:xsd="http://www.w3.org/2001/XMLSchema"
    xmlns:sql="urn:schemas-microsoft-com:mapping-schema">
  <xsd:element name="Emp" sql:relation="Employees" >
   <xsd:complexType>
     <xsd:sequence>
        <xsd:element name="FName"
                     sql:field="FirstName"
                     type="xsd:string" />
        <xsd:element name="LName"
                     sql:field="LastName"
                     type="xsd:string" />
     </xsd:sequence>
     <xsd:attribute name="EmployeeID" type="xsd:integer" />
   </xsd:complexType>
  </xsd:element>
</xsd:schema>
<!-- end of MySchema.xml -->
```

Although this is interesting from a "use XML everywhere" point of view, what actually happens when this command is executed is that the SQLOLEDB provider processes the XPath statement and mapping schema to produce a SQL FOR

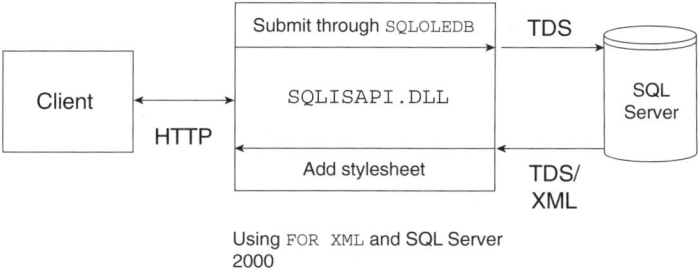

Using FOR XML and SQL Server 2000

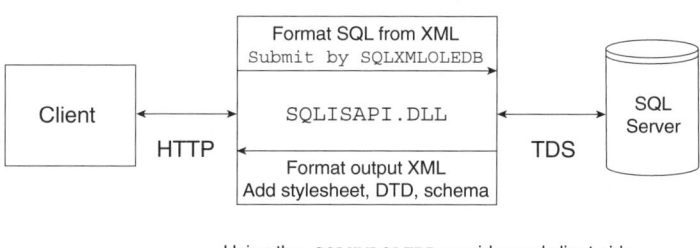

Using the SQLXMLOLEDB provider and client-side processing

Figure 7–4   Database versus client transformations

XML EXPLICIT query, which is sent to SQL Server. In addition, an XML result (wrapped in a TDS packet) is returned from SQL Server to the client. Both of these behaviors might combine to make the execution quite a bit slower than using a SQL query and processing the result into XML (or HTML) on the client. When client processing is preferable, you can specify the Command.Client-SideXml property. When you use Command.ClientSideXml, the client (usually a Web server) must have SQL Server client libraries installed. The difference in processing is shown in Figure 7–4.

The SqlXmlAdapter has three constructors. One takes a single parameter, a SqlXmlCommand. The other two take three parameters. The first parameter is either a textual command or a CommandStream. The other two parameters are the same in both constructors: a CommandType (SqlXmlCommandType.Sql, XPath,

Template, or TemplateFile), and a ConnectionString. The SqlXml-Adapter implements single Fill and Update methods, each using XML to read or update based on all the DataSet's tables. Listing 7–45 shows an example of using SqlXmlAdapter.

Listing 7–45 Using SqlXmlAdapter

```
SqlXmlAdapter da;
SqlXmlCommand cmd = new SqlXmlCommand(
  "provider=sqloledb;uid=sa;server=localhost;" +
  "database=northwind");
cmd.RootTag = "ROOT";
cmd.CommandText = "Emp";
cmd.CommandType = SqlXmlCommandType.XPath;
cmd.SchemaPath = "MySchema.xml";
//load data set
DataSet ds = new DataSet();
da = new SqlXmlAdapter(cmd);
da.Fill(ds);
DataRow row = ds.Tables["Emp"].Rows[0];
row["FName"] = "Bob";
da.Update(ds);
```

Finally, SQLXML Web Release 2 and the SqlXml data provider support using DiffGrams, in addition to updategrams, to update SQL Server. This is supported both through SqlXmlCommand and through the ISAPI application. When you use SqlXmlCommand, DiffGram is supported as SqlXmlCommandType.Template or TemplateFile. To use a DiffGram to perform updates, you must specify an XSD format mapping schema to map the DiffGram to database tables. Unlike an updategram, the DiffGram format does not include sync elements, so you are more constrained in using transactions than you are with the updategram. Also, when exceptional conditions occur when you update SQL Server through updategrams or DiffGrams, an exception is not thrown in the provider code. Instead, the resulting XML output contains the XML nodes not used, such as the nodes that were used to attempt to add a row to the database where the add failed. Listing 7–46 shows an example of updating using a Diff-Gram, mapping schema, and HTTP endpoint.

Listing 7–46   Using a DiffGram to update SQL Server

```
try
{
SqlDataAdapter da = new SqlDataAdapter(
  "select CustomerID, CompanyName, " +
  "ContactName from customers",
  "server=localhost;uid=sa;database=northwind");

DataSet ds = new DataSet();
da.Fill(ds, "Customers");

// map this to an XML Attribute
// to match the mapping schema
ds.Tables[0].Columns[0].ColumnMapping =
  MappingType.Attribute;

// update the ninth row
ds.Tables[0].Rows[9][1] = "new customer name";
DataSet ds2 = ds.GetChanges();

HttpWebRequest r = (HttpWebRequest)WebRequest.Create(
  "http://zmv43/northwind/");
r.ContentType = "text/xml";
r.Method = "POST";

// MUST add mapping schema reference
String rootelem = "<ROOT " +
 "xmlns:sql='urn:schemas-microsoft-com:xml-sql'" +
 " sql:mapping-schema='diffgram1.xml'>";

String rootend = "</ROOT>";

StreamWriter s = new StreamWriter(
  r.GetRequestStream());
s.Write(rootelem, 0, rootelem.Length);
ds2.WriteXml(s, XmlWriteMode.DiffGram);
s.Write(rootend, 0, rootend.Length);
s.Close();

HttpWebResponse resp =
    (HttpWebResponse)r.GetResponse();
StreamReader rdr = new StreamReader(
    resp.GetResponseStream());
```

```
Console.WriteLine(rdr.ReadToEnd());
}
catch (Exception e)
{
  Console.WriteLine(e.Message);
}

<!-- here's the mapping-schema -->
<xsd:schema xmlns:xsd="http://www.w3.org/2001/XMLSchema"
  xmlns:sql="urn:schemas-microsoft-com:mapping-schema">

<xsd:annotation>
  <xsd:documentation>
    Diffgram Customers/Orders Schema.
  </xsd:documentation>
</xsd:annotation>

<xsd:element name="Customers" sql:relation="Customers">
  <xsd:complexType>
    <xsd:sequence>
      <xsd:element name="CompanyName" type="xsd:string"/>
      <xsd:element name="ContactName" type="xsd:string"/>
    </xsd:sequence>
    <xsd:attribute name="CustomerID"
      type="xsd:string" sql:field="CustomerID"/>
  </xsd:complexType>
</xsd:element>

</xsd:schema>
<!-- end of mapping-schema -->
```

7.9 Where Are We?

You've completed your in-depth exploration of ADO.NET by looking at the XML capabilities built into the data access stack at all levels. You've looked at integration of ADO.NET and XML in DataSet (including using XSD schemas to generate typed DataSets) and the XmlDocument/DataSet hybrid called XmlDataDocument, including its implementation of an XPathNavigator class. Finally, you've seen that SQL Server directly supports SELECT, INSERT, UPDATE, and DELETE operations using XML. This support is built into two data providers: the SqlClient data provider and the new SqlXml managed classes.

What I hope you take away from this exposition is that ADO.NET not only supports relational data through the data provider, `DataSet`, and `Adapter` architecture but also adds support for all types of nonrelational data through its integration with XML. ADO.NET provides a wide integration layer between relational and nonrelational data via XML and also provides direct XML support of relational data.

You've learned the basic concepts of ADO.NET, but unless you started programming data access yesterday, you already have some data access code written using some other API. You may even have code that exposes your data through OLE DB providers. Chapter 8 discusses strategies for provider writers in the new .NET world and explores the ways existing OLE DB providers work with the `OleDb` managed provider. Chapter 9 explains migration strategies for consumer writers who use existing APIs.

Chapter 8

Providers: ADO.NET and Data Providers

The data provider architecture is a new provider model for data access. Database vendors and data store administrators can continue to expose their data through OLE DB, or they can move to .NET data providers or XML-based Infoset providers.

8.1 What Are Your Choices?

In the days of OLE DB and ODBC, drivers and providers were implemented for a variety of reasons. Sets of data could be exposed through a common set of graphical user interface controls when a provider was implemented. Reporting programs, data exchange programs, and other data consuming products used the common API. The ADO `Recordset` and Remote Data Services were used as a de facto standard for data exchange, so some teams wrote providers only to produce ADO `Recordset`s. There was even the promise of "write-once, use with everything" generic data clients. Providers and drivers were implemented even if the data access method corresponded little or not at all with the API or object model. Examples of the latter include the ODBC driver for text that exposed "SQL" over text files and the OLE DB Simple Provider architecture.

Companies built OLE DB providers using a variety of data sources and provider styles. Some were written by database vendors such as Oracle, IBM, and Unisys. Merant (now DataDirect Technologies) released a comprehensive suite of providers and a middle-tier service architecture known as OLE DB Direct. ISG

Software released a middle-tier solution with support for a plethora of data sources—relational and nonrelational—known originally as ISG Navigator. There is an OLE DB provider for ODBC (known as MSDASQL, the original provider released by Microsoft) as well as ODBC drivers for OLE DB providers released by DataDirect Technologies and ISG Software. The ODBC drivers for OLE DB were meant to be an ODBC gateway for OLE DB provider vendors who did not bother writing ODBC drivers for their databases; the goal was to ensure compatibility with third-party products that did not yet support OLE DB but did support ODBC.

Less well known were the providers over proprietary data access methods, such as those from Advantage Software and Centura Software and Reuters' market data provider. In addition, an entire series of providers was developed as solutions for obtaining data from in-house application systems, hardware devices, and proprietary protocols. I've corresponded with developers around the world who built OLE DB providers as the solution for ordinary and unique data access.

These providers were developed to obtain access to third-party tools such as Crystal Reports or to achieve seamless integration with Microsoft and other third-party ActiveX controls. With the extremely tight integration between OLE DB and SQL Server 7 and later, some companies used OLE DB providers as a means of implementing distributed queries or accessing the SQL Server query engine, or of using SQL Server Data Transformation Services.

These companies have an important decision in light of the new .NET platform if they wish to retain the competitive advantage they've obtained by implementing OLE DB providers. They ask, what now? The .NET platform suggests three main strategies for those individuals and corporations that wish to retain integration with the new .NET generation of APIs, services, and products built on them.

- Retain your existing OLE DB provider. This is the most obvious as well as the easiest to implement. The OleDb data provider permits entry to the DataSet class and the rest of the .NET world for most existing OLE DB providers. Not all advanced customizations for OLE DB providers may be supported through the OleDb data provider, but in many of these cases, the COM ADODB library is available by using the interoperability between .NET and COM.

- Write a new .NET data provider. Not only should it run faster, in general, than using OLE DB interoperability, but also you can write it completely without leaving the .NET APIs if your proprietary APIs can support it. `SqlClient` is an example of such a provider.

- Expose your data as XML. This may be the most misunderstood approach, but it is the simplest to implement and is also the gateway to the new universal data access, universal data representation, or both. This does not mean that you must expose your data encased in angle brackets in `<name>value</name>` format, as you will see.

8.2 Staying with OLE DB: A Summary of OLE DB Concepts

Before we discuss the option of retaining an existing OLE DB provider, it is helpful to explain the major concepts of the OLE DB object model.

The OLE DB object model consists of a series of well-defined abstract objects called cotypes and a set of well-factored interfaces for each cotype. To implement a provider, only three cotypes are required, and each cotype (including optional cotypes) has required and optional interfaces.

A set of optional, special-purpose cotypes are individually implemented at the provider's discretion. For example, the OLE DB `Command` cotype is optional, required only if the provider supports a command language. If a provider implements the `Command` cotype, there is a set of required interfaces on the `Command` as well as optional interfaces. The set of common cotypes and interfaces is defined by the OLE DB specification.

In addition, provider writers are free to add custom interfaces on each cotype and even expose custom cotypes. Functionality is determined by the consumer at runtime through a normal COM `QueryInterface` method call.

Figure 8–1 shows a simplified version of the four major OLE DB objects. Not all interfaces are shown in the figure.

In OLE DB, providers can obtain data directly from a data store (for example, `SQLOLEDB`) or through a native provider-specific API (such as `OraOLEDB.Oracle` using OCI calls). The `MSDASQL` provider implements an OLE DB object model over any ODBC data source using any ODBC driver.

In addition, OLE DB supports the notion of service providers. A *service provider* can be middleware that communicates with each data source through a

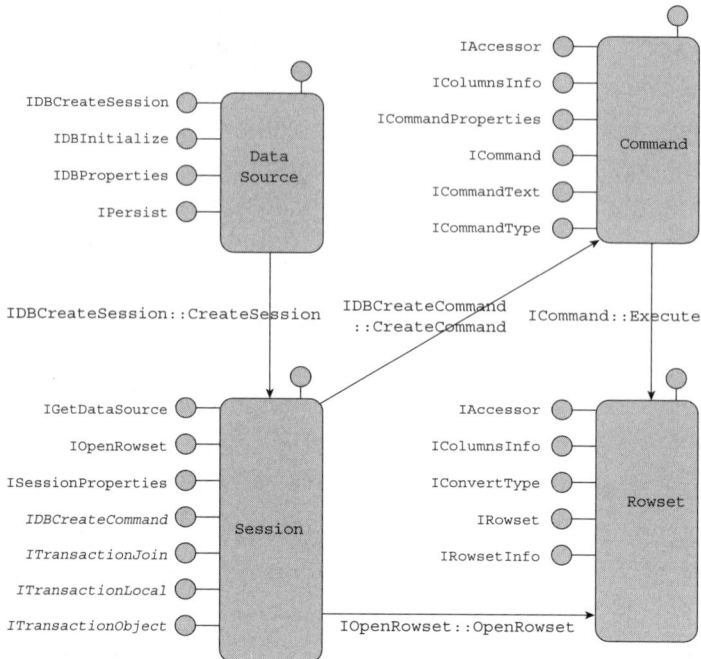

Figure 8–1 The OLE DB object model

native API (such as DataDirect Technologies' OLE DB Direct). A service provider can also act as a consumer of other OLE DB providers' data, optionally reformat it, and expose the result as a provider. An example is the MSDataShape provider, which consumes multiple rowsets and can optionally reformat them into hierarchies and expose aggregates. Technically, the SQLOLEDB provider (and MSDASQL when the SQL ODBC driver is used) is a service provider. It gets its data from the SQL Server relational manager, which, by virtue of being able to consume OLE DB Rowsets from the SQL Server storage manager or any linked server, is also a service provider. Figure 8–2 shows the service provider architecture.

Microsoft provides some OLE DB classes for specific purposes. For example, the OLE DB Root Enumerator produces a Rowset of information about OLE DB providers available on a specific machine. The OLE DB Root Binder can invoke a provider through a URL if this functionality is supported by the provider. In addition, a series of built-in services supports connection pooling on a per-provider basis, as well as automatic distributed transaction enlistment (if the

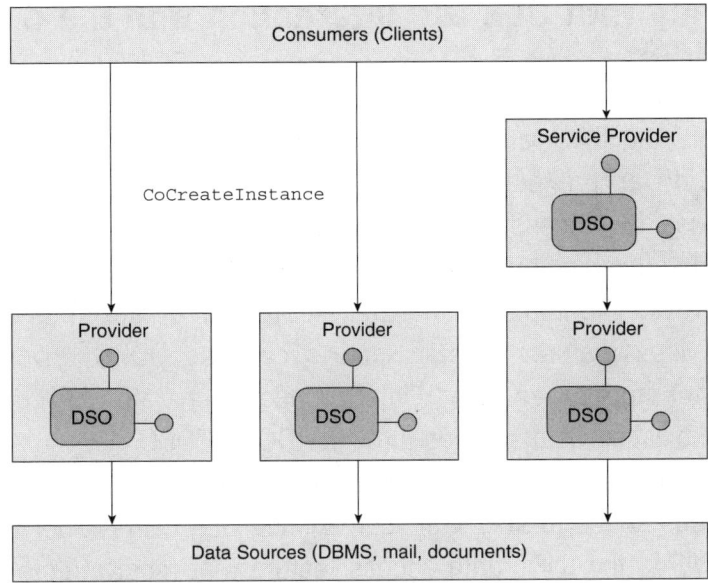

Figure 8–2   OLE DB service provider architecture

provider supports OLE transactions) and client-side scrollable `Rowsets`. These services work through custom cotypes and COM aggregation and live in `OLEDB32.DLL` and `MSDACE.DLL`.

OLE DB goes beyond ODBC in the case of nonrelational, nonrectangular data. Support of the SQL language (or any command language, for that matter) is not required. OLE DB can handle homogeneous and heterogeneous hierarchies. Homogeneous hierarchies are supported by means of a specific data type called a `Chapter`, which represents rows in a sublevel of the hierarchy. Heterogeneous hierarchies are supported by means of the `Row` object and its interfaces, such as the oddly named `IScopedOperations`, which exposes methods for obtaining sets of heterogeneous children. Extensions to the object model, such as new metadata schemas and an additional cotype, handle multidimensional (OLAP) data and data mining.

Now let's look at some of the issues, from a provider writer's perspective, of staying with OLE DB and attempting to interoperate with the `OleDb` data provider in the .NET framework. I concentrate on the `Command` and `Rowset` instances but mention other points of possible functionality differences.

8.3 Staying with OLE DB: Interaction with the `OleDb` Data Provider

ODBC and OLE DB providers have the advantage of being directly hooked into other Microsoft and third-party products. Microsoft Access, for example, can use any ODBC driver to directly expose data as though it came from Access databases, for use by Access applications. SQL Server permits OLE DB data sources to be used in distributed queries. SQL Server 7.0 and later can also use any OLE DB provider to import, export, and transform data with its Data Transformation Services feature. Crystal Reports can use ODBC drivers or ADO `Recordset`s for input to reporting. Other products generate OLAP data or XML schemas from existing data sources through ADO or ODBC.

These and other examples make writing OLE DB providers or ODBC drivers attractive. If you choose to stay with your existing OLE DB provider but want to use the .NET APIs, the .NET data access feature that most affects you is the `OleDb` data provider. Let's take a closer look at this provider from an OLE DB provider writer's point of view. Chapter 9 looks into ODBC and the `Odbc` data provider Web release.

Note that "OLE DB" (all uppercase letters with a space) refers to the OLE DB API, whereas `OleDb` (Pascal case, no space, Courier typeface) refers to the `OleDb` data provider in .NET.

Data providers replace OLE DB providers as the most integrated way to use databases with the rest of the platform. For vendors that have already written OLE DB providers, the `OleDb` data provider acts as a bridge between the COM-based OLE DB world and the managed world. Like the `SqlClient` data provider, the `OleDb` data provider exposes .NET-compliant managed types and interfaces. Unlike `SqlClient`, the `OleDb` data provider makes many trips through COM-callable wrappers because the underlying OLE DB provider is not managed code, as shown in Figure 8–3. You also lose code safety and .NET code access security because unmanaged code is being allowed to execute in-process with managed code. In some ways the `OleDb` data provider is analogous to the OLE DB provider for ODBC in that they both provide a bridge from new to older technologies.

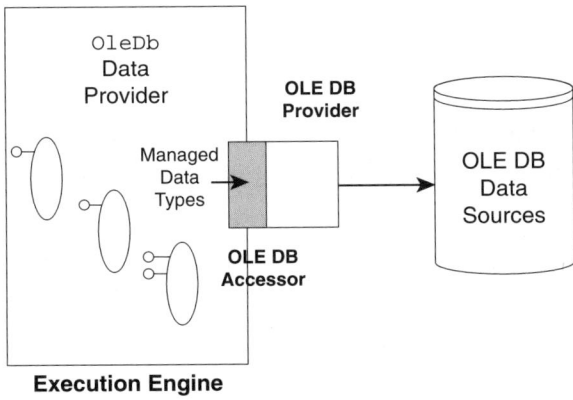

Execution Engine

Figure 8–3 `OleDb` **managed provider and managed classes**

The `OleDb` data provider uses OLE DB interfaces and methods directly, rather than go through ADO. Very few interfaces are exposed in `OLEDB32.DLL`'s type library. For that reason, few developers will go through the hassle required to use OLE DB directly through COM interoperability in .NET programs without using the data provider. To be most useful, functionality must be accessible through `OleDb` directly. Because ADO classic exposes all its functionality through a type library, you can also use ADO classic through COM interoperability.

8.3.1 Main Cotypes and Type Mapping

The `OleDb` data provider uses the OLE DB provider's `Data Source`, `Session`, and `Command` cotypes to connect to the data source and submit commands. `DataReader` and `DataAdapter` are the closest to, but do not directly correspond to, the OLE DB `Rowset`. Only a subset of the `Rowset`'s interfaces is used with both of these classes. `DataReader` keeps an array of the underlying provider's accessors as a private variable.

Native OLE DB is pointer- and offset-based; the offsets of the data buffer used when `IRowset::GetData` is called point to the equivalent managed types. The information used in producing those types is provided by calling `IColumnsRowset::GetColumnsRowset`, if exposed by the provider. `IColumnsInfo::GetColumnInfo` is used to provide a subset of metadata if `IColumnsRowset` is not available.

8.3.2 Accessors

Strongly typed getters in `OleDbDataReader`, discussed in Chapter 3, permit direct access to the managed types. Unlike OLE DB—in which the accessor can specify a different type than the native database type (and the provider will do the conversion)—the OLE DB accessor used by `OleDbDataReader` uses the native type corresponding to the type reported by `IColumnsInfo` or `IColumnsRowset` only. Attempting to use a strongly typed getter of the wrong type will fail, as shown in Listing 8–1, even if the OLE DB provider could do the conversion. A single accessor is used in the `OleDb` data provider for all the `Rowset`'s columns, and this accessor binds only the data and status for each column. The length portion, which is especially useful for BLOB and CLOB columns, can be returned by using `OleDbDataReader.GetBytes` or `GetChars` and specifying a null buffer.

Listing 8–1   Using strongly typed getter with the wrong data type fails

```
OleDbDataReader rdr;

// issue SELECT statement

// this will fail if column empno is not a VARCHAR (String)
// even if it could be converted to a string
string s = rdr.GetString(rdr["empno"]);
```

8.3.3 Executing `Commands`, Returning Results, and Using `OpenRowset`

The `OleDb` data provider supports obtaining counts of rows affected through `OleDbCommand` and resultsets through `OleDbDataReader`. The `OleDbCommand ICommand::Execute` method supports relational providers through SQL commands and also provides a series of extensions, such as `CommandType.TableDirect`, for providers that use alternative means of obtaining data.

The `OleDb` data provider supports the OLE DB `Command` object, including parameterized queries. The `OleDbCommand` object can use stored procedures directly and also can use parameterized queries or stored procedures invoked through textual commands. Whether a command is issued as a stored procedure or as a command is indicated through `CommandType`. The `OleDb` data provider supports only positional parameters, although OLE DB allows you to get parameter names using parameter ordinals, and the data provider uses the question mark as a parameter marker in the query. Using `CommandType.StoredProcedure` or `CommandType.Text` results in `ICommand::Execute` being issued by the provider. The data provider also supports `CommandType.TableDirect`, which uses `IOpenRowset::OpenRowset`.

8.3.4 `Command` Results Format and Behaviors

OLE DB's `ICommand::Execute` is highly overloaded; depending on which pointer is asked for, it can return an OLE DB `Row`, `Dataset`, `Rowset`, `MultipleResults`, or `Stream` pointer. A subset of this functionality, along with other extended command functionality, is supported by `OleDbCommand`'s `CommandBehavior` property. Asking for a single row (`CommandBehavior.SingleRow`) will use the OLE DB `IRow` interface to return a `Row` object, which is represented as a one-row `DataReader`. Asking for the single result (`CommandBehavior.SingleResult`) requests `IRowset`, and the default is to request `IMultipleResults` from providers that support it. Support for multiple results is determined from the `DBPROP_MULTIPLERESULTS` OLE DB informational property.

Using `CommandBehavior.SchemaOnly` results in issuing `ICommandPrepare` followed by `IColumnsInfo` or `IColumnsRowset` if command preparation is supported. Returning an OLE DB 2.5 `Stream` pointer directly is not supported by the `OleDb` provider, although the `SqlXml` managed data classes expose this functionality for SQL Server. When you use `OleDbDataAdapter.Fill` and retrieve multiple results through a `DataReader`, the `CommandBehavior.SequentialAccess` parameter is used. This behavior permits only sequential iteration through the columns of a rowset in column order, facilitating the use of `ISequentialStream` to read BLOB columns. It is also the fastest way to access a resultset.

8.3.5 Command Dialects

Secondary command dialects are not available because OLE DB's command dialect property is not directly supported. This affects the `SQLOLEDB` provider most of all because none of the new XML dialects is supported. The `SqlXml` managed data classes were introduced just to provide this functionality. The fact that secondary command dialects are unavailable also disallows the use of SQL and MDX commands through the SQL Server OLAP provider because these were specified as command dialects.

The MSOLAP provider works around this in two ways. The provider attempts to recognize the command dialect and submit it through the correct command parser. In addition, MSOLAP 8.0 permits you to specify a default primary dialect as a connection string parameter (`Default GUID Dialect`) and adds support for a third dialect, Data Mining language. However, when you use OLAP providers with `OleDb`, there is no support for the OLE DB for OLAP `Dataset` object (note the lowercase s). This object is an OLE DB cotype, not to be confused with the .NET `DataSet`. An OLAP provider using a `DataReader` can retrieve only rectangular results.

8.3.6 Hierarchical Data

In OLE DB, hierarchical data is exposed as two `Rowset`s that use a column of a special data type, `DBTYPE_CHAPTER`, to represent the parent-child relationship. Reading the child `Rowset` through the chapter column in the parent results in only the subset of rows that corresponds to that parent's children. The `OleDb` data provider supports the chapter concept by use of the `OleDbData-Reader.GetData` method. As with reading through the chapter column in OLE DB, `GetData` returns the child rows of a single parent.

OLE DB 2.5 extends hierarchy support to heterogeneous hierarchies by allowing providers to return a `Rowset`, `Row`, or `Stream` pointer from an accessor and by implementing the `IScopedOperations` interface. This interface is not supported in ADO.NET when the `OleDb` data provider is used.

8.3.7 Updating from a `Rowset`

`OleDbCommandBuilder` uses schema information, especially `BASECATALOG`, `BASETABLENAME`, and `BASECOLUMN`. These are exposed as special metadata columns using `IColumnsRowset` if this is supported by the provider. The requirements for an OLE DB provider to be usable by `OleDbCommandBuilder` are almost identical to the requirements for exposing `IRowsetUpdate` using the OLE DB client cursor engine in traditional OLE DB or ADO.

The `OleDb` data provider does not support direct updates through a `Rowset` using OLE DB's `IRowsetChange` and `IRowsetUpdate` interfaces. Neither does

`OleDb` support scrolling forward and backward (indicated in OLE DB by support of certain `Rowset` properties) or using `IRowsetScroll` or `IRowsetUpdate` directly on a `Rowset`. Some of this functionality is supported by the .NET `DataSet`, but OLE DB providers must support updating through `Command`s (and therefore, a command language) to use `DataSet`'s update capabilities. For example, any provider written using the OLE DB Simple Provider architecture (known as OSP), uses direct updating and does not support a `Command` object or a command language. Such providers are read-only (using `CommandType.TableDirect`) and are not scrollable when exposed through `OleDb`.

8.3.8 Errors

`OleDb` exposes errors as exceptions but exposes warnings through an event handler that does not interrupt program flow. If the data provider for OLE DB can determine the difference between a success error code that can return error information and a fatal error, the error handling will distinguish between the two.

8.3.9 Unsupported Functions

Some OLE DB functionality has no direct support in the `OleDb` data provider. It does not support the URL binder, setting or getting most OLE DB properties, and provider-specific errors and cotypes. However, `OleDb` has private variables that contain OLE DB interface pointers. These variables—in conjunction with reflection (if permitted by the security settings) and manual mapping of unsupported OLE DB interfaces to .NET interfaces and methods—may permit you to use these methods, but it is not recommended. Because direct support for `ITransactionJoin` is not available in the data provider model, the only supported way to use distributed transactions is through `System.EnterpriseServices`.

8.3.10 Supported and Unsupported Providers

The only providers directly supported as tested for use with the OLE DB data provider are `SQLOLEDB, Jet OLE.DB.4.0`, and `MSDAORA`. Certain constants in the `OleDb` data provider keep track of whether one of these providers is in use and perform special handling in some cases. The OLE DB provider for ODBC is specifically *not* supported; its use is disallowed and will cause an exception. The Exchange and WEBDAV OLE DB providers are not supported. They can be used to produce `Rowsets` of metadata, but not BLOB data through the OLE DB `stream`. With these providers, using ADODB through COM interoperability is a better choice.

Table 8–1 shows OLE DB cotypes, interfaces, and some properties, along with the `OleDb` data provider equivalents, if they exist. Appendix A maps OLE DB `DBTYPES` to .NET types.

Table 8–1   Mapping OLE DB to the `OleDb` data provider

Object/Interface	`OleDb` Provider
*Data Source**	*Connection*
IDBInitialize	Open/Close
IDBProperties	—
IDBCreateSession	—
IPersist/IPersistFile	—
IDBAsynchStatus	—
IDBDataSourceAdmin	—
IDBInfo	Info used by CommandBuilder
Session	*Connection, Transaction*
IOpenRowset	CommandType.Table
IDBCreateCommand	Connection.CreateCommand
ITransactionLocal/ITx	BeginTransaction
ITransactionJoin/ITx	Enterprise Services attributes only
IGetDataSource	—
ISessionProperties	—
IDBSchemaRowset	Connection.GetOleDbSchemaTable
IIndex/TableDefinition	—
Command	*Command*

Table 8–1 Mapping OLE DB to the `OleDb` data provider (Continued)

Object/Interface	`OleDb` Provider
`IAccessor`	*Parameters* on Command
`IColumnsInfo`	`CommandBehavior.SchemaOnly`
`ICommand`	`ExecuteReader`
	`ExecuteNonQuery`
`ICommandText`	`CommandText` property
`IConvertType`	—
`IColumnsRowset`	`CommandBehavior.SchemaOnly`
`ICommandPrepare`	`Prepare`
`ICommandWithParms`	`Parameters` metadata, `CommandBehavior.RefreshSchema`
`ICommandPersist`	—
`ICommandStream`	`SqlXml` managed classes only
`ICommandProperties`	`SqlXml` managed classes only
Rowset	*DataReader*
`IAccessor`	Indexers, getters
`IColumnsInfo`	`GetSchemaRowset`
`IRowset`	`DataReader.Read` (forward only)
`IColumnsRowset`	`GetSchemaRowset/` `CommandBehavior.SchemaOnly`
`IChapteredRowset`	`GetData`
Remaining Interfaces	Unsupported, moved to *DataSet*
Extended Errors	*Exception/Errors*
Data_Links	Unsupported
Enumerator	Unsupported
Binder	Unsupported

(continues)

Table 8–1 Mapping OLE DB to the `OleDb` data provider (Continued)

Object/Interface	`OleDb` Provider
MultipleResults	`DataReader.NextResult`
Row	`CommandBehavior.SingleRow`
Stream	`SqlXml` managed classes only
View	Moved to *DataView*
Dataset (OLAP Support)	No equivalent
Index	Not supported
MSDAInitialize (pooling)	OLE DB Services / `SqlClient` connection string
Notifications	*Delegates* on `Connection` only
Proxy/Stubs	Derived from *MarshalByRefObject*
RowPosition Object	Moved to *XPathDataNavigator*
DataConversion	—

* Italics indicate cotype (COM) or class (.NET). Lack of italics indicates interface (COM) or method or property (.NET).

Table 8–2 lists OLE DB interfaces and functionality and their implementation in the disconnected or client-side model.

Table 8–2 Mapping OLE DB to the .NET `DataSet`

Object/Interface	Disconnected Model
Data Source*	*DataSet* and related classes only
IDBDataSourceAdmin	*DataSet* new
IDBInitialize	*DataSet* new
Others	Not supported
Session	
ITableDefinition	*DataTable* new
IIndexDefinition	`DataView.IList`
IAlterTable	`DataColumn.Add`

Table 8–2   Mapping OLE DB to the .NET `DataSet` (Continued)

Object/Interface	Disconnected Model
`DBCOLUMNDESC` structure	`DataColumn`
Column property set	Properties of `DataColumn`
`ITableDefinitionWithCon-` `straints`	`ConstraintCollection`
	`DataRelationCollection`
`Command`	Interaction with `DataAdapter`
`Rowset`	
`IAccessor`	`DataColumn/DataTable`
`IColumnsInfo`	`DataColumn` properties
`IConvertType`	—
`IRowset::GetNextRows`	Array-based access
`IRowset::GetData`	Array, named, or typed column access
`IChapteredRowset`	`Relations` collection
`IColumnsRowset`	`DataColumnProperties`
`IRowsetInfo`	`DataTable` properties
`IGetRow`	`DataTable.Row` indexer
`IRowsetChange::Insert`	`DataTable.Add`
`IRowsetChange::Update`	`DataTable` change column values
`IRowsetChange::Delete`	`DataTable.Delete`
`IRowsetUpdate::Undo`	`DataTable.RejectChanges`
`IRowsetUpdate::GetOrigi-` `nalRows`	`DataTable.RejectChanges`
`IRowsetUpdate::GetPending` `Rows`	`DataTable` filter by `Status`
`IRowsetUpdatee::Update`	`DataAdapter.Update`

(continues)

Table 8–2 Mapping OLE DB to the .NET `DataSet` (Continued)

Object/Interface	Disconnected Model
`IRowsetFind`	DataView.Find
`IRowsetIdentity`	`RowStates`
`IRowsetIndex`	IList
`IRowsetRefresh`	`DataSet.Merge`
`IRowsetResynch`	`DataSet.Merge`
`IRowsetScroll`	Index-based
`IRowsetView`	`DataTable.Select`, *DataView*
View	*DataView*

8.4 Writing a Data Provider

A more labor-intensive alternative to staying with your custom OLE DB provider is to write a new data source-specific .NET data provider. In addition to the generic data providers for OLE DB and ODBC, Microsoft has written two data providers (`SqlClient` and `SqlXml`) for SQL Server. Microsoft is currently working on custom data providers for Oracle, and DataDirect Technologies has announced data providers for Oracle and Sybase, with perhaps more to come. Although no "standard" is set in stone for .NET data providers, enough information is available for third parties to begin building their own.

The .NET SDK documentation includes details on how to build a data provider, what types and interfaces make up a standard provider, and how the interface methods should act to encourage standardization and interoperability among custom data providers. In addition, the SDK includes a sample data provider that exposes a custom data store. Although it isn't a complete specification, the information codifies how a data provider should behave. It shows how to implement the standard types and interfaces defined in `System.Data` and use some of the public helper base classes in `System.Data.Common`.

In Visual C++ 6.0, Microsoft introduced a set of classes that enable programmers to write OLE DB providers, based on the ActiveX Template Library (ATL). The ATL OLE DB provider templates ship with a wizard that uses the ATL infrastructure and produces a sample provider that exposes the `WIN32_FIND_DATA` structure, which consists of information about files and directories, using OLE DB cotypes and interfaces. I have used this provider in demos so often that I've given it a standard name, `DirProv`, which stands for the OLE DB provider for directory information. Because .NET ships with a set of classes that exposes similar functionality, I reproduce this example as a data provider and call it managed dirprov. The data provider appears in its entirety on the book's Web site.

Throughout the implementation, I use some simple coding conventions. Properties provide access to private member fields that begin with an underscore character (" _"). Exceptions are thrown by calling the appropriate private method when functionality is either `NotSupported` or `NotImplemented`.

Writing a data provider for ADO.NET is a much more straightforward task than writing the equivalent OLE DB provider. ADO.NET interfaces are well defined; if you implement a class to expose certain functionality, you should implement the corresponding interface. At a bare minimum, you should implement the following four major classes:

- `Connection`: This class is required even if you don't actually connect to a data source. Other classes, such as the `Command` class, require a `Connection` class for basic functionality. `DataAdapters` call `Open` and `Close` on the `Connection` class in the process of filling a `DataTable` in `DataSet`.

- `Command`: This class serves at least two purposes. `Commands`, in the command language of your choice, are supported to directly affect the data store. An example is a SQL `INSERT`, `UPDATE`, or `DELETE` command. In addition, you can submit commands that return results, such as a SQL `SELECT` command.

- `DataReader`: This class processes results from a `Command`. Its methods allow the consumer to iterate, in a forward-only manner, through rows of one or more sets of results. It also provides methods to get the data in the columns of those rows into variables of .NET types.

- `DataAdapter`: This class fills `DataSet` with results from `Commands`. In addition, it can provide updates using `Commands`, and an event model for fine-tuning updates.

Figure 8–4 shows these four required classes and some of the relationships among them. Not all relationships are shown; for example, you can create a `Command` class not only by calling `Connection.CreateCommand` but also by

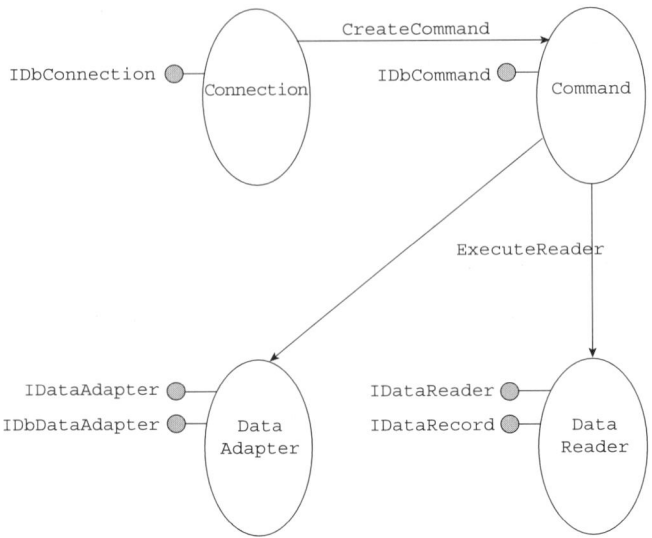

Figure 8–4 **Basic data provider classes**

specifying the `Connection` in an overload of the `Command`'s constructor. The reason that this is the smallest number of classes you can realistically implement is that some of the classes depend on the existence of other classes.

Let's implement a read-only provider that exposes these classes for a start. After you have defined the base functionality, you can layer additional functionality on top of the existing required classes or define it through ancillary classes.

8.5 Implementing the `Connection` Class

To implement the `Connection` class, you start by implementing `IDbConnection`, shown in Listing 8–2. Note that `IDbConnection` inherits from `IDisposable`.

Listing 8–2 **The `IDbConnection` interface**

```
public interface IDbConnection : IDisposable
{
    IDbTransaction BeginTransaction(IsolationLevel iso);
    IDbTransaction BeginTransaction();
    bool ChangeDatabase(string newdb);
    void Close();
    IDbCommand CreateCommand();
    void Open();
```

```
// properties
  string ConnectionString {get; set;}
  int ConnectionTimeout {get; set;}
  string Database {get; set;}
  ConnectionState State {get;}
}
```

8.5.1 Specification

IDbConnection has six public methods. The most obvious are Open and Close. Because the .NET runtime does not include the concept of deterministic destruction, the user must explicitly call Close rather than just release all the interface pointers as you would do with OLE DB. You use ChangeDatabase if your data source includes the concept of connecting to a different database. You use the BeginTransaction method to start a local transaction. Begin-Transaction returns an IDbTransaction interface through which the user calls Commit or Rollback. An overload of BeginTransaction takes a transaction isolation level. If your data source does not support local transactions, you do not need to support BeginTransaction. The IDbCreateCommand interface creates your provider's Command object and returns an IDbCommand interface reference. Finally, because IDbConnection inherits from IDisposable, you will need an implementation of the Dispose method.

IDbConnection exposes four public properties. ConnectionString, ConnectionTimeout, and Database are the most commonly used properties. A critical property is State, which is a get-only property returning a ConnectionState enumerated value, as shown in Table 8–3. The meaning of Opened and Closed is obvious. Opening and Closing can be used if your data source supports asynchronous initialization, and Fetching can be exposed if the data source supports asynchronous fetch at connection time. Broken is a state that represents the state of a connection that was opened but is not operational because, for example, the database it is using has been shut down by a system administrator.

8.5.2 Implementation

Decide what you are connecting to and what information you need. If it corresponds to the information used in a DBMS system, so much the better. If it does

Table 8–3   ConnectionState enumeration

Member Name	Description
Broken	The object is broken. This can occur only after the connection has been opened. A connection in this state can be closed and then reopened.
Closed	The object is closed.
Connecting	The object is connecting.
Executing	The object is executing a command.
Fetching	Data is being retrieved.
Open	The object is open.

not, you must add additional properties and fields. For the simplest "directory information" connection, I have implemented a simple `Open` and `Close` (which do nothing except set the correct `ConnectionState`) but no connection string, current database, or transaction.

Your `Connection` class should be a publicly creatable class. You should have at least a no-arg constructor and one constructor that takes a `String` (the connection string). Because my data provider does not use a connection string, I implemented only the no-arg constructor. A newly created `Connection` should be initialized to the state `ConnectionState.Closed`; this is accomplished by initializing the private `_ConnectionState` variable.

8.5.3   Specialization

The OLE DB spec allows providers to implement custom provider-specific interfaces. You can also do this when using .NET data providers. In addition, you can implement provider-specific instance methods or extra overloads. As with OLE DB, generic clients may choose not to use your provider-specific methods. The most dependable way to find capabilities is via runtime discovery by casting for interfaces or classes. You use interfaces whose methods define the custom features; discovery is then a matter of simply attempting a cast to the custom interface, much as you do in using `QueryInterface` in OLE DB. In addition, specialized clients can discover your provider-specific methods, overloads, and properties at runtime through reflection without explicit prior knowledge, subject to permission considerations. Because these methods are discovered at runtime, neither one gives the consumer any insight as to the semantics of your specializations.

An example of specialization in a `Connection` is the connection string parameter series supported by `SqlClient`. In addition to the standard connection string parameters—such as `Data Source`, `User ID`, and `Password` (taken from the OLE DB spec)—`SqlClient` supports SQL Server-specific parameters such as `Network Library` and `TDS buffer size`. A more complex specialization is to provide an implementation of connection pooling to enable better sharing of connections in a three-tier environment, such as a Web server scenario. Using different semantics, both `OleDb` and `SqlClient` provide connection pooling.

8.6 Implementing the `Command` Class

Commands must implement `IDbCommand`, which is shown in Listing 8–3. `IDbCommand` inherits from `IDisposable`.

Listing 8–3 The `IDbCommand` interface

```
public interface IDbCommand : IDisposable
{
  public void Cancel();
  public IDbDataParameter CreateParameter();
  public int ExecuteNonQuery();
  public IDataReader ExecuteReader();
  public IDataReader ExecuteReader(CommandBehavior b);
  public object ExecuteScalar();

  public string CommandText {get; set;}
  public int CommandTimeout {get; set;}
  public CommandType CommandType {get; set;}
  public IDbConnection Connection {get; set;}
  public IDataParameterCollection Parameters {get;}
  public IDbTransaction Transaction {get; set;}
  public UpdateRowSource UpdatedRowSource {get; set;}
}
```

8.6.1 Specification

`IDbCommand`'s main purpose is to submit commands or queries to the data store. Commands that affect the data store but do not produce results are submitted through `IDbCommand.ExecuteNonQuery`. This method returns the number of rows affected by the command. Commands that are queries return resultsets through the `DataReader` class. The method `IDbCommand.ExecuteReader` returns an `IDataReader` interface on your `DataReader` class. `ExecuteScalar` returns the first column of the first row but can also be used to return a scalar result. A possible use might to retrieve a "resultset" that is actually a single object instance or document.

An overload of `IDbCommand.ExecuteReader` takes a `CommandBehavior` parameter. The `CommandBehavior` indicates whether a `DataReader` provides data or metadata, or whether additional behavior is desired. The `CommandBehavior` enumeration is shown in Table 8–4.

Commands need a `CommandText` (the command itself) and `CommandType`. These are exposed as public properties. In addition, you can specify a `CommandText` string and a `Connection` instance in overloaded constructors, as specified in the documentation. The only `CommandType` that you must support is `CommandType.Text`. Other types include stored procedures and the use of simple table names instead of commands. (`SqlClient` does not support this because using only table names is an OLE DB-ism.) Commands can be canceled directly with the `Cancel` method, or they can time out by exceeding the `CommandTimeout` property.

Table 8–4 `CommandBehavior` **enumeration**

Member Name	Description
CloseConnection	When the command is executed, the associated `Connection` object is closed when the associated `DataReader` object is closed.
KeyInfo	The query returns column and primary key information.
SchemaOnly	The query returns column information only and does not affect the database state.
SequentialAccess	The results of the query are read sequentially to the column level.
SingleResult	The query returns a single result. Execution of the query may affect the database state.
SingleRow	The query is expected to return a single row. Execution of the query may affect the database state.

Command types integrate and contain references to other types in the object model. A `Command` must have an associated `Connection` through an `IDbConnection` reference, which can be set in the constructor or directly as a property. There is also an optional associated `Transaction` through an `IDbTransaction` reference, and this `Transaction` reference can be set in the constructor or by using the `Command`'s `Transaction` property, but it must be set explicitly. The `Transaction` reference cannot be inherited from the underlying `Connection`. Stored procedures or parameterized queries use sets of `Parameters`. `Parameters` are exposed as a .NET type and a collection. The `Parameters` collection is a property of `Command`, and `Command` includes the `CreateParameter` method. Finally, the `UpdatedRowSource` indicates which version of a `DataRow` is used when updates are performed through a `DataAdapter`.

8.6.2 Implementation

In the sample data provider, a directory name can be used as input to the `FileSystemInfos` API. This directory name must be specified as the `CommandText` type of command. Because transactions, parameterized queries, updates, and cancelable commands are not supported, most of the implementation is handled in the command execution methods. Both `ExecuteNonQuery` and `ExecuteReader` instantiate a `DataReader`, call its internal `GetDirectory` method, and return either the number of directory entries (the number of rows affected) or a `DataReader` over the set of entries.

The most complex method to code is the overload of `ExecuteReader` that takes a `CommandBehavior`. Because some of the behaviors can be logically or'd together, individual bits must be checked in the implementation. It is possible to request `KeyInfo` or `SchemaOnly`, but schema info is returned (through the `DataReader`'s `GetSchemaInfo` method) each time. Data is also returned each time.

The only difference in implementation occurs when `CommandBehavior.CloseConnection` is specified. This invokes a different overloaded constructor of `DataReader`, which stashes the associated `Connection`. Then, when `Close` is called on the `DataReader` class, `Close` is also called on the associated `Connection`, as mandated by the `CloseConnection` bit. Listing 8–4 shows the implementation of `ExecuteReader(CommandBehavior)`.

Listing 8–4 `IDbCommand.ExecuteReader(CommandBehavior)`

```csharp
public IDataReader ExecuteReader(CommandBehavior b)
{
  Debug.WriteLine(
    "MDirCommand.ExecuteReader(b)", "MDirCommand");

  // must have a valid and open connection
  if (_Connection == null ||
      _Connection.State != ConnectionState.Open)
        throw new InvalidOperationException(
          "Connection must be valid and open");

  if ((b & CommandBehavior.KeyInfo) > 0)
    Debug.WriteLine("Behavior includes KeyInfo");

  if ((b & CommandBehavior.SchemaOnly) > 0)
    Debug.WriteLine("Behavior includes SchemaOnly");

  // only implement CloseConnection and "all other"
  if ((b & CommandBehavior.CloseConnection) > 0)
  {
    Debug.WriteLine("Behavior includes CloseConnection");
    MDirDataReader reader =
      new MDirDataReader(_CommandText, _Connection);
    reader.GetDirectory(_CommandText);
    return reader;
  }
  else
  {
    MDirDataReader reader =
      new MDirDataReader(_CommandText);
    reader.GetDirectory(_CommandText);
    return reader;
  }
}
```

8.6.3 Specialization

The `SqlClient` and `OleDb` data providers implement almost all the functionality of `IDbCommand`. Because it's often faster for databases to produce singleton results than a resultset that contains a single row, both providers make use of the `SingleRow` command behavior. Both providers implement a `Prepare` method, which allows you to submit the command to the database for parsing separately from query plan preparation.

SqlClient extends the Command in a unique way. Because SQL Server 2000 can return streamed results in XML format, SqlClient exposes an ExecuteXml-Reader method, which returns an XmlReader rather than an IDataReader.

8.7 Implementing the DataReader Class

DataReader classes do not have a public constructor. They must implement both the IDataReader and the IDataRecord interface. The DataReader class allows the user to read in a forward-only, row-at-a-time fashion and get typed data or generic types from the columns in each row. Listing 8–5 shows IDataReader and IDataRecord.

Listing 8–5 IDataReader and IDataRecord

```
public interface IDataReader
{
// IDataReader methods
public DataTable GetSchemaTable();
public void Close();
public bool NextResult();
public bool Read();

// IDataReader properties
public int Depth
public bool IsClosed
public int RecordsAffected
}

public interface IDataRecord
{
// IDataRecord methods
public bool GetBoolean(int i);
public byte GetByte(int i);
public int GetBytes(int i, int fieldoffset, byte[] buffer,
      int length, int bufferoffset);
public char GetChar(int i);
public int GetChars(int i, int fieldoffset, char[] buffer,
      int length, int bufferoffset);
public IDataReader GetData(int i);
public string GetDataTypeName(int i);
```

```
public DateTime GetDateTime(int i);
public decimal GetDecimal(int i);
public double GetDouble(int i);
public Type GetFieldType(int i);
public float GetFloat(int i);
public Guid GetGuid(int i);
public short GetInt16(int i);
public int GetInt32(int i);
public long GetInt64(int i);
public string GetName(int i);
public int GetOrdinal(string name);
public string GetString(int i);
public object GetValue(int i);
public int GetValues(object[] values);
public bool IsDBNull(int i);

// IDataRecord properties
public int FieldCount
public object this[string name]
public object this[int i]
}
```

8.7.1 Specification

The IDataReader interface can iterate over results in a resultset using the Read method, which returns false when it runs out of rows. Multiple resultsets can be returned in a single command execution; a NextResult method moves to the next resultset.

Some consumers require a description of the information contained within the resultset, known as *resultset metadata*. IDataReader can return a single DataTable of metadata about each resultset through the method GetSchemaTable. The GetSchemaTable method exposes some standardized information and some provider-specific information.

IDataRecord exposes methods that allow providers to return a strongly or loosely typed data item for every column. A series of strongly typed getters take a zero-based column ordinal, and generic GetValue and GetValues methods return type object. The IDataRecord interface always returns .NET managed types; therefore, it is this interface that encapsulates mapping the data source type system to the .NET type system. In addition, IDataRecord contains column iterators (exposed as two overloads of the property `Item`) that can get a specific column by name or zero-based ordinal.

8.7.2 Implementation

The `DataReader` class contains the only provider-specific implementation method, `GetDirectory`, which calls the managed API `System.IO.DirectoryInfo.GetFileSystemInfos`. The data provider exposes a subset of the information retrieved: `Name`, `Size`, `Type` (file or subdirectory), and `CreationDate`. The `Name` and `Type` columns are type `String`, the `Size` column is `Int64`, and `CreateDate` is a `DateTime`. Because the metadata is fixed (each resultset returns the same metadata), the results are encoded into four arrays: `types` (the managed type of a single column), `sizes` (the sizes of those types), `names` (the column name), and `cols` (values of type `object`). Although `cols` is an array of type `object`, each column is an instance of the correct type; in other words, not all of them are exposed as `Variant`, as they are in ADO classic. Because the metadata is always the same, `GetSchemaTable` is hard-coded. Listing 8–6 shows the protected implementation for the `DataReader` class and the `Read` method.

Listing 8–6 `MDirProv DataReader` implementation details

```
// IDataReader.Read()
public bool Read()
{
  Debug.WriteLine("MDirDataReader.Read", "MDirDataReader");
  if (_ie != null)
  {
    bool notEOF = _ie.MoveNext();
    if (notEOF == true)
    {
      _CurrentRow++;
      if (_fsi[_CurrentRow] is FileInfo)
      {
        FileInfo f = (FileInfo)_fsi[_CurrentRow];
        _cols[0] = f.Name;
        _cols[1] = f.Length.ToString();
        _cols[2] = "File";
        _cols[3] = f.CreationTime.ToString();
      }
```

```
      else
      {
        DirectoryInfo d = (DirectoryInfo)_fsi[_CurrentRow];
        _cols[0] = d.Name;
        _cols[1] = "0";
        _cols[2] = "Directory";
        _cols[3] = d.CreationTime.ToString();
      }
    }
    return notEOF;
  }
  return false;
}


// MDirDataReader
// Implementation
// used by MDirCommand.Execute and MDirCommand.ExecuteReader

/*
 * We keep track of the connection to implement the
 * CommandBehavior.CloseConnection flag. null means
 * normal behavior (don't automatically close)
 */
private    IDbConnection _Connection = null;

internal  DirectoryInfo _dir;
internal  FileSystemInfo[] _fsi;
internal  int _CurrentRow;
internal  IEnumerator _ie;

internal  String[] _names = {"Name",
                             "Size",
                             "Type",
                             "CreationDate" };
internal  Type[] _types = {typeof(String),
                           typeof(long),
                           typeof(String),
                            typeof(DateTime) };
internal  object[] _cols = new object[4];

// maximum size in bytes
internal  Int32[] _sizes = { 1024, 8, 9, 8 };
```

```
internal void GetDirectory(String command)
{
        _dir = new DirectoryInfo(command);
        _fsi = _dir.GetFileSystemInfos();

        _RecordsAffected = _fsi.Length;

        _CurrentRow = -1;
        _ie = _fsi.GetEnumerator();
        _isClosed = false;
}
```

The strongly typed getters are implemented by simple type casting. Casting to a different type (for example, using `GetInt32` on a `String` column) produces an `InvalidCastException`, as it does in the `SqlClient` and `OleDb` data providers. Because all data values returned in a `FileSystemInfo` structure are already managed types, no conversion from data store-specific to managed types is required. The `Item` properties are implemented through C# indexers. The provider does not expose multiple resultsets from a single command.

To be usable with databound controls, `DataReaders` should implement `IEnumerable`. I've chosen to implement `IEnumerable` by using the `DbEnumerator` class in `System.Data.Common`. This class is used by both `SqlClient` and `OleDb`. To implement `IEnumerable`'s `GetEnumerator` method, I return a new `DbEnumerator` instance obtained by passing my `DataReader` instance to the `DbEnumerator` constructor. This is shown in Listing 8–7.

Listing 8–7 Using `System.Data.Common` `DbEnumerator`

```
IEnumerator System.Collections.IEnumerable.GetEnumerator()
{
  return ((IEnumerator) new DbEnumerator(this));
}
```

8.7.3 Specialization

The `OleDb` and `SqlClient` providers map to managed types in different ways. `SqlClient` has a `SqlDbType` enumeration as well as a `System.Data.Sql-Types` namespace that expose SQL Server-specific types. In addition to the strongly typed getters (such as `GetInt32`) that map SQL Server data types to .NET types, `SqlClient` also has a series of getters (such as `GetSqlInt32`) that expose the native `System.Data.SqlTypes` without any conversion. Using this technique is faster than converting to managed types, and it's especially useful when you're writing a data provider that runs inside SQL Server. When used inside the database itself, these types eliminate the impedance mismatch between SQL Server and .NET types.

The `OleDb` data provider maps OLE DB `DBTYPES` to managed types because the data store's types are mapped to OLE DB `DBTYPES` in the provider. The only interface of particular interest is `IDataRecord.GetData`, which returns an `IDataReader`. In OLE DB this maps to the chapter concept, in which hierarchical data is exposed through a special column of type `chapter` that relates the parent and child rowsets. `IDataRecord.GetData` would return a `DataReader` over the child row, based on a particular parent row. The same concept could have been used in the `MDirProv` data provider to recurse into subdirectories in the file system.

8.8 Implementing the `DataAdapter` Class

Because there is a canned implementation of a `DataAdapter` in `System.Data.Common`, it's relatively straightforward to implement your custom `DataAdapter` as a specialization of the base. In our case, the fact that the data provider is read-only makes implementation trivial.

8.8.1 Specification

The `DataAdapter` class is one of the few data provider classes that are implemented through a common base. Provider-specific `DataAdapters` inherit from `DbDataAdapter`, which inherits from `DataAdapter`. These classes implement `IDataAdapter`—which defines `Fill` and `Update` methods that interact with `DataSet`—and `IDbDataAdapter`. The latter exposes a set of four `Commands`—`SelectCommand`, `UpdateCommand`, `InsertCommand`, and `DeleteCommand`—to define the interaction between the provider and `DataSet` in terms of `Commands`. Also, a standard pair of events and delegates enables the consumer to receive notification and possibly modify behavior, before as well as after update (update being considered `Insert`, `Delete`, or `Update` in the data store). Figure 8–5 shows this hierarchy of classes and interfaces.

8.8.2 Implementation

The `DataAdapter` in the `MDirProv` data provider is a very lightweight implementation because the provider exposes read-only data. It supports only a `SelectCommand` because it does not need any updating or command-submitting logic nor `Updating` events or delegates. The `Updating` events and delegates are never used.

The base class, `DbDataAdapter`, provides almost all the methods that are needed (`Fill`, `FillSchema`, and others) for our `MDirDataAdapter`. However, our class does work as specified, allowing the consumer to `Fill` the `DataSet` and exposing the `SelectCommand`. In tracing through the provider, you'll note that

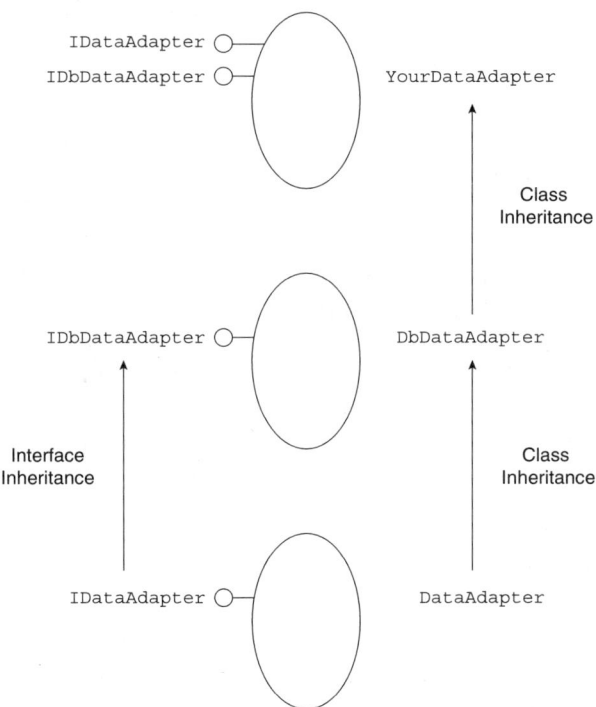

Figure 8–5 `DataAdapter` **class and interface inheritance**

`DbDataAdapter`'s implementation of `Fill` calls `Command.ExecuteReader-` `(CommandBehavior)` with behavior of `SequentialAccess`, and its `FillSchema` implementation uses the behavior `CommandBehavior.KeyInfo` and `Command-` `Behavior.SchemaOnly`.

8.8.3 Specialization

Both the `SqlClient` and the `OleDb` data providers implement subclasses of the `Updating/UpdatedEventArgs` and delegates. As a final specialization, `OleDb` implements a special overload of `Fill` that allows you to fill a `DataSet` or `DataTable` from a (classic) ADO `Recordset`.

8.9 Adding Enhanced Functionality

This brings us to the end of the major required common objects of the data provider object model. I should add that the `MDirProv` data provider is fully instrumented and can be extended to serve as a trace of higher-level calls inside the ADO.NET managed data stack. The entire source code and a sample program are downloadable from the book's Web site.

This provider implements only the base set of types and interfaces, and, as with OLE DB providers, you can add extended functionality. To complete your tour through the model, I'll mention the extended types available and common base definitions and implementations. Note that the `SqlClient` and `OleDb` data providers implement provider-specific variations of these types as well as provider-specific data type enumerations.

- `Transaction` types: These types encapsulate local transaction semantics that can be invoked from outside the data provider. Both `OleDb` and `Sql-Client` have `Transaction` types that implement `IDbTransaction`.

- `Parameter` and `ParameterCollection`: These classes implement collections of parameters used in stored procedures and parameterized queries. Parameters must map .NET types to database types in a method similar to `IDataReader`. The `SqlParameter` and `OleDbParameter` classes implement the common `IDbDataParameter` interface. The collection classes implement `IDataParameterCollection` as well as the collection interfaces `IEnumerable`, `ICollection`, and `IList`.

- `CommandBuilder`: This class assists in building default `InsertCommand`, `UpdateCommand`, and `DeleteCommand` members of a `DataAdapter` from database metadata. Both `SqlClient` and `OleDb` implement a version of this, but there is no common interface or base class. Both `CommandBuilder` classes use a common private `CommandBuilder` class in `System.Data.Common` in their implementations.

- Error handling types: A difficulty in any data access API is mapping flow of control based on error handling and accounting for multiple errors. Both `SqlClient` and `OleDb` implement `Error` and `ErrorCollection` types. These types do not extend a common base. They do, however, implement the collection interfaces. Both providers throw a provider-specific exception (`OleDbException` or `SqlException`) and also implement an event or delegate for warnings and informational messages (`Sql/OleDbInfoMessageEventArgs/Delegate`) so that warnings need not interrupt the flow of control in the calling program.

- `Permission` types: To be consistent with the .NET security architecture and because clients should not be allowed to perform secure functions just because they are using a high-level API, a data provider should implement `Permissions` and `PermissionsAttribute` types. `System.Data.Common` contains a set of base classes—`DBDataPermission` and `DBDataPermissionAttribute`—for this purpose.

8.10 Implementing XML Infoset Providers

Since the introduction of ODBC, all generic data access methods have been based on relational concepts. APIs based on connections, statements (commands), and resultsets were the only choice. Since the introduction of XML, however, the XML Infoset has been the preferred object model for exposing data because of its tight integration with HTML-based Web pages and its availability on almost every computing platform. Web presentation itself has evolved from the notion of combining data and presentation in HTML pages to splitting presentation (HTML) from data (XML or other data object models). Therefore, an alternative to exposing data as resultsets using OLE DB providers or data providers is to expose data as XML. In the .NET set of APIs, arbitrary data is exposed as XML using either the `XmlReader` or the `XPathNavigator` model. `XmlReader` and `XPathNavigator` are abstract base classes; in each case, custom data sources are exposed as a concrete derived class. These derived classes are known as XML data providers or Infoset providers.

For provider writers who do not expose the concepts of connection or sign-on to a data source, transactions, or commands with parameters, an XML Infoset provider is a viable alternative to a data provider. In addition, you get access to the other XML API tools (on the client, if you are implementing a server-based data source) that provide similar functionality to that usually performed in a database server. For example, you could expose your custom data as an `XmlReader`, read it into an `XmlDocument` class for `DataSet`-like functionality, issue subqueries against the resulting nodesets using XPath, and transform it to a different XML vocabulary with XSLT. Infoset providers can be used with flat, relational, hierarchical, or any of the other data models we've talked about so far.

Both `XmlReader` and `XPathNavigator` expose data, for the most part, as elements, attributes, and text nodes. The first task in writing an Infoset provider is to map arbitrary data to the XML Infoset; will the custom data source map to a variety of user-defined schemas, or will it instead map to a fixed schema? Microsoft's SQL for XML (discussed in Chapter 7) can map to user-defined schemas. Some readers and navigators map each data source (registry, file system, zip file) to a fixed XML representation. For example, Aaron Skonnard's registry navigator maps the registry to an XML document, as shown in Listing 8–8. This mapping task should not be taken lightly. Functionality, ease of XPath query, and bandwidth considerations affect whether data should be mapped to element or attribute data. This has been a subject of great debate within the XML community, and I won't wade into that discussion here.

Listing 8–8   Mapping the Windows registry to an XML representation

```
<result>
  <xmlfile EditFlags="AAABAA==">XML Document
    <BrowseInPlace/>
    <CLSID>{48123bc4-99d9-11d1-a6b3-00c04fd91555}</CLSID>
    <DefaultIcon>C:\WINNT\system32\msxml.dll,0</DefaultIcon>
    <shell>Open
      <Open>&amp;Open
        <command>
        "C:\Program Files\IE\iexplore.exe" -nohome
```

```
        </command>
        <ddeexec>"file:%1",,-1,,,,,
            <application>IExplore</application>
                <topic>WWW_OpenURL</topic>
        </ddeexec>
      </Open>
    </shell>
  </xmlfile>
</result>
```

After determining the schemas you mean to expose, you must then decide on namespaces for your data. Namespaces in XML scope data in XML Infosets, just as namespaces in .NET assemblies scope type definitions in the .NET API. In other words, it is possible to distinguish between two elements with a local name of `Person` if they come from different namespaces. If any of your data comes from a specific namespace (or namespaces) defined by an XML schema—for example, your data includes part numbers from a companywide part-numbering schema or namespace—you must account for this in the Infoset representation. If you are starting afresh, you can define your own data source-specific namespace or use `no namespace` in your Infoset instances. Microsoft data representations commonly use annotations from Microsoft-specific namespaces (such as `MSData`), and that can permit out-of-band processing hints to the consumer. You should avoid these unless you choose to document their intended use.

After the Infoset representation (or domain of multiple related representations) is settled, all that is required is to implement the appropriate `XmlReader` or `XPathNavigator`. The `XmlReader` class exposes a forward-only stream of nodes. `XmlReader` nodes are read-only, and the model uses the concept of a *current node*. This is very similar to the `DataReader` in the data provider space. Although XML Infosets are hierarchical, `XmlReaders` use depth-first traversal to expose a sequential set of nodes, as shown in Figure 8–6.

On the other hand, `XPathNavigator` exposes a model that allows not only forward-only reading but also backward, first, and last navigation. This functionality is most similar to that of a scrollable cursor in a relational database. As opposed to fixed, depth-first sequential traversal, `XPathNavigator` exposes ancestor navigation and navigation between parent and child and between siblings in a set.

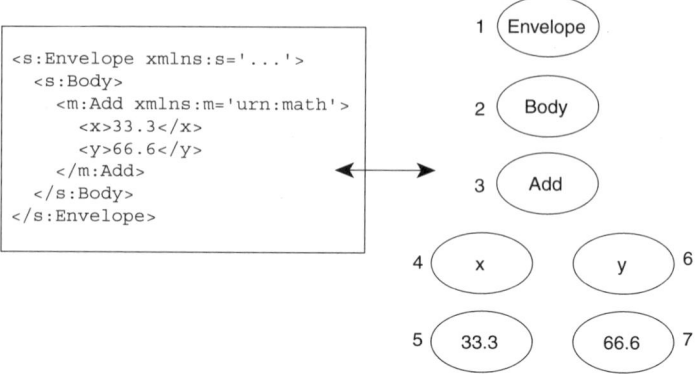

Figure 8–6   Depth-first traversal in `XmlReader`

Because `XmlReader`'s functionality is a subset of `XPathNavigator` (although `XmlReader` is not a subclass of `XPathNavigator`), you can layer `XmlReader` functionality over an existing `XPathNavigator`. If only forward navigation is allowed (that is, ancestor and parent axis and preceding node navigation are prohibited), you can build an `XPathNavigator` over the `XmlReader` as well. A set of Infoset provider sources released by Aaron Skonnard includes examples of both the generic `Navigator`-over-`Reader` and generic `Reader`-over-`Navigator` concepts.

8.11   Implementing `XmlReader`

Because I illustrate how to write data providers with an example of a simple provider of file system information, I'll illustrate `XmlReader` using the same data source. The Infoset provider based on `XmlReader` appears in its entirety on the book's Web site. XML documents make great use of hierarchies, however, and therefore the file system reader will be able to recurse into child levels of the file system hierarchy. I could have exposed this functionality in a data provider using `IDataReader.GetData`, but with data providers, it is less important in terms of the overall model.

`XmlReader` is a complex class, containing functionality in a few discrete areas. Some of the functionality is related to the division of data in XML into elements, attributes, and text. `XmlReader` contains functionality for reading each data type. In addition, you can inspect the content of the current node. The main functional areas of `XmlReader` are as follows:

- Inspecting the current node
- Exposing Infoset-level properties
- Reading methods for all node types
- Reading attributes and attribute text
- Using document fragment reading methods
- Using utility methods and methods for dealing with noncontent and entity nodes

`XmlReader` recognizes many different node types using the enumeration `XmlNodeType`, as shown in Listing 8–9. Node types mostly represent Infoset information items, although some node types—such as `EndElement` and `EndEntity`—are artificial, a result of exposing a hierarchical data structure as a sequential set. The placement of `EndElement`, for example, lets you determine which items are children of a given parent. The parent's `EndElement` node does not occur in the stream until the end of all contained child elements. Using the file system as an example, if files and directories are exposed as elements, each directory is a parent node containing child nodes (files and subdirectories). The `EndElement` node is returned when the end of a specific directory is reached.

Listing 8–9 `XmlNodeType` **enumeration**

```
public enum XmlNodeType
{
  Attribute,
  CDATA,
  Comment,
  Document,
  DocumentFragment,
  DocumentType,
  Element,
  EndElement,
  EndEntity,
  Entity,
  EntityReference,
  None,
  Notation,
```

```
ProcessingInstruction,
SignificantWhitespace,
Text,
Whitespace,
XmlDeclaration
}
```

I've separated the required methods and properties of `XmlReader` into roughly the six categories defined earlier. In addition, I've separately listed the methods that you need not implement because they have implementations in the base class. The properties and methods are categorized as follows:

- Properties implemented by base class: `CanResolveEntity`, `HasAttributes`

- Methods implemented by base class: `IsName`, `IsNameToken`, `IsStartElement`, `MoveToContent`, `ReadElementString`, `ReadEndElement`, `ReadStartElement`

- Properties of the current node: `AttributeCount`, `BaseURI`, `Depth`, `HasValue`, `IsDefault`, `IsEmptyElement`, `LocalName`, `Name`, `NamespaceURI`, `NodeType`, `Prefix`, `Value`

- Document properties: `EOF`, `NameTable`, `QuoteChar`, `ReadState`, `XmlSpace`, `XmlLang`

- Attribute methods: `GetAttribute` (three overloads), `MoveToAttribute` (three overloads), `MoveToFirstAttribute`, `MoveToNextAttribute`, `ReadAttributeValue`, indexer (three overloads)

- Reading methods: `MoveToElement`, `ReadString`, `Read`

- Fragment reading methods: `InnerXml`, `OuterXml`

- Utility methods: `Close`, `LookupNamespace`, `ResolveEntity`

Although you need not reimplement the methods defined in the base class, you would implement them (they are virtual in C#) if your implementation could provide some performance gains or your provider has unique requirements. Some of the default implementations are defined in terms of a series of calls into other `XmlReader` methods.

Let's first discuss implementing the most straightforward subsets of methods and properties. The document-specific properties (`QuoteChar`, `XmlSpace`) are hard-coded, although EOF is a Boolean switch. Note that, for simplicity, I don't use an XmlNameTable. The XmlNameTable method is an optimization that can keep atom-value pairs of frequently used strings. This technique improves performance because you can optimize string compares to comparing the atoms (think addresses in memory) and you need keep only one copy of the string. The document-fragment reading methods (InnerXml and OuterXml) are convenience methods for consumers. For simplicity, I've chosen not to implement them. Utility methods are hard-coded as well.

When implementing an XmlReader with more than one hierarchical level (more than one level of hierarchy below the root element), you must keep multiple currency positions (in the provider) to accommodate moving down and up a level during depth-only traversal. I've implemented this recursive state by using the System.Collections.Stack class because only one level of hierarchy is "live" at a given time. The state is kept in a Stack of instances of the DirState class, as shown in Listing 8–10.

Listing 8–10   Class to keep state of a single hierarchy

```
internal class DirState
{
   internal int              _CurrentRow;
   internal DirectoryInfo    _dir;
   internal FileSystemInfo[] _fsi;
   internal IEnumerator      _ie;

   internal DirState(string name)
   {
     _dir = new DirectoryInfo(name);
     _fsi = _dir.GetFileSystemInfos();

     _CurrentRow = -1;
     _ie = _fsi.GetEnumerator();
   }
}
```

In the Read method, when the end of any level of hierarchy is reached, an EndElement node is generated and returned. The next time Read is called, the state (DirState instance) of the previous level of hierarchy is popped off the stack. Listing 8–11 shows the Read method.

Listing 8-11 `FSReader.Read` **method implementation**

```
public override bool Read()
{
  // We're not on a text node any more
  _ReadText = false;

  // Or an attribute...
  _CurrentAttr = -1;

  // If we are done, get out
  if ((what == What.EndElement) && (Depth == 0))
  {
    _ReadState = ReadState.EndOfFile;
    _EOF = true;
    return false;
  }

  if (what == What.EndElement)
    ds = (DirState)dstack.Pop();

  // if it's the initial state, populate the root
  if (_ReadState == ReadState.Initial)
    {
      dstack = new Stack();
      ds = new DirState(_startingPath);
      what = What.Root;
      _ReadState = ReadState.Interactive;
      _cols[0] = ds._dir.FullName;
      _cols[1] = "0";
      _cols[2] = ds._dir.CreationTime.ToString();
      return true;
    }

  // if we're on a directory, go down a level
  if (what == What.Directory)
  {
    dstack.Push(ds);
    ds = new DirState(_cols[0]);
    _Depth++;
  }

  if (_Depth == 0)
    _Depth++;
```

```
if (ReadNextItem(ds) == false)
{
  _Depth--;
  what = What.EndElement;
}

return true;
}
```

The properties that expose the current node are interesting in that they can return different things based on node type. For example, `HasValue` returns `true` for my attributes and text nodes, but `false` for element nodes. Because I can have two different main element node values (`directory` and `file`) and can distinguish the root node from other directories, I keep track via an enumeration (the `What` enumeration) and a set of switches (`_CurrentAttr` and `_ReadText`). Listing 8–12 shows the `What` enumeration.

Listing 8–12 The `What` enumeration keeps track of my item types.
```
enum What
{
  None,
  Root,
  Directory,
  File,
  EndElement
}
What what = What.None;
```

Using the set of switches also assists in dealing with attributes and their values. Because all my elements are either empty elements (file) or parent elements (most directories), I need not be concerned with element text. Attributes require special handling, however, and a subset of methods applies only to attributes. In fact, you can simplify your provider by not modeling any data item as an attribute. Attributes are a special case because `Xml-Reader.Read` does not read attribute nodes or attribute values directly. Instead, attributes appear on the element node and are "read" using special attribute inspection methods. Reading attributes does not change the current element position.

In addition, implementing the `MoveToFirstAttribute` and `MoveToNext-Attribute` methods means that you must keep track of the "current attribute" in addition to current element. The attribute methods include indexers for reading attributes by ordinal, local name, or local name-namespace pairs.

The custom `XmlReader` implementation is fairly simple and straightforward. The data model, however, is related to the complexity of the Infoset provider. The distinction between elements, attributes, and text value nodes means that the provider must keep many positions of currency. Because of `XmlReader`'s depth-first traversal, you can do little to optimize an `XmlReader` other than to read a level of hierarchy only when it is needed. You must keep data from previous hierarchical levels if they are still in scope. This doesn't usually cause a performance problem because usually you've already read it. The `XmlReader` class is truly efficient if the data is laid out as an XML document, a navigation database, or a desktop database, where currency pointers point to local memory addresses.

8.12 Implementing `XPathNavigator`

`XPathNavigator` is a cursor-based model, optimized to be useful with the XPath query language. Because `XPathNavigator` uses XPath's object model, the `NodeType` enumeration is a little different from the `NodeType` enumeration used with `XmlReader`.

Listing 8–13 shows the possible `XPathNodeType`s. Note that `XPathNodeType` contains significantly fewer node types than `XmlNodeType` and does not contain the synthetic `EndElement` and `EndEntity` node types. Implementing an `XPathNavigator` over an arbitrary data source is similar to implementing an `Xml-Reader` with respect to the design considerations (fixed versus varying schema, elements versus attributes and namespace usage) described earlier.

Listing 8–13 `XPathNodeType` **enumeration**

```
public enum XPathNodeType
{
  All,
  Attribute,
  Comment,
  Element,
  Namespace,
  ProcessingInstruction,
  Root,
```

```
    SignificantWhitespace,
    Text,
    Whitespace
}
```

XPathNavigator shares a large subset of its implementation concepts with XmlReader. Many of the properties are identical, although some properties (such as QuoteChar) are omitted because they are specified by the XPath engine implementation. Table 8–5 compares the properties in XmlReader and XPathNavigator.

XPathNavigator also shares most of the methods for moving through the attributes collection with XmlReader, although XPathNavigator does not expose as many choices. In addition to attribute collection and navigation methods, XPathNavigator provides a series of namespace navigation methods that expose navigation among the collection of namespaces. This is required because XPath queries can be based on the namespace axis.

Most of the added functionality in XPathNavigator occurs in its series of Move methods, which move in any direction as well as hierarchically, on a node-by-node basis:

MoveTo

MoveToAttribute

MoveToFirst

MoveToFirstAttribute

MoveToFirstChild

MoveToFirstNamespace

MoveToId

MoveToNamespace

MoveToNext

MoveToNextAttribute

MoveToNextNamespace

MoveToParent

MoveToPrevious

MoveToRoot

Table 8–5 Mapping `XmlReader` to `XPathNavigator`

Property	In `XmlReader` Only	In `XPathNavigator` Only	In Both
Property of Current Node			
AttributeCount	X		
BaseURI			X
Depth	X		
HasAttributes			X
HasValue	X		
IsDefault	X		
IsEmptyElement			X
LocalName			X
Name			X
NamespaceURI			X
NodeType			X
Prefix			X
Value			X
HasChildren		X	
Property of Document			
CanResolveEntity	X		
EOF	X		
Item	X		
QuoteChar	X		
ReadState	X		
XmlSpace	X		
XmlLang			X
NameTable			X

Note that most of them look very similar to the series of methods exposed by IMS or IDMS in Chapter 1. To accommodate these move methods, you must keep more state than with `XmlReader`. Although state is kept on a level-of-hierarchy basis in `XmlReader`, in `XPathNavigator` you must keep state on a per-node basis. Because reading must be sequential at a level of hierarchy, as well as up or down the hierarchy tree, you must keep the parent node and children nodes, as well as the current position of the child node collection, in node-specific state.

The difference between using an `XmlReader` and using an `XPathNavigator` is the difference between reading an entire document (beginning to end) and navigating through a hierarchical set of data, as would be done by a hierarchical database engine. If you're working with data sources in which the access API directly reflects the navigational model of the data engine, the `XPathNavigator` is an excellent choice. There is much more chance for optimization in `XPathNavigator` because most of the methods are implemented by the base class. The following methods are the ones that are most commonly called by the XPath query engine:

```
Compile
Evaluate
Select
SelectAncestors
SelectChildren
SelectDescendants
```

You can optimize the `XPathNavigator` in two ways:

- Read only the subset of data being worked on.
- Request the data at a very granular level.

For example, if you request an `XmlReader` that will read the file system, you must request a starting point. If you use the root directory of the file system as a starting point, `XmlReader` assumes that you're going to read all of it! `XPathNavigator` need only read the subset of directories needed as you use the `Move` methods, "paging in" the information when required. Subsets of data returned by XPath queries, using `Select`, are reminiscent of SQL resultsets. They are returned via `XPathNavigator` using an `XPathNodeIterator` over a set of nodes. `XPathNavigator.Evaluate` returns scalar values, as does the `ExecuteScalar` method in the `Command` class of a data provider.

One final feature of the `XPathNavigator` (or at least the `Document-XPathNavigator` and `DataDocumentXPathNavigator` implemented as private classes in `System.Xml`) is that there is a model to accomplish in-place updating. This model is not available in an `XmlReader` or `XPathDocument` or, for that matter, in a `DataReader` or `DataAdapter`. The way these navigators allow in-place updating, on a node-by-node basis, is to implement the `IHasXml-Node` interface on the items returned by an `XPathNodeIterator`. If the iterator implements `IHasXmlNode` on an item, this can return an updatable node. You can imagine an analogous case where `IHasFile` can return an updatable file or `IHadIMSNode` could return an updatable record in an IMS database.

8.13   Implementation Alternatives: Conclusions

What are the alternatives? What is the best choice? Let's review these questions in light of the reasons for exposing data through a OLE DB provider, data provider, or Infoset provider: data exchange, integration with GUI components, and third-party product support.

Data provider writers have at least four major choices to hook into the .NET compatibility space:

- Write a .NET data provider. This is a good choice for a data source (usually a relational or other database) that uses a proprietary protocol that can be parsed using a set of managed classes. The immediate example is `SqlClient`, which includes a TDS parser, or the `OleDb` data provider, which encapsulates a COM-based API. For maximum benefit and support of local transactions, parameterized queries, customizable commands, and nonstandard error collections, your data source should be updatable using a command language. The ideal data source would support multiple rectangular resultsets, batching of commands, and command-based updates. Note that current providers have no intrinsic support for in-place (non-command-based) updates or server cursors.

- Write a custom `XmlReader` or `XPathNavigator`. This option is especially good if your data is hierarchical (or, more correctly, nonrectangular) and uses navigation-based access (cursors) rather than set-based access. Data sources that can be optimized by subsetting reads (reading only a portion of the hierarchy) benefit greatly from a custom `XPathNavigator` implementation. In addition, not only navigation but also XPath queries and XSLT transforms can be used directly with your data.

- Write a "legacy" OLE DB provider or ODBC driver. Eventually, their importance may diminish, but this is still your best bet for doing distributed queries with SQL Server by using SQL Server DTS (data transformation services), direct enlistment in MSDTC transactions, and other integration processes. Both APIs also expose an update-in-place cursor model. With an OLE DB provider, you have almost 100 percent integration into the new .NET world through the `OleDb` data provider.

- Programmatically populate `DataSet` or `XmlDocument` using the appropriate data-specific APIs. If all you want is a set of data, both APIs are directly programmable. You need not expose navigation, updatability, or connections and commands unless you need them.

The .NET `DataSet` can be used for data exchange, providing functionality similar to an ADO `Recordset`. It is supported directly for use in Web services and marshals by value. But the key point is how the `DataSet` marshals by value. Unlike the ADO `Recordset`, which uses a proprietary binary format (advanced data tablegram, or ADTG), the `DataSet` class marshals as XML, as does almost everything else in the .NET framework. XML, rather than ADTG or `DataSet`, is the universal marshaling and data exchange format in .NET. So there is no need to implement a data provider to `Fill` the `DataSet` to facilitate data exchange.

You could implement the same functionality using a custom `XmlReader` or `XPathNavigator` that accesses an XML Infoset rather than a `DataSet`. An Infoset is an in-memory opaque representation of the data in an XML document and is often a more efficient representation of an XML document. You need not use the XML serialization format as long as the data can be exposed using the XML Infoset model. In addition, the XML Infoset is a better fit for nonrelational data such as homogeneous and heterogeneous hierarchies and semistructured data (that is, structured document data). In addition to directly exposing data as XML, keep in mind that you can fill the `DataSet` programmatically, as you can the ADO `Recordset`, without the need of a `Connection-Command-Data-Reader` model.

Because the Visual Studio team had input into the data access stack from the beginning, it is easy to integrate controls, not only with data providers but also with any data source. The .NET databound controls work with any type that implements `IEnumerable` or `ICollection`. The Visual Studio designers also support this integration. A data provider need not be written for the purpose of control support.

Some third-party products are beginning to support .NET directly. For example, Crystal Reports .NET, shipped with Visual Studio .NET, supports the use of `DataSets`, in addition to ODBC drivers and ADO `Recordsets`, for reporting. You'll most likely see this as a continuing trend.

8.14 Is a Single Universal Data Access Model Possible?

Chapter 1 briefly mentioned the concept of universal data access. Now it's time to revisit it in light of ADO.NET and recent development in access patterns and storage trends for data. Universal data access is not really about data access; instead, it's a means to an end. The end is distributed data storage and management. Universal data access, as a concept, started with ODBC, which was invented as a standardization layer to enable "write once, use with any database" portability. It grouped desktop databases, client-server databases, and other data stores under a common API. There were two prerequisites in the ODBC arena. The first was support (or mapping to) database concepts such as connecting to a central data store, executing commands, grouping multiple operations as transactions, and returning counts of rows affected and sets of results (relational rowsets). The second was support for the "universal query language," that is, SQL.

OLE DB was invented for two reasons. The first was that layering a SQL query parser on arbitrary files and nonrelational data stores was an unnecessary distraction. OLE DB did not mandate that the data providers support SQL; any query language or no query language would do. It did, however, mandate (until version 2.5) that providers expose data as sets of homogeneous rows. The second reason for the invention of OLE DB was that the illusion of universal data access could be strengthened if component layers leveled the playing field. This was to be accomplished by service providers that could add similar services to any OLE DB provider, usually by means of COM containment or aggregation. OLE DB mandated that providers implement all data access through a standard set of COM cotypes and interfaces because all Microsoft APIs were implemented this way at the time.

Then object-oriented databases gained popularity because of the way they handled nonrelational data, such as structured files—multimedia, time series, and others—and the representation of information as classes of objects. These databases abstracted the differences between the object and relational models by providing centralized storage of data as objects: instances of application classes. A different, navigation-based access was needed by every program that used object databases, and this lessened the need for optimized query parsers. Vendors of relational databases attempted to integrate objects into their databases by extending their data access models to incorporate different access types. They deemed their databases "object-relational" and accommodated nonrelational data types by using special "data cartridges," "data blades," and "extenders."

The large database vendors have always believed that all data should be kept in a central repository. This is largely for centralized control, security, ease of query, and ease of administration. With the addition of nonrelational data types, these databases were known as *universal servers* because any data could be stored, managed, and queried there. Only one data access API need be used: that of the specific database vendor. This meant two things:

- Data was kept in (or replicated to) large central repositories.
- The company was locked in to a specific database by virtue of being locked in to the API.

Universal data access was a reaction to this trend. OLE DB extended universal data access by support of simple data providers. Softening the requirement for SQL support made this support easier, but implementation of standard COM interfaces (making OLE DB Microsoft-centric) and the user expectation of greater than lowest common denominator functionality (the OLE DB minimum requirement) stood in the way of adoption on a global scale. But OLE DB did enable data access without deployment of a universal server.

Because XML is ubiquitous in the .NET framework and is supported on every major platform, XML takes up the mantle of universal data access. At the same time, every major database vendor, including Microsoft, is moving toward a universal server approach for data storage. Soon, there will be only three major universal servers left: the corporate database, files on a local or network file system, and information available on the Internet. Note that there are currently rumors of a future Windows operating system (code-named Blackcomb) using SQL Server to control the file system. This operating system would leave us with only two universal servers.

Each of these universal servers can be exposed, and data can be exchanged and processed, as XML. Because the XML space includes at least one query language (XPath), a data definition language (XML schemas), an object model (Infoset), some standard APIs (DOM and SAX), and a transformation, reporting, and programming language (XSLT), the future of interoperable data is indeed XML-based, if not XML-centric.

8.15 Where Are We?

You've assessed the available choices for data providers moving into the .NET-centric programming world, and you've gained some insight about a few choices for exposing your data through XML. Although the concept of Infoset providers is currently .NET-centric, it may become more mainstream in exposing both nonrelational and relational data as XML.

Chapter 9

Consumers: ADO.NET Migration for Consumers

Providing a migration path is crucial for the success of any new API stack. This chapter examines the migration paths for consumers and also the parts of the data access picture not covered by ADO.NET.

9.1 ADO.NET Migration Paths

ADO.NET is part of the new .NET framework, and it is likely that most new programs from a certain point in your company's history will be written to use .NET. If you're a programmer of data consumer programs, you have choices that are analogous to those who write data providers (see Chapter 8). Your choices are as follows:

- Continue to use your existing data access API while migrating your programs to use the rest of the .NET framework classes.
- Convert your data access to ADO.NET as you convert the rest of the program.

Although conversion to ADO.NET is most likely, ADO.NET currently provides only the most-used subset of data access functionality. Some functionality, such as server cursors and in-place resultset updating, is not currently exposed in ADO.NET data classes. Some data sources, such as Exchange mail stores and multidimensional data, do not yet have equivalents to enable access in the .NET framework.

Some programmers might like to continue to use vendor-specific data access libraries such as Sybase's DBLIB or Oracle's OCI. If you do not wish to convert, there are two possibilities. First, if your API is COM-based (as are most Microsoft APIs since around 1992) and is also type library-based (most COM implementers provide a type library to be usable by languages such as Visual Basic), you can use COM interoperability. This chapter discusses this mechanism with respect to ADO classic and ADOMD, the library for multidimensional data. If your current data access method uses native Windows (Win32) API calls, they can be executed from managed .NET code using platform invoke (PInvoke). You'll use this mechanism if you wish to, for example, retain your existing OCI code.

Most programmers will eventually convert their data access code to ADO.NET. For the most common cases, it will be a direct conversion. To assist those programmers, this chapter addresses converting programs from the most commonly used pre-.NET APIs:

- OLE DB: Native OLE DB code is used by some C++ programmers, especially those who use ATL consumer templates.

- ADO: ActiveX Data Objects is the most used API in recent (Microsoft platform) history, and a few special interoperability hooks have been built into ADO.NET to assist conversion.

- ODBC: Some programmers have chosen to stick with ODBC through the COM era because of ODBC's relative simplicity and the availability of ODBC drivers for nearly every data source imaginable. Microsoft has released a bridge data provider for ODBC users.

- JDBC: Programmers converting to .NET from Java will need to be especially aware of the difference between the JDBC and ADO.NET models.

The RDO and DAO COM-based predecessors to ADO can be used through COM interoperability but are outside the scope of this book

9.2 ADO.NET for OLE DB Programmers

Because there were a number of programmers that used OLE DB, especially since the introduction of the OLE DB consumer templates in Visual C++, it's instructive to compare native OLE DB types, interfaces, and methods to ADO.NET classes and interfaces. Let's investigate this, with a special emphasis on using the `OleDb` data provider. Similar information for provider writers can be found in Chapter 8.

9.2.1 Cotype Equivalents

The ADO.NET data provider classes are related to OLE DB as shown in Figure 9–1. OLE DB `DataSource` and `Session` are parallel to ADO.NET `Connection`. OLE DB `Command` is almost equivalent to ADO.NET `Command`. OLE DB `Rowset`

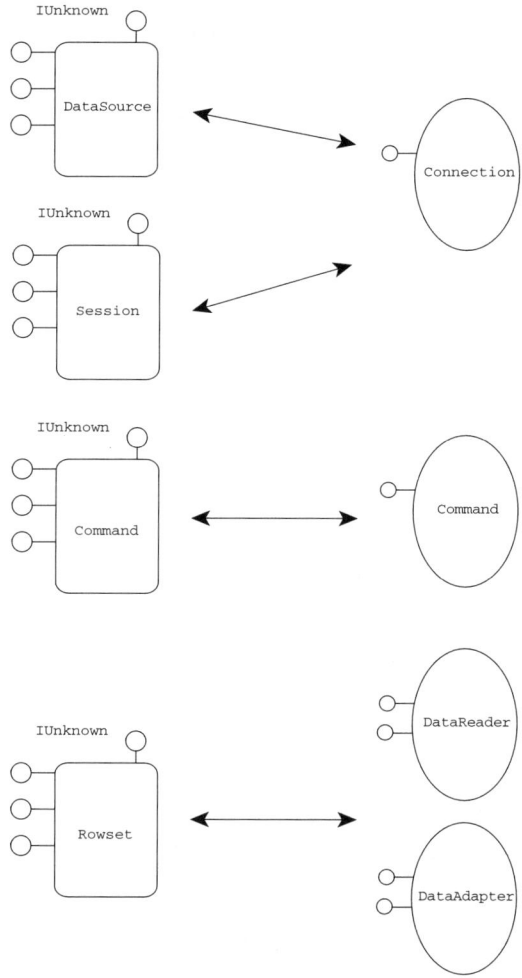

Figure 9–1   Mapping OLE DB cotypes (left) to ADO.NET classes

functionality is a superset of ADO.NET `DataReader`, which exposes only streaming (or forward-only cursor) mode. Not shown in the figure are OLE DB `Transaction` (actually defined in the OLE TX spec), which is analogous to ADO.NET `Transaction`, and the OLE DB `Error` objects, which are similar in purpose to the ADO.NET data provider's `Error` class.

9.2.2 Data Provider Transparency

OLE DB providers implement cotypes so that, in theory, you can use the same code with multiple providers by changing only properties. For example, the code in Listing 9–1 should be usable with any provider by changing only the connection string.

Listing 9–1   OLE DB generic code

```
CDataSource ds;
CSession session;
CCommand<CDynamicAccessor, CRowset> cmd;

HRESULT hr;
hr = ds.OpenFromInitializationString(L"connectstring");
if (FAILED(hr))
return hr;

hr = session.Open(ds);
if (FAILED(hr))
goto cleanup;

hr = cmd.Create(session, W2T(bstrQuery));
if (FAILED(hr))
goto cleanup;

hr = cmd.Open(NULL, NULL, false);
if (FAILED(hr))
goto cleanup;

// process rowset pointer cmd.m_spRowset
```

Each cotype has a standard set of interfaces, which are defined by the OLE DB specification as required or optional interfaces. Although providers can invent new nonstandard cotypes, this is rarely done. Instead, new functionality is exposed through provider-specific interfaces. OLE DB attempts to define a superset of interfaces in anticipation of every provider and consumer requirement.

The ADO.NET data provider model, on the other hand, is based on a standard set of classes with a common interface associated with each class. This interface exposes only base functionality; any provider-specific extensions are exposed at the class level, although provider writers may add additional interfaces. Even if only the interfaces are used, at least a typed `Connection` object must be instantiated, as shown in Listing 9–2. OLE DB accomplishes this by using `CoCreateInstance` or `DataSource::CreateInstance`, a variant that adds transparent services. You can, of course, maintain OLE DB provider transparency if you choose to use only the `OleDb` data provider.

Listing 9–2 ADO.NET needs a typed connection.

```
// this won't work
IDbConnection conn = new IDbConnection(connString);

// this is required
IDbConnection conn =
  (IDbConnection)new SqlConnection(connString);
```

9.2.3 Using Provider-Specific Functionality

Because classes are visible in ADO.NET—as opposed to using only interfaces and a single visible data source class as in OLE DB—data providers expose unique functionality as additional methods on the "standard" data classes. An example you've explored in detail is `SqlClient`'s implementation of `SqlCommand.ExecuteXmlReader`. There is even a completely nonstandard class, `CommandBuilder`, that is more or less unique for each provider, although Microsoft's implementations derive from a common base class.

9.2.4 Error Handling

OLE DB errors are exposed through well-defined COM HRESULTS that are returned on each method. Their meanings are defined in the specification (the OLE DB programmer's guide). HRESULTS have a severity, and OLE DB exposes both severe (`DB_E_xxx`) and nonsevere (`DB_S_xxx`) HRESULTS as well as `S_OK`

(HRESULT=0). In addition, a special error class allows OLE DB providers to expose multiple error messages from a single call.

Whether or not an error interferes with the program's flow of control is entirely determined by programmers. They may decide to ignore these HRESULTs if enough information has been returned to continue processing or interrupt processing at the first error. ADO.NET handles this implementation concept by using typed Exceptions, typed Error classes (which can be collections of errors), and a special EventHandler that exposes similar functionality to some nonzero success HRESULTs.

9.2.5 System-Supplied Services

OLE DB includes the notion of transparent context-based additional functionality, known as OLE DB Services. The three OLE DB services are as follows:

- Connection pooling
- Automatic enlistment in distributed transactions
- A *client cursor* provider, which is actually a COM component

These services are intended to be exposed without needing to be explicitly requested, based on default per-provider registry settings or connection string properties. Because they are "transparent," the services cause a good deal of confusion for beginning programmers. To further confuse the issue, by default the OLE DB consumer wizard provided by Visual C++ 6.0 does not use the services, thus convincing beginners that the services do not work as advertised, although they work correctly in the Visual Studio .NET OLE DB consumer wizard.

The data provider for OLE DB behaves like OLE DB with respect to services—it uses the underlying OLE DB provider's services settings—but the SqlClient provider makes them explicit and uses an improved connection pooling model. Declarative transactions and connection pooling parameters are specified in the connection string only when the SqlClient provider is used.

9.2.6 System-Supplied Components

OLE DB includes a few components that can enumerate the providers installed on a specific machine. One is GUI-based and can be used as a standard technique to configure provider connection strings or prompt the user. ADO.NET does not include this functionality.

9.2.7 Service Providers

OLE DB introduced the notion of service providers: providers written especially to use most of the facilities of an underlying provider, but adding functionality either by aggregation or containment. Microsoft shipped some service providers as part of the data access stack. Examples include the data shaping provider (`MSDataShape`), which uses a special command language to expose multiple SQL results as hierarchies or aggregates, and the remote provider, which allows any installed provider to be exposed to remote clients.

The remote provider functionality is the basis of a subtechnology known as RDS (Remote Data Services), which allows remote transmission of database commands and query results. Although such functionality can be exposed using ADO.NET data providers, it is not explicitly part of the model. Remoting of `DataSet`s in ADO.NET uses the XML format.

9.2.8 Marshaling

OLE DB marshals interface pointers by reference, as is the default in COM. However, specialized providers—namely, the client cursor provider—can marshal OLE DB `Rowset`s by value, using a `Recordset` class under the covers, in a well-defined but nonstandard binary format known as ADTG (advanced data tablegram). ADO.NET's `Connection`, `Command`, and `DataReader` classes extend `MarshalByReferenceObject` but are not marshaled out of process. For maximum interoperability, however, ADO.NET's disconnected `DataSet` (the equivalent of the client cursor provider) marshals in a number of different formats using XML.

9.3 A Brief Overview of ADO

Although the basic data access technology supplied by Microsoft for provider writers in the COM era is OLE DB, application programmers have been encouraged to adopt ADO in their programs. Before we look into migration paths, it is instructive to go over some of the basics of ADO.

ADO is a simplified version of (and an extra layer on top of) the OLE DB API. ADO is based on dual interfaces, making it usable by Visual Basic and ASP programmers as well as C++ programmers. The ADO `Connection` object encapsulates a combination of the OLE DB `Data Source` and OLE DB `Session` objects. The ADO `Command` object encapsulates OLE DB `Command`, and the ADO `Recordset` object encapsulates OLE DB `Rowset`. The ADO objects contain the corresponding OLE DB objects; native OLE DB interfaces are not visible through `Query Interface`. Figure 9–2 shows the ADO object model as a refinement of the OLE DB object model.

ADO adds object types for certain OLE DB structures. `Fields` and `Parameters` are exposed as collections in ADO, in place of OLE DB's accessor model. OLE DB's custom error object, which can handle a stack of errors, is exposed through the ADO `Errors` collection. The entire ADO 2.5 object model is shown in Figure 9–3. The `Record` and `Stream` objects were added in version 2.5 and are implemented over the OLE DB `Row` and `Stream` objects.

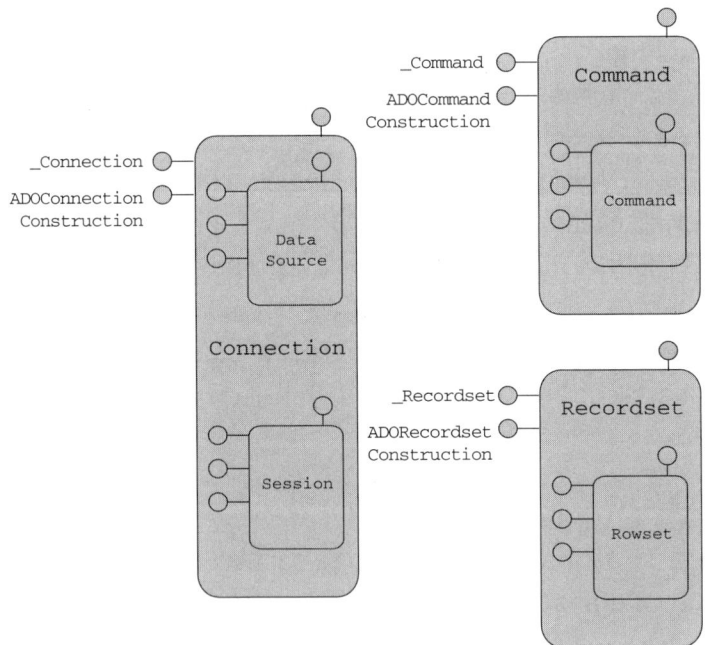

Figure 9–2   ADO encapsulates OLE DB objects

ESSENTIAL ADO.NET

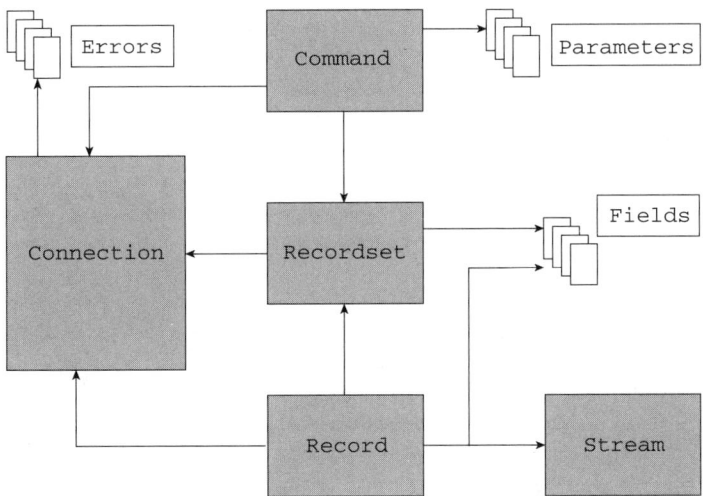

Figure 9–3   The ADO 2.5 object model

Because there is effectively one interface per object, ADO exposes new functionality by versioning interfaces. This is arguably the greatest cause of frustration when you're programming (or using products that use) ADO. ADO's type library names the current interface by prefixing with an underscore. For example, _Connection is the current Connection, and previous versions are available with the version number appended (Connection15, Connection20). Each version has a different IID, as is required by the rules of COM. Visual Basic and script programmers "see" a single object named Connection (logically Connection25 or _Connection). The drawback of this versioning method is that programs can fail (with "Error 429, ActiveX cannot create component") if the developer is using a newer version of ADO than the user has installed. A fragment of the ADO IDL (from the type library) illustrates this:

```
// current version
[
  odl,
  uuid(00000550-0000-0010-8000-00AA006D2EA4),
          dual
]
  interface _Connection : Connection15 {
    HRESULT Cancel();
```

```
      };

  // old version
  [
    odl,
    uuid(00000515-0000-0010-8000-00AA006D2EA4),
    hidden,
    dual,
  ]
    interface Connection15 : _ADO {
      [id(00000000), propget, helpcontext(0x0012c918)]
       HRESULT ConnectionString([out, retval] BSTR* pbstr);
      [id(00000000), propput, helpcontext(0x0012c918)]
  // more propeties, methods deleted for clarity
```

9.4 ADO.NET for ADO Programmers

ADO exposes a rich subset of the OLE DB model, so many of the comparisons we've already made to OLE DB programming also apply to ADO. However, because ADO exposes only a subset of OLE DB, ADO.NET goes beyond ADO in some areas. ADO always uses all OLE DB services by default and hides the client cursor engine as an option of `Recordset`.

9.4.1 Class Equivalences

The ADO.NET object model will be familiar to ADO programmers because the names and functionality of some of the classes correspond:

- ADO `Connection` to ADO.NET `Connection`
- ADO `Command` to ADO.NET `Command`
- ADO `Recordset` (default cursor type and location) to ADO.NET `Data-Reader`

Table 9–1 shows equivalents between the ADO and ADO.NET data models.

Table 9–1   Mapping ADO classes to ADO.NET classes

ADO Object/Property/Method	OleDb Data Provider
Connection*	*OleDbConnection*
Open/Close	Open/Close

Table 9–1 Mapping ADO classes to ADO.NET classes (Continued)

ADO Object/Property/Method	`OleDb` Data Provider
`BeginTransaction`	`BeginTransaction`
`Commit/RollbackTx`	`IDbTransaction.Commit/Rollback`
`Cancel`	—
`Execute`	Not supported on `Connection`
`OpenSchema`	`Connection.GetOleDbSchemaTable`
`ConnectionString`	`ConnectionString`
`ConnectionTimeout`	`ConnectionTimeout`
`CommandTimeout`	Only on `Command` class
`CursorLocation`	No exact equivalent
`DefaultDatabase`	`Database`
`Errors` collection	*`OleDbError/OleDbException`* not specific to connection
`IsolationLevel`	On `OleDbTransaction`
`Mode`	On connection string only
`Properties`	Most not available
`State`	`State`
`Version` (ADO Version)	—
—	.NET `Connection Version` = ADO `Connection.Properties("DBMS Version")`
`Async Events`	—
An Error in Errors	`InfoMessage` `Event`
`Connection Events`	Only `StateChange` event
`Command`	*`OleDbCommand`*
`Execute`	`ExecuteReader, ExecuteNonQuery`

(continues)

Table 9–1 Mapping ADO classes to ADO.NET classes (Continued)

ADO Object/Property/Method	OleDb Data Provider
Cancel	Cancel
CreateParameter	CreateParameter
ActiveConnection	Connection
CommandStream	SqlXml managed classes only
CommandText	CommandText
CommandTimeout	ResetCommandTimeout method
CommandType	CommandType
Dialect	—
Name	—
NamedProperties	True only in SqlClient provider, false for OleDb provider
Parameters	Parameters
Prepared	Prepare method
Properties	—
State	—
Parameter	*OleDbParameter*
Attributes	—
Direction	Direction
Name	ParameterName
NumericScale	Scale
Precision	Precision
Properties	IsNullable
Size	Size
Type	*DbType, OleDbType*

Table 9–1   Mapping ADO classes to ADO.NET classes (Continued)

ADO Object/Property/Method	`OleDb` Data Provider
`Value`	`Value`
`AppendChunk`	—
`Recordset`	*`DataReader`*
EOF	`DataReader.Read` return code indicates this
`Fields` collection	`FieldCount`
`RecordCount`	`RecordsAffected`
`State`	`IsClosed`
`Close`	`Close`
`MoveNext`	`Read`
`NextRecordset`	`NextResult`
`Field`	Indexer by name or ordinal, strong getters
	Columns in `DataReader.GetSchemaTable` (metadata)
`Error`	*`OleDbException/OleDbError`*
`Record`	`CommandBehavior.SingleRow`
`Stream`	`SqlXml` managed classes only
`Recordset`	*`DataSet`*
`EditMode`	`DataTable.BeginEdit`
`Filter`	`DataView.Filter`
`Index`	Collection class-specific (`IList`)
`Sort`	`DataView.Sort`
`StayInSync`	`DataSet.Relations`
`AddNew`	`DataTable.NewRow`

(continues)

Table 9–1   Mapping ADO classes to ADO.NET classes (Continued)

ADO Object/Property/Method	`OleDb` Data Provider
`CancelBatch`	`ContinueUpdateOnError` property of `DataAdapter`
`CancelUpdate`	`ContinueUpdateOnError` property of `DataAdapter`
`Clone`	`DataTable.Clone`
`Delete`	`DataTable.Delete`
`Find`	`DataView.Find`
`GetRows`	`DataAdapter.Fill`
`Move`	`Indexer on DataTable.Rows`
`Requery`	`DataAdapter.Fill`
`Resync`	`DataAdapter.Fill`
`Seek`	`DataView.Seek`
`Update`	`DataAdapter.Update`
`UpdateBatch`	`DataAdapter.Update` (no batching supplied)
Recordset Events	*DataSet/DataAdapter.Events*
`WillChangeRecordset/` `RecordsetChange-` `Complete`	`DataAdapter.OnRowUpdating/` `OnRowUpdated`
`WillChangeField/` `FieldChangeComplete`	`DataColumnChangeEvent` `DataRowChangeEvent`

*Italics indicate class (ADO) or class (.NET). Lack of italics indicates interface (COM) or method or property (.NET).

Listing 9–3 is a simple comparison example. It shows how to connect to a database, execute a command, and process the resultset.

Listing 9–3   Simple example in ADO and ADO.NET

```
' ADO (Visual Basic 6)
Dim conn as New ADODB.Connection
Dim cmd as New ADODB.Command
Dim rs as Recordset
```

```
conn.Open("connectionstring")
set cmd.ActiveConnection = conn
cmd.CommandText = "select * from mytable"
set rs = cmd.Execute()

' ADO is positioned at the first record
' when Execute returns,
while not rs.EOF
'process row
  rs.MoveNext
wend

rs.Close
cmd.Close
conn.Close

' ADO.NET (VB.NET)
Dim conn as OleDbConnection = _
  new OleDbConnection("connectionstring")
Dim cmd as OleDbCommand = _
  new OleDbCommand("select * from mytable", conn)
Dim rdr as OleDbDataReader

conn.Open()
rdr = cmd.ExecuteReader()

while (rdr.Read() = True)
  'process row
end while

rdr.Close()
cmd.Dispose()
conn.Close()
```

9.5 ADO Connections, Commands, and Transactions

Connected access and simple statement execution consists of using Connections and Commands. Local transactions are supported by using methods of the Connection class. As opposed to OLE DB, in ADO (classic) Connections and Commands are creatable classes. Let's go over the parallel of this usage in ADO.NET.

9.5.1 Connections and Connection Strings

You establish connections in ADO by instantiating a Connection and using a connection string to point to the data source. Because the ADO Connection is a generic object, the specific provider is specified as part of the connection string. In ADO.NET, you instantiate a strongly typed provider class, such as SqlConnection or OleDbConnection. Because the class is data-provider-specific, you need not specify the data provider in the connection string, although you must specify the OLE DB provider in the connection string when using the OleDb data provider. With SqlConnection, specifying the provider in the connection string is not permitted. In ADO.NET, you must use a wrapper method that returns an IDbConnection interface reference if you wish to write generic code. Future versions of ADO.NET may include a generic *connection factory* class that reincorporates the data provider and connection parameters.

9.5.2 Using Transactions

The Connection.BeginTransaction method is the same in ADO.NET as in ADO, but ADO does not use a Transaction object, as in ADO.NET. The difference stems from the fact that ADO.NET supports a richer local transaction model than ADO; ADO.NET includes support for nested transactions (in the OleDb data provider if supported by the underlying OLE DB provider) and savepoints (in the SqlClient data provider).

In addition, in ADO.NET each Command instance must be associated with the appropriate Transaction instance, as opposed to ADO, where it is tied only to the Connection. As a result, ADO.NET supports more than one Transaction at a time if the underlying data source permits it; however, it is confusing to programmers who are used to seeing a Transaction associated with a Connection.

9.5.3 Commands and Command Behaviors

In ADO, you can submit a command through the ADO Connection object (Connection.Execute), the ADO Command object (Command.Execute), the ADO Recordset object (Recordset.Open), and the ADO Record object (Record.Open). ADO conveniently instantiates the additional objects that are required. In ADO.NET, on the other hand, you must submit all commands through the `Command` class or through a `DataAdapter`. Using the `DataAdapter` is somewhat equivalent to using ADO's `CursorLocation = adUseClient`.

ADO.NET's `CommandType` and `CommandText` properties are directly analogous to those of ADO, although `CommandType.TableDirect` corresponds to `Connection.Execute` using the `adTableDirect` option parameter. ADO.NET supports a subset of ADO's `Options` (usually the last parameter on `Connection.Execute`, `Command.Execute`, or `Recordset.Open`) through its `CommandBehavior` enumeration. However, there is not an equivalent option to ADO's `adCmdStream` that returns an ADO `Stream` object.

9.5.4 Hierarchical Data

ADO handles hierarchies by using the `chapter` column (exposed as a `variant`) as though it were a `Recordset`. This has a direct analogy in ADO.NET's `IDataRecord.GetData`. ADO 2.5 introduced the `CopyRecord`, `DeleteRecord`, `MoveRecord`, and `GetChildren` methods to support the use of heterogeneous hierarchical operations. These operations are not supported in ADO.NET.

9.5.5 Asynchronous Operations

ADO has specific support for asynchronous operations and defines an event model for asynchronous `Connection`s and `Command`s as well as for filling a `Recordset` asynchronously. This support is not explicit in ADO.NET, although in some cases you can achieve equivalent functionality using .NET synchronization classes. The cancelable `Command` example in Chapter 3 shows how this would work in practice.

9.5.6 Properties

ADO exposes all OLE DB properties, including provider-specific properties, by using the `Properties` collection property. These properties are available on the `Connection`, `Command`, `Recordset`, and `Field` classes. Very few of these properties are exposed by ADO.NET when the `OleDb` data provider is used.

9.6 ADO.NET Versus ADO Disconnected Model

You've used the ADO disconnected `Recordset` class as a universal data representation mechanism in the classic ADO API. In addition to offline manipulation of resultsets and cross-component marshaling, you've also used it to populate databound controls. Let's compare this to the equivalent functionality in ADO.NET.

9.6.1 Class Equivalents

The disconnected model in ADO.NET is not hidden behind the facade of a client-side cursor but instead is exposed directly through the `DataSet` class. ADO's client cursor `Recordset` has quite a few things in common with a single `DataTable` in an ADO.NET `DataSet`. Both the `DataSet`/`DataTable` and the `Recordset` are createable classes that can expose tabular data. ADO programmers can instantiate empty `Recordset`s, define columns, and fill them with data while totally disconnected from any database. Listing 9–4 shows the parallel between creating a synthetic `Recordset` and using a synthetic `DataTable` in ADO.NET.

Listing 9–4   Creating a synthetic `Recordset`/`DataSet`

```
' ADO (Visual Basic 6)
Dim rs as New ADODB.Recordset
rs.Fields.Append "id", adInteger
rs.Fields.Append "name", adVarChar, 50
' ready to add data

' ADO.NET (VB.NET)
Dim ds as DataSet = new DataSet()

' DataTable can also be created standalone
Dim table as DataTable = new DataTable()
ds.Tables.Add(table)

table.Columns.Add("id", Type.GetType("Int32"))
table.Columns.Add("name", Type.GetType("String"))
' ready to add data
```

As with `DataSet`, a single table in a `Recordset` can be filled with data from a database and then disconnected by closing the connection, as shown in Listing 9–5.

Listing 9–5   Disconnected `Recordset`

```
' ADO - VB6
Dim rs as New ADODB.Recordset
rs.CursorLocation = adUseClient
```

```
rs.Open "select * from mytable", "connstring"

' Recordset still usable after this
rs.ActiveConnection.Close
```

Using the `DataAdapter` with a previously opened connection will leave the connection open, as happens in ADO if the connection is not explicitly closed or disconnected (see Listing 9–6). Note that keeping a connection open is the default pattern of access in ADO, but the default in ADO.NET is to have the `Data-Adapter` open and close the connection immediately during the `Fill` method.

Listing 9–6   Disconnected data in ADO.NET
```
' ADO.NET VB.NET
Dim ds as DataSet = new DataSet()
Dim da as OleDbDataAdapter = _
   new OleDbDataAdapter("select * from mytable", _
                        "connect string")
da.Fill(ds)
' data and disconnected and connection close here
```

9.6.2   Navigation

ADO's method of movement through rows in a `Recordset` uses a navigation paradigm through the `MoveNext, MovePrevious, MoveFirst`, and `Move-Last` methods. ADO.NET uses array-based access more in keeping with a relational set. The array-based usage is somewhat of a niggling point in that the `Recordset` supports `Move(n)`, and `MoveNext` functionality can be easily replicated in ADO.NET with a `for` loop and an index; nevertheless, the fact that navigation APIs are not used makes the model's purpose and functionality (providing access to a disconnected array) more explicit.

The `Move` methods in ADO's `Recordset` are necessary because ADO supports server cursors (client access to database cursors) using the same model. ADO.NET does not require this because client access to database cursors is not currently part of the model. It will be added later, perhaps when the internal SQL Server data provider that uses the existing connection is provided for executing .NET-based stored procedures, triggers, and user-defined functions inside SQL Server 2003 (code-named Yukon). Aside from a few edge cases, support of cursor-based access is most useful inside the database.

9.6.3 What Happened to `GetRows` in ADO.NET?

The ADO `Recordset` has a method called `GetRows` that can retrieve a set of rows into a two-dimensional variant array. This method is known to be very fast as well as a convenience if a two-dimensional array is the desired presentation. `GetRows` can specify an optional starting point and the number of rows to retrieve, as well as a subset of fields to retrieve. `GetRows` can be useful in a few specific situations: when you're using server-side cursors and when you're using XBase databases, such as Microsoft Access. When you're using server-side cursors, you need retrieve only a subset of the rows. When you're using XBase databases, you can set a next record to read through a pointer to an offset in a (hopefully) local file.

Server-side cursors are at odds with the scalability goal of the ADO.NET model. XBase databases do not scale well for large applications or Internet applications, which are the focus of ADO.NET. Because of the way SQL Server works, there is no optimization for positioned or partial retrieval except for a server cursor or `top N` query. Oracle can use a query to `rownumber` (the position in the resultset), but because Oracle always opens a cursor, the optimization of this also is questionable.

You can use server-side cursors, at least in SQL Server, by using `Command.ExecuteNonQuery` and `Command.ExecuteReader` to issue cursor statements directly to the database. Although this technique works, it is slower than ADO's server cursor API because you can fetch only one row at a time using the SQL `FETCH` statement. The `SQLOLEDB` provider and the ODBC driver for SQL Server use undocumented system stored procedures, such as `sp_cursorfetch`, to enable optimizations based on fetching more than one row at a time. You can attempt to achieve similar performance gains by using SQL Profiler to hack the format of `sp_cursorfetch` and managing the fetch buffering yourself as ADO does; as with any dependence on undocumented semantics, however, this is a perilous undertaking.

Listing 9–7 shows a simple example using cursors and SQL Server. The next release of ADO.NET may provide the `ISqlResultset` interface to reinstate this functionality. Like the ADO `Recordset`, the `ISqlResultset` interface will contain move and update-in-place methods.

Listing 9–7   Using server cursors in ADO.NET

```
SqlConnection conn = new SqlConnection(
  "server=localhost;database=pubs;uid=sa");
SqlCommand cmd = new SqlCommand();
conn.Open();
cmd.Connection = conn;

cmd.CommandText =
  "DECLARE aucursor " +
  "SCROLL CURSOR FOR " +
  "select * from authors FOR UPDATE;" +
  "OPEN aucursor";
cmd.ExecuteNonQuery();

cmd.CommandText =
  "FETCH NEXT FROM aucursor";
SqlDataReader dr = cmd.ExecuteReader();
while (dr.Read())
  // Use the reader
  Console.WriteLine("column 0 is " + dr[0]);
dr.Close();

cmd.CommandText =
  "FETCH ABSOLUTE 3 FROM aucursor";
cmd.ExecuteNonQuery();

cmd.CommandText =
  "UPDATE authors set au_fname = 'Bob' " +
  "WHERE CURRENT OF aucursor";
cmd.ExecuteNonQuery();

cmd.CommandText =
  "CLOSE aucursor; DEALLOCATE aucursor";
cmd.ExecuteNonQuery();
```

The `DataTable` is ADO.NET's data-centric two-dimensional array class. For data sources in which `GetRows` is actually an optimization, the `DataAdapter` class exposes an overload of `Fill` that can take a starting position and maximum number of rows to fill. In most cases, this causes the provider to fetch all the rows and the `DataAdapter` class, discarding a subset of them. Although fetching a subset of columns from an existing resultset may be an optimization in some databases, this optimization is not used by `DataAdapter`.

9.6.4 Updates

ADO supports two ways of doing database updates through a `Recordset`. Although the code for each is almost identical, the default (`Recordset.CursorLocation = adUseServer`) uses an updatable database cursor. This is not supported at all by ADO.NET. When you're using disconnected updates (through `Recordset.CursorLocation = adUseClient`), you use an entirely different mechanism. Calls to `Recordset.Update` or `Recordset.UpdateBatch` cause ADO to generate SQL statements and submit them to the database.

ADO has a choice of four variations of update statements that can be automatically generated, based on the (disconnected) `Recordset`'s `UpdateCriteria` property. ADO.NET's `CommandBuilder`s also generate SQL update statements, but only a single variation is supported. Listing 9–8 shows the default statements generated for a SQL update by ADO and ADO.NET.

Listing 9–8 Disconnected updates generated by ADO and ADO.NET

```
/* ADO generated updates -  */
/* job_desc field updated in pubs database */
/* adCriteriaUpdCols - default in ADO */
update jobs
  set job_desc = @newdesc
  where job_id = @oldid and job_desc = @olddesc

/* adCriteriaAllCols - ADO option */
/* only update statement auto-generated */
/* by ADO.NET CommandBuilder */
update jobs
  set job_desc = @newdesc
  where job_id = @oldid and job_desc = @olddesc
    and min_lvl = @oldmin and max_lvl = @oldmax

/* adCriteriaKey - ADO option */
update jobs
  set job_desc = @newdesc
  where job_id = @oldid

/* adCriteriaTimeStamp - ADO option */
/* note: this only is possible */
/* if you add a timestamp to jobs table */
update jobs
  set job_desc = @newdesc
  where job_id = @oldid and timestamp_col = @oldts
```

Note that for disconnected updates to be useful in ADO, the OLE DB provider must support the SQL command language. In ADO.NET, the data provider must support a command language (which need not be SQL); otherwise, disconnected updates (as well as `IDbCommand`-based updates) are not possible.

9.6.5 Update Statement Creation

In ADO.NET, `CommandBuilder` generates only the default update statements, but consumer-supplied updates are also available. Because the `Insert`, `Update`, and `Delete` commands are public and the multiple row versions are directly accessible, it's straightforward to specify custom insert, update, and delete commands. Customized ADO.NET statements can even specify stored procedures and permit updates through a `DataTable` produced via a SQL `JOIN`.

9.6.6 Batch Updates

One final difference is that ADO exposes a *batch update* mode, in which batches of SQL statements are issued. This method is useful only with the SQL Server OLE DB provider; with all other providers, one SQL statement for each update (and one round-trip to the data store) is the only behavior available. ADO.NET always issues one SQL statement per update; commands must be batched manually outside the model or not at all. Both ADO and ADO.NET permit further customization of the disconnected update (and possible conflict resolution) process through an event model.

9.6.7 ADO.NET `DataSet` Extensions

The `DataSet` class extends the ADO disconnected `Recordset` model by permitting you to combine multiple `DataTable`s, including data from different data sources, in a single `DataSet`. You can also define relationships between arbitrary `DataTable`s in a `DataSet`. A special OLE DB service provider, MS-DataShape, combines multiple relational results into aggregates or hierarchies, so this subset of the `DataSet` functionality is available in ADO. Moreover, the `DataSet` class goes far beyond this functionality by allowing multiple unrelated tables from multiple data sources in a single `DataSet`, while also allowing relationships. `DataSet` also permits the consumer to specify a cascading policy.

9.6.8 Column and Table Naming

The column names in ADO `Recordsets` are the column names provided by the OLE DB provider, usually by virtue of being the column names used in the SQL statement. This means that the programmer or control writer must map names in order to display more meaningful names in data controls such as grids. The programmer also can specify aliases directly in the SQL statement. In ADO.NET, this functionality is built in through the `TableMapping` and `ColumnMapping` collections.

9.6.9 Sorting and Filtering

ADO.NET's `DataView` functionality is exposed in the `Recordset` object in the disconnected `Recordset` model. This is based on the fact that ADO's client cursor provider (the `FX.Rowset` component) supports OLE DB's `View` cotype, which has interfaces and methods for providing sorting and filtering in memory. ADO's `Find` (which is supported only by the `Jet` provider) is similar to `DataView`'s `Find` or `DataTable`'s `Select` method. Listing 9–9 compares them. Although `DataView` supports the .NET `IList` interface, this interface provides by default a single index based on primary key. ADO client cursor `Recordsets` can index on any field via the `Optimized` property.

Listing 9–9 ADO `Find` versus ADO.NET `Select`

```
' ADO VB6
' Only works with Jet 4 provider and database
Dim conn as New ADODB.Connection
Dim rs as ADODB.Recordset
conn.Open "Provider=Microsoft.Jet.OLEDB.4.0;" & _
          "Data Source=C:\Nwind4.mdb"
set rs = conn.Execute("customers",adCmdTableDirect)
rs.Find "customerid like A%"

' ADO VB.NET
Dim ds as DataSet = new DataSet()
Dim da as OleDbDataAdapter = _
  new OleDbDataAdapter("select * from mytable", "connstr")
da.Fill(ds)
ds.Tables(0).Select("myid > 5")

' This works if myid is primary key
ds.Tables(0).DefaultView.ApplyDefaultSort = true
ds.Tables(0).DefaultView.Find("myid > 15")
```

9.7 ADO DB Interoperability

Much code has been written using classic ADO. Rather than insist that programmers throw away existing code or port everything to ADO.NET at once, .NET provides a few different types of interoperability with classic ADO. First, because ADO is a library based on COM dual interfaces, you can use existing ADO code directly in .NET, even in languages such as C# and VB.NET. The TLBIMP utility lets you use COM-callable wrappers and existing COM libraries. Here is the TLBIMP command for producing a .NET assembly from `msado15.dll`:

```
tlbimp c:\program files\common files\system\ado\msado15.dll
 /out:net_msado15.dll
```

In fact, Microsoft ships a pre-generated wrapper for ADO in the .NET developers' SDK. Listing 9–10 shows how to use classic ADO to process a server cursor in C# through interoperability.

Listing 9–10 Processing a server-side cursor through ADO (C#)

```
ADODB.Connection cn;
ADODB.Recordset rs;

String strConn =
  "Provider=SQLOLEDB;Data Source=(local);" +
  "UID=sa;Database=pubs;";
cn = new ADODB.Connection();

cn.ConnectionString=strConn;
cn.Open(strConn,"","",-1);

rs= new ADODB.Recordset();
rs.Open("select * from titles", cn,
   ADODB.CursorTypeEnum.adOpenKeyset,
   ADODB.LockTypeEnum.adLockOptimistic,
   (int)ADODB.CommandTypeEnum.adCmdText);

if (rs.BOF || rs.EOF)
  Console.WriteLine("no records found");
else
   rs.MoveNext();
```

There are only a few general tricks to using classic ADO in .NET programs through interoperability. These are not all necessary if you are using VB.NET, which can use optional parameters, but with other languages (such as C#), they are essential.

- You must use the enumerated constants in every case. This is more like programming ADO through C++ than using Visual Basic 6, where optional parameters can be left to default.

- Because the enumerated constants must be used (or the program will not even compile), make sure that you know which enumerated constant is the default that you are accustomed to using.

- Specify missing parameters in ADO calls `Type.Missing` rather than using `null` (or `DBNull`, for that matter). This is the .NET equivalent of `Variant` type `VT_EMPTY`.

- ADO interface and class definitions exist in the compatibility library. For example, in classic ADO, the class name is `Recordset`, but the interface is named `_Recordset`. In the ADODB .NET wrapper library, the class is named `RecordsetClass` and the interface is named `Recordset`. You can use either one in your programs.

Listing 9–11 shows the equivalent program to use a server cursor in VB.NET. Note that in VB.NET, as in Visual Basic 6, optional arguments need not be specified.

Listing 9–11   Processing a server-side cursor through ADO (VB.NET)

```
Dim cn As ADODB.Connection
Dim rs As ADODB.Recordset

Dim strConn As String = _
  "Provider=SQLOLEDB;Data Source=(local);" & _
  "UID=sa;Database=pubs;"
cn = New ADODB.Connection()

cn.ConnectionString = strConn
cn.Open(strConn)

rs = New ADODB.Recordset()
rs.Open("select * from titles", cn, _
    ADODB.CursorTypeEnum.adOpenKeyset, _
    ADODB.LockTypeEnum.adLockOptimistic)

If (rs.BOF = True Or rs.EOF = True) Then
```

```
    Console.WriteLine("no records found")
Else
    rs.MoveNext()
End If
```

Certain providers, such as the `Exchange` OLE DB provider and the `WebDav` provider, usually use URLs as locators to produce a `Recordset` or a `Record`; these providers are not well supported when you're using the `OleDb` data provider. There is another way to use interoperability if you have ADO `Recordset`s and want ADO.NET `DataSet`s. The `OleDb` data provider's `DataAdapter` class has an overload of the `Fill` method that accepts an ADO classic `Recordset` or `Record` as input. Listing 9–12 shows examples of using an ADO `Record` with the `WebDav` provider.

Listing 9–12   Filling a `DataSet` from the `WebDav` provider
```
ADODB.Record rec = new ADODB.Record();

rec.Open("", "URL=http://myhost/default.htm",
  ADODB.ConnectModeEnum.adModeRead,
  ADODB.RecordCreateOptionsEnum.adFailIfNotExists,
  ADODB.RecordOpenOptionsEnum.adOpenRecordUnspecified,
  "myuserid", "mypassword");

OleDbDataAdapter da = new OleDbDataAdapter();
DataSet ds = new DataSet();

// Fill using the ADODB Record object
da.Fill(ds, (object)rec, "mytable");
```

The interoperation between `DataSet`s and `Recordset`s is one-way, however, and methods to produce `Recordset`s or `Record`s from `DataTable`s are not provided. You can easily work around this, provided that you use the ADO-compatible subset of data types in the `DataSet`. After the ADO `Recordset` is read into the `DataSet` through the `OleDbDataAdapter`, you use the `DataAdapter`'s `InsertCommand`, `UpdateCommand`, and `DeleteCommand` properties and the `Update` method to write back to the database (if the provider supports it).

In addition to using ADO `Recordset` and `Record` in .NET programs, you can use the OLE DB Services component library (`MSDASC.dll`)—which includes a component that exposes a method for prompting users for a connection string—in .NET through COM interoperability. Although this technique somewhat compensates for the lack of this functionality in .NET data providers, only OLE DB-compliant connection strings can be generated. Because the `SqlClient` provider can use OLE DB connection string syntax (except for the `provider=` parameter), you can use the generated connection string as a starting point when connecting to `SqlClient`. Listing 9–13 shows an example.

Listing 9–13 Prompting the user for a connection

```
ADODB.Connection cn = new ADODB.Connection();
OleDbConnection oconn = new OleDbConnection();

// prompt the user to fill in the connection string
MSDASC.DataLinks dl = new MSDASC.DataLinks();
object o = (object)cn;
dl.PromptEdit(ref o);

if (cn.ConnectionString != null)
{
 oconn.ConnectionString = cn.ConnectionString;
}
```

ADO can persist `Recordset`s in a binary format (advanced data tablegram), and also in XML format. The XML format used by ADO is a special one, consisting of a specific type of XDR format schema followed by the `Recordset`'s data. Extended information (such as the OLE DB data type of each column) is defined in this schema by means of annotations (information exposed outside the XDR schema definition) in a Microsoft-specific namespace. The schema is followed by the data in the `Recordset`. Each row is represented by an XML `row` element. Each column is represented as an attribute of the `row` element. If the column contains a (database) null value, the corresponding attribute is not present. The set of row elements is the child of an `rs:data` element that represents the `Recordset`. Listing 9–14 shows an example of the XML produced (and consumed) by the ADO `Recordset`.

Listing 9–14 ADO format XML for a `Recordset`

```
<xml xmlns:s='uuid:BDC6E3F0-6DA3-11d1-A2A3-00AA00C14882'
         xmlns:dt='uuid:C2F41010-65B3-11d1-A29F-00AA00C14882'
         xmlns:rs='urn:schemas-microsoft-com:rowset'
         xmlns:z='#RowsetSchema'>
```

```
<s:Schema id='RowsetSchema'>
  <s:ElementType name='row' content='eltOnly'
                 rs:updatable='true'>
      <s:AttributeType name='au_id'
        rs:number='1' rs:writeunknown='true'
        rs:basecatalog='pubs' rs:basetable='authors'
          rs:basecolumn='au_id' rs:keycolumn='true'>
            <s:datatype dt:type='string' rs:dbtype='str'
            dt:maxLength='11' rs:maybenull='false'/>
      </s:AttributeType>
        <s:AttributeType name='au_lname'
        rs:number='2' rs:writeunknown='true'
        rs:basecatalog='pubs' rs:basetable='authors'
        rs:basecolumn='au_lname'>
        <s:datatype dt:type='string' rs:dbtype='str'
           dt:maxLength='40' rs:maybenull='false'/>
        </s:AttributeType>
        <s:AttributeType name='au_fname'
                    rs:number='3'
                    rs:writeunknown='true'
        rs:basecatalog='pubs' rs:basetable='authors'
        rs:basecolumn='au_fname'>
            <s:datatype dt:type='string' rs:dbtype='str'
            dt:maxLength='20' rs:maybenull='false'/>
        </s:AttributeType>
    <s:extends type='rs:rowbase'/>
  </s:ElementType>
</s:Schema>
<rs:data>
  <z:row au_id='172-32-1176'
         au_lname='White'
         au_fname='Bob' />
  <z:row au_id='213-46-8915'
         au_lname='Green'
         au_fname='Marjorie'/>
  <!-- rest of rows elided for clarity -->
</rs:data>
</xml>
```

ADO.NET can use the information in ADO-format XML—to a point. The information in ADO-XML's schema is ignored, and the XmlReader does not understand the meaning of the annotations. The information in the row elements can be read into a DataSet, XmlDocument, or XmlDataDocument. If it is used in the

`DataSet`, the schema is ignored and schema inference is used to infer the shape of the `DataTables` in the `DataSet`. The XML document shown in Listing 9–14 results in two `DataTables` in the `DataSet`: one named `data` and having no rows, and one named `row` and containing the data.

In addition to the columns contained in the XML file, the `DataSet`'s schema inference produces an extra column, `data_Id`, as illustrated in Listing 9–15. Note that although the data is present, each column in the `DataTable` is data type `String`. The synthesized `data_Id` column is type `Int32`.

Listing 9–15   Using ADO's XML in the `DataSet`

```
// this program
DataSet ds = new DataSet();
ds.ReadXml("c:\\authors.xml",
  XmlReadMode.InferSchema);
Console.WriteLine(
  "there are {0} tables in the dataset",
  ds.Tables.Count);
Console.WriteLine(
  "there are {0} relations",
  ds.Relations.Count);
foreach (DataTable t in ds.Tables)
{
  Console.WriteLine(
    "table {0} has {1} columns and {2} rows",
     t.TableName, t.Columns.Count, t.Rows.Count);
  foreach (DataColumn c in t.Columns)
    Console.WriteLine(
      " column {0} has data type {1}",
      c.ColumnName, c.DataType);
}

// produces this output
there are 2 tables in the dataset
there are 1 relations
table data has 1 columns and 1 rows
 column data_Id has data type System.Int32
table row has 4 columns and 23 rows
 column au_id has data type System.String
 column au_lname has data type System.String
 column au_fname has data type System.String
 column data_Id has data type System.Int32
```

When used with hierarchical OLE DB providers, such as the `MSDataShape` provider, ADO can produce hierarchical XML. Listing 9–16 shows an example of the XML produced by hierarchical data shaping. When read into the `DataSet`, this code produces multiple `DataTables`, with a relationship between the tables that were nested in the XML document.

Listing 9–16 ADO format XML for a hierarchical `Recordset`

```
<xml xmlns:s='uuid:BDC6E3F0-6DA3-11d1-A2A3-00AA00C14882'
          xmlns:dt='uuid:C2F41010-65B3-11d1-A29F-00AA00C14882'
          xmlns:rs='urn:schemas-microsoft-com:rowset'
          xmlns:z='#RowsetSchema'>
<s:Schema id='RowsetSchema'>
  <s:ElementType name='row' content='eltOnly'
        rs:CommandTimeout='30' rs:updatable='true'
        rs:ReshapeName='DSRowset1'>
     <s:AttributeType name='au_id' rs:number='1'
                       rs:writeunknown='true'
        rs:basecatalog='pubs' rs:basetable='authors'
        rs:basecolumn='au_id' rs:keycolumn='true'>
        <s:datatype dt:type='string' rs:dbtype='str'
           dt:maxLength='11' rs:maybenull='false'/>
     </s:AttributeType>
     <s:AttributeType name='au_lname' rs:number='2'
                       rs:writeunknown='true'
        rs:basecatalog='pubs' rs:basetable='authors'
        rs:basecolumn='au_lname'>
        <s:datatype dt:type='string' rs:dbtype='str'
           dt:maxLength='40' rs:maybenull='false'/>
     </s:AttributeType>

     <!-- hierarchy column -->
     <s:ElementType name='chapter' content='eltOnly'
       rs:CommandTimeout='30' rs:updatable='true'
       rs:ReshapeName='chapter'
       rs:relation='01000000010000000000000'>
      <s:AttributeType name='au_id' rs:number='1'
       rs:writeunknown='true'
       rs:basecatalog='pubs' rs:basetable='titleauthor'
       rs:basecolumn='au_id' rs:keycolumn='true'>
       <s:datatype dt:type='string' rs:dbtype='str'
                   dt:maxLength='11'
                   rs:maybenull='false'/>
```

```
    </s:AttributeType>
    <s:AttributeType name='title_id' rs:number='2'
     rs:writeunknown='true'
     rs:basecatalog='pubs' rs:basetable='titleauthor'
     rs:basecolumn='title_id' rs:keycolumn='true'>
     <s:datatype dt:type='string' rs:dbtype='str'
        dt:maxLength='6' rs:maybenull='false'/>
    </s:AttributeType>
    <s:extends type='rs:rowbase'/>
  </s:ElementType>
 <s:extends type='rs:rowbase'/>
 </s:ElementType>
</s:Schema>
<rs:data>
        <z:row au_id='172-32-1176' au_lname='White'>
            <chapter au_id='172-32-1176'
                title_id='PS3333'/>
        </z:row>
        <z:row au_id='213-46-8915' au_lname='Green'>
            <chapter au_id='213-46-8915'
                title_id='BU1032' />
            <chapter au_id='213-46-8915'
                title_id='BU2075' />
        </z:row>
</rs:data>
</xml>
```

A further synthesized column called `row_Id` is created to tie the parent and child rows. This is in addition to the column that contains the actual relationship. Listing 9–17 shows the `DataSet` produced by the document shown in Listing 9–16.

Listing 9–17 Using ADO's XML hierachies in the `DataSet`

```
// this program (same as program above)
ds.ReadXml(@"c:\authors.xml",
  XmlReadMode.InferSchema);
Console.WriteLine(
  "there are {0} tables in the dataset",
  ds.Tables.Count);
Console.WriteLine(
  "there are {0} relations",
  ds.Relations.Count);
foreach (DataTable t in ds.Tables)
{
```

```
Console.WriteLine(
  "table {0} has {1} columns and {2} rows",
   t.TableName, t.Columns.Count, t.Rows.Count);
foreach (DataColumn c in t.Columns)
  Console.WriteLine(
    " column {0} has data type {1}",
    c.ColumnName, c.DataType);
}

// produces this output
there are 3 tables in the dataset
there are 2 relations
table data has 1 columns and 1 rows
 column data_Id has data type System.Int32
table row has 5 columns and 23 rows
 column row_Id has data type System.Int32
 column au_id has data type System.String
 column au_lname has data type System.String
 column au_fname has data type System.String
 column data_Id has data type System.Int32
table chapter has 3 columns and 25 rows
 column au_id has data type System.String
 column title_id has data type System.String
 column row_Id has data type System.Int32
```

Because ADO.NET does not expose the database tables and index creation functionality of ADO, interoperability is also useful for this functionality. Later versions of ADO ship with a library known as ADOX, which provides the ability to directly define database tables and indexes for those data stores that do not support DDL (data definition language). The OLE DB provider for Jet provides full support for this library. Because this functionality does not exist in ADO.NET, adox.dll can be used through TLBIMP. Microsoft has announced that this functionality will be added in future releases of ADO.NET.

9.8   ADO.NET for ODBC Programmers

ODBC was the first generic data access API. This API is still the API of choice among many programmers for the following reasons:

- ODBC is easier to use than OLE DB/ADO because ODBC doesn't have as many choices about how to manage sets of results. In addition, many C++

programmers have trouble with OLE DB's extremely factored interfaces model and reference counting in COM.

- Microsoft Foundation Classes has direct support for ODBC through `CRecordset` and friends.

- Many manufacturers of ODBC drivers have not built OLE DB providers for their data sources. On occasion, when they have, the performance of these providers is not as good as that of the corresponding ODBC drivers.

- ODBC is perceived as being faster than OLE DB, given the same data source. Until very recently, Microsoft's own scaling test (the MTS/COM+ performance toolkit) showed ODBC as scaling better and outperforming OLE DB with SQL Server.

Although SQL Server consumers should be converting to the `SqlClient` data provider, others may continue to use ODBC drivers. For these programmers, Microsoft originally recommended using the `OleDb` data provider and the OLE DB provider for ODBC. Before the release of .NET, that support was discontinued (you will get a runtime error if you attempt to use this provider), and an ODBC-specific bridge provider, the `Odbc` data provider, was introduced. For programmers attempting to determine whether to convert to ADO.NET, as well as those who have made the decision, it's most illustrative to study how the `Odbc` data provider maps ODBC calls to ADO.NET classes. That is the approach I'll use to explore ODBC-to-ADO.NET conversion.

9.8.1 Handles and Environment

ODBC programmers allocate *handles* (opaque numbers representing resources) to encapsulate functionality groups. These handles are the equivalent of classes in a class-based model. The most common handles and their equivalents are as follows:

- ODBC `Environment` handle: No direct equivalent
- ODBC `Connection` handle: ADO.NET `Connection` class
- ODBC `Statement` handle: ADO.NET `Command` and `DataReader` classes, along with `IDataReader`-specific methods
- ODBC `Descriptor` handle: ADO.NET `DataReader` class and `IDataRecord` interfaces

The first thing that an ODBC program must do is to allocate an ODBC `Environment` handle. In the `Odbc` managed provider, this is accomplished in the constructor of the `OdbcConnection` class. An ODBC environment handle is kept in the `ODBCGlobalEnv` class, an embedded class of `OdbcConnection`. The `OdbcConnection` class uses a connection string to populate the ODBC connection string and calls `SQLDriverConnect` to connect to the ODBC driver specified. ODBC DSNs are supported in the connection string in addition to series of name-value connection string pairs. Because ODBC DSNs do not store the user ID and password in the registry, the user ID and password must always be included on the connection string, as shown in Listing 9–18.

Listing 9–18   Connection string for the `Odbc` data provider

```
// connection string must contain user id and password
// even if DSN is specified
  OdbcConnection conn = new OdbcConnection(
    "DSN=pubdsn;UID=sa;PWD=sapass");
```

The `OdbcConnection` also allocates an ODBC `Connection` handle. The current database and connection timeout parameters are the only attributes on the connection handle; the `OdbcConnection` constructor calls down to ODBC's `SQLSetConnectAttr`. ODBC's `SQL_AUTO_COMMIT` attribute is set off, except when a transaction is explicitly started by using `OdbcConnection.BeginTransaction`. As with the limitation mentioned earlier regarding OLE DB and ADO, ADO.NET does not have an equivalent of `SQLBrowseConnect` that enables selection of an ODBC driver at runtime. In an equivalent manner, you can use the OLE DB GUI components through COM interoperability, select the OLE DB provider for ODBC, and strip the provider name from the resulting connection string to obtain a valid connection string for the `Odbc` data provider.

9.8.2   Commands

The `OdbcCommand` class supports execution of parameterized stored procedures. The `Parameters` collection uses ODBC's `SQLBindParameter` directly. The data provider doesn't support the use of multiple parameter sets in a single command or stored procedure execution. `OdbcCommand` also supports text commands, including ODBC escape clauses, which are passed to the driver.

Direct table access (using `CommandBehavior.TableDirect`) is not supported because it is not supported by ODBC. `OdbcCommand` uses either `SQLExecute` or `SQLExecDirect` to execute commands, based on the `CommandBehavior` specified. Cancelable commands are supported.

9.8.3 Fetching Data

`OdbcDataReader` always uses `SQLFetch` and `SQLGetData` to read forward-only cursors. Scrollable or updatable cursors are not supported by the ADO.NET framework. Multiple results are exposed using the `SQLMultiple` function if the driver supports it. The number of rows affected by a `SELECT` statement is not available, but you can use `SQLRowCount` to retrieve the number of rows affected by insert, update, or delete commands.

Bulk fetching (`SQLBulkOperations`), and advanced fetch capabilities such as `SQLExtendedFetch` and `SQLFetchScroll`, are not supported. The `Odbc` data provider does enable setting the buffer size if it can be set on the connection string. ODBC's `SQL_TYPES` map to .NET types using an internal `TypeMap` class. The exact type mappings are exposed in the `OdbcType` enumeration, and this is summarized in Appendix A.

9.8.4 Metadata and Schema Information

Currently, the `Odbc` data provider does not expose either ODBC provider information—such as most of the attributes obtainable through `SQLGetInfo`—or data source metadata, such as `SQLTables`, `SQLProcedures`, or `SQLProcedureColumns`. This deficiency may be addressed in future updates of this data provider. `OdbcDataReader`'s `GetSchemaTable` uses `SQLGetDescField` to get basic metadata after the execution of a resultset-returning command.

`OdbcDataAdapter`'s `FillSchema` and use of the `MissingSchemaAction.AddWithKey` option of `OdbcDataAdapter.Fill` employ a variety of methods to get metadata. `SQLPrimaryKeys`, `SQLSpecialColumns`, and `SQLStatistics` are used to get key and extended column information. This information is also used by `OdbcCommandBuilder`. The `CommandBuilder` class also uses `SQLGetInfo` to obtain driver-specific information, such as the character to be used as a quotation mark character.

9.8.5 Errors

ODBC error conditions map to `OdbcExceptions` in the data provider using a special internal `OdbcHandleError` call after each ODBC call. A special `Odbc-Error` class encapsulates the information obtained by calling `SQLDiagInfo`, including the ODBC state code. By using `OdbcHandleError`, you can separate fatal from nonfatal errors; the data provider exposes an `OdbcInfoMessage` handler for nonfatal errors.

Table 9–2 maps ODBC functions to their equivalent ADO.NET functionality.

Table 9–2 Mapping the ODBC API to ADO.NET methods

Function	ADO.NET
Connecting to Data Source	*OdbcConnection**
SQLAllocHandle	Constructors
SQLConnect	Connection.Open
SQLDriverConnect	Connection string
SQLBrowseConnect	—
Get Data Source/ Driver Info	
SQLDataSources	—
SQLDrivers	—
SQLGetInfo	—
SQLGetFunctions	—
SQLGetTypeInfo	—
Getting/Setting Driver Attributes	
SQLGet/SetConnectAttr	Connection string, Connection properties
SQLGet/SetEnvAttr	Connection string
SQLGet/SetStmtAttr	Command properties

(continues)

Table 9–2   Mapping the ODBC API to ADO.NET methods (Continued)

Function	ADO.NET
Getting/Setting Descriptor Fields	
SQLGet/SetDescField	OdbcDataReader.GetSchemaTable (DataColumn)
SQLGet/SetDescRec	OdbcDataReader.GetSchemaTable
Preparing SQL Requests	*OdbcCommand* and *OdbcParameterCollection*
SQLPrepare	Prepare
SQLBindParameter	ParametersCollection
SQLGet/SetCursorName	—
SQLSetScrollOptions	—
Submitting Requests	*OdbcCommand*, *OdbcParameterCollection*, *OdbcDataReader*
SQLExecute	ExecuteNonQuery/ExecuteReader + Prepare
SQLExecDirect	ExecuteNonQuery/ExecuteReader
SQLNativeSql	—
SQLDescribeParm	OdbcCommandBuilder.RefreshSchema
SQLNumParms	OdbcCommandBuilder.RefreshSchema
SQLParamData	*OdbcParameterCollection* on *OdbcCommand*
SQLPutData	—
Retrieving Results and Result Info	*OdbcDataReader*
SQLRowCount	RowsAffected

Table 9–2   Mapping the ODBC API to ADO.NET methods (Continued)

Function	ADO.NET
SQLNumResultColumns	FieldCount
SQLDescribeCol	GetSchemaInfo
SQLColAttribute	GetSchemaInfo
SQLBindCol	Indexers, getters
SQLFetch	—
SQLFetchScroll	—
SQLGetData	Indexers, getters
SQLSetPos	—
SQLBulkOperations	—
SQLMoreResults	NextResult
SQLGetDiagField	*OdbcExceptions*/*OdbcError*/ *OdbcInfoMessage*
SQLGetDiagRec	*OdbcExceptions*/*OdbcError*/ *OdbcInfoMessage*
Obtaining Catalog Information	
Terminating a Statement	
SQLFreeStmt	OdbcDataReader.Close
SQLCloseCursor	OdbcCommand.Dispose
SQLCancel	OdbcCommand.Cancel
SQLEndTran	OdbcTransaction.Commit
Terminating a Connection	
SQLDisconnect	OdbcConnection.Close
SQLFreeHandle	OdbcConnection.Dispose/ garbage collection

*Italics indicate class (.NET). Lack of italics indicates function or method or property (.NET).

Table 9–3 shows a list of ODBC attributes and their ADO.NET equivalents.

Table 9–3 ODBC Attributes and ADO.NET Equivalents

ODBC Attribute	ADO.NET
Environment Attribute	
SQL_ATTR_CONNECTION_POOLING	In `OdbcConnection` constructor
SQL_ATTR_CP_MATCH	Match by properties or connect string
SQL_ATTR_ODBC_VERSION	—
SQL_ATTR_OUTPUT_NTS	—
Connection Attribute	
SQL_ATTR_ACCESS_MODE	—
SQL_ATTR_ASYNC_ENABLE	—
SQL_ATTR_AUTOCOMMIT	`Connection.BeginTransaction`
SQL_ATTR_CONNECTION_TIMEOUT	`Connection.ConnectionTimeout`
SQL_ATTR_CURRENT_CATALOG	`Connection.Database`
SQL_ATTR_LOGIN_TIMEOUT	`Connection.ConnectionTimeout`
SQL_ATTR_METADATA_ID	—
SQL_ATTR_ODBC_CURSORS	—
SQL_ATTR_PACKET_SIZE	Connection string
SQL_ATTR_QUIET_MODE	—
SQL_ATTR_TRACE	—
SQL_ATTR_TRACEFILE	—
SQL_ATTR_TRANSLATE_LIB	—
SQL_ATTR_TRANSLATE_OPTION	—
SQL_ATTR_TXN_ISOLATION	`Transaction.IsolationLevel`
Statement Attributes	
SQL_ATTR_APP_PARAM_DESC	—

Table 9–3   ODBC Attributes and ADO.NET Equivalents (Continued)

ODBC Attribute	ADO.NET
SQL_ATTR_APP_ROW_DESC	—
SQL_ATTR_ASYNC_ENABLE	—
SQL_ATTR_ATTR_CONCURRENCY	—
SQL_ATTR_CURRENT_CATALOG	Connection.Database
SQL_ATTR_CURSOR_SCROLLABLE	—
SQL_ATTR_CURSOR_SENSITIVITY	—
SQL_ATTR_CURSOR_TYPE	—
SQL_ATTR_FETCHBOOKMARK_PTR	—
SQL_ATTR_KEYSET_SIZE	—
SQL_ATTR_MAX_LENGTH	—
SQL_ATTR_MAX_ROWS	—
SQL_ATTR_METADATA_ID	—
SQL_ATTR_NOSCAN	—
SQL_ATTR_TXN_ISOLATION	Command.Transaction.Isolation-Level
SQL_ATTR_PARAM_XXX_PTR	—
SQL_ATTR_PARAMSET_SIZE	—
SQL_ATTR_QUERY_TIMEOUT	Command.ResetCommandTimeout

Listing 9–19 shows a simple program using the Odbc .NET data provider. Note that it is identical in structure to an analogous program written for the OleDb or SqlClient data providers.

Listing 9–19   Simple program using Odbc data provider

```
void doODBC()
{
  // SQL Server DSN
  String strConn = "DSN=PUBS;UID=sa";
```

```
String strCmd  = "select * from authors";

OdbcConnection conn = new OdbcConnection(strConn);
OdbcCommand cmd = new OdbcCommand(strCmd, conn);
IDataReader rdr=null;

try
{
  conn.Open();
  rdr = cmd.ExecuteReader();

  Console.WriteLine(
    "fieldcount = {0}", rdr.FieldCount);
  while (rdr.Read())
  {
    for (int i=0;i<rdr.FieldCount;i++)
      Console.WriteLine(
        "Field {0}: {1}", i+1, rdr[i]);
    Console.WriteLine("*** end of row ***");
  }
}
catch (OdbcException ex)
{
 for (int i=0; i < ex.Errors.Count; i++)
 {
  Console.WriteLine("Index #" + i + "\n" +
    "Message: " + ex.Errors[i].Message + "\n" +
    "Native: " + ex.Errors[i].NativeError.ToString() +
                "\n" +
    "Source: " + ex.Errors[i].Source + "\n" +
    "SQL: " + ex.Errors[i].SQLState + "\n");
 }
}
finally
{
if (rdr != null)
  rdr.Close();
if (conn.State == ConnectionState.Open)
  conn.Close();
}
}
```

9.9 ADO.NET for JDBC Programmers

JDBC is related in concept to ODBC and shares some additional features with OLE DB and ADO. JDBC's three main interfaces are `Connection`, `Statement`, and `ResultSet`. There are two additional subclasses of the `Statement` interface: `PreparedStatement` (statements that can use input parameters) and `CallableStatement` (statements that can return output parameters).

The three main JDBC interfaces most closely correspond to ADO.NET's `IDbConnection`, `IDbCommand`, and `IDataReader`. JDBC also defines `RowSet`, an interface that inherits from `ResultSet`. It is meant for implementing disconnected `ResultSet` operations, although the exact semantics of this class differ with each implementation. Some available beta implementations of `RowSet` correspond to a subset of ADO.NET `DataSet`-like functionality.

9.9.1 Generic Code

Like OLE DB, ADO, and ODBC, JDBC is more geared toward writing interoperable code and minimizing vendor extensions by defining more in the specification than ADO.NET. For example, no hard specification yet exists for ADO.NET data provider writers, but guidelines exist. The Oracle JDBC driver is a good example of a driver that adds many nonportable, vendor-specific extensions to the JDBC specification. It is possible to write generic code in either ADO.NET or JDBC, but ignoring vendor extensions tends to make this code the lowest common denominator. ADO.NET gives you only a single path through the `Connection/Command/DataReader` classes that you can use to provide generic code with only one cast required; all other paths require classes of a specific provider type and many casts of specific classes to generic interfaces.

9.9.2 Provider Types

JDBC categorizes providers by means of their behaviors and use of native code. A type 1 JDBC driver is a bridge driver, such as the ODBC-JDBC bridge. A type 2 JDBC driver uses native (nonmanaged) code through API interoperability; an example is the Oracle type 2 driver, which uses native OCI calls. Type 3, such as DataDirect Technologies' JDBC Direct, can use middleware as a connection to multiple data sources. Type 4 is defined as a driver that uses 100 percent native code (every call is managed code, including socket calls); providers of this type are most flexible because they are most likely to work across operating systems and Java Virtual Machines.

Using these definitions, `OleDb`, `Odbc`, and the `SqlXml` managed data classes (which uses OLE DB underneath) are all classified as type 1 drivers because they provide a bridge to other APIs. The `SqlClient` provider would have to be classified as type 2 because it requires unmanaged SQL Server netlibs, although, because TDS protocol processing is done in managed code, it is very similar in concept to a JDBC type 4 driver. DataDirect Technologies will release ADO.NET data providers that use 100 percent managed code; these will be the equivalent of JDBC type 4 drivers.

ADO.NET data providers, like JDBC drivers, provide concrete implementations of the defined interfaces. The concrete implementations can add functionality beyond the interface definition. ADO.NET classes, except for the initial `Connection` class, can be created using the following factory pattern:

```
IDbConnection conn = new SqlConnection("connectionstring");
IDbCommand cmd = conn.CreateCommand();
```

JDBC also adds a level of indirection to the `Connection` class. You must first register the class object of your JDBC driver with the JDBC driver manager or instantiate the driver class itself, thereby causing it to be registered:

```
Class.forName("oracle.jdbc.driver.OracleDriver");
```

You can also register a special factory object through the Java Naming and Directory Interface (JNDI) API by using a directory service. In ADO.NET, the initial `Connection` instance is created by using the `new` operator, as shown in the preceding example. In JDBC, to open a connection object you must either specify connection parameters or use a URL-style connection string that contains a user ID and password. The driver manager then passes the connection string to all registered drivers until one is found.

The alternative method, using JNDI, causes a trip to a directory service, where the connection information is stored. ADO.NET's `Connection` string enables the underlying provider to connect directly to the data source. No middleman need be consulted. On the other hand, it is not possible to write a single method that connects to any data provider; this must be provided by programmatic *case* statements. If you need single source code capability, you can use the `OleDb` data provider with almost all OLE DB providers.

9.9.3 Connection Pooling

Connection pooling is implemented differently in JDBC than in ADO.NET. In JDBC, a standard `ConnectionPoolDataSource` interface is implemented by driver writers to provide connection pooling. Also, the JDBC specification defines a standard behavior for connection pooling. This is similar to the OLE DB dispenser manager architecture that is used in `OleDbConnection`. The `SqlClient` provider uses a different style of connection pooling, and no standard is yet defined by the spec. A recent addition to the JDBC 3.0 specification allows driver writers to include such pooling parameters as minimum and maximum pool size, similar to the connection pooling parameters in the ADO.NET `SqlClient` provider.

9.9.4 Nonrelational Data Types

The JDBC specification has support for SQL-99 nonrelational data types, such as arrays and "object" types. JDBC provides for mapping "objects" to member variables in classes by using a `DataMap` and the `SqlData` interface. Although this functionality is not explicitly a part of ADO.NET, you can do approximately the same thing by using the loosely typed getter `GetValue`, which returns an `Object` data type.

You can define the ADO.NET `DataTable` columns to accept data typed as an arbitrary class, as shown in Chapter 4. Also, functionality similar to that of `DataMap` is available through strongly typed subclasses of `DataSet`; this is related to defining a `DataSet` as an XML schema, and the use of .NET's native serialization format. In addition, both APIs allow provider and driver writers the freedom to define additional provider- or driver-specific data types with provider-specific access methods for them, as in the `SqlClient` support of SQL Server data types.

9.9.5 Object Databases

The Java object serialization format has spawned a series of *Java-relational databases* (JDBMS) that store serialized Java objects or object graphs as the database's native format. Also, extensions to the API enable storage of serialized object instances in the BLOB fields of nonobject databases, subject to the limitation that the individual instance properties are not exposed to SQL query statements. Because .NET has a common serialization format based on XML, it is possible to store .NET objects in a similar fashion in CLOB fields (TEXT in SQL Server) or XML-based databases. It will be interesting to see how (or whether) this .NET object storage concept progresses.

9.9.6   Other SQL-99 Extensions

Neither API mandates support for the object-oriented extensions to SQL defined as part of the SQL-99 specification. JDBC drivers are expected to support the SQL command language; ADO.NET does not mandate any such support. In fact, the OLE DB specification enables support of any query language and allows simple access to data by table name; the `OleDb` data provider supports this through `CommandBehavior.TableDirect`.

9.9.7   Metadata

`DatabaseMetaData` is a specific JDBC interface—obtainable from `Connection`—that supports a tabular view of metadata as `ResultSets` in the format defined by the SQL-92 and SQL-99 information schema. This interface closely corresponds to OLE DB's `IDBSchemaRowset`, which is directly exposed in the ADO.NET `OleDb` data provider as `OleDbConnection.GetOleDbSchema-Table`. In the `SqlClient` provider, the user is instructed to directly issue a `SELECT` statement against SQL Server's `INFORMATION_SCHEMA`.

9.9.8   Transactions

JDBC uses an `AutoCommit` property of the `Connection` interface to expose local transactions. The `Connection` also contains methods to `commit` and `rollback` local transactions. For greater flexibility when different transaction types are used, ADO.NET exposes the transaction as a separate interface (`IDbTransaction`). The `Command` classes can take an `IDbTransaction` reference in their constructors, and nested transactions are supported in the `OleDb` data provider through `IDbTransaction.BeginTransaction` for those OLE DB providers that support it.

Both the JDBC 3.0 specification and the ADO.NET `SqlClient` provider have direct support for named savepoints in transactions. JDBC mandates the use of the XA protocol for distributed transactions and has a set of specific interfaces (`XAConnection`) that can provide distributed transactions in addition to connection pooling. This is similar to the support for automatic distributed transactions using the OLE TX protocol in OLE DB providers, and it's supported by the `OleDb` data provider. Support for automatic distributed transactions in a COM+ environment is also supported by the `SqlClient` data provider for SQL Server.

9.9.9 Commands and Behaviors

JDBC factors support for SQL command execution into three interfaces: `Statement`, `PreparedStatement`, and `CallableStatement`. Only `CallableStatement` supports output parameters. In ADO.NET a single `IDbCommand` interface seems to suffice, along with the `CommandType` property and `CommandBehavior`s for refinements. The JBDC 1.0 specification states that columns in a `ResultSet` need only be accessible in ordinal order; although this is not a part of later JDBC specifications. ADO.NET supports this through `CommandBehavior.SequentialAccess`, and it happens to be the behavior used by the `Fill` method of `SqlDataAdapter` and `OleDbDataAdapter`.

Additional `CommandBehavior` choices in ADO.NET include obtaining key or schema information, a single scalar value, or a singleton row. The last two choices result in performance gains in some providers.

9.9.10 Executing Queries and Returning Results

JDBC exposes four methods that return results from `Statement`s—namely, `execute`, `executeBatch`, `executeQuery`, and `executeUpdate`. The most often used are `executeQuery`, which returns one or more resultsets, and `executeUpdate`, which returns a single count of rows affected. `execute` is a special-purpose method that can return multiple results, each result consisting of a possible count of rows affected, and you can use `ResultSet.executeBatch` for explicitly batching queries.

ADO.NET supports three methods: `ExecuteReader`, `ExecuteScalar`, and `ExecuteNonQuery`. The `ExecuteReader` method returns a `DataReader`, which can contain the output from multiple statements. Each statement can return the number of rows affected, `IDataReader.RecordsAffected`, and tabular results. As long as you're using multiple results and `ExecuteReader`, the number of rows affected is a running, cumulative total. None of the current data providers will return results that consist only of the number of rows affected. `ExecuteNonQuery` is similar to JDBC's `executeUpdate`.

9.9.11 Server Cursors

JDBC 2.0 adds support for server cursors to the model. This feature was purposely omitted from the first version of ADO.NET because of ADO.NET's focus on disconnected, scalable applications, and because few databases support server cursors that are manipulable from a client API. However, OLE DB and SQL Server both support this functionality; moreover, an `ISqlResultset` interface was presented at PDC and will be added to the `SqlServer` internal provider—and possibly also to the `SqlClient` provider—in the future.

Server cursors are usable (although probably suboptimal) when you're writing stored procedures, triggers, or user-defined functions that live inside the database. A feature that may be added in the next version of SQL Server (Yukon) will enable use of CLR languages for these functions, as does the "internal" Oracle JDBC driver.

9.9.12 Errors

Both ADO.NET and JDBC separate errors into fatal errors, which throw exceptions, and nonfatal errors, which do not interrupt program flow. JDBC's `SqlException` contains similar information to the `OleDb` data provider's `OleDbException`, and `SqlClient` adds some SQL Server-specific information. JDBC's `getWarnings` and ADO.NET's `InfoMessage` delegates must be specifically looked for and do not interrupt program flow.

Table 9–4 shows JDBC classes, interfaces, and methods and their equivalents in ADO.NET.

Table 9–4 Mapping JDBC classes to ADO.NET classes

Interface/Method	ADO.NET
*Connection**	*Connection* and *Transaction*
createStatement	CreateCommand
prepareStatement	CreateCommand + Command.Prepare
prepareCall	CreateCommand + Command.Prepare
get/setAutoCommit	Depends on whether transaction in progress
commit	IDbTransaction.Commit
rollback	IDbTransaction.Rollback
close	Close
isClosed	State
getMetaData	OleDbConnection.GetOleDbSchemaTable (OleDb provider only)
setReadOnly	Mode on connection string
isReadOnly	—
get/setCatalog	Database
getWarnings	*InfoMessageEvent*
clearWarnings	—
get/setTypeMap	—
get/setTransaction-Isolation	IDbTransaction.Isolation
nativeSQL	—
PooledConnection	Automatic OLE DB Services /SqlClient connect string

(continues)

Table 9–4 Mapping JDBC classes to ADO.NET classes (Continued)

Interface/Method	ADO.NET
XAConnection	Automatic OLE DB Services /SqlClient connect string
DatabaseMetaData	OleDbConnection.GetOleDbSchemaTable (OleDb provider only)
Statement	*Command*
executeQuery	ExecuteReader
executeUpdate	ExecuteNonQuery
close	Dispose
getWarnings	*InfoMessageEvent*
clearWarnings	—
get/setMaxFieldSize	—
get/setMaxRows	—
setEscapeProcessing	—
get/setQueryTimeout	ResetCommandTimeout
add/clear/ executeBatch	—
getConnection	Connection
getResultSetConcur- rency	—
getResultSetType	—
get/setFetchDirection	Only forward allowed
get/setFetchSize	—
cancel	Cancel
setCursorName	—
execute	—
getResultSet	DataReader return value from ExecuteReader

Table 9–4 Mapping JDBC classes to ADO.NET classes (Continued)

Interface/Method	ADO.NET
getUpdateCount	RowsAffected
getMoreResults	DataReader.NextResult
PreparedStatement	*Command + ParameterCollection*
executeQuery	ExecuteReader
executeUpdate	ExecuteNonQuery
execute	—
addBatch	—
getMetaData	—
parameterSetters	Parameter.Value
CallableStatement	*Command + ParameterCollection*
registerOutputPara-meter	Parameter.ParameterDirection
ParameterGetters	Parameter.Value
wasNull	IsDBNull
ResultSet	*DataReader*
close	Close
wasNull	IsDBNull
next/previous/first/last	DataReader.Read (forward only)
absolute/relative	—
cursorPosition Methods	—
updateMethods	DataAdapter.Update

(continues)

Table 9–4   Mapping JDBC classes to ADO.NET classes (Continued)

Interface/Method	ADO.NET
insert/update/ deleteRow	Supported only in `DataSet/DataTable`
cancelRowUpdates	`DataSet.CancelChanges`
rowInserted/ Updated/Deleted	`DataAdapter.RowUpdatedEvent`
getType	—
getConcurrency	—
get/setFetchDirection	—
get/setFetchSize	—
getMetaData	`GetSchemaRowset`
getWarnings	*InfoMessageEvent*
clearWarnings	—
findColumn	—
ResultSetMetaData	`DataReader.GetSchemaRowset`
DriverManager/ Driver	—

*Italics indicate interface (Java) or class (.NET). Lack of italics indicates method or property.

Table 9–5 lists JDBC interfaces and functionality and their implementation in the disconnected or client-side model.

Table 9–5   JDBC and .NET disconnected model

Rowset	DataSet
get/setDataSource Name	(no data source)
get/setURL	(no data source)
get/setPassword	—

Table 9–5   JDBC and .NET disconnected model (Continued)

Rowset	DataSet
get/setUsername	—
get/setTransac- tionIsolation	DataAdapter.Command.Transaction
get/setTypeMap	—
execute	—
getCommand	—
get/setMaxField- Size	—
get/setMaxRows	—
get/setEscape- Processing	—
isReadOnly/ setReadOnly	—
*get/setQueryTime- out**	Command.ResetCommandTimeout
setConcurrency	—
setType	—
clearParameters	—
moveMethods	Indexers on DataTables, DataView
moveToInsertRow	DataTable.NewRow
Getters/update methods	Update/Delete on DataRow
RowsetListener	*DataSet/DataTable/DataAdapter* events

*Italics indicate an interface (Java) or class (.NET). Lack of italics indicates method or property.

Table 9–6 shows the data types defined by JDBC and their ADO.NET equivalents.

Table 9–6   JDBC versus ADO.NET data types

JDBC Data Type	ADO.NET Data Type
Char	AnsiStringFixedLength/StringFixedLength
Varchar	AnsiString/String
LongVarchar	String (max length = 8000)
Binary	Byte Array
*Varbinary**	Byte Array
LongVarbinary	Byte Array
Bit	Boolean
TinyInt	Byte
SmallInt	Int16
Integer	Int32
BigInt	Int64
Real	Double
Double	Double
Float	Float
Decimal, Numeric	Numeric
Date, Time, Timestamp	Date, Time, DateTime
Blob	Byte Array
Clob	Char Array
Array	—
Distinct	—
Struct	—

Table 9–6   JDBC versus ADO.NET data types (Continued)

JDBC Data Type	ADO.NET Data Type
Ref	—
Java_Object	Object

*Italics indicate cotype (COM) or class (.NET). Lack of italics indicates interface (COM) or method or property (.NET).

Listing 9–20 shows a simple sample program that exposes similar functions to those of our ADO.NET sample program, this time in JDBC. As you can see, it is almost identical in structure to the two ADO.NET programs that you analyzed in Chapter 2.

Listing 9–20   Comparing JDBC and ADO.NET programs

```
// typed exception declared
public static void main(String[] Args) throws SQLException
{
Connection conn = null;
Statement stmt = null;
PreparedStatement pstmt = null;
ResultSet rs = null;
String sqlstmt;
int theId;

try {

// get connection through driver mgr
// based on connection string
DriverManager.registerDriver(
  new oracle.jdbc.driver.OracleDriver());
conn = DriverManager.getConnection(
 "jdbc:oracle:thin:@localhost:1521:orcl",
 "dmuser", "dmuser");

// uses positional parms with '?' markers
sqlstmt = "UPDATE Clients SET address1 = ? " +
  "WHERE id = ?";

// driver can choose when to prepare
pstmt = conn.prepareStatement(sqlstmt);
```

```java
// set parameters
// strongly typed setters, no parameters collection
pstmt.setString(1, "Somewhere else");
pstmt.setInt(2, theId);

// executeUpdate is for updates
pstmt.executeUpdate();
System.out.println("Number of rows updated: " +
  pstmt.getUpdateCount());

sqlstmt = "SELECT firstname, lastname " +
  "FROM Clients " +
  "WHERE id > ?";
pstmt = conn.prepareStatement(sqlstmt);
pstmt.setInt(1, 771);

// executeQuery returns resultset
rs = pstmt.executeQuery();
if (rs.next())
  System.out.println("First client named: " +
    rs.getString(1) + " " + rs.getString(2));
else
  System.out.println("Unable to retrieve client");
rs.close();
}
catch (SQLException e) {
  System.out.println("Error: " + e.getMessage());
}
catch (Exception e) {
  System.out.println("Error: " + e.getMessage());
}
finally
{
  if (rs != null) rs.close();
  if (pstmt != null) pstmt.close();
  if (conn != null) conn.close();
}
```

9.10 ADO.NET JDBC Programmers and the Disconnected Model

The JDBC disconnected model consists of the RowSet interface, which extends ResultSet. Beta versions of three Rowset implementations are available from

Sun, and third parties can write their own. `CachedRowSet` is most similar in concept to an ADO.NET `DataTable`, providing a single disconnected set of rows that can be marshaled across a network. `CachedRowSet` can be updated offline; methods for flushing changes back to the database in batches are available in the model, as are some listeners.

`WebRowSet` adds the capability to marshal in a single XML format; it's more similar to ADO's disconnected `Recordset` than to ADO.NET's `DataSet`. The functionality of `HttpRowSet` is similar to the Remote Data Services function in ADO classic and, with the acceptance of XML as a universal marshaling format, is probably less functional than marshaling as XML. The ADO.NET `DataSet` and `XmlDataDocument`, with support for multiple tables, relationships, and constraints, go far beyond the `DataTable` or JDBC `RowSet` in functionality. The JDBC `RowSet` has the limitation of being able to support only a single rowset and a single hierarchy level.

9.11   SQL/J Part 0 and Typed `DataSets`

JDBC `ResultSets`, like the ADO.NET `DataReader` and all other dynamic SQL APIs equivalents, will produce runtime errors if the specified column name or column number does not exist at runtime. This problem is discussed in Chapter 7 in conjunction with the ADO.NET strongly typed `DataSet` class, a subclass of `DataSet`, which provides compile-time checking based on database metadata.

Although JDBC does not have the concept of strongly typed subclasses, an addition to the SQL-99 spec known as "SQL/J part 0" provides equivalent functionality by supporting embedded SQL, that is, escaped SQL statements embedded within program code. The embedded SQL is processed by a preprocessor, so SQL clauses can contain actual Java variables.

In addition to strong typing and compile-time type checking, SQL/J lets you check and optimize `Statements` against an exemplar database at compile time. Although the ADO.NET typed `DataSet` does not enable checking against an exemplar database at compile time, a combination of executing the SQL statement desired, generating XML schema from the resultset, and using an in-line invocation of the `XSD.exe` program can provide analogous functionality.

Perhaps the next release of SQL Server will enable even richer compile-time optimization and type checking.

9.12   Where Are We?

In this chapter you've compared existing data access technologies. Hopefully, you have some insights into how and why to convert your existing data access programs to ADO.NET, and how to use existing APIs if you need to.

Chapter 10

ADO.NET and Various Types of Data

Having started our journey by surveying the various data models, we turn, in this chapter, to examining what ADO.NET has to offer each type of data modeler.

10.1 Evolution in Data Access

You've taken a tour of data access and have learned how the new ADO.NET API works. You've looked at various access patterns and investigated the design nuances of the ADO.NET model. But programmers and system architects are usually interested in more mundane issues such as these:

- Which database do I choose?
- How do I get my data to integrate with my Web site? How can I make data access as fast as possible and also plan for scaling up to perhaps huge numbers of users?
- What is the best way to structure data storage in my application?
- What is the best way to structure data for presentation?
- What is the best and easiest way to exchange data with business partners?

Hopefully, this book has given you enough detailed information to answer these questions on a case-by-case basis by using ADO.NET—but ADO.NET and technology in general continue to evolve. Some programmers or system architects have enough leverage in their organizations to get to answer meta-questions such as, "What is the best data storage system?" and "What is the best data programming paradigm to use?" If you are a system architect or might be cast in that role in a future project, the simplest answer, before examining the problem in detail, is to say, "It depends."

This is not a trivial answer; the solution really does depend on the problems (and future problems) to be solved. There is no "one best answer" or set of rules set in stone. Here are few examples of the kinds of data problems we can expect to see and the kinds of solutions available:

- Most systems lend themselves in some way to some sort of relational design. In a typical situation, designers gather data elements and user requirements and decompose all the data elements into tables that satisfy the relational model.

- Any solution requiring maximum portability will probably use XML. The XML format has established itself as extremely flexible and well supported on almost every platform. XML can represent any type of data structure, including relational, hierarchical, object (as well as object graphs), and even CODASYL-like structures. XML is currently the major technology for bridging the gap between data and documents. The .NET framework provides two serializers based on XML format for transporting the persisted states of its own classes.

- Problems that entail storing large, mostly opaque objects (BLOBs and CLOBs) of nonrelational data—such as multimedia presentations or entire documents (regardless of format)—can benefit from the use of an object-relational model. These large objects can access their special data type domains by means of a special user type definition and a series of user defined functions.

- Certain data structures—such as bills of materials and the data generated in computer aided drafting and manufacturing—can benefit greatly from an object storage structure, such as an object-based database. Best performance is achieved if large object graphs are mapped to memory locations. This is analogous to old-style hierarchies that use a physical disk cylinder and track numbers as keys, with the physical memory location being the locator in object databases.

- Systems that use large pieces of hardware and need maximum performance regardless of cost can use hierarchical or CODASYL databases dating back 20 years or so. This idea is not as far-fetched as it sounds; airline reservations systems still rely on this technology for best performance and robustness. This type of system is best for single-record or heavily batch-oriented processing and has excellent transactional and recovery capabilities.

- Disconnected systems based on transactional *sagas* (series of transactions that can be rolled back in parts or as a whole) with manual compensation will become more mainstream with the increasing popularity of HTTP-based communication (using protocols such as SOAP) and definitions (using XML schema and Web Service Description Language (WSDL)). The disconnected nature of the participants produces a large time lag in parts of the process, and as a result, distributed transactions using lock-based concurrency schemes are not feasible. These systems will probably need semantics that require manual compensation in case of failure and will probably use XML as a data transport mechanism.

- We will see wider use of decision support or analysis systems using OLAP processing with multidimensional data. These systems are also used for input to data mining systems that perform algorithm-based meta-analysis.

If you experience these kinds of problems and use mostly Microsoft platforms, you have the following tools at your disposal in .NET:

- The ADO.NET data access stack (`System.Data`) and the XML stack (`System.Xml`) for data access and transmission

- Transaction processing systems APIs (`System.ComponentServices`) and Web-based processing systems (`System.Web.Services`) for gluing together multiple operations

- ASP.NET Web Forms (`System.Web.UI`) and Windows Forms (`System.Windows.Forms`) for data presentation

This book focuses on data access, so we finish by attempting to map the .NET data access solutions to these data storage types, data design types, and problem domains.

10.2 ADO.NET with Server- and File-Based RDBMS

Because of the popularity of relational databases, ADO.NET with server- and file-based RDBMS is what most projects will be using. Like all other generic data APIs, ADO.NET has a data provider architecture based on connections, commands, and transactions. In online transaction processing systems, all you may need is a way to issue commands and obtain results through stored procedure output parameters or as scalar values, especially in systems that involve heavy data entry—for example, Web site signup or sign-on processing.

For queries through large relational databases—using simple queries, multiple results, or join-based results—the `DataReader` class is optimal. Further optimizations are available using providers and data sources that are optimized for singleton results. These solutions use the `CommandBehavior.SingleRow` or `Command.ExecuteScalar` method.

Traditional transaction-based systems can use either local or distributed transactions. Distributed transactions must be declarative; the only way to use the distributed transaction APIs in ADO.NET is through `System.Enterprise-Services`. Because ADO.NET uses a separate transaction class, you can have more than one transaction executing concurrently in the same program, using the same connection, for data sources that support this. Nested transactions using the OLE TX protocol, named savepoints, and configurable transaction isolation levels are also part of the model.

The `DataSet` class is meant for disconnected operation, but it can also be used in pessimistic concurrency operations. A connection that is open when `DataAdapter.Fill` is called remains open, and it can hold locks if a transaction has been started. This makes it possible, although awkward, to perform operations that lock data while that data is being updated offline and flushed back to the database using `DataSet`s.

`DataSet` is more usable in an optimistic concurrency situation. In this case, no locks are held when the data is fetched, and update statements are shaped to allow the desired degree of optimistic concurrency. For example, if the application needed "last writer wins" semantics, the update statement would look like this:

```
UPDATE authors set au_lname = @newname where au_id = @oldID
```

But suppose that the application concurrency semantics allow users to update some columns if other columns in the row have been updated in the meantime, but not if any updated columns have been updated—in other words, overwriting at the column level is not permitted. In that case, the update statement would look like this:

```
UPDATE authors set au_lname = @newname
```

where `au_id = @oldID` and `au_lname = @oldname`. The difference is that the current user is not allowed to overwrite other changes at the column level.

If row-based concurrency is required—the user is not allowed to change anything in the row if *any* column value has changed—then each column can be specified in the where clause, or a timestamp column can be used in the where clause. The Visual Studio .NET designer lets you visually configure a `Data-Adapter` to distinguish between two types of optimistic concurrency. Your system design can also support optimistic concurrency by using business rules, user-defined locks, and manual compensation actions. As distributed updates are used between data sources that are farther apart geographically and in terms of network transport (such as over the Web), concurrency using business rules, user-defined locks, and manual compensating actions will become more commonplace.

Desktop databases and data stores that normally work in connected mode will not fare well under this model. Because the "connection" to the database usually consists of direct pointers into the data itself, scrolling rowset applications rely on the data being local. `DataSet` updating could benefit from the use of stored procedures, but Microsoft Access has only a simple model of procedural code through `Query` objects. Access is only one example of a data source that uses a "connected updatable rowset" model; many more appear in systems commonly in use today.

The Visual Studio documentation mentions these limitations and suggests that the use of ADO.NET with the `Jet` OLE DB provider be restricted to single-user applications. To use Access-specific functionality, Access users are advised to employ ADO or DAO through COM interoperability or to upgrade to MSDE or SQL Server as a data engine. The current Access product has accommodations for replacing the Jet engine with an MSDE engine, but the two engines use two different dialects of SQL and two different programming models, as discussed in Chapter 1.

Past APIs that dynamically generated update statements for optimistic concurrency made two invalid assumptions. One was that the SQL dialects of all relational databases were almost identical. This turned out not to be the case. For example, updates generated by the OLE DB client cursor engine in ADO or OLE DB programs would often fail when a DB2 database was used. This incompatibility made this solution unworkable for some databases and for application packages that must run on different databases.

The second invalid assumption was that any relational database could provide metadata for any resultset consisting of columns such as "base table name," "base column name," and so on. Not all relational databases (or OLE DB providers or ODBC drivers) support this functionality, making such API-generated updates inoperable. But an ADO.NET feature now makes this functionality workable. It permits users to define update statements on a per-operation basis by specifying a `DataAdapter`'s `InsertCommand`, `UpdateCommand`, and `DeleteCommand`. By specifying these commands as stored procedures, users can even include business rules that execute as part of the update or abstract away differences among query dialects when unlike databases are used. This solution assumes, though, that only a common subset of stored procedure semantics is used. But that isn't always the case. For example, not all databases support the return of multiple resultsets from stored procedures.

When deciding whether to use the ADO.NET `DataSet` object in general, you'll find it helpful to remember that `DataSet` is a highly specialized collection class. It uses collections of collections and array syntax, and it permits customized XML persistence. You would no more use a `DataSet` when an array would suffice than you would use a `Stack` class when its special semantics were not required. In addition, remember that for the semantics of updating through a `DataSet` to be useful, you must keep `DataSet` intact at all times while updates are being performed on the set of data it contains. This requirement makes `DataSet` less useful when combined with the ASP.NET data grid, which flattens `DataSet`'s structure into data values only and stores the values in ASP.NET's `Viewstate`. Components that bind directly to the `DataSet`'s structure (such as the Windows Forms grid) make it more attractive to update through `DataSet`.

10.3 ADO.NET with Homogeneous Hierarchical Data and ORDBMS

The ADO.NET model supports hierarchical data or those ORDBMS that use concepts such as embedded tables and homogeneous object graphs. The support takes three major forms:

- Hierarchies can be factored into multiple relational tables and can be used with the `DataSet`'s concept of relationships.

- `DataReader` lets you read true hierarchical data through the `IData-Record.GetData` method.
- Hierarchical data can be used with XML Infoset providers.

The data provider and `DataSet` object models and semantics were designed with relational data stores in mind and are a continuation of the relational-centric property of common database APIs. Data providers can support nonrelational semantics, however, and the use of SQL as a query language is not dictated by the API. `DataSets` support object data types and embedded tables with difficulty, although the model supports them with ease. It is easy to define a `DataColumn` of type `Person` or type `DataTable`, but, as you saw in Chapter 4, you must use special semantics to support XML persistence and sorting and filtering of these items.

As you saw in Chapter 5, nonrelational types can be supported using a `DataAdapter` and a custom provider (remember the `SQL_VARIANT` type) if the support is programmed into the data provider, as support for `SQL_VARIANT` is in the `SqlClient` provider. SQL Server 2000 and earlier versions have little direct support for nonrelational data, but other ORDBMS, such as Oracle 8i, use these constructs and need this kind of support. With Microsoft working on an Oracle data provider, it will be interesting to see whether these constructs make their way into the ADO.NET model, as they have with, for example, JDBC.

10.4 ADO.NET and Network Data: Object Graphs, ODBMS, and Network DBMS

ADO.NET supports persistence for objects and object graphs through XML serialization of two types. The classes in the `System.Xml.Serialization` namespace appear to be more XML-centric in persisting objects than those in `System.Runtime.Serialization`. The persistence and object mapping mechanism that you use will depend on your desire for interoperability (`XmlSerialization`) versus nearly perfect mapping of .NET data types (`Runtime.Serialization`). In addition, the .NET XML APIs—especially `XmlReader`, `XmlNavigator`, and `XmlSchemas`—map almost directly to the ODBMS and IDMS style of data access. In this approach, relational APIs (such as `DataReader` and `DataSet`) have limited support for any but the simplest parent-child data models. Manufacturers of OODBMS and network DBMS (although network DBMS is mostly a thing of the past) would be best served to support their data through XML Infoset providers.

An interesting thing about the `XmlSerialization` APIs and the XSD utility is their tendency not to support data models that cannot be modeled both as object type paradigms (the `XSD.exe /c` option to produce object graphs) and as relational type paradigms (the `XSD.exe /d` option to produce a typed `DataSet`). Valid XML schema concepts that do not fit into this model, such as mixed content and derivation by restriction, do not work well (or at all) with this library.

Because most vendors have settled on using relational databases but object-oriented programming systems, there has been great interest in *object-relational mapping*. This process maps persisted object data—stored as LOBs (large object types) or multiple relational tables—directly to objects in the programming system. JDBMS attempt to support this process directly by persisting object graphs using Java binary serialization, and this functionality is accommodated in JDBC by a set of object-table mappings (in the `Connection` object) and by having object implementers expose a JDBC mapping method called `SQLData`. Perhaps a .NET object-relational mapping library—using relational tables or perhaps XML Infoset as a single object model—will make an appearance, allowing integration with the current model.

If you're searching for direct integration with the ODBMS standard APIs (from Object Data Management Group, or ODMG) or SQL-99 extensions, you will not find it in the current version, or probably any version, of the .NET APIs. The major vendors of relational databases appear to be moving toward accommodation with both relational mapping and XML. For example, the eXcelon database and others use XML-based APIs such as XPath and XSLT for storing, querying, and processing data, and provide an XML view of data from many sources, relational databases among them.

At the October 2001 Professional Developers Conference, Microsoft presented a technology preview of ObjectSpaces, an object-relational mapping library for .NET. ObjectSpaces allows relational data designs, including multitable relationships, to be mapped to .NET `Object` data types by means of XML-based descriptors. This adds a layer of abstraction to the ADO.NET data access model. How popular the library will be remains to be seen.

10.5 ADO.NET and Structured Files, Multidimensional Data, and ORDBMS

The .NET APIs do not directly provide anything for retrieval and query of multimedia data types, time series, or multidimensional data. Microsoft made a rather successful attempt to standardize multidimensional data access using a two-pronged standard: OLE DB for OLAP as an API, and the MDX (Multidimensional Extensions to SQL) query language. In addition, a simplified API that was compatible with the type library—that is, usable by Visual Basic 6 and ADO.NET—was modeled on classic ADO. This API, called ADOMD (ADO for Multidimensional), was not ported to interoperate with ADO.NET. This means that it must be used through interoperability between .NET and COM, using TLBIMP to produce a .NET wrapper library.

In a nod toward the future of the multidimensional data access space, Microsoft has introduced the XML for Analysis and XML for Data Mining specifications. There is an implementation of XML for Analysis, and SQL Server 2000 contains support for XML for Data Mining. Although the current XML specs are a thin wrapper around OLE DB for OLAP and OLE DB for Data Mining, the exposure of data (although perhaps not its internal access or storage) appears to be moving toward being XML-based in this area.

Multimedia, time-series, and similar data is exposed by most relational databases using Extender, DataBlade, or DataCartridge technology. These extenders usually combine a special set of functions and a user-defined type. The data being processed can reside inside the database as LOBs or, in the case of Oracle 8, as a distinct data type (a reference to a file system object) known as a BFILE type. Databases that support this technology declare themselves as object-relational databases. They may also accommodate object data types and embedded tables. With the ability of SQL Server Yukon to host the .NET runtime, Microsoft may move into this arena as well, enabling you to write .NET libraries that run inside SQL Server to process these structured types. Also, Microsoft may integrate SQL Server with a file system, making it easier to manage large data using SQL Server utilities.

10.6   ADO.NET Flat Files and Semistructured Files

Flat files are commonly used for data transfer between businesses. Semistructured data pertains to any format (usually a document) that combines data and metadata and includes HTML and XML mixed-content models. There is even a standard called XHTML that supports exposing HTML in an XML-compliant format (that is, the HTML is a well-formed XML document).

In the past, business exchange of flat files was a specialized type of data access that required writing a new program for each new data format encountered. Standards such as EDI (Electronic Data Interchange) and EDIFACT (Electronic Data Interchange for Administration Commerce and Transport) codified certain data exchange formats. The need for standardization is addressed in the .NET data access space by support of the XML APIs. No longer must flat files be exposed as OLE DB simple providers using an extension of the `Connection`/`Command`/`Recordset` paradigm and possibly SQL. This was not a particularly good data access fit because programmers had to implement a new provider for each new data type and then graft on the different, mostly unusable, semantics.

Increasingly, flat file and semistructured data is being exposed as XML documents. XML's beginnings as a document-centric data format come in handy here, and products such as BizTalk and repositories such as OASIS deal with flat and semistructured file transmission using XML format and XSLT transformations.

Data providers benefited by stretching to adapt to the `Connection`/`Command`/`Recordset` model, mainly in the ability they gained to support transactional semantics in their data exchange. Within an organization, where a certain quality of service can be guaranteed, distributed transactions between unlike systems are a possible solution. This concept contributed to the initial popularity of technologies such as Microsoft Transaction Server and Enterprise Java Beans; they built on the intra-organization legacy of transaction processing systems such as IBM's CICS and IMS.

With distributed data access moving to adopt the pattern of loosely coupled organizations communicating over the Internet (with its great potential for denial of service attacks and unpredictable quality of service), however, distributed transactions may not be as viable as within a single organization. In this environment, the norm may become the exchange of messages (probably in XML format) that represent operations with strong typing but loosely coupled semantics (Web Services). Transactional systems will need to shift away from, on the one hand, a distributed transaction based on each resource keeping locks to, on the other hand, a loose transaction system based on optimistic concurrency and direct compensating actions. Systems such as BizTalk have already incorporated this model for transactions and compensation. Look for this model to be codified and incorporated in the .NET data APIs as we move forward.

10.7 Where Are We Going?

This book is about .NET, ADO.NET, and data access. In the past, data access was implemented via a relational database and a simple model; the goal was to make the model general enough to be useful by various relational databases and to give programmers and their organizations the ability to move among various relational databases. Hopefully, you've seen by now that programmers who work with data access are going to be involved in more diverse activities than coding SQL SELECT statements and optimizing connections and cursors. One of the goals of this book is to help you to explore the reasons for using certain APIs and the programming paradigms that are used in various data access scenarios.

As the future unfolds, we'll be using ADO.NET's Connections, Commands, and Transactions as we always have but, in addition, integrating this access with XML in disconnected, distributed data scenarios. This situation may look new or foreign at first, but the "new" data access methods, such as XML and compensating transactions, may look familiar to those whose experience predates the relational revolution. Programmers with experience in nonrelational techniques will feel right at home (or at least comfortable) with this revolution, but those who have never seen a flat file or a hierarchy should take the time to study them. You'll be dealing with XPath as well as SQL, XSLT as well as stored procedures.

And that's only the beginning. A hybrid is emerging from the W3C organization. Known as XQuery, it will attempt to bridge the gap between SQL commands over relational architecture and XML, with its support for diverse formats. Microsoft has released a .NET library that supports an early version of the XQuery specification.

As usual, we are in for interesting times.

Appendix A

Data Types and Type Mappings

A.1   `DbType` **Enumeration**

Table A–1 is the `DbType` enumeration from the `System.Data` namespace.

Table A-1   `DbType` **enumeration members and meanings**

Member Name	Description
`AnsiString`	A variable-length stream of non-Unicode characters ranging between 1 and 8,000 characters.
`Binary`	A variable-length stream of binary data ranging between 1 and 8,000 bytes. Note: ADO.NET cannot correctly infer the type if the byte array is greater than 8,000 bytes. Explicitly set the object when working with byte arrays larger than 8,000 bytes.
`Boolean`	A simple type representing Boolean values of `true` or `false`.
`Byte`	An 8-bit unsigned integer.
`Currency`	A currency value ranging from -2^{63} (or −922,337,203,685,477.5808) to $2^{63}-1$ (or +922,337,203,685,477.5807) with an accuracy to a ten-thousandth of a currency unit.
`Date`	Date and time data ranging in value from January 1, 1753 to December 31, 9999 to an accuracy of 3.33 milliseconds.
`DateTime`	A type representing a date and time value.
`Decimal`	A simple type representing values ranging from 1.0×10^{-28} to approximately $7.9 \infty 10^{28}$ with 28–29 significant digits.

(continues)

Table A-1 **DbType enumeration members and meanings (Continued)**

Member Name	Description
Double	A floating point type representing values ranging from approximately $5.0 \infty 10^{-324}$ to $1.7 \infty 10^{308}$ with a precision of 15–16 digits.
Guid	A globally unique identifier (or GUID).
Int16	An integral type representing signed 16-bit integers with values between −32,768 and 32,767.
Int32	An integral type representing signed 32-bit integers with values between −2,147,483,648 and 2,147,483,647.
Int64	An integral type representing signed 64-bit integers with values between −9,223,372,036,854,775,808 and 9,223,372,036,854,775,807.
Object	A general type representing any reference or value type not explicitly represented by another DbType value.
SByte	An integral type representing signed 8-bit integers with values between −128 and 127.
Single	A floating point type representing values ranging from approximately $1.5 \infty 10^{-45}$ to $3.4 \infty 10^{38}$ with a precision of 7 digits.
String	A type representing Unicode character strings.
StringFixedLength	A fixed-length stream of Unicode characters.
Time	Date and time data ranging in value from January 1, 1753 to December 31, 9999 to an accuracy of 3.33 milliseconds.
UInt16	An integral type representing unsigned 16-bit integers with values between 0 and 65,535.
UInt32	An integral type representing unsigned 32-bit integers with values between 0 and 4,294,967,295.
UInt64	An integral type representing unsigned 64-bit integers with values between 0 and 18,446,744,073,709,551,615.
VarNumeric	—

A.2 Mapping SQL Server Data Types to `SqlTypes` and `SqlDbTypes`

Table A–2 maps the members of the `System.Data.SqlTypes` namespace to Microsoft SQL Server data types and to the members of the `SqlDbType` enumeration.

Table A-2   Mapping SQL Server data types to .NET types

Native SQL Server	.NET Framework SqlTypes	.NET Framework SqlDbType
binary	SqlBinary	Binary
Bigint	SqlInt64	BigInt
Char	SqlString	Char
datetime	SqlDateTime	DateTime
decimal	SqlDecimal	Decimal
Float	SqlDouble	Float
image	SqlBinary	Image
Int	SqlInt32	Int
Money	SqlMoney	Money
nchar	SqlString	NChar
Ntext	SqlString	NText
nvarchar	SqlString	NVarChar
Numeric	SqlDecimal	Numeric
Real	SqlSingle	Real
smalldatetime	SqlDateTime	SmallDateTime
smallint	SqlInt16	SmallInt
smallmoney	SqlMoney	SmallMoney
sql_variant	Object	Variant

(continues)

Table A-2   Mapping SQL Server data types to .NET types (Continued)

Native SQL Server	.NET Framework `SqlTypes`	.NET Framework `SqlDbType`
sysname	SqlString	VarChar
text	SqlString	Text
timestamp	SqlBinary	TimeStamp
tinyint	SqlByte	TinyInt
varbinary	SqlBinary	VarBinary
varchar	SqlString	VarChar
uniqueidentifier	SqlGuid	UniqueId

A.3   Mapping of OLE DB DBTYPEs to .NET data types

Table A–3 maps the members of the `OleDbType` enumeration to OLE DB DB-TYPEs and the .NET type system.

Table A-3   `OleDbType` enumeration

Member Name	Description
BigInt	A 64-bit signed integer (DBTYPE_I8). This maps to Int64.
Binary	A stream of binary data (DBTYPE_BYTES). This maps to an Array of type Byte.
Boolean	A Boolean value (DBTYPE_BOOL). This maps to Boolean.
BSTR	A null-terminated character string of Unicode characters (DBTYPE_BSTR). This maps to String.
Char	A character string (DBTYPE_STR). This maps to String.
Currency	A currency value ranging from -2^{63} (or –922,337,203,685,477.5808) to $2^{63} -1$ (or +922,337,203,685,477.5807) with an accuracy to a ten-thousandth of a currency unit (DBTYPE_CY). This maps to Decimal.
Date	Date data, stored as a double (DBTYPE_DATE). The whole portion is the number of days since December 30, 1899, while the fractional portion is a fraction of a day. This maps to DateTime.

Table A-3 `OleDbType` enumeration (Continued)

Member Name	Description
DBDate	Date data in the format yyyymmdd (`DBTYPE_DBDATE`). This maps to `DateTime`.
DBTime	Time data in the format hhmmss (`DBTYPE_DBTIME`). This maps to `TimeSpan`.
DBTimeStamp	Date and time data in the format yyyymmddhhmmss (`DBTYPE_DBTIMESTAMP`). This maps to `DateTime`.
Decimal	A fixed precision and scale numeric value between $-10^{38}-1$ and $10^{38}-1$ (`DBTYPE_DECIMAL`). This maps to `Decimal`.
Double	A floating point number within the range of $-1.79E+308$ through $1.79E+308$ (`DBTYPE_R8`). This maps to `Double`.
Empty	No value (`DBTYPE_EMPTY`). This maps to `Empty`.
Error	A 32-bit error code (`DBTYPE_ERROR`). This maps to `Exception`.
Filetime	A 64-bit unsigned integer representing the number of 100-nanosecond intervals since January 1, 1601 (`DBTYPE_FILETIME`). This maps to `DateTime`.
Guid	A globally unique identifier (or GUID) (`DBTYPE_GUID`). This maps to `Guid`.
IDispatch	A pointer to an `IDispatch` interface (`DBTYPE_IDISPATCH`). This maps to `Object`. Note: This data type is not currently supported by ADO.NET. Usage may cause unpredictable results.
Integer	A 32-bit signed integer (`DBTYPE_I4`). This maps to `Int32`.
IUnknown	A pointer to an `IUnknown` interface (`DBTYPE_UNKNOWN`). This maps to `Object`. Note: This data type is not currently supported by ADO.NET. Usage may cause unpredictable results.
LongVarBinary	A long binary value (`OleDbParameter` only). This maps to an `Array` of type `Byte`.
LongVarChar	A long string value (`OleDbParameter` only). This maps to `String`.

(continues)

Table A-3 `OleDbType` enumeration (Continued)

Member Name	Description
LongVarWChar	A long null-terminated Unicode string value (`OleDbParameter` only). This maps to `String`.
Numeric	An exact numeric value with a fixed precision and scale (`DBTYPE_NUMERIC`). This maps to `Decimal`.
PropVariant	An automation `PROPVARIANT` (`DBTYPE_PROP_VARIANT`). This maps to `Object`.
Single	A floating point number within the range of −3.40E +38 through 3.40E +38 (`DBTYPE_R4`). This maps to `Single`.
SmallInt	A 16-bit signed integer (`DBTYPE_I2`). This maps to `Int16`.
TinyInt	An 8-bit signed integer (`DBTYPE_I1`). This maps to `SByte`.
UnsignedBigInt	A 64-bit unsigned integer (`DBTYPE_UI8`). This maps to `UInt64`.
UnsignedInt	A 32-bit unsigned integer (`DBTYPE_UI4`). This maps to `UInt32`.
UnsignedSmallInt	A 16-bit unsigned integer (`DBTYPE_UI2`). This maps to `UInt16`.
UnsignedTinyInt	An 8-bit unsigned integer (`DBTYPE_UI1`). This maps to `Byte`.
VarBinary	A variable-length stream of binary data (`OleDbParameter` only). This maps to an `Array` of type `Byte`.
VarChar	A variable-length stream of non-Unicode characters (`OleDbParameter` only). This maps to `String`.
Variant	A special data type that can contain numeric, string, binary, or date data, as well as the special values `Empty` and `Null` (`DBTYPE_VARIANT`). This type is assumed if no other is specified. This maps to `Object`.
VarNumeric	A variable-length numeric value (`OleDbParameter` only). This maps to `Decimal`.
VarWChar	A variable-length, null-terminated stream of Unicode characters (`OleDbParameter` only). This maps to `String`.
WChar	A null-terminated stream of Unicode characters (`DBTYPE_WSTR`). This maps to `String`.

A.4 Mapping of ODBC Types

Table A–4 maps the members of the `OdbcType` enumeration to ODBC data types and the .NET type system.

Table A-4 The `OdbcType` enumeration

Member Name	Description
BigInt	Exact numeric value with precision 19 (if signed) or 20 (if unsigned) and scale 0 (signed: $-2[63] <= n <= 2[63] - 1$, unsigned: $0 <= n <= 2[64] - 1$) (SQL_BIGINT). This maps to Int64.
Binary	A stream of binary data (SQL_BINARY). This maps to an Array of type Byte.
Bit	Single bit binary data (SQL_BIT). This maps to Boolean.
Char	A fixed-length character string (SQL_CHAR). This maps to String.
DateTime	Date data in the format yyyymmdd (SQL_TYPE_TIMESTAMP). This maps to DateTime.
Decimal	Signed, exact, numeric value with a precision of at least p and scale s, where $1 <= p <= 15$ and $s <= p$. The maximum precision is driver-specific (SQL_DECIMAL). This maps to Decimal.
Double	Signed, approximate, numeric value with a binary precision 53 (zero or absolute value 10[–308] to 10[308]) (SQL_DOUBLE). This maps to Double.
Image	Variable length binary data. Maximum length is data source–dependent (SQL_LONGVARBINARY). This maps to an Array of type Byte.
Int	Exact numeric value with precision 10 and scale 0 (signed: $-2[31] <= n <= 2[31] - 1$, unsigned: $0 <= n <= 2[32] - 1$) (SQL_INTEGER). This maps to Int32.
NChar	Unicode character string of fixed string length (SQL_WCHAR). This maps to String.

(continues)

Table A-4 The `OdbcType` enumeration (Continued)

Member Name	Description
NText	Unicode variable-length character data. Maximum length is data source–dependent (SQL_WLONGVARCHAR). This maps to String.
Numeric	Signed, exact, numeric value with a precision p and scale s, where 1 <= p <= 15, and s <= p (SQL_NUMERIC). This maps to Decimal.
NVarChar	A variable-length stream of Unicode characters (SQL_WVARCHAR). This maps to String.
Real	Signed, approximate, numeric value with a binary precision 24 (zero or absolute value 10[–38] to 10[38]) (SQL_REAL). This maps to Single.
SmallDateTime	Date and time data in the format yyyymmddhhmmss (SQL_TYPE_TIMESTAMP). This maps to DateTime.
SmallInt	Exact numeric value with precision 5 and scale 0 (signed: –32,768 <= n <= 32,767, unsigned: 0 <= n <= 65,535) (SQL_SMALLINT). This maps to Int16.
Text	Variable length character data. Maximum length is data source–dependent (SQL_LONGVARCHAR). This maps to String.
Timestamp	A stream of binary data (SQL_BINARY). This maps to an Array of type Byte.
TinyInt	Exact numeric value with precision 3 and scale 0 (signed: –128 <= n <= 127, unsigned: 0 <= n <= 255) (SQL_TINYINT). This maps to Byte.
UniqueIdentifier	A fixed-length, globally unique identifier (GUID) (SQL_GUID). This maps to Guid.
VarBinary	Variable length binary. The maximum is set by the user (SQL_VARBINARY). This maps to an Array of type Byte.
VarChar	A variable-length stream character string (SQL_CHAR). This maps to String.

A.5 Parameter.DbType

The .NET data provider type of a `Parameter` object is inferred from the .NET framework type of the `Value` of the `Parameter` object or from the `DbType` of the `Parameter` object, as shown in Table A–5.

Table A-5 Mapping `Parameter.DbType` to parameter values in .NET

.NET Framework Type	System.Data. DbType	SqlDbType	OleDbType
bool	Boolean	Bit	Boolean
byte	Byte	TinyInt	Unsigned-TinyInt
byte[]	Binary	VarBinary. This implicit conversion will fail if the byte array is greater than the maximum size of a VarBinary, which is 8,000 bytes. For byte arrays larger than 8,000 bytes, explicitly set the SqlDbType.	VarBinary
char		Inferring a SqlDbType from char is not supported.	Char
DateTime	DateTime	DateTime	DBTimeStamp
Decimal	Decimal	Decimal	Decimal
double	Double	Float	Double
float	Single	Real	Single

(continues)

Table A-5 Mapping `Parameter.DbType` to parameter values in .NET (Continued)

.NET Framework Type	System.Data. DbType	SqlDbType	OleDbType
Guid	Guid	Unique-Identifier	Guid
int		Int	Integer
Int16	Int16	SmallInt	SmallInt
Int32	Int32	Int	Int
Int64	Int64	BitInt	BigInt
long		BigInt	BigInt
object	Object	Variant	Variant
short		SmallInt	SmallInt
string	String	NVarChar. This implicit conversion will fail if the string is greater than the maximum size of an NVarChar, which is 4,000 characters. For strings greater than 4,000 characters, explicitly set the SqlDbType.	VarWChar
UInt16	UInt16	Inferring a SqlDbType from UInt16 is not supported.	Unsigned-SmallInt
UInt32	UInt32	Inferring a SqlDbType from UInt32 is not supported.	UnsignedInt

ESSENTIAL ADO.NET

Table A-5 Mapping `Parameter.DbType` to parameter values in .NET (Continued)

.NET Framework Type	System.Data. DbType	SqlDbType	OleDbType
UInt64	UInt64	Inferring a SqlDbType from UInt64 is not supported.	Unsigned-BigInt
	AnsiString	VarChar	VarChar
	Currency	Money	Currency
	Date	DateTime	DBDate
	SByte	TinyInt	TinyInt
	Time	DateTime	DBTime
	VarNumeric	Inferring a SqlDbType from VarNumeric is not supported.	VarNumeric

Appendix B

Expression Syntax

The following is a description from the .NET documentation of the column expression syntax. This syntax is used not only in column expressions, but in filter expressions in DataViews.

When creating an expression, use the ColumnName property to refer to columns. For example, if the **ColumnName** for one column is "UnitPrice," and another "Quantity," the expression would be:

```
"UnitPrice * Quantity"
```

When creating an expression for a filter, enclose strings with single quotes:

```
"LastName = 'Jones'"
```

The following characters are special characters and must be escaped, as explained below, if they are to be used in a column name:

\n (newline)

\t (tab)

\r (carriage return)

~

(

)

#

\

/

```
=
>
<
+
-
*
%
&
|
^
'
"
[
]
```

If a column name contains one of the above characters, the name must be wrapped in brackets. For example to use a column named "Column#" in an expression, you would write "[Column#]":

```
Total * [Column#]
```

Because brackets are special characters, you must use a slash ("\") to escape the bracket, if it is part of a column name. For example, a column named "Column[ ]" would be written:

```
Total * [Column[\]]
```

(Only the second bracket must be escaped.)

B.1 User-Defined Values

User-defined values may be used within expressions to be compared against column values. String values should be enclosed within single quotes. Date values should be enclosed within pound signs (#). Decimals and scientific notation are permissible for numeric values. For example:

```
"FirstName = 'John'"
"Price <= 50.00"
"Birthdate < #1/31/82#"
```

For columns that contain enumeration values, cast the value to an integer data type. For example:

```
"EnumColumn = 5"
```

B.2 Operators

Concatenation is allowed using Boolean AND, OR, and NOT operators. You can use parentheses to group clauses and force precedence. The AND operator has precedence over other operators. For example:

```
(LastName = 'Smith' OR LastName = 'Jones') AND FirstName = 'John'
```

When creating comparison expressions, the following operators are allowed:

<

>

<=

>=

<>

=

IN

LIKE

The following arithmetic operators are also supported in expressions:

+ (addition)

– (subtraction)

* (multiplication)

/ (division)

% (modulus)

B.3 String Operators

To concatenate a string, use the + character. Whether string comparisons are case-sensitive or not is determined by the value of the DataSet class's CaseSensitive property. However, you can override that value with the **DataTable** class's CaseSensitive property.

B.4 Wildcard Characters

Both the * and % can be used interchangeably for wildcards in a LIKE comparison. If the string in a LIKE clause contains a * or %, those characters should be escaped in brackets ([ ]). If a bracket is in the clause, the bracket characters should be escaped in brackets (e.g., [[ ] or [ ]]). A wildcard is allowed at the beginning and end of a pattern, or at the end of a pattern, or at the beginning of a pattern. For example:

```
"ItemName LIKE '*product*'"
"ItemName LIKE '*product'"
"ItemName LIKE 'product*'"
```

Wildcards are not allowed in the middle of a string. For example, 'te*xt' is not allowed.

B.5 Parent/Child Relation Referencing

A column in a child table may be referenced in an expression by prepending the column name with "Child." For example, "Child.Price" would reference the column named Price in the child table.

If a table has more than one child, the syntax is: Child(RelationName). For example, if a table has two child tables named Employee and Titles, and the DataRelation objects are named "Publishers2Employee: and "Publishers2Titles," the reference would be:

```
Child(Publishers2Employee).fname
Child(Publishers2Titles).title
```

A parent table may be referenced in an expression by prepending the column name with "Parent." For example, the "Parent.Price" references the parent table's column named "Price."

B.6   Aggregates

The following aggregate types are supported:

Sum (Sum)

Avg (Average)

Min (Minimum)

Max (Maximum)

Count (Count)

StDev (Statistical standard deviation)

Var (Statistical variance)

Aggregates are usually performed along relationships. Create an aggregate expression by using one of the functions listed above and a child table column as detailed in PARENT/CHILD RELATION REFERENCING above. For example:

```
Avg(Child.Price)
Avg(Child(Orders2Details).Price)
```

An aggregate can also be performed on a single table. For example, to create a summary of figures in a column named "Price":

```
Sum(Price)
```

Note: If you use a single table to create an aggregate, there would be no group-by functionality. Instead, all rows would display the same value in the column.

If a table has no rows, the aggregate functions will return a null reference (**Nothing** in Visual Basic).

Data types can always be determined by examining the DataType property of a column. You can also convert data types using the Convert function, shown below.

B.7   Functions

The following functions are also supported:

CONVERT

Description	Converts given expression to a specified .NET Framework Type.
Syntax	Convert(*expression*, *type*)
Arguments	*expression* — The expression to convert.
	type — The .NET Framework type to which the value will be converted.

Example: myDataColumn.Expression="Convert(total, 'System.Int32')"

All conversions are valid with the following exceptions: **Boolean** can be co-erced to and from **Byte**, **SByte**, **Int16**, **Int32**, **Int64**, **UInt16**, **UInt32**, **UInt64**, **String**, and itself only. **Char** can be coerced to and from **Int32**, **UInt32**, **String**, and itself only. **DateTime** can be coerced to and from **String** and itself only. **TimeSpan** can be coerced to and from **String** and itself only.

LEN

Description	Gets the length of a string.
Syntax	LEN(*expression*)
Arguments	*expression* — The string to be evaluated.

Example: myDataColumn.Expression="Len(ItemName)"

ISNULL

Description	Checks an expression and either returns the checked expression or a replacement value.
Syntax	ISNULL(*expression*, *replacementvalue*)
Arguments	*expression* — The expression to check. *replacementvalue* — If expression is a null reference (**Nothing**), *replacementvalue* is returned.

Example: myDataColumn.Expression="IsNull(price, -1)"

IIF

Description	Gets one of two values depending on the result of a logical expression.
Syntax	IIF(*expr*, *truepart*, *falsepart*)
Arguments	*expr* — The expression to evaluate. *truepart* — The value to return if the expression is true. *falsepart* — The value to return if the expression is false.

Example: myDataColumn.Expression = "IIF(total>1000, 'expensive,' 'dear')"

TRIM

Description	Removes all leading and trailing blank characters like\r,\n,\t, ' '
Syntax	TRIM(*expression*)
Arguments	*expression* — The expression to trim.

SUBSTRING

Description	Gets a substring of a specified length, starting at a specified point in the string.
Syntax	SUBSTRING(*expression, start, length*)
Arguments	*expression* — The source string for the substring. *start* — Integer that specifies where the substring begins. *length* — Integer that specifies the length of the substring.

Example: myDataColumn.Expression = "SUBSTRING(phone, 7, 8)"

Note: You can reset the **Expression** property by assigning it a null value or empty string. If a default value is set on the expression column, all previously filled rows are assigned the default value after the **Expression** property is reset.

Appendix C

Schema Inference Rules

The relational structure, or schema, of a **DataSet** is made up of tables, columns, constraints, and relations. When loading a **DataSet** from XML, the schema can be pre-defined, or it can be created, either explicitly or through inference, from the XML being loaded. For more information about loading the schema and contents of a **DataSet** from XML, see Loading a DataSet from XML and Loading DataSet Schema Information from XML.

If the schema of a **DataSet** is being created from XML, the preferred method is to explicitly specify the schema using either the XML Schema Definition language (XSD) (as described in Generating DataSet Relational Structure from XSD) or the XML-Data Reduced Language (XDR). If no XSD or XDR schema is available in the XML, the schema of the **DataSet** can be inferred from the structure of the XML elements and attributes.

This section describes the rules for **DataSet** schema inference by showing XML elements and attributes and their structure, and the resulting inferred **DataSet** schema.

C.1 Excluding Information

Not all attributes present in an XML document should be included in the inference process. Namespace-qualified attributes may include metadata that is important for the XML document but not for the **DataSet** schema. Using **DataSet.InferXmlSchema**, you can set specific namespaces to be ignored during the inference process. For more information, see Loading DataSet Schema Information from XML.

C.2 Summary of the Inference Process

The inference process first determines, from the XML document, which elements will be inferred as tables. From the remaining XML, the inference process determines the columns for those tables. For nested tables, the inference process generates nested **DataRelations** and **ForeignKeyConstraints**.

Following is a brief summary of inference rules:

- Elements that have attributes are inferred as tables.
- Elements that have child elements are inferred as tables.
- Elements that repeat are inferred as a single table.
- If the document, or root, element has no attributes, and no child elements that would be inferred as columns, it is inferred as a **DataSet**. Otherwise, the document element is inferred as a table.
- Attributes are inferred as columns.
- Elements that have no attributes or child elements, and do not repeat, are inferred as columns.
- For elements that are inferred as tables that are nested within other elements also inferred as tables, a nested **DataRelation** is created between the two tables. A new, primary key column named "TableName_Id" is added to both tables and used by the **DataRelation**. A **ForeignKeyConstraint** is created between the two tables using the "TableName_Id" column.
- For elements that are inferred as tables and that contain text but have no child elements, a new column named "TableName_Text" is created for the text of each of the elements. If an element is inferred as a table and has text, but also has child elements, the text is ignored.

C.3 Tables

When inferring a schema for a **DataSet** from an XML document, ADO.NET first determines which XML elements represent tables. The following XML structures will result in a table for the **DataSet** schema.

C.4 Elements with Attributes

Elements that have attributes specified in them will result in inferred tables. For example, consider the following XML:

```
<DocumentElement>
  <Element1 attr1="value1"/>
  <Element1 attr1="value2">Text1</Element1>
</DocumentElement>
```

The inference process will produce a table named "Element1."

DataSet: DocumentElement

Table: Element1

attr1	Element1_Text
value1	
value2	Text1

C.5   Elements with Child Elements

Elements that have child elements will result in inferred tables. For example, consider the following XML:

```
<DocumentElement>
  <Element1>
    <ChildElement1>Text1</ChildElement1>
  </Element1>
</DocumentElement>
```

The inference process will produce a table named "Element1."

DataSet: DocumentElement

Table: Element1

ChildElement1
Text1

The document, or root, element will result in an inferred table if it has attributes or child elements that will be inferred as columns. If the document element has no attributes and no child elements that would be inferred as columns, the element will be inferred as a **DataSet**. For example, consider the following XML:

```
<DocumentElement>
  <Element1>Text1</Element1>
  <Element2>Text2</Element2>
</DocumentElement>
```

The inference process will produce a table named "DocumentElement."

DataSet: NewDataSet
Table: DocumentElement

Element1	Element2
Text1	Text2

Alternatively, consider the following XML:

```
<DocumentElement>
  <Element1 attr1="value1" attr2="value2"/>
</DocumentElement>
```

The inference process will produce a **DataSet** named "DocumentElement" that contains a table named "Element1."

DataSet: DocumentElement
Table: Element1

attr1	attr2
value1	value2

C.6 Repeating Elements

Elements that repeat will result in a single inferred table. For example, consider the following XML:

```
<DocumentElement>
  <Element1>Text1</Element1>
  <Element1>Text2</Element1>
</DocumentElement>
```

The inference process will produce a table named "Element1."

DataSet: DocumentElement
Table: Element1

Element1_Text

Text1

Text2

C.7 Columns

When inferring a schema for a **DataSet** from an XML document, after ADO.NET has determined which elements to infer as tables it then determines, from the remaining XML elements and attributes, what columns to infer for those tables. Because data type information is only available with an inline schema, the data type of an inferred column is **System.String**. The following XML structures will result in table columns.

C.8 Attributes

As defined in Inferring Tables, an element with attributes will be inferred as a table. The attributes of that element will then be inferred as columns for the table. The **ColumnMapping** property of the columns will be set to **MappingType.Attribute**, to ensure that the column names will be written as attributes if the schema is written back to XML. The values of the attributes are stored in a row in the table. For example, consider the following XML:

```
<DocumentElement>
  <Element1 attr1="value1" attr2="value2"/>
</DocumentElement>
```

The inference process will produce a table named "Element1" with two columns, "attr1" and "attr2." The **ColumnMapping** property of both columns will be set to **MappingType.Attribute**.

DataSet: DocumentElement

Table: Element1

attr1	attr2
value1	value2

C.9 Elements without Attributes or Child Elements

If an element has no child elements or attributes, it will be inferred as a column. The **ColumnMapping** property of the column will be set to **MappingType.Element**. The text for child elements is stored in a row in the table. For example, consider the following XML:

```
<DocumentElement>
  <Element1>
    <ChildElement1>Text1</ChildElement1>
    <ChildElement2>Text2</ChildElement2>
  </Element1>
</DocumentElement>
```

The inference process will produce a table named "Element1" with two columns, "ChildElement1" and "ChildElement2." The **ColumnMapping** property of both columns will be set to **MappingType.Element**.

DataSet: DocumentElement
Table: Element1

ChildElement1	ChildElement2
Text1	Text2

C.10 Relationships

If an element that is inferred as a table has a child element that is also inferred as a table, a **DataRelation** will be created between the two tables. A new column with a name of "ParentTableName_Id" will be added to both the table created for the parent element, and the table created for the child element. The **ColumnMapping** property of this identity column will be set to **MappingType.Hidden**. The column will be an auto-incrementing primary key for the parent table, and will be used for the **DataRelation** between the two tables. The data type of the added identity column will be **System.Int32**, unlike the data type of all other inferred columns, which is **System.String**. A **ForeignKeyConstraint** with **DeleteRule = Cascade** will also be created using the new column in both the parent and child tables.

For example, consider the following XML:

```
<DocumentElement>
  <Element1>
    <ChildElement1 attr1="value1" attr2="value2"/>
    <ChildElement2>Text2</ChildElement2>
  </Element1>
</DocumentElement>
```

The inference process will produce two tables: "Element1" and "ChildElement1."

The "Element1" table will have two columns: "Element1_Id" and "ChildElement2." The **ColumnMapping** property of the "Element1_Id" column will be set to **MappingType.Hidden**. The **ColumnMapping** property of the "ChildElement2" column will be set to **MappingType.Element**. The "Element1_Id" column will be set as the primary key of the "Element1" table.

The "ChildElement1" table will have three columns: "attr1," "attr2," and "Element1_Id." The **ColumnMapping** property for the "attr1" and "attr2" columns will be set to **MappingType.Attribute**. The **ColumnMapping** property of the "Element1_Id" column will be set to **MappingType.Hidden**.

A **DataRelation** and **ForeignKeyConstraint** will be created using the "Element1_Id" columns from both tables.

DataSet: DocumentElement
Table: Element1

Element1_Id	ChildElement2
0	Text2

Table: ChildElement1

attr1	attr2	Element1_Id
value1	value2	0

DataRelation: Element1_ChildElement1
ParentTable: Element1
ParentColumn: Element1_Id
ChildTable: ChildElement1
ChildColumn: Element1_Id

Nested: True
ForeignKeyConstraint: Element1_ChildElement1
Column: Element1_Id
ParentTable: Element1
ChildTable: ChildElement1
DeleteRule: Cascade
AcceptRejectRule: None

C.11   Element Text

If an element contains text and has no child elements to be inferred as tables (such as elements with attributes or repeated elements), a new column with the name "TableName_Text" will be added to the table that is inferred for the element. The text contained in the element will be added to a row in the table and stored in the new column. The **ColumnMapping** property of the new column will be set to **MappingType.SimpleContent**.

For example, consider the following XML:

```
<DocumentElement>
  <Element1 attr1="value1">Text1</Element1>
</DocumentElement>
```

The inference process will produce a table named "Element1" with two columns: "attr1" and "Element1_Text." The **ColumnMapping** property of the "attr1" column will be set to **MappingType.Attribute**. The **ColumnMapping** property of the "Element1_Text" column will be set to **MappingType.Simple-Content**.

DataSet: DocumentElement
Table: Element1

attr1	Element1_Text
value1	Text1

If an element contains text, but also has child elements that contain text, a column will not be added to the table to store the text contained in the element. The text contained in the element will be ignored, while the text in the child elements is included in a row in the table. For example, consider the following XML:

```
<Element1>
  Text1
  <ChildElement1>Text2</ChildElement1>
  Text3
</Element1>
```

The inference process will produce a table named "Element1" with one column named "ChildElement1." The text for the "ChildElement1" element will be included in a row in the table. The other text will be ignored. The **ColumnMapping** property of the "ChildElement1" column will be set to **MappingType.Element**.

DataSet: DocumentElement

Table: Element1

ChildElement1
Text2

C.12   Limits

The process of inferring a **DataSet** schema from XML is not deterministic, in that different instances of XML documents having the same intended schema can result in different schemas depending on the XML elements in each document. For example, consider the following XML documents:

Document1:

```
<DocumentElement>
  <Element1>Text1</Element1>
  <Element1>Text2</Element1>
</DocumentElement>
```

Document2:

```
<DocumentElement>
  <Element1>Text1</Element1>
</DocumentElement>
```

For "Document1," the inference process will produce a **DataSet** named "DocumentElement" and a table named "Element1," because "Element1" is a repeating element.

DataSet: DocumentElement

Table: Element1

Element1_Text

Text1

Text2

However, for "Document2," the inference process will produce a **DataSet** named "NewDataSet" and a table named "DocumentElement." "Element1" will be inferred as a column because it has no attributes and no child elements.

DataSet: NewDataSet

Table: DocumentElement

Element1

Text1

These two XML documents may have been intended to produce the same schema, but the inference process produces very different results based on the elements contained in each document.

To avoid the discrepancies that can occur when generating schema from an XML document, it is recommended that you explicitly specify a schema using XML Schema Definition language (XSD) or XML-Data Reduced Language (XDR) when loading a **DataSet** from XML. For more information about explicitly specifying a **DataSet** schema with XSD, see Generating DataSet Relational Structure from XSD.

Bibliography

Box, Don, Aaron Skonnard, and John Lam. 2000. *Essential XML.* Boston, MA: Addison-Wesley.

Brown, Keith. 2001. "Security in .NET: Enforce Code Access Right with the Common Language Runtime." MSDN, Feb., pp. 117–128.

Date, C. J. 1981. *An Introduction to Database Systems,* Third Edition. Boston, MA: Addison-Wesley.

Ewald, Tim. 2001. *Transactional COM+: Building Scalable Applications.* Boston, MA: Addison-Wesley.

Ewald, Tim. 2001. "COM+ Integration: How .NET Enterprise Services Can Help You Build Distributed Applications." *MSDN,* Oct., pp. 42–50.

Gray, Jim, and Andreas Reuter. 1993. *Transaction Processing: Concepts and Techniques.* San Mateo, CA: Morgan Kaufmann Publishers.

Kent, William. 1982. A Simple Guide to the Five Normal Forms in Relational Design Theory. http://home.earthlink.net/~billkent/Doc/simple5.htm.

Onion, Fritz. Forthcoming. *Essential ASP.NET.* Boston, MA: Addison-Wesley.

Skonnard, Aaron, and Martin Gudgin. 2002. *Essential XML Quick Reference.* Boston, MA: Addison-Wesley.

Index

A

AcceptChanges, DataSets, 183
Access. *See* Microsoft Access
Accessors
    OleDb data providers, 358
    strongly typed, 98–99
ACID (atomicity, consistently, isolation, and durability) properties, 2–3, 150–151
ActiveX Template Library (ATL), 366
ADO, 415–417. *See also* interoperability, ADO with ADO.NET
    asynchronous operations, 417
    class equivalences with ADO.NET, 410–414
    COM-based approach, 23
    commands, 416–417
    connections, 416
    disadvantage of, 409–410
    example using, 414–415
    hierarchical data, 417
    integration in OleDbDataAdapter, 195–196
    object model of, 409
    OLE DB and, 408
    properties, 417
    transactions, 416
    XML and, 277
ADO disconnected model, 417–424
    class equivalences, 418–419
    column and table names, 424
    DataSets extensions, 423
    filtering and sorting, 424
    GetRows, 420–421
    navigation, 419
    updates, 422–423
ADO Extensions. *See* ADOX (ADO Extensions)
ADO for Multidimensional (ADOMD), 467
ADO-format XML, 428–433
    DataSet example, 430–431
    hierarchical DataSet example, 432–433
    hierarchical Recordset example, 431–432
    Recordset example, 428–430
ADO programmers
    class equivalences, 410–414
    example comparing ADO to ADO.NET, 414–415
ADO Recordset. *See* Recordsets
ADOMD (ADO for Multidimensional), 467
ADO.NET
    architecture for data access, 25–26
    building upon OLE DB and ADO, 23–24
    connected vs. disconnected access methods, 26–27
    data access styles in, 25
    layout of managed data classes, 65–67
    support for nonrelational data, 13
ADO.NET, connected mode, 27–42
    console application example, 29–34
    cursors and, 41–42
    generic data access code, 35–40
    OleDb and SqlClient data providers, 34–35
    SQL and OleDb connection strings, 27–29
ADO.NET data providers
    Command class, 371–375
    Connection class, 368–371
    DataAdapter class, 380–382
    DataReader class, 375–380
    enhancing functionality of, 382–383
    overview of, 396
    writing, 352–353, 366–368
ADO.NET, disconnected mode
    JDBC and, 452–453
    updates, 42–46
ADOX (ADO Extensions)
    CommandBuilder, 218–219
    DDLs and, 433
    library, 23

ADTG (Advanced Data TableGram), 23, 428
Aggregate types, 487
AND operator, 485
ANSI standards, SQL schema, 74
APIs (Application programming interfaces). *See also*
    XML APIs
    data access, 1
    database access, 3
    evolution of, 19–24
    writing, 21
Architecture, ADO.NET, 25–26
Arithmetic operators, 485
Asynchronous operations, ADO vs.ADO.NET, 417
ATL (ActiveX Template Library), 366
Atomicity. *See* ACID (atomicity, consistently, isola-
    tion, and durability) properties
Attributes
    mapping ODBC attributes to ADO.NET, 440–441
    relational model and, 5
    schema inference and, 492–493, 495–496
Authentication, 4
Authorization, 4
AutoIncrement columns, 137–138

B

Basic Direct Access Method (BDAM), 9
Batch optimistic concurrency, 227
Batch updates, 219–220, 423
BDAM (Basic Direct Access Method), 9
Binary formats, 428. *See also* ADTG (Advanced Data
    TableGram)
Binary large objects. *See* BLOBs (binary large
    objects)
BLOBs (binary large objects)
    connected model and, 101
    managed types and, 358
    metadata and, 446
    object-relational model and, 460
    storing data as, 12
Boolean operators, 485
Bulk loading, XML to SQL Server, 339

C

C#
    console application example, 29
    processing server-side cursor, 425–426

Cancel methods, Command class, 92
Cascading updates, 160–161
CASPOL command-line utility, 125
Catch blocks, exceptions, 32
Changes
    AcceptChanges, 183
    RejectChanges, 287–288
Child elements, 493–494, 496. *See also* Parent-
    child
Class equivalents
    ADO and ADO.NET, 410–414
    ADO disconnected model and ADO.NET,
        418–419
    JDBC and ADO.NET, 449–452
Client cursor library, 41
Client-server applications, 16–17
CLOBs
    connected model and, 101
    managed types and, 358
    metadata and, 446
    object-relational model and, 460
Clone method, DataRows, 149–150
Close method, connection classes, 71
CLR data types, 171–172
CLS (Common Language Specification), 37
Clustered indexes, 6
CODASYL model, 9, 171, 460
Codd, E. F., 5
Code
    access security, 125
    declarative code, DataGrid, 260–262
    declarative code, DataList, 257–259
    generic code, JDBC, 443
    generic code, OLE DB, 404
    interoperability with legacy code, 25
    stored procedures examples, 85–86
Column values
    field indexers and, 99–100
    fields as array of objects, 99
    large data columns, 101–103
    strongly typed accessors, 98–99
Columns. *See also* DataColumns
    attributes of elements inferred as, 495
    elements without attributes inferred as, 496
    expression syntax, 483–484
    mapping information, 186–188
    names, 424
COM-callable wrappers, 25, 425

COM (Component Object Model)
    interoperability, 402
    libraries, 425
    ODBC and, 22
Command-based data models. *See* Connected data
    access model
Command cotype, OLE DB, 353
Command dialects, OleDb data providers, 359–360
Command instances, DataAdapter, 179
CommandBehavior parameters, 81–82, 372–374
CommandBuilder class, 199–206
    DeriveParameters and, 205–206
    extended functionality with, 383
    InsertCommand, UpdateCommand, and Delete-
        Command, 199
    populating DataAdapter with, 200–201
    rebuilding commands, 201–202
    table names containing spaces and, 202
    updates generated by, 202–205
    using, 200
Command.ExecuteReader, 79
Command.ExecuteScalar, 81
Commands, 371–375
    ADO vs. ADO.NET, 416–417
    as basic data provider class, 367–368
    customized, ADOX CommandBuilder, 218–219
    customized, batch updates, 219–220
    IDbCommand interface, 371
    implementation, 373–374
    JDBC vs. ADO.NET, 447
    ODBC vs. ADO.NET, 435–436
    OleDb data providers, 358–359
    specialization, 374–375
    specification, 371–373
Commands, connected model, 77–82
    behaviors, 81–82
    Command.ExecuteScalar, 81
    initializing, 77–78
    multiple results, 80–81
    preparation, cancellation, and cleanup, 92–94
    returning total number of rows affected, 79
    switching connections, 78
CommandText, 79, 86
CommandTimeout, 92
CommandType, DataSets, 66
Commit transactions, 107
Common Language Specification (CLS), 37
Comparison operators, 485
Compile-time type checking, 457

Component Object Model. *See* COM (Component
    Object Model)
Composition, XML, 334
Compute method, DataSets, 145–146
Concurrency
    checking, 197–198
    optimistic vs. pessimistic, 177–178,
        462–463
Connected data access model
    as ADO.NET data access method, 8
    ADO.NET data providers and, 69–70
    connection classes, 70–73
    declarative transactions, 121–124
    error handling, catching errors and warnings,
        106–107
    error handling, Sqlclient, 104–106
    metadata methods, 74–77
    permission classes, 124–126
    relational databases and, 463
    streaming data through DataReaders, 94–97
    vs. disconnected model, 2, 26–27
Connected data access model, column values
    field indexers, 99–100
    fields as array of objects, 99
    large data columns, 101–103
    strongly typed accessors, 98–99
Connected data access model, commands
    behaviors, 81–82
    canceling, 92–93
    Command.ExecuteScalar, 81
    disposing of, 93–94
    initializing, 77–78
    multiple results, 80–81
    Prepare method, 92
    returning number of rows affected, 79
    switching connections, 78
Connected data access model, connection pooling
    Min Pool Size, 119–121
    overview of, 115–118
    parameters, 73–74
    sample listing, 118–119
Connected data access model, parameters
    adding to collection, 86–87
    overview of, 82–83
    retrieving result and output parameters, 84–85
    SqlParameter, 87–88
    stored procedures and, 85–86, 91
    using with OleDb data provider, 89–90
    using with SQL Server provider, 89–90

Connected data access model, transactions
    distributed, 111–113
    EnterpriseServices, 112–115
    named savepoints, 110
    nested, 109–110
    simple example, 107–109
Connected mode, ADO.NET, 27–42
    console application example, 29–34
    cursors, 41–42
    generic data access code, 35–40
    OleDb and SqlClient data providers, 34–35
    SQL and OleDb connection strings, 27–29
Connection attributes, ODBC, 440
Connection classes, 367–371
    as basic data provider class, 367–368
    connected model and, 70–73
    implementation, 369–370
    specialization, 371
    specification, 369
Connection Lifetime parameter, 120
Connection pooling, 115–121
    JDBC vs. ADO.NET, 445
    Min Pool Size, 119–121
    overview, 73, 115–118
    parameters, 74
    sample listing, 118–119
Connection strings
    ADO/ADO.NET interoperability, 416, 427–428
    connected mode and, 27–29
    Odbc data provider, 435
Connection Timeout, 120
Connection.Dispose method, 71
ConnectionState, 369–370
ConnectionTimeout property, 71
Consistency. See ACID (atomicity, consistently, isolation, and durability) properties
Console application example, 29–34
Constraints. See also Primary keys
    creating, 141
    overview of, 140
    relaxing, 142
ContinueUpdateOnError property, 198–199
Control types, data binding, 233–235
Conversion, to ADO.NET, 401–402
Copy method, DataRows, 149–150
Cotypes
    mapping OLE DB to ADO.NET, 403–404
    mapping OLE DB to OleDb data provider, 362–364

OLE DB, 23, 353
    OleDb data providers, 357
Crystal Reports, 356
Currencies positions, 11
Cursors, 41–42. See also Server cursors

D

DAO (Data Access Objects), 22
Data access
    data provider model for, 351
    styles in ADO.NET, 25
    traditional, 273–274
Data Access Objects (DAO), 22
Data binding, 227–243
    control types, 233–234
    to DataReader, 241–243
    with DataSet, 243–246
    HTMLControls, 233–237
    multiple results, 243
    overview, 227–230
    Web Form types, 230–233
    WebControls, 233–235, 237–241
Data definition language. See DDL (Data definition language)
Data directed routing, 78
Data Form Wizards, 270–271
Data manipulation language, 9
Data mining, 13, 360
Data models
    flat file, 9
    hierarchical, 9–11
    modern nonrelational, 11–12
    multidimensional, 12–13
    overview of, 1–2
    relational, 5–8
Data presentation. See GUIs (graphical user interfaces)
Data providers, 60–65, 351–400
    ADO.NET. see ADO.NET data providers
    base classes of, 190
    choices, 351–353, 396–398
    connected model and, 69–70
    JDBC vs. ADO.NET, 443–445
    new architecture for, 25–26
    nonrelational data and, 465
    OLE DB vs. ADO.NET, 405
    OleDb. see OleDb data providers

OleDb connection strings and, 27–29
SqlClient. *see* SqlClient data providers
transparency of, 404–405
XML. *see* XML Information Set (Infoset) providers
data source name (DSN) files, 71
Data storage, 399
Data types. *See also* Managed data types
    mapping JDBC to ADO.NET, 454–455
    mapping Odbc to ADO.NET, 476–478
    mapping OleDb to ADO.NET, 474–476
    mapping Parameter.DB to ADO.NET, 479–481
    mapping SQL Server to ADO.NET, 473–474
    SQL and OLE DB, 87–88
    supported by DataColumns, 131–132
Data warehouses, 13
DataAdapters, 177–223, 380–382
    as basic data provider class, 367–368
    command instances, base classes, and inter-
        faces, 179
    customized commands, 218–220
    DataReader and, 221–223
    disconnected model and, 8, 177–178
    implementation, 381–382
    nonrelational types, 220–221
    OleDbDataAdpter, 195–196
    specialization, 382
    specification, 380–381
    synchronizing function of, 177
DataAdapters, event model
    refreshing DataSets, 216–218
    RowUpdating handlers, 214–215
    turning off errors during batches, 215–216
DataAdapters, Fill method
    error handling, 188–190
    how it works, 190–195
    overloads, 182–183
    pessimistic concurrency and, 181–182
    populating DataSets, 179–181
    schema and mapping information and, 183–188
DataAdapters, Update method
    CommandBuilder class and, 199–206
    concurrency checking, 197–198
    ContinueUpdateOnError property, 198–199
    disconnected mode and, 196–197
    hand coded example, 208–209
    how it works, 212–214
    overview of, 45
    retrieving identity columns and, 211–212

specifying row version, 206–207
    timestamp construction, 209–211
Database administrator accounts, 126
Database cursors. *See* Server cursors
Databases
    authorization and authentication methods, 4–5
    as data management mechanism, 1
    DataSets vs. in-memory databases, 128
    fundamentals of, 2–3
    object-oriented, 399
    physical records, 9
    update methods, 177–178
Databound controls, 26. *See also* data binding
DataColumns. *See also* Columns
    accessing and updating, 146
    adding to DataTables, 134–136
    computed, 134, 255–256
    DataAdapter.Fill and, 192–193
    DBNull and default values and, 132–133
    errors, 163–164
    mapping, 254–255
    overview, 131–132
    referencing, 303
    schema information, 183
    XML-specific properties of, 133
DataDocumentXPathNavigator, 331
DataExceptions. *See also* Exceptions
    error handling, 163–164
    list of, 161–162
DataGrid, 259–265
    binding to SqlDataReader, 241–242
    custom pager, 263–264
    declarative code, 260–262
    overview, 259–260
    sorting, 264–265
    updating, 262–263
DataList, 256–259
    declarative code, 257–259
    templates, 256–257
Datamarts, 13
DataReaders, 375–380
    as basic data provider class, 367–368
    binding to, 241–243
    function of, 69
    IDataReader and IDataRecord and, 375–376
    implementation, 377–379
    interfaces for, 94
    OleDb data providers and, 357

DataReaders *(continued)*
    querying large relational databases with, 462
    specialization, 379–380
    specification, 376–377
    streaming data through, 94–97
    vs. DataAdapters, 190, 221–223
    vs. DataSets, 245
    vs. XmlReader, 47
DataRelations. *See also* Relationships
    counting relations, 142–143
    defining, 141
    inference process and, 492
    nested, 282–283
    specification of cardinality and, 143
    XML and, 282
DataRows
    adding to DataTables, 136
    Copy and Clone methods, 149–150
    DataRowState and DataRowVersions, 154–158
    deleting, 147
    editing, 151–152
    errors, 163–164
    filtering, 249
    inserting, 148
    overview, 131
    updates and versions, 196–197
    working with, 146
DataRowState, 154–158, 249–250
DataRowVersions, 154–158
    changing order of inserts with, 213–214
    current, default, original, and proposed, 155
    disconnected mode and, 196–197
    functions of, 158–159
    specifying, 206–208
DataSet object model, 129–167
    array of objects in, 139
    events, list of, 165–166
    events, sample program, 166–171
    filling DataSets programmatically, 138–139
    ImportDataRow method, 148–150
    keys and constraints, 139–140, 142
    LoadDataRow method, 148–150, 158–159
    merges, 152–154
    nonrelational types, 171–175
    row versions, 158–159
    rules and relationships, 159–161
    synopsis of classes in, 129–131
    updates and changes, 150–152

DataSet object model, DataColumns
    accessing and updating, 146
    computed, 134
    overview of, 131–132
    using DBNull and default value with, 132–134
DataSet object model, DataRelations
    counting relations, 142–143
    defining, 141
DataSet object model, DataRows
    Copy and Clone methods, 149–150
    deleting, 147
    editing, 151–152
    inserting, 148
    overview of, 131, 136
    state and versions, 154–158
    working with, 146
DataSet object model, DataTables
    adding columns, 134–136
    adding rows, 136–138
    overview of, 131
    retrieving and updating values, 146
DataSet object model, error handling
    causing exceptions, 163–164
    list of errors thrown, 161–162
    processing errors, 164–165
DataSet object model, navigation methods
    getting child rows, 144
    hierarchies, 144–145
    using Select and Compute, 145–146
DataSet.InferXmlSchema, 491
DataSet.Merge, 217
DataSets
    ADO-format XML, 430–433
    CommandType, 66
    data binding with, 243–246
    disconnected mode, 8, 44
    extensions to ADO Recordset, 423
    filling from DataAdapter, 180–181
    filling from WebDav provider, 427
    functions of, 129
    integration with XML stack, 274
    interoperability with Recordsets, 427–428
    mapping OLE DB to, 364–366
    overview of, 127–128
    pessimistic vs. optimistic concurrency, 462
    populating programmatically, 397
    producing XML with, 60–62
    PropertyCollection, 129

ESSENTIAL ADO.NET

refreshing with Update and Merge, 216–218
schema, defining, 174–176, 274–277
schema, inferring. see Schema inference rules
schema, refining for XML, 280–283
specialized use of, 464
updates using, 42–46
vs. DataReaders, 245
vs. in-memory database, 128
DataSets, XML and, 324
loading, 324
reading XML into DataSet, 283–288
use of XML properties, 281–282
writing XML data, 292–298
writing XML schemas, 288–291
XmlDataDocument class, 326–327
DataSet.WriteXml method, 292–293
DataTables
AutoIncrement columns and, 137–138
columns, adding, 134–136
DataAdapter.Fill and, 193
disconnected mode, 44–45
embedded, 173–174
event model, 214
filling from SQL statements, 191
mapping, 254–255
methods, 148
overview, 131
primary keys, 139–140
references, 303
retrieving and updating values, 146
rows, adding, 136
schema, 183–185
views, 246, 248
DataViewManager, 250, 252–254
DataViews, 246–254
DataViewManager, 252–254
DefaultView, 246–247
disconnected mode, 44–45
filtering and sorting, 249–250
modifying DefaultView, 251
nonrelational data, 265–266
reading items, 249–250
restricting editing, 248–249
two views on same DataTable, 248
vs. database views, 175–176
Date, C. J., 5, 7
Date values, 484
DB2, 333

DbDataAdapter base class, 179, 380–381
DbDataAdapter.Update. See Update method
DBDataPermission, 125
DbEnumerator class, 379
DBNull
columns and, 132–134
exceptions and, 162
DbType, 87, 471–472
DDL (data definition language)
ADOX and, 433
SQL, 53
XML schemas as, 400
Decision support, data warehouses, 13
Declarative code
DataGrid, 260–262
DataList, 257–259
Declarative data binding, 230
Declarative transactions, 121–124
Decomposition, relational model, 8
DefaultView, DataViews, 246–247, 251
DELETE method, DataTables, 148
DeleteCommand
customizing, 206
DataAdapter Command instances, 179
Update method and, 199
DeriveParameters, CommandBuilder class, 205–
206
Designer libraries, 266
DiffGram
applying, 295–297
changes and, 293–295
format of, 284
row changes in, 284–286
SQL Server and, 342, 347–348
XML representation of DataSet and, 293
Disconnected data access model
ADO, 419
ADO.NET, 8
advantages of, 461
vs. connected data access model, 2, 26–27
Disconnected mode, ADO.NET, 42–46, 196–197,
422–423
Dispenser manager (DispMan), 116
Distributed transactions
ADO.NET support for, 469
connected model and, 111–113
relational databases and, 462
DL/1, 9–10

DLLs (Dynamic link libraries), 34
Document composition, XML, 334
document type definitions (DTDs), 14
DOM (Document Object Model), 15, 323
DSN (data source name) files, 71
DTDs (document type definitions), 14
Durability. See ACID (atomicity, consistently, isola-
        tion, and durability) properties
Dynamic link libraries (DLLs), 34

E

EDI (Electronic Data Interchange), 468
EDIFACT (Electronic Data Interchange for Administra-
        tion Commerce and Transport), 468
EJB (Enterprise Java Beans), 115, 468
Electronic Data Interchange (EDI), 468
Electronic Data Interchange for Administration Com-
        merce and Transport (EDIFACT), 468
Embedded applications, ADO.NET support for, 16
Embedded DataTables, 173–174, 464
Enterprise Java Beans (EJB), 115, 468
EnterpriseServices transactions, 112–115
Entities, data representation, 5
Environment attributes, ODBC, 440
Environment handle, ODBC, 435
Error handling
    causing exceptions, 163–164
    connected model, 103–107
    connected model, catching errors and warnings,
        106–107
    connected model, Sqlclient, 104–106
    Fill method and, 188–190
    list of errors thrown, 161–162
    OLE DB vs. ADO.NET, 405–406
    processing errors, 164–165
    types, 383
Errors
    ADO.NET classes, 406
    JDBC vs. ADO.NET, 448
    ODBC vs. ADO.NET, 437
    OleDb data providers, 361
Essential ASP.NET (Onion), 233
Essential XML (Box, Skonnard, and Lam), 16
Event handlers, 361
Event model
    refreshing DataSets, 216–218
    RowUpdating handlers, 214–215

turning off errors during batches, 215–216
Events
    list, 165–166
    sample program, 166–171
Exceptions. See also DataExceptions; errors
    ADO.NET classes, 406
    catching, 32
    error handling, 163–164
    list of, 161–162
    subclasses for OleDb and SqlClient, 103–104
Exchange mail stores, 401
ExecuteReader, IDbCommand, 374
ExecuteStream, SqlXml, 343
ExecuteToStream, SqlXml, 343–344
ExecuteXmlReader, 340–341
Expression syntax, 483–500
    aggregates, 487
    column and filter expressions, 483–484
    functions, 487–489
    operators, 485
    parent/child references, 486
    string operators, 486
    user-defined values, 484–485
    wildcard characters, 486
Extensible Markup Language. See XML (Extensible
        Markup Language)

F

Fetching data, ODBC, 436
Field indexers, 99–100
Fields, as array of objects, 99
File-based RDBMS, 461–464
Fill method
    error handling, 188–190
    how it works, 190–195
    overloads, 182–183
    pessimistic concurrency and, 181–182
    populating DataSets, 179–181
    schema and mapping information and, 183–188
FillErrorEventArgs class, 188–189
FillSchema, 191, 436
Filter expressions, syntax, 483–484
Filtering and sorting
    ADO vs. ADO.NET, 424
    DataGrids, 264–265
    DataViews, 249–250
Finally blocks, exceptions, 32

Find (ADO), vs. Select (ADO.NET), 424
First normal form, 7
Flat file systems
    ADO.NET support for, 468–469
    vs. relational models, 6–7
FMTONLY option, SQL Server, 194
FOR XML keyword, 335–336, 339
Foreign keys, 141, 492
Functions, 487–489

G

GetChanges, 295–297
GetChildRows, 144
GetElementFromRow, 325–326
GetRows, 420–421
GIF (Graphics Interchange Format), 11–12
Globally unique identifiers (GUIDs), 6
Graphical user interface. See GUIs (Graphical user
        interfaces)
Graphics Interchange Format (GIF), 11–12
Grids. See DataGrid
GUIDs (Globally unique identifiers), 6
GUIs (Graphical user interfaces)
    Data Form wizards, 270–271
    data presentation, 226–227
    table and column mappings, 254–256
    Visual Studio integration, 266–270
    Window Forms and Web Forms, 225–226
GUIs (Graphical user interfaces), data binding, 227–
        243
    control types, 233–235
    to DataReader, 241–243
    with DataSet, 243–246
    HTMLControls, 234–237
    multiple results, 243
    overview of, 227–230
    Web Form, 230–233
    WebControls, 235, 237–241
GUIs (Graphical user interfaces), DataGrid, 259–265
    custom pager, 263–264
    declarative code for, 260–262
    overview of, 259–260
    sorting, 264–265
    updating, 262–263
GUIs (Graphical user interfaces), DataList, 256–259
    declarative code for, 257–259

templates, 256–257
GUIs (Graphical user interfaces), DataViews, 246–
        254
    DataViewManager, 252–254
    DefaultView, 246–247
    filtering and sorting, 249–250
    modifying DefaultView, 251
    nonrelational data and, 265–266
    reading items, 249–250
    restricting editing, 248–249
    two views on same DataTable, 248

H

Handles, ODBC vs. ADO.NET, 434–435
Heterogeneous data stores, 19
Heterogeneous hierarchies, 11
Hierarchical data
    ADO vs. ADO.NET, 417
    advantages of, 460
    heterogeneous hierarchies, 11
    homogeneous hierarchies, 9
    OleDb data providers, 360
    overview of, 1–2
    parent-child structure of, 9
    use of ADO.NET with, 464–465
Homogeneous hierarchies, 9, 464–465
HRESULTS, OLE DB error handling, 405–406
HTML (Hypertext Markup Language)
    Infoset providers and, 383
    screen scraping and, 14
HTMLControls, 234–237
    HTMLSelect, 235–237
    list of, 233–234
HTMLSelect, 235–237

I

IBM, data access methods, 9
IDataAdapter, 179, 380
IDataReader
    DataReader class, 94, 375–376
    using with Shape provider, 100–102
IDataRecord
    DataReader class, 94, 375–376
    reading column values, 97
    strongly typed accessors and, 98–99

IDbCommand
  ExecuteReader, 374
  ExecuteScalar, 80
  interface, 77, 371
  parameterized queries and, 85
  Prepare method, 92
IDbConnection
  ADO vs. ADO.NET, 416
  interface, 368–369
  methods and properties, 369
  System.Data namespace, 66
  transaction method, 107
IDbTransaction, 107–109
Identity columns
  retrieving, 211–212
  updates and, 204
IDMS (Information Management System/Database),
    9–10
IEnumerator, 379
IgnoreSchema, 285
ImportDataRow method, 148–150
in-memory database, 128
In-memory network library, 16
Indexed Sequential Access Method (ISAM), 9
InferSchema, 285
InfoMessageEvent, 105
Information Management System/Database (IDMS),
    9–10
Information schema, DataSets, 174–176
Informix 9, 333
Infoset. See XML Information Set (Infoset) providers
INSERT method, DataTables, 148
InsertCommand
  customizing, 206
  DataAdapter Command instances, 179
  retrieving identity columns with, 211–212
  Update method and, 199
Interfaces. See also APIs (Application programming
        interfaces); GUIs (Graphical user inter-
        faces)
  DataReaders, 94
  IDbCommand, 77, 368–369, 371
  JDBC, 443
  mapping JDBC to ADO.NET equivalents, 452–453
Interoperability
  COM interoperability, 402
  legacy code and, 25
  Windows APIs and, 402

interoperability, ADO with ADO.NET, 425–433
  ADO-format XML and, 428–433
  connection strings and, 427–428
  DataSets and RecordSets, 427
  list of tips, 426
  server cursors and, 425, 426–427
An Introduction to Database Systems (Date), 7
ISAM (Indexed Sequential Access Method), 9
ISAPI application, SQL Server, 342
ISG Navigator, 352
Isolation. See ACID (atomicity, consistently, isolation,
        and durability) properties

J

Java Naming and Directory Interface (JNDI), 444–445
Java objects, 445–446
Java-relational databases (JDBMS), 46, 445–446
JDBC
  Direct, 443–444
  disconnected model, 456–457
  drivers, 443–444
  sample program, 455–456
JDBC programmers, ADO.NET for
  commands and command behavior, 447
  connection pooling, 445
  disconnected model and, 456–457
  errors, 448
  example program, 455–456
  generic code, 443
  mapping classes to ADO.NET, 449–452
  mapping data types to ADO.NET, 454–455
  mapping interfaces to ADO.NET, 452–453
  metadata, 446
  nonrelational data types, 445
  object databases, 445–446
  provider types, 443–445
  queries, 447–448
  server cursors, 448
  SQL-99 extensions, 446
  SQL/J part 0, 457–458
  transactions, 446–447
JDBMS (Java-relational databases), 46, 445–446
Jet engine, 22, 463
JIT (Just-in-time) optimization, 12
JNDI (Java Naming and Directory Interface), 444–445
Join tables, 7
Just-in-time (JIT) optimization, 12

K

Key columns, relational data stores, 6
Keys, primary, 139–140

L

large object types. See LOBs (large object types)
LDAP readable directories, 273
Libraries
    ActiveX Template Library (ATL), 366
    ADOX (ADO Extensions), 23
    Client cursors, 41
    COM, 425
    designer libraries, 266
    DLLs (Dynamic link libraries), 34
    In-memory network library, 16
    Jet Engine Library, 22
    XML classes, 298
LIKE comparisons, 486
Listbound controls, 232–233
Lists. See DataList
LoadDataRow method, 148–150, 158–159
LOBs (large object types)
    column values and, 101–103
    object-relational mapping and, 466
    storing, 11
Local transactions, relational databases, 462
Lookup tables, DataSets, 127

M

Managed data types
    accessing, 358
    JDBC and, 444
    layout of, 65–67
    mapping to OleDb and SqlClient, 379–380
Many-to-many relationships, 7
Mapping information
    Fill method and, 183–188
    tables and columns and, 186–188, 254–256
Marshaling
    OLE DB vs. ADO.NET, 407
    XML, 298–302
MDirProvDataReader, 377–379
MDX (Multidimensional Extensions to [SQL]), 13, 467
Merges, DataSets, 152–154
Metadata
    collecting, 201

JDBC vs. ADO.NET, 446
    methods, 74–77
    multiple results and, 185–186
    ODBC vs. ADO.NET, 436
    relational databases and, 464
    requesting from data providers, 194
Methods, mapping ODBC to ADO.NET,
        437–439
Microsoft Access, 356, 420
Microsoft, data access APIs, 22
Microsoft Distributed Transaction Coordinator
        (MSDTC), 111
Microsoft Foundation Classes, 434
Microsoft Management Console snap-in, 125
Microsoft-specific annotations, XML, 291–292
Microsoft Transaction Server (MTS), 115–116, 468
Microsoft Visual Studio. See Visual Studio
Migration paths, 401–402
Min Pool Size, 119–121
Move methods
    ADO Recordset, 419
    XPathNavigator, 393
MSDASQL, 352, 353
msdata:ConstraintName="Constraint1", 292
msdata:Is-DataSet="true", 291–292
msdata:IsNested="true", 292
MSDE engine, 463
MSDTC (Microsoft Distributed Transaction Coordina-
        tor), 111
MSOLAP provider, 360
MSSQLXML, 342
MTS (Microsoft Transaction Server), 468
    connection pooling and, 115–116
Multidimensional data
    ADO.NET and, 401, 467–468
    OLAP and, 461
    overview of, 12–13
Multidimensional Extensions to [SQL] (MDX), 13,
        467
Multimember sets, 10
Mutator functions, SQL-99, 265–266

N

Named savepoints, 109–110, 462
Namespace
    annotations, DataSet schema, 291
    defining, 385

Navigation
    ADO disconnected model vs. ADO.NET, 419
    facilities, 55–56
Navigation-based data access, 2
Navigation methods, DataSets
    getting child rows, 144
    hierarchies, 144–145
    using Select and Compute, 145–146
Nested DataRelations, 282–283
Nested transactions, 109–110, 462
Netlibs, SQL Server, 17
Network data, 465–466
NO_BROWSETABLE option, SQL Server, 194
Nonrelational data, 171–174
    data providers and, 465
    DataAdapters and, 220–221
    DataViews and, 265–266
    embedded DataTables and, 173–174
    examples of, 273
    JDBC vs. ADO.NET, 445
    object types and, 172–173
Normal form rules, 7
NOT operator, 485
NT File System, 273
Numeric values, 484–485

O

Object Data Management Group (ODMG), 466
Object database management systems (ODBMS),
    12, 465–466
Object models
    ADO, 409
    XML Information Set (Infoset), 400
Object-oriented databases
    data structures benefiting from, 460
    JDBC vs. ADO.NET, 445–446
    popularity of, 399
Object Query Language (OQL), 3
Object-relational database management systems
    (ORDBMS), 12, 464–465
Object-relational mapping, 466
Object-relational model, 460
Object types, DataSets, 172–173
ODBC
    advantages of, 433–434
    client-side pooling in, 18
    data providers, 69, 356

legacy providers and, 397
mapping data types to ADO.NET, 476–478
OLE DB provider for, 352
relationship to JDBC, 443
universal data access and, 22, 398
Odbc data provider
    example program, 441–442
    metadata and schema information and, 436
ODBC-JDBC bridge, 443
ODBC programmers, 433–442
    benefits of ODBC, 433–434
    commands, 435–436
    errors, 437
    example program, 441–442
    fetching data, 436
    handles and environment, 434–435
    mapping ODBC attributes to ADO.NET, 440–441
    mapping ODBC methods to ADO.NET, 437–439
    metadata and schema information, 436
OdbcCommand, 435–436
OdbcConnection, 435
OdbcDataReader, 436
OdbcExceptions, 437
OdbcHandleError, 437
OdbcType enumeration, 476–478
ODBMS (Object database management systems),
    12, 465–466
ODMG (Object Data Management Group), 466
OLAP (Online analytical processing)
    data analysis process, 13
    OLE DB for, 467
    providers, 360
OLE DB
    ADO and, 408
    classes and purposes, 354–355
    client-side pooling, 18
    COM-based data access, 23
    components, 406–407
    development of, 398–399
    generic code, 404
    heterogeneous and homogeneous hierarchies, 355
    legacy providers, 397
    mapping data types to ADO.NET, 474–476
    mapping to DataSets, 364–366
    mapping to OleDb data providers, 362–364
    object model, 352–355
    properties, exposed in ADO, 417
    services, 406

OLE DB programmers, 402–407
    cotype equivalents, 403–404
    data provider transparency, 404–405
    error handling, 405–406
    marshaling, 407
    provider-specific functionality, 405
    service providers, 407
    system-supplied components, 406–407
    system-supplied services, 406
OleDb-Command, 77
OleDb data providers
    accessors, 358
    command dialects, 359–360
    command execution, 358–359
    command preparation, cancellation, and
        cleanup, 92–94
    command results, 359
    connected mode, 34–35, 36, 69
    connection pooling, 73, 118
    cotypes and type mapping, 357
    data access methods and, 27
    DbDataAdapter base class, 179
    errors and unsupported functions, 361
    exceptions, 103–104
    hierarchical data, 360
    IDbCommand and, 374
    mapping to managed types, 379–380
    mapping to OLE DB, 362–364
    metadata information, 74–76
    overview of, 356–357
    parameters, 88–90
    retaining existing, 352
    supported and unsupported providers, 361–362
    transparency, 405
    types, 351–352
    updating, 360–361
OleDbCommand object, 358
OleDbCommandBuilder class, 200
OleDbConnection, 416
OleDbDataAdpter, 195–196
OleDbDataReader, 358
OleDbPermission, 125
OleDbTransaction, 107–109
OleDbType enumeration, 474–476
OleTX, 111–112
Online analytical processing. See OLAP (Online ana-
        lytical processing)
Open method, 71
OpenRowset, 359

OpenXML, 336
Operators, 485
Optimistic concurrency. See also Disconnected data
        access model
    conflict resolution and, see, 177–178
    DataSets and, 462–463
    defined, 177
    updates, 178, 207
Optimistic data models. See Disconnected data
        access model
OQL (Object Query Language), 3
OR operator, 485
Oracle, 182
ORDBMS (Object-relational database management
        systems), 12, 464–465
Ordering, relational model, 6
Output parameters, 84–85
Overload methods, XML, 279–280, 283

P

Paging, DataGrid, 263–264
Parameter classes, 382
ParameterCollection, 382
Parameter.DbType, 479–481
Parameterized statements, 4, 82–83, 206
Parameterized updates, 188
Parameters, connected model, 82–91
    adding to collections, 86–87
    OleDb data provider and, 89–90
    overview, 82–83
    result and output parameters, 84–85
    SQL Server provider and, 89–90
    SqlParameter, 87–88
    stored procedures, 85–86, 91
Parent-child. See also Child elements
    grids, 253
    references, 486
Permission classes, 124–126
Permission types, 383
PermissionAttribute, 124
Persistent stored modules. See Stored procedures
Person class, 301–302
Pessimistic concurrency. See also Connected data
        access model
    DataSets and, 462
    defined, 177
    Fill method and, 181–182
Physical database records, 9

Platform invoke (PInvoke), 25, 402
Pooling. *See* Session pooling
Prepare method, IDbCommand, 92
Primary keys. *See also* constraints
    defining, 139–140
    populating, 191
    relational data model and, 7
    updating, 159
Programmers, ADO. *See* ADO programmers
Programmers, JDBC. *See* JDBC programmers
Programmers, ODBC. *See* ODBC programmers
Programmers, OLE DB. *See* OLE DB programmers
Properties, ADO vs. ADO.NET, 417
Property Builder, 270
PropertyCollection, DataSets, 129

Q

Queries
    JDBC vs. ADO.NET, 447–448
    large relational databases, 462
    multimedia data types, 467
    parameters for, 4–5, 82–83
    XPathNavigator methods, 395

R

RCWs (Runtime callable wrappers), 25
RDBMS (Relational database management systems)
    ADO.NET and, 2, 461–464
    SQL commands and, 3–4
RDO (Remote Data Objects), 22
RDS (Remote Data Services), 23, 351, 407
ReadSchema, 286
ReadXml, 284–287
Recordsets
    ADO-format XML, 428–432
    creating, 418
    data exchange with, 351
    disconnected, 418–419
    extensions, 423
    GetRows method, 420
    interoperability with DataSets, 427–428
    navigation, 419
    update support in, 422
    vs. DataSets, 417–418
RejectChanges, 287–288
Relational data, mapping XML to, 277

Relational database management systems. *See*
    RDBMS (Relational database management systems)
Relational databases
    restricted formats of, 333
    vs. DataSets, 127
Relational model, 5–8
    advantages of, 7–8, 460
    design rules for, 6–7
    features of, 5–6
    support in ADO.NET, 8
    vs. flat file systems, 6–7
Relationships. *See also* DataRelations
    counting, 142–143
    defining, 141
    navigating through, 143–146
    relational data model and, 7
    rules, 159, 496–498
    types of, 143
Remote Data Objects (RDO), 22
Remote Data Services (RDS), 23, 351, 407
Remote method calls, SOAP, 46
Remote procedure calls (RPCs), 46
Repeater control, WebControls, 239–241
Request for Comments (RFCs), 51
Result parameters, 84–85
RFCs (Request for Comments), 51
Rollback transactions, 107
Round-trip updates, XML, 297–298
Rows (tuples), relational model, 5. *See also*
    DataRows
Rowset
    disconnected model and, 456–457
    updating from, 360–361
    vs. DataSets, 452–453
RowState. *See* DataRowState
RowUpdating events, 214–216
RPCs (Remote procedure calls), 46
Runtime callable wrappers (RCWs), 25
Runtime.Serialization, 465

S

Savepoints, named, 110, 462
Schema inference rules, 491–500
    columns, 495–496
    excluding information, 491
    lack of determinism in, 499–500

relationships, 496–498
    summary of, 492
    tables, 492–495
    text, 498–499
Schema information
    changing using column mapping, 280–281
    Fill method and, 183–188
    ODBC vs. ADO.NET, 436
Schema Object Model (SOM), 54
Schemaless data, 14
Screen scraping, 14, 273
Scrolling-rowset presentation, 227
SDK documentation, data providers and, 366
Second normal form, 7
Security
    code access security, 125
    database security, 126
Segments, hierarchical databases, 9
Select method, DataSets
    navigation with, 145–146
    returning an iterator with, 59
    vs. ADO Find, 424
SelectCommand, 179, 201
Self-referencing tables, 7
Semistructured data
    ADO.NET support for, 468–469
    defined, 14
Serialization, XML, 298–302
    ADO.NET libraries for, 298–299
    ISerializable, 299–301
    object databases and, 278
    object persistence and, 465–466
Server-based RDBMS, 461–464
Server cursors
    GetRows method, 420
    JDBC vs. ADO.NET, 448
    processing in C#, 425–426
    processing in VB.NET, 426–427
    unsupported by ADO.NET, 41–42, 70
    using in ADO.NET, 421
Server Explorer, Visual Studio, 267
Server-side cursors. See Server cursors
Service providers
    OLE DB support for, 353–354
    OLE DB vs. ADO.NET, 407
Session pooling, 18
Set-based data access, 2, 231

Simple Object Access Protocol (SOAP), 46, 461
Single-record presentation, 226–227
Skonnard, Aaron, 384
SOAP (Simple Object Access Protocol), 46, 461
SOM (Schema Object Model), 54
Sorting and filtering
    ADO vs. ADO.NET, 424
    DataGrids, 264–265
    DataViews, 249–250
Special characters, 483–484
SQL-99 standard
    DataSet schema, 174–175
    JDBC and, 445, 446
    Mutator functions, 265–266
SQL-CLI (SQL Call Language Interface), 19
Sql exception types, 32
SQL/J part 0, JDBC, 457–458
SQL Query Builder, 268–269
SQL Server
    bulk loading, 339
    concurrency checking, 197–198
    cursors, 420–421
    Fill method and, 193–194
    FOR XML keyword, 335–336
    ISAPI application, 342
    mapping data types to ADO.NET, 473–474
    nonrelational data, 465
    OLE DB and, 356
    OpenXML and, 336
    pessimistic concurrency, 181
    provider parameters, 89–90
    Server Explorer connection to, 267–268
    SQLOLEDB provider, 336
    SqlXml managed classes, 337
    SqlXml Web application, 337
    SQLXMLOLEDB Provider, 339
    updategrams, 337–338
    updating with DiffGram, 347–348
SQL (Structured Query Language)
    accessing data via, 1
    commands, examples, 4
    commands, filling DataTables from, 191
    commands, list of basic, 3
    commands, syntax of, 3–4
    connection strings, 27–29
    dialects, 463
    information schema, 74–75
    use of SQL commands by APIs, 3

SqlClient data providers
    command preparation, cancellation, and
        cleanup, 92–94
    connected mode, 34–35, 69
    connection pooling, 73, 118
    data access methods and, 27–28
    DbDataAdapter base class, 179
    error handling, 104–106
    exceptions, 103–104
    ExecuteXmlReader support, 340–341
    IDbCommand and, 374–375
    mapping to managed types, 379–380
    metadata information, 76–77
    parameter specification, 88–90
    SQL Server and, 366
SqlClientPermission, 125
SqlCommand, 77
SqlCommandBuilder class, 43, 200, 202–205
SqlConnection, 32, 416
SqlDataAdapter class, 43–44
SqlDataReader
    binding DataGrid to, 241–242
    connected mode, 32–33
    disconnected mode, 43
    getting fields as arrays of objects, 99
    using field indexers, 99–100
SQLFetch, 436
SQLGetData, 436
SQLOLEDB provider, 336, 354
SqlParameter, 87–88
SqlTransaction, 107–109
SQL_VARIANT type, 220
SQLXML, 339–348
    ExecuteStream, 343
    ExecuteToStream, 343–344
    ExecuteXML Reader, 340–341
    SqlXmlAdapter, 346
    XPath query and, 344–346
SqlXml data provider, 366
SqlXml managed classes, 337, 359–360
SqlXml Web application, 337
SqlXmlAdapter, 346
SQLXMLOLEDB Provider, 339
Standards. See also SQL-99 standard
    ANSI standards, SQL schema, 74
    SQL command language, 3
    W3C standards, XSD, 52–53

State
    of database entities, 5
    DataRowState, 154–158, 249–250
Statement attributes, ODBC, 440–441
Stored procedures
    adding to databases, 334
    applying as CommandText, 86
    calling, 91
    client-server applications and, 17
    code examples of, 85–86
    DeriveParameters and, 205–206
    parameters, 85, 91
    queries, 83
    SQL statements and, 3
Streaming data, DataReaders, 94–97
Streaming mode, SQL Server, 95
String operators, 486
String values, 484
Strong typing
    accessors, 98–99
    DataSets, 304–305
    JDBC and, 457
Structured file systems, 467–468
Syntax. See Expression syntax
System. Web.Services, 461
System. Windows.Forms, 461
System.Data namespace, 66
System.Runtime.Serialization, 13, 298–301
System.Xml, 461
System.Xml.dll, 67
System.Xml.Serialization, 13, 298–301

T

Tables. See also DataTables
    elements with attributes are inferred as tables,
        492–493
    elements with child elements are inferred as
        tables, 493–494
    mapping information, 186–188
    names, ADO vs. ADO.NET, 424
    repeating elements are inferred as single table,
        494–495
TDS (Tabular data stream) packets, 29, 193
Templates, DataList, 256–257
Text, schema inference rules, 498–499
Third normal form, 7

Three-tier applications, 17–19
Timestamps, 204, 209–211
TLBIMP, 467
Transactions
    ADO vs. ADO.NET, 416
    extended functionality with, 382
    JDBC vs. ADO.NET, 446–447
    relational databases and, 462
Transactions, connected model
    declarative, 121–124
    distributed, 111–113
    EnterpriseServices and, 112–115
    named savepoints, 110
    nested, 109–110
    simple example, 107–109
Transformations, XSLT, 59–60, 400
Try-catch-finally blocks, exceptions, 32
Tuples (rows), in relational model, 5
type mapping, OleDb data providers, 357
Typed DataSets
    applying, 317–322
    defined, 302–303
    producing input for, 305
    strong typing, 304–305
    subclass generated by XSD.exe, 305–317
    table and column references, 303

U

UDA (universal data access), 19–21, 398–400
UDFs (User defined functions), 83, 334
UDL (universal data link) files, 71
UDTs (User-defined types), 334
Uniform resource identifier (URI), 51
Uniform resource locator (URL), 51
Universal data access (UDA), 19–21, 398–400
Universal data link (UDL) files, 71
Universal servers, 19–20, 399
Update method
    CommandBuilder class, 199–206
    concurrency checking, 197–198
    ContinueUpdateOnError property, 198–199
    DataAdapter class, 45
    databases and, 177–178
    DataTables and, 148
    disconnected mode, 196–197
    hand coded example, 207–209

how it works, 212–214
    retrieving identity columns, 211–212
    specifying row version, 206–207
    timestamp construction, 209–211
Update statements, 423
UpdateCommand
    customizing, 206
    DataAdapter Command instances, 179
    Update method and, 199
Updategrams, 337–338, 342
Updates
    ADO vs. ADO.NET, 422–423
    batch updates, 423
    cascading updates, 160–161
    CommandBuilder class and, 202–205
    DataSets, 150–152
    disconnected mode, 42–46
URI (uniform resource identifier), 51
User defined functions (UDFs), 83, 334
User-defined types (UDTs), 334
User-defined values, 484–485

V

VB.NET, 426–427
Visual C++, 366
Visual Studio
    concurrency and, 463
    integration with, 266–270, 398
    typed DataSets and, 304–305
    XML schema support, 53

W

W3C (World Wide Web Consortium), 52
Web browsers, 27, 42
Web Forms
    binding data to arrays, 232
    binding List box to SqlDataReader, 231–232
    as data binding control class, 228–230
    overview of, 225–226
    types, 230–233
    vs. Window Forms, 226
Web Service Description Language (WSDL), 461
WebControls, 237–241
    data binding, 235
    DataFormatString Property, 238–239

WebControls (continued)
    list of, 235
    overview of, 237–238
    Repeater control, 239–241
WebDav, 427
What enumeration, XmlReader, 391
Wildcard characters, 486
Window Forms
    as data binding control class, 228–230
    overview of, 225–226
    vs. Web Forms, 226
Windows registry, mapping to XML, 384–385
Windows (Win32), migration to ADO.NET, 402
World Wide Web Consortium (W3C), 52
WSDL (Web Service Description Language), 461

X

XBase applications, 17, 420
XDR (XML Data Reduced)
    as predecessor of XSD, 277
    specifying DataSet schema with, 491
    XML schema support, 52
XML APIs, 46–65
    overview of, 46–47
    XML, mixing with data providers, 60–65
    XML schemas, 51–54
    XmlDocument, XPath, and XPath Navigators,
        54–60
    XmlReader, 47–51
XML Data Reduced (XDR)
    as predecessor of XSD, 277
    specifying DataSet schema with, 491
    XML schema support, 53
XML DataBlade, 333
XML Extender, 333
XML (Extensible Markup Language)
    ADO classic and, 277
    advantages, document composition, 353
    advantages, universal support, 333
    advantages, XML as distinct type, 333–334
    bridging data models with, 2
    features of, 14–15
    flat files and semistructured data and, 6, 468
    interoperability with nonrelational data, 13
    mapping to relational data, 277
    mapping to Windows registry, 384–385
    method for reading XML data, 279–280

Microsoft-specific annotations, 291–292
    portability and, 460
    serialization and marshaling, 298–302
    universality of, 15–16
    XSD schemas and, 277–279
XML (Extensible Markup Language), DataSets and
    defining schema, 274–277
    reading XML to, 283–288
    refining schema, 280–283
    writing XML data from, 292–298
    writing XML schemas from, 288–291
XML (Extensible Markup Language), SQL Server and
    bulk loading, 339
    ISAPI application, 342
    OpenXML, 336
    SQLOLEDB provider, 336
    SqlXml managed classes, 337
    SqlXml Web application, 337
    SQLXMLOLEDB Provider, 339
    updategrams, 337–338
    updating with DiffGram, 347–348
    FOR XML keyword, 335–336
XML (Extensible Markup Language),
        SQLXML and
    ExecuteStream, 343
    ExecuteToStream, 343–344
    ExecuteXML Reader, 340–341
    SqlXmlAdapter, 346
    XPath query, 344–346
XML (Extensible Markup Language), typed DataSets
        and
    applying, 317–322
    defined, 302–303
    input for, 305
    strong typing, 304–305
    subclass generated by XSD.exe, 305–317
    table and column references, 303
XML for Analysis specification, 13, 467
XML for Data Mining, 467
XML Information Set (Infoset) providers, 383–396
    DTDs and, 14
    not limited to homogeneous data, 324
    as object models, 400
    overview of, 383–386
    XmlReader, implementing, 386–392
    XPathNavigator, implementing, 392–396
XML Schema Definition Language. See XSD (XML
        Schema Definition Language)

XML schemas
    compiler, 274
    as data definition language (DDL), 400
    example, 62–65
    refining for DataSet, 280
    writing from DataSet, 288–291
    XML APIs and, 51–54
XML transformation language. *See* XSLT (XML transformation language)
XmlDataDocument, 322–333
    bridging data models with, 2
    creating, 326–327
    DataSets and, 324
    disconnected model and, 8
    GetElementFromRow, 325–326
    loading, 327–328
    merging data, 328–329
    merging documents, 329–331
    missing columns, 323–324
    mixed content, 324
    overview, 322–324
    XPathNavigator and, 331–333
XmlDocument
    members, 56–57
    navigation methods, 55–56
    populating, 397
    as XML APIs, 54–60
XmlNode
    document traversal, 56
    DOM model and, 323
    members, 56–57
XmlNodeType, 387–388
XmlReader, 386–392
    customizing, 392, 396–397
    document properties, 388–389
    exposing data, 384–386
    functional areas of, 387
    hierarchy levels and, 389
    mapping to XPathNavigator, 394
    node recognition by, 387–388
    properties and methods, 388
    SqlClient and, 339
    streaming XML, 47–51
    What enumeration, 391

XmlReadMode, 285–286
XmlSerializer, 300
XmlTextReader, 48–51
XmlTextWriter, 48–51
XmlWriter, 48–49
XPath
    nodes or nodesets, 323
    overview of, 54–60
    queries, 54–55, 65, 344–346
    as XML API, 14–15
XPathNavigator, 392–396
    applying, 331–332
    bridging data models with, 2
    customizing, 396–397
    DataDocumentXPathNavigator and, 331
    exposing data, 384–386
    in-place updating, 396
    loading, 57–58
    mapping to XmlReader, 394
    members for document traversal, 58
    Move methods, 393
    navigating XML documents, 323
    optimizing, 395–396
    query methods, 395
    updating with, 332–333
    as XML API, 15, 54–60
    XPathNodeTypes and, 392–393
    XSLT and, 59–60
XPathNodeTypes, 392–393
XSD (XML Schema Definition Language)
    flexibility of, 278
    specifying DataSet schema with, 491
    vs. DTDs, 14
    XDR as predecessor of, 277
    XML integration with ADO.NET, 277–279
XSD.exe
    object and relational paradigms and, 466
    strongly typed subclass, 53
    typed DataSets, 302, 305–317
XSLT (XML transformation language)
    as transformation language, 400
    transforming XML documents with, 323
    XPathNavigator and, 59–60

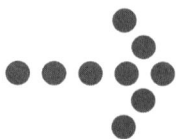

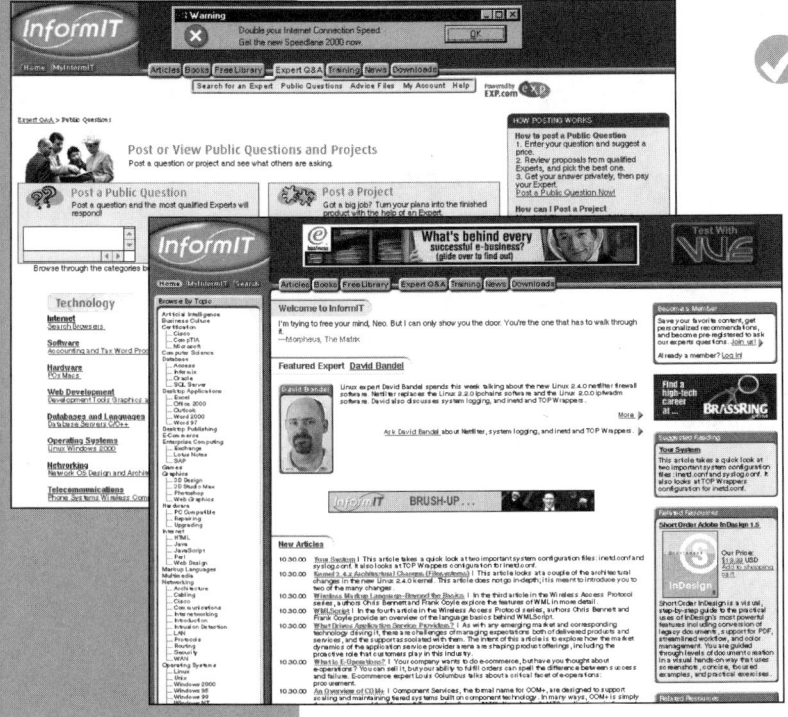

Register
Your Book
at www.aw.com/cseng/register

You may be eligible to receive:

- Advance notice of forthcoming editions of the book
- Related book recommendations
- Chapter excerpts and supplements of forthcoming titles
- Information about special contests and promotions throughout the year
- Notices and reminders about author appearances, tradeshows, and online chats with special guests

Contact us

If you are interested in writing a book or reviewing manuscripts prior to publication, please write to us at:

Editorial Department
Addison-Wesley Professional
75 Arlington Street, Suite 300
Boston, MA 02116 USA
Email: AWPro@aw.com

Addison-Wesley

Visit us on the Web: http://www.aw.com/cseng